Reading and Writing Short Arguments

Third Edition

WILLIAM VESTERMAN

Rutgers University

Mayfield Publishing Company
Mountain View, California
London • Toronto

Copyright © 2000, 1997, 1994 by Mayfield Publishing Company
All rights reserved. No portion of this book may be reproduced in any
form or by any means without written permission of the publisher.

Library of Congress Cataloging-in-Publication Data

Reading and writing short arguments / [compiled by] William Vesterman.
— 3rd ed.
    p.   cm.
  ISBN 0-7674-1136-6
    1. English language—Rhetoric.   2. Persuasion (Rhetoric)
3. College readers.   4. Report writing.   I. Vesterman, William.
PE1431.R43   1999
808'.0427—dc21   99-20919
                                                                    CIP

Manufactured in the United States of America
10 9 8 7 6 5 4 3 2

Mayfield Publishing Company
1280 Villa Street
Mountain View, California 94041

Sponsoring editor, Renée Deljon; developmental editor, Rick Roehrich;
production, Hockett Editorial Service; manuscript editor, Loralee
Windsor; design manager and cover designer, Susan Breitbard; cover art,
Gary Overacre; manufacturing manager, Randy Hurst. The text was set in
11/12 Bembo by G & S Typesetters, Inc., and printed on 50# Butte des
Morts by The Banta Book Group.

Acknowledgments and copyrights appear at the back of the book on
pages 347–349, which constitute an extension of the copyright page.

 This book is printed on acid-free, recycled paper.

PREFACE

Purpose and Principles

Reading and Writing Short Arguments, Third Edition, is an introductory text for courses that emphasize critical reading, critical thinking, and argumentative writing. The book begins with an Introduction to Argument and Persuasion, followed by 58 short, lively essays on controversial current issues by a variety of contemporary writers. Moving to Longer Arguments offers three classic longer essays. Next, A Minicasebook on Censoring Rock and Rap provides material for more extensive student research and writing, material that ranges from an editorial cartoon to two formal academic essays complete with footnotes. A Guide to Finding and Using Information allows the student to avoid the purchase of a separate handbook. The book concludes with a sample research paper in MLA and APA formats, a glossary, and an index.

The main group of selections addresses each of sixteen controversial issues from three divergent points of view. This organization should discourage any belief that simply choosing sides makes for either an adequate analysis of the arguments of others or a satisfactory method of forming arguments of one's own. Each reading is followed by discussion questions that invite the student to analyze the author's appeals to logic, character, and emotion. In each group, the major claim of one of the essays is presented in diagrammatic form according to the Toulmin method of logic. (The *Instructor's Manual* that accompanies the text includes, along with other material, diagrams for all the readings.) Each group of essays ends with Intertextual Questions and Suggestions for Writing. The goal of the apparatus in every case is to make the reading and writing of arguments easier by constantly encouraging analysis before the students synthesize their own views.

For further flexibility in instruction, the next section consists of ten topics represented by a single essay without accompanying apparatus— enabling students to practice on their own the skills they have acquired. Next, three longer arguments by Jonathan Swift, M. F. K. Fisher, and Martin Luther King, Jr., provide material for courses that move toward the study of longer essays. Finally, the Minicasebook and the Guide to Finding and Using Information offer ways of incorporating longer and more extensively researched arguments into a course without the need for purchasing extra books.

Changes in the Third Edition

In response to reviewers' suggestions, many successful essays have been kept in this edition, yet more than fifty percent of the material is new. New topics with three essays include *What Should We Do about Tobacco? Hate Crimes and Justice, Should Blood Alcohol Percentages for Drunken Driving Be Lowered? Giving Computers the Boot, Affirmative Action in College and Business, Global Warming, The Rich—Saints or Sinners? Toys for Tots,* and *Modern Manners.* Five of the ten single essays are new, as is the Mini-casebook on Censoring Rock and Rap. The guide to library research has been expanded to include additional material on doing research on the Internet and has been updated to reflect current MLA and APA documentation formats.

Acknowledgments

Many people have helped in the development of this book throughout its three editions. I wish now to thank the staff at Mayfield who have helped with this edition, particularly April Wells-Hayes, Susan Breitbard, Rick Roehrich, and Renée Deljon, my editor. I also thank Loralee Windsor for her able copyediting and Rachel Youngman of Hockett Editorial Service for her expert production management.

I also thank once again the reviewers of the first edition: Robert H. Bentley, Lansing Community College; Sue E. Cross, Mission College; Jean F. Goodine, Northern Virginia Community College; Edward McCarthy, Harrisburg Area Community College; Paul J. McVeigh, Northern Virginia Community College; Thomas A. Mozola, Macomb Community College; Joseph Nassar, Rochester Institute of Technology; Kathleen O'Shea, Monroe Community College; Teresa M. Purvis, Lansing Community College; and Richard J. Zbaracki, Iowa State University. And to their names I add, with thanks, the names of the reviewers who helped with advice on the second edition: Angela Berdahl, Portland Community College; Curt Bobbitt, College of Great Falls; Susan Brodie, University of Wisconsin Center; Sue E. Cross, Mission College; Collett B. Dilworth, East Carolina University; Rose Gruber, Gloucester County College; Susan Hoyne, Centralia College; Jill Marie Karle, Piedmont Virginia Community College; Lutz Kramer, Rogue Community College; Colleen McGuigan, University of Wisconsin Center at Manitowoc; Nancy Montgomery, Sacred Heart University—Connecticut; Dan Pearce, Ricks College; Phoebe Reeves, San Francisco State University; Howard Sass, Roosevelt University; Greg Scholtz, Wartburg College; and James Strickland, Slippery Rock University. My thanks as well to to those who thoughtfully reviewed the third edition: Kathryn E. Dobson, University of Maryland; Barry M. Maid, University of Arkansas at Little Rock; Patricia R. McClure, West Virginia State College; Marianne F. Pollack, Eastern New Mexico University; Michael W. Shurgot, South Puget Sound Community College; Stephen Wilhoit, University of Dayton; and William Zeiger, Slippery Rock University.

CONTENTS

Part I: Current Controversies from Three Points of View *27*

1. *What Should We Do about Tobacco?* *29*

2. *Hate Crimes and Justice* *38*

Introduction to Argument and Persuasion

MOTIVES AND METHODS OF ARGUMENT

Why Argue?

To human beings, forming opinions is as natural and necessary as breathing. Birds never have to decide what kind of nest to build, but humans decide how to build everything from a house to a society on the basis of thought and opinion. Because a diversity of opinion has always characterized human activities, listening to arguments and forming arguments of one's own are necessary ways of deciding among competing opinions.

We are not born with opinions but form them through our own mental and emotional lives and our interactions with the lives of others. At first we may receive most of our opinions unquestioningly, but very soon we begin to question even the views of our parents. The sounds of "Why?" and "Because!" echo throughout every childhood. However unsatisfactory that primitive dialogue may be (for both parties), those words present the basic structure of inquiry, and they begin to suggest some of the ways we form opinions. We want to know *why*—we want some reasons to follow the *because*—so that we can decide for ourselves whether we agree or disagree.

But our opinions are not just personal decisions. However confident we might have been of our views, and however inevitably convincing they might have seemed to us, "I wish that I had thought to say . . . !" is a common refrain when we find ourselves alone again after a dispute with other people. And merely announcing our views on a topic is seldom enough to convince anyone that we are right to think as we do. Dialogue rather than **assertion** is the basis of the process. If we want others to take our views seriously, let alone be persuaded by them, we have to argue our positions effectively and responsibly and find answers to reasonable objections.

We ourselves don't change our minds unless we are persuaded by responsible arguments. Yet we don't need to be convinced to benefit from a dialogue. Though hearing other views and the arguments that support them may not change our minds, having to answer the arguments of others may clarify and strengthen our own opinions. As educated people we should never be satisfied to know what we already know, and we need all the clarity and mental strength we can get to face serious and complex issues. Clarification for ourselves and for others, rather than "winning," is a goal to which both parties in a dialogue can aspire.

Clarity and strength of opinion are necessary not only for education but also for the world of work and action. Thinking critically about problems and explaining suggested solutions are activities that play a large part in any business or profession. Even in a field as concerned with physical facts as engineering, for example, those who succeed are those who are able to explain to their superiors the importance of their work and to argue in support of the ideas they propose. The same skills are required at every level of government, from the smallest local committee to the largest national legislature. Public opinion ultimately controls democratic government, and effectively argued views ultimately control public opinion.

What We Don't Argue About

Argument is a term often incorrectly applied to quarrels, in which mere assertion and name calling replace the rational presentation of opinion and the responsible meeting of opposing viewpoints. Quarrels can take place over any issue, but responsible and effective argument is impossible in certain areas:

- We can't argue about *facts*. For example, that the American Revolution occurred is beyond dispute; we are no longer ruled by Great Britain. While it is possible to argue about the significance of facts or the probability that an assertion actually is a fact, verified matters are not matters of opinion.
- We can't argue about the *impossible*. For example, that men should be responsible for bearing children is not an arguable position.
- We can't argue about *preferences*. Preferences resemble opinions, but they are neither formed nor changed by logic. For example, that rap music is better than rock music, that baseball is more graceful than ballet, and that long hair is ugly on men are all matters of preference, not matters of rational debate.
- We can't argue about *beliefs* that lie beyond rational or empirical proof, such as religious faith.

What We Do Argue About

We argue about *opinions* because arguing is the process by which opinions are formed. For this reason, opinion is not the end of rational discussion but the beginning of a dialogue with others and with yourself. In fact, it is safe to say that the process of learning to argue in responsible and effective ways will expand, modify, and strengthen many of the opinions you have now.

Why Analyze the Arguments of Others?

Arguing is an activity requiring skill, and, as in most activities, you acquire skill by imitation as well as by instruction. As you read the essays in this book, the discussion questions following them will invite you to analyze how and why the writers' arguments work. Having done this, you should be able to imitate their methods to make your own arguments more effective. Simply having opinions is not enough. You must also decide how to organize and express them and how to counter your opponent's objections. The discussion questions will help you master this task by encouraging a dialogue between you and authors of short essays like those you will be asked to write.

The essays here have been chosen because they address a variety of current topics that you can discuss, preliminarily at least, without further research. Some of the essays in this book provide instances of what to *avoid* as an effective writer of arguments. These flawed essays may be just as useful as those better argued in stimulating the growth of your argumentative skills.

Argument and Persuasion

Since arguments offer reasons for taking a position on an issue, **argument** is often distinguished from **persuasion,** since we may be persuaded by means other than evidence or logic. These other means of persuasion are generally divided into (a) matters of *character*—the trustworthiness we may grant to the reputation, ethics, or clarity and strength of mind of the writer or speaker—and (b) matters of *feeling*—the emotional agreement we may come to feel with the speaker or writer. In ancient Greece, where these distinctions were first proposed, the appeal of the moral character of the arguer, or speaker, was called **ethos,** while **logos** referred to the powers of logic or reason in the argument, and **pathos** referred to the ways emotion persuaded the audience to agree. The Greeks called the study of persuasive argument **rhetoric** just as we do in English.

The following diagram, called the Rhetorical Triangle, may clarify the interaction of the three means of persuasion. To each point of the triangle have been added the terms of the **Toulmin system** of logic to which you will shortly be introduced.

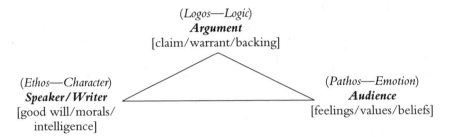

(*Logos—Logic*)
Argument
[claim/warrant/backing]

(*Ethos—Character*)
Speaker/Writer
[good will/morals/
intelligence]

(*Pathos—Emotion*)
Audience
[feelings/values/beliefs]

Argument is the first aspect of the rhetorical triangle that we will discuss. **Claim, warrant,** and **backing** are terms the Toulmin system uses to talk about this aspect of rhetoric.

THE WRITER AND LOGIC: APPEALS TO REASON

Logical is a word people often use informally to mean "reasonable." But the word *logic* also refers to formal systems of reasoning that depend on definite rules to determine the truth or falsity of an argument. In the West, formal logical theory began with the syllogism of Aristotle (see p. 7), and modern logicians have created various symbolic systems and techniques to meet needs for rigorous proof like those of mathematics. In ordinary verbal arguments, however, such strict proof is made extremely difficult not only by the complexity of life but also by the inherent ambiguities of language.

The Toulmin System of Logic

The feeling that logical theory was becoming too far removed from verbal arguments as they really took place among ordinary people caused British philosopher Stephen Toulmin to propose a new system of logic. Toulmin's method aimed not at the absolute truth of mathematical operations but at the kind of truth produced by argument within the legal system of English-speaking countries. In such legal argument a preponderance of evidence suggests a conclusion to a jury, and guilt needs to be proved, not beyond all conceivable doubt, but beyond a reasonable doubt. Legal argument, therefore, is close to the kind of argument used elsewhere in life. It depends for its persuasiveness on convincing an audience of the general strength of a case rather than on the rigorous but narrow standards of absolute proof used in mathematics or other formally constructed logical systems.

Toulmin's Terms

Let us look at Toulmin's names for the different parts of a logical argument before analyzing some examples to see how the parts go together. Toulmin breaks the structure of an argument into six parts:

- **Data:** what prompts you to make a claim, that is, the facts that lead you to believe your claim is true.
- **Claim:** what you believe your whole argument proves.
- **Qualifier:** the part of the argument that measures the strength or force of the claim. For example, is the claim *always* true? true *in the United States?* true *in modern times?*
- **Warrant:** an assumption that you expect your audience will share. The warrant supports the claim by connecting it to the data.
- **Backing:** any facts that give substance to the warrant. Not all arguments make use of explicit backing.
- **Rebuttal:** the part of an argument that allows for exceptions without having to give up the claim as generally true. The rebuttal does not so much refute your point as anticipate and answer attempts by someone else to refute it. For example, you could claim that most geese fly south for the winter, while admitting that a few are still found in the north. The very fact that *few* are found helps to prove your general point that *most* migrate.

An Example of the Toulmin System

Let us put the terms to work and illustrate them by analyzing an example Toulmin himself uses. Suppose, he suggests, you find yourself forced to argue something you thought was fairly obvious. You claim in the course of conversation that a man mentioned in the newspaper, Sven Petersen, is probably not a Roman Catholic. In a friendly dialogue, someone doubts your claim, asking, "What makes you say that?" You reply, "I think Sven Petersen is almost certainly not a Roman Catholic, because he's Swedish and very few Swedes are Catholics." Sorted out, the elements of this simple argument are:

- **Data:** Petersen is a Swede.
- **Claim:** Sven Petersen is not a Roman Catholic.
- **Qualifier:** "almost certainly."
- **Warrant:** A Swede can generally be taken not to be a Roman Catholic.
- **Backing:** The proportion of Catholics in Sweden is very low. (If you researched the religious proportions of Sweden, you might find something like the following to use as backing: "According to Whittaker's Almanac, less than 2% of Swedes are Roman Catholic.")
- **Rebuttal:** unless Petersen is one of the 2%.

The Toulmin Diagram

The structure of the argument may be clearer in diagrammatic form:

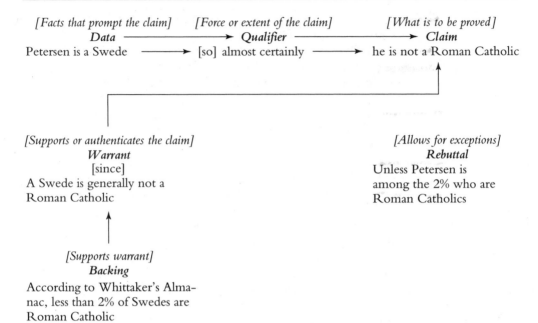

[Facts that prompt the claim]   *[Force or extent of the claim]*   *[What is to be proved]*

Data ⟶ **Qualifier** ⟶ **Claim**

Petersen is a Swede ⟶ [so] almost certainly ⟶ he is not a Roman Catholic

[Supports or authenticates the claim]

Warrant

[since]

A Swede is generally not a
Roman Catholic

[Allows for exceptions]

Rebuttal

Unless Petersen is
among the 2% who are
Roman Catholics

[Supports warrant]

Backing

According to Whittaker's Almanac, less than 2% of Swedes are
Roman Catholic

Of course not all arguments are so clear-cut. And most writers argue for several things in the course of a single essay. Further, one or more of the elements of an argument may be implicit or lacking altogether. For example, in analyzing an argument you may be unable to find the backing for one claim because the author took for granted that the warrant was so obvious as not to need further evidence. In the following passage, the qualifier is not explicitly stated, though it seems to have the force of something like "always."

The passage that follows is a single paragraph of "Government Is the Problem" by Walter E. Williams, an essay that appears in full later in this book (p. 203). In the course of arguing the main point suggested by his title, Williams devotes many single paragraphs to particular examples of what he sees as the general governmental "problem." Here is paragraph 6:

> Government control, such as the attempt to establish an official language, frequently leads to conflict, including wars and civil unrest, as we've seen in Quebec, Belgium, South Africa, Nigeria and other places. As our government creates bilingual legislation, we are seeing language become a focal point for conflict such as the ugly, racist-tainted "English Only" political campaigns in several states. The best state of affairs is to have no language laws at all.

Analyzed with the Toulmin system, the elements of Williams's argument are:

- **Data:** As our government creates bilingual legislation, we are seeing language become a focal point for conflict such as the ugly racist-tainted "English only" political campaigns in several states.
- **Claim:** The best state of affairs is to have no language laws at all.
- **Qualifier:** Always [implied].
- **Warrant:** [since] Government control, such as the attempt to establish an official language . . . leads to conflict. (Implied warrant) And it is best to avoid conflict.
- **Backing:** as we have seen in Quebec, Belgium, South Africa, Nigeria, and other places.
- **Rebuttal:** frequently.

Diagramed, the argument looks like this:

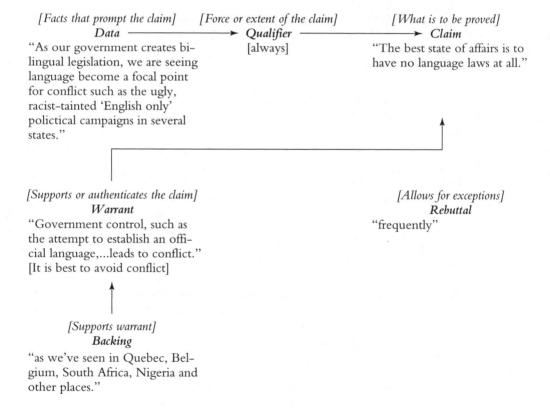

[Facts that prompt the claim]
Data   →

[Force or extent of the claim]
Qualifier   →
[always]

[What is to be proved]
Claim

"As our government creates bilingual legislation, we are seeing language become a focal point for conflict such as the ugly, racist-tainted 'English only' politcal campaigns in several states."

"The best state of affairs is to have no language laws at all."

[Supports or authenticates the claim]
Warrant
"Government control, such as the attempt to establish an official language,...leads to conflict." [It is best to avoid conflict]

[Allows for exceptions]
Rebuttal
"frequently"

[Supports warrant]
Backing
"as we've seen in Quebec, Belgium, South Africa, Nigeria and other places."

Aristotle's Syllogism

Let us illustrate Toulmin's system further by briefly comparing its methods with the ways in which the classical **syllogism** invented by

Aristotle might analyze the same argument. A syllogism is made up of three parts:

- **Major premise:** Conflict is bad.
- **Minor premise:** Government language laws create conflict.
- **Conclusion:** Therefore government language laws are bad.

Syllogistic reasoning assumes that if both premises are accepted as true, the conclusion must also be accepted as true. That is, if an entire class of facts is true, and if the case in question is a member of that class, the case in question must also be accepted as true, since what is true of a class must also be true of the members of that class.

You may notice that Williams's paragraph does not look like a syllogism and that the words used in the sample syllogism are sometimes not exactly his words. In fact, Aristotle says that most syllogisms are embedded in or implied by real-life arguments. He calls the implied syllogisms **enthymemes** (EN-thuh-meems). Teasing out the syllogisms from the enthymemes of a given argument is a skill that users of classical logic must acquire, just as arranging the writer's language and its implications into Toulmin's categories can often be a tricky matter at first and is always subject to differences of opinion on details.

Inductive and Deductive Reasoning

Whether analyzed by the Toulmin system or by Aristotelian logic, Williams's specific argument within the sample paragraph is an example of **deductive reasoning.** He deduces his conclusion about a specific problem from general premises. That is, his argument moves from a general proposition (conflict is bad) to a particular instance (government control of language is bad).

On the other hand, as you will see, Williams's essay as a whole is an example of **inductive reasoning**—the kind that scientists employ. Inductive arguments reason from particulars (government control of language is bad) to the general (government control is always bad). Williams gives example after example of the problems that he considers are caused by governmental interference; he expects us then to agree that government control makes a general "problem," one extending well beyond the examples he cites to all or most examples.

Inductive reasoning does not claim the strengths of absolute proof but seeks to establish a high degree of *probability* for the general truths it infers from the observation of particular facts. For instance, scientists have not examined every molecule of water to see whether it is composed of hydrogen and oxygen, but since all the water molecules that *have* been examined show the same results, they conclude that all other water molecules would too.

Kinds of Arguments

Like Williams in "Government Is the Problem," many writers employ both the inductive and the deductive methods of reasoning at different times in the same essay. And whether analyzing arguments or forming them yourself, you will find that the arguments in an essay also tend to fall into some different general categories. Because often several of the categories appear within a given essay, it will pay you both as a reader and as a writer to understand the categories.

ARGUMENTS ABOUT THE NATURE OF SOMETHING — IS IT **x?** Arguments about the nature of something are based on definition. For example, in the section on drunken driving, the real issue is not drunkenness (which each of the writers opposes) but whether drunkenness can be properly defined by one or another percentage of blood alcohol.

Guidelines Definition usually plays a subordinate part in a larger argument, but it is important to develop a sense of when you need to define your terms and when you can take them for granted. In general you should always define terms that are new to you, ones you suspect will be new to your audience, ones you are conscious of using in a special sense, or ones you suspect an opponent will use to question your case. Imagining your opponent's potential questions in a fair-minded way will serve you well in this as well as other areas of argumentative discourse. In defining your own important terms, there are several reliable methods:

- *Dictionary definitions.* The most common (and perhaps the most overused) technique is simply to repeat what a dictionary says: for example, "According to *Webster's Third International Dictionary, drunkenness* is defined as. . . ."
- *Stipulative definitions.* A writer can simply state the particular sense in which he or she will be using a word. For example, in the section "What Should We Do About Tobacco?" (p. 29), Sally Chen provides a stipulative definition of *sophisticated* when she says that nonsmoking teenagers are "really sophisticated in the true sense of that word. They have a real 'knowledge of life and how to live in the world.'"
- *Definition by synonym.* You can define a word by means of synonyms. But choose carefully. *Home* is used by real estate agents as a synonym for *house,* but a poet tells us that: "It takes a heap of livin'/ To make a house a home."
- *Definitions by image or verbal picture.* For example, in one of the essays in the section "Animal Testing," medical researcher Ron Karpati attempts to show what he understands *cruelty* to mean by

describing the suffering of children he has known as patients. After doing so, he argues that such cruelty might be avoided by medical advances based on a lesser degree of suffering undergone by animals in controlled experiments.

- *Definition by extended description.* For example, in "Ethnic Studies Are a Delusion" (p. 109), Jeffrey Hart gives many examples of what he defines as "ethnic studies" rather than history per se.
- *Operational definition.* This is a kind of definition designed to make clear distinctions about terms based on actions that define what they mean. For example, in "Serving Time the Old-Fashioned Way" (p. 00), Dick Boland describes activities available to convicts that can hardly be defined as "punishment."

ARGUMENTS OF CAUSE AND EFFECT — HOW DID X COME TO BE? If arguments of definition generally respond to the issue of "what," arguments of cause and effect seek to answer the questions "how?" and "why?" Cause and effect can organize your argument in either direction:

- *From cause to effect.* For example, in "Needed: Techies Who Know Shakespeare" (p. 00), Ellen Ullman argues that a literary education makes people better technical workers.
- *From effect to cause.* For example, in "Public Servants Often Behave Like Masters" (p. 167), Stephen Chapman argues that incivility in civil servants is an effect traceable to their status as workers in a public monopoly.
- *Antecedent and consequence.* This relation is useful in analyzing situations that may be deceptively similar to those involving cause and effect. Turning 18 does not cause you to become a voter: Acquisition of the right to vote is a consequence of that event but is not caused by it.

Guidelines Cause and effect reasoning is as tricky as it is important in forming effective and responsible arguments. Keep these general principles in mind:

- *An effect always follows a cause.* For example, thunder follows lightning, so the cause and effect relation must be that of "lightning-thunder" and never the other way round.
- *For repeated effects, the most likely cause is the common factor.* For example, if several children attending the same school become ill while their friends from other schools remain healthy, they most likely contracted the sickness at their school.
- *If the effect increases and decreases, you must find a cause that acts similarly.* If violent crime increases and decreases proportionally with

the size of the male population 15–25 years old, you can make a good argument that connects characteristics of young males and violent crime.

ARGUMENTS OF EVALUATION—IS X BETTER OR WORSE THAN Y? Many larger arguments contain issues of evaluation that present special difficulties. Our senses of value go so deep that we tend to treat them as self-evident warrants. Yet the well-known saying, "Everyone is entitled to his or her own opinion" need not end the discussion of values, which include beliefs about good/bad, right/wrong, moral/immoral.

In the first place, differences of opinion are seldom so widespread that there is not a great deal of common ground. For example, most people come up with similar lists of the leading qualities that define good writing, and "clarity" is usually first on the list. In the second place, disagreements about values are often based on a lack of understanding about what the argument is about. Being clear about your own and others' bases of judgment and understanding what is being judged are basic requirements of discussion. In "On Reading Trash" (p. 159), for example, Bob Swift concedes the differences of quality in literature but argues that reading "bad" books is good for children because it leads to a love of reading that will later lead to a love of "classics."

Guidelines Some general philosophical principles are often evoked directly or indirectly as standards for judging value.

- The German philosopher Kant held in his "categorical imperative" that no human being should be used merely as a means to the ends of another.
- The British philosopher Bentham held that the greatest good for the greatest number should be the principle on which to judge actions.

Of course, more particular bases for judgment do exist, and you should be aware of distinctions among them.

- Naive egoism, for example—what's good for me is obviously good—is a poor basis for argument.
- In judging that something is bad, you should make clear the basis of your negative judgment. For example, is what you condemn bad because it is a sin, a wrong, or a crime—or is it some combination of these different categories? In "Raking It In" (p. 80), convicted bookie Peter Alson questions why New York State punishes his gambling activities as crimes but does not consider its own similar activities to be wrongs.

ARGUMENTS OF POLICY—SHOULD WE OR SHOULDN'T WE DO X? Arguments of policy are very common and are among the main modes of argument in almost all the selections in this book. As you will see, this kind of argument often makes use of the other kinds we have been reviewing, but you should be aware of some common checkpoints that will give additional help.

Guidelines Since arguments of policy generally respond to a "problem," your analysis in this regard needs to be thorough.

- Make sure you clearly designate the problem that the policy you recommend or reject addresses.
- Spell out the consequences that will ensue if the problem is not solved and any reasons that make the need for a solution especially pressing.
- Propose the solution and make specific recommendations of the procedures that will lead to the solution while explaining how they will do so.
- Consider opposing arguments and make sure you answer them.
- Support your proposal with solid backing and evidence, but don't neglect the moral and emotional supports for your policy and for the policies you reject.

Counterarguments

A part of most arguments is taken up not with advancing the reasons for your own views but with answering the reasoning of your opponents. In general you should seek to test opposing views on the same bases you use to test your own; the series of policy argument guidelines just given will be helpful in this regard as well.

Some Common Forms of Fallacious Reasoning

In the course of analyzing both your own arguments and those of others, you should be aware of some common errors of reasoning. You should be sure both to avoid these errors yourself and to point them out in the arguments of others when you make your counterarguments. It is important to note that fallacious reasoning does not necessarily make the claim wrong. That is a question you must decide by examining the whole issue for yourself.

FAULTY GENERALIZATION The error of faulty generalization comes from treating all members of a class or category as if they were defined by criteria that apply only to some members. For example, in "Whose Canon Is It Anyway? It's Not Just Anglo-Saxon" (p. 161), Henry Louis Gates, Jr., argues that the list of "great books" has been formed by the tastes of only part of the reading population.

BEGGING THE QUESTION Users of the fallacy of **begging the question** try to take for granted the issues that need to be proved. They often use words and phrases like "obviously," "of course," and "simply" to preface unproved assertions. For example, in "Eliminate the Minimum Drinking Age" (p. 51), Doug Bandow argues that to tinker with penalties for drunkenness is to beg the question of how to promote responsible drinking.

FAULTY ANALOGY Comparing one issue to another is an effective and indispensable technique of argument, but an **analogy** is always open to question, and you should be sure that your comparisons are as solid as possible. For example, in "A World of Virtual Reality" (p. 71), Thomas Sowell argues that nowhere in the history of the earth have "races" been represented in economic activities in any way analogous to the percentages they represent in the general population.

POST HOC ERGO PROPTER HOC The Latin phrase **post hoc ergo propter hoc** means roughly "after this, therefore because of this." The fallacy is a mainstay of superstitious reasoning that claims causal connection for events that merely succeed one another in time—seeing a black cat and experiencing misfortune, for example. But the issues are not always so clear-cut. In "On Reading Trash" (p. 159), for example, Bob Swift argues against the idea that reading "trashy" books when young leads to "trashy" tastes in adulthood.

ARGUMENT *AD HOMINEM* The Latin **ad hominem** means "to the man," and the fallacy involves attacking someone personally as a way of attacking that person's views. For example, the controversy over the performer called Ice-T that appears in the Minicasebook on Censoring Rock and Rap (p. 000), revolves in part around the man himself.

ARGUMENT *AD POPULUM* An attempt to appeal "to the people" and their presumed common values and emotions may be another diversionary tactic designed to advance or oppose arguments unfairly. This tactic often uses what are called "God-words" (*pro-, help, family,* etc.) and "Devil-words" (*anti-, greed, mean-spirited,* etc.). In "Offering Euthanasia Can Be an Act of Love" (p. 145), Derek Humphry implies that opponents who compare mercy killing to Nazi exterminations are guilty of using both a faulty analogy and an argument **ad populum.**

RED HERRING The figure of speech that describes this fallacy comes from the fact that a red herring has a strong odor and can be dragged across the scent trail left by humans or animals to confuse persuing dogs. For example, in "The Quota Bashers Come in from the Cold" (p. 66), Brent Staples argues that calling affirmative action "discrimination" is a red herring because it attempts to distract the public from the social justice that affirmative action is designed to achieve.

EQUIVOCATION To equivocate is to use terms in differing senses in an attempt to deceive. For example, in " 'Global Warming' Is a Grab for Power" (p. 121), Thomas Sowell points out that the average temperature in 1990 was the same as that in 1980. By picking hotter or colder years in between to begin with, anyone can demonstrate a "trend" down or up toward the temperature of 1990, when in fact the decade as a whole shows no trend at all.

PROVING A NEGATIVE Arguments often take something like the following form: "If we do as you propose, what guarantees do we have that something awful will not occur as a result at some time in the future?" Negative propositions cannot be proved to an absolute degree because we can never know the future, or anything else, to an absolute degree. Recall Toulmin's example and remember that our system of logic is designed to prove only a preponderance of probability. One can argue the highly likely proposition that Sven Petersen is not a Roman Catholic without having to prove that it is impossible for him to be a member of that faith.

The foregoing examples of fallacious reasoning do not exhaust the category of logical fallacies, just as the brief introduction to logic itself is designed only to get you started. The next section looks beyond logic at other methods of presenting your views.

PERSUASION BY OTHER THAN LOGICAL MEANS

Let's look again at the Rhetorical Triangle to emphasize once more that, as important as logic is to human beings, reason is not the only attribute of human nature and therefore not the only means by which we express or respond to opinions.

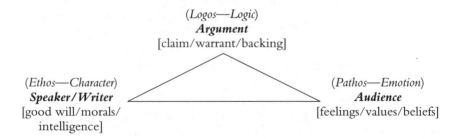

(*Logos—Logic*)
Argument
[claim/warrant/backing]

(*Ethos—Character*)
Speaker/Writer
[good will/morals/
intelligence]

(*Pathos—Emotion*)
Audience
[feelings/values/beliefs]

Character: The Writer's Personal Persuasion

As the diagram suggests, the strength of effective argumentation relies not only on reason but also on the credibility of the reasoner, and that credibility needs to be established with an audience. Establishing credentials is the function of the appeal to the writer's general character and personality. This "ethical appeal" acts with the appeals to logic and emotion to convince the reader that the writer's arguments are persuasive.

Classical rhetoric holds that writers and speakers should give their audiences an overall impression of a good character, including high intelligence, high moral standards, and an attitude of general good will. The audience gains its knowledge of these inward and spiritual virtues from the outward and visible signs of the writer's reputation and style and the format of the essay. Each of these elements in turn may make its ethical appeal by several means.

REPUTATION Intelligence and expertise can be shown through public credentials, which may strongly influence our responses one way or another. Most of the writers whose essays are included in this book are briefly identified in the "Annotated Table of Contents," and you might try the following experiments to test the force of the ethical appeal. Open the book at any point and read an essay without referring to its author's description in the table of contents. Then read the brief biographical identification and rethink your response. As another experiment, simply remind yourself of the attitudes that new acquaintances seem to take toward you when you explain what your college major is or might be!

STYLE Even without elaborate public reputations, all writers can express character through their writing styles. Carefully formed sentences and paragraphs argue intelligence in general, but you must also adapt your tone of voice and manner of presentation to the occasion at hand. For example, consider how you automatically change your presentation of the same anecdote when recounting it to your grandmother and your close friends.

Adopting an appropriate style expresses not only your relation to your audience but also your respect and consideration for its time and attention. For example, how do you feel about a fellow student's argument, regardless of its rationale, when that speaker adopts a belligerent or blustering manner in class? To take another example: Public speakers are usually invited because they are presumed to know more about the topic in question than the audience they address, but many speakers begin their talks with a joke to display a character that does not consider itself above its listeners.

One final example of the ethical appeal through style can be seen in the Declaration of Independence. Signing that document meant death to its signers if the revolution failed; yet it ends with the pledge of "our lives, our fortunes, and our sacred honor." By putting "lives" in the least important position in the list and "honor" in the climactic place, the signers affirmed a hierarchy of values that shows high ethical standards as well as personal courage.

Your own stylistic choices should aim at establishing not only your intelligence but also your good faith, rationality, fair-mindedness, and benevolence. Without sounding like a know-it-all or a show-off, you should try both to connect your personal views to wider categories of public importance and to refer to publicly acknowledged authorities who agree with you. But you can achieve all the goals of the ethical appeal most easily if you try to write in a natural style rather than the artificial grandiosity often associated with "English papers." For example, few students have ever spoken the word *thus,* though many have written it.

FORMAT The format and mechanical correctness of writing is also taken to express the character of its author. Neatness counts! And so does accuracy. Remember how widely ridiculed Vice President Quayle once was when he misspelled *potato*. If your essay is mechanically sloppy, your grammar careless, and your spelling poor, your **audience** will respond to those elements, whatever the strength of your reasoning might be.

Guidelines In checking your efforts to establish the impression of a character that includes intelligence and common sense, ask yourself:

- Have I used arguments that I myself believe? Have I qualified or modified them for my audience as I would for myself?
- Have I overstated the case or used inappropriate language or **clichés**?
- Have I allowed for doubts and uncertainties and acknowledged the good faith of other viewpoints?
- In trying to establish good character and good will, have I made my own beliefs clear?
- Have I connected my views to other **authorities** and larger contexts?
- Have I shown consideration and respect for my audience?
- Have I reviewed any potential points of disagreement?
- Have I tried to show off?
- Have I avoided name-calling?
- Have I shown that I assume my audience's sincerity and common sense?
- Have I defined questionable terms and distinguished between my facts and the opinions they are to support?

Looking forewoard to voting?
why?

Emotion: The Writer and Persuasive Feelings

In expressing their views, people often use the phrase "I feel that" as equivalent to "I think that"—and while thought and emotion may be separated for purposes of discussion, they are closely intertwined in an audience's response to your views. In the first place, while it may hardly need saying that emotions are not subject to logic, they do have a rationale of their own. As Pascal says, "the heart has its reasons that reason knows not of." Here are some examples of the emotional appeal at work:

- In "Curbing the Sexploitation Industry" (p. 248), Tipper Gore attempts to **appeal** to the reader's sympathy for children as a way of answering those who accuse her of unconstitutional censorship.
- Very early in the modern debate on abortion, the sides ceased to describe themselves as *antiabortion* or *antiregulation,* and began to use *prolife* and *prochoice* instead. The change was an acknowledgment of the greater force of positive terms in such an emotion-filled debate.
- Freedom is a concept commonly applauded, while hatred is an attitude commonly disapproved, so *free speech* and *hate speech* are often used by differing sides to describe the same phenomenon.

Emotions need not be so extreme or dramatically founded as some of the preceding examples to play an effective part in argumentative writing; many emotional appeals are more subtle. For example, absolute terms of assertion like *certainly* and *without a doubt* can evoke a mild annoyance in your readers that might lead them to hunt for minor exceptions to your argument. By avoiding them you may keep attention focused on the general strength of your case.

Avoiding negatively emotive words is only one side of a style formed to appeal to an audience's emotions. Figurative language is loaded with implied emotional appeals that can work positively—even if a term is negative in itself. For example, in "On 'Junk Food for the Soul': In Defense of Rock and Roll" (p. 000), Frank Zappa playfully admits the negative implication of "junk food" into his title, the better to express his confidence in his ability to act "In Defense of Rock and Roll."

In checking your emotional appeals, remember that emotions play a very strong part in the process of persuasion and that logical reasoning alone is seldom enough to stir an audience to action or deep conviction. As a reader of your own and others' arguments, try to sort out the emotional appeals from the logical reasoning. As a writer, remember that you cannot command the emotions of others. Let the connotations of the words you choose and the metaphors, images, and description you employ speak for themselves.

GUIDELINES One part of the discussion questions following each essay in this book examines the many ways in which the emotional appeal operates in persuasive writing. The idea is to gain as many effective techniques for your own writing as you can by carefully observing the techniques of professional writers. For general purposes, keep in mind a simple checklist:

- Ask yourself: "Have I given examples that might prompt positive or negative emotions such as pride or indignation?"
- Use images, figures of speech, and concrete examples to elicit the emotions in your audience. Avoid abstract words or direct assertions that *tell* your audience directly how to feel, such as "Every right-thinking person will be appalled at this state of affairs." *Show* your readers that the state of affairs in question is appalling and let them do the feeling for themselves. For example, in "The Trials of Animals" (p. 83), Cleveland Amory tells us of laboratory monkeys that "first nerves in their limbs were removed and then stimuli—including electric shocks and flames—were applied to see if they could still use their appendages." He doesn't need to tell us this is horrifying; we are horrified.
- Ask yourself: "Have I taken care not to insult my audience's values and assumptions?"
- Ask yourself: "Have I defined my position on the issues in a way that will appeal to my audience's general sense of fairness and justice?"

READING AND WRITING ARGUMENTATIVE ESSAYS

This introduction and the discussion questions that follow each essay are designed to foster your skills as both reader and writer. These skills are mutually supportive: By becoming a better reader of arguments made by others, you will learn how to form better arguments of your own. At the same time, the critical thinking you do in composing your own arguments will stimulate your analytical abilities as a reader. The discussion questions will invite you to write at least three kinds of essays prompted by your reading: (1) Essays in which you critique the various appeals made by different writers on the same topic; (2) topical essays that you write without needing more information than the selections provide or you already know; and (3) essays that you write using information from outside sources such as the library. For any of these writing tasks, learning to be a better reader of arguments is a sensible first step.

Reading Arguments

While the discussion questions will provide you with particular approaches to each topic, some general advice for you as a reader of arguments is in order here. First of all, drop that highlighter, pick up a pencil, and open your dictionary! The arguments in this book are short enough to be read several times, and taking notes in the margin will be much more effective than reminding yourself to reread what you will reread anyway.

In your first reading, mark the words you don't know or are unsure of while you proceed rapidly through the essay. Next use your dictionary to make sure you understand the particular ways in which the writer uses his or her terms. Get in the habit of noting definitions in the margin and making other notes there as well.

Then read the essay carefully, several times if necessary, while making more elaborate notes. For example, translating a writer's arguments into summaries is worth a dozen rereadings, because you are reading the material actively. As an active reader, you will form, modify, and strengthen your own opinions on the topic as you participate in a mental dialogue with the writer.

Some other ways of improving your reading skills include what is sometimes called *prereading*—making notes (mental or written ones) on your own view of a given topic before reading the essays on that issue. This exercise will give you a firm basis for response and help you see more clearly how writers present and back up their positions. You can even prepare for prereading. Try keeping an idea log or journal as you read to note points of view or effective techniques. When you begin to write, you will have practice and material to depend on, and if you know your topic in advance, reading any other essay will suggest ways of meeting your particular task.

You may also try the technique of rereading an essay from a point of view opposite to yours. This should sharpen your sense of how firmly argued views include attention to answering opponents. Attending to all the differing points of view in each of the topical units of the book will give you useful practice in gaining this skill.

To sum up: Learning to be an active and effective reader in the ways suggested here is part of the initial process of learning to be an active and effective *writer* of your own arguments.

Reading with the Help of Discussion Questions

The discussion questions for each essay are designed to help you become a more active reader by prompting you to pay attention to the ways in which the essayist appeals to logic, character, and emotion in the course of arguing a case. All the questions fall into some general modes of inquiry that you can employ as a reader of any argument, while the questions for a given case attempt to lead you to more particular answers.

In general the questions on logic will ask you to focus on the following:

- What are the data that prompt the claim?
- What are the warrants for making the claim, and what backing is offered for the warrants?
- What provision is made for rebuttals or qualifiers?
- Has a writer used appropriate analogies and provided needed definitions?

Questions on character include:

- How does the writer attempt to establish his or her general competence for dealing with the issue?
- How do particular uses of language establish an impression of good character?
- What values, **assumptions**, and beliefs underlie the writer's position?

Some general questions on emotion are:

- To what emotions in the audience does the writer appeal?
- What particular uses of language invite or evoke emotional responses, and how do they do so?

Finally, questions at the end of each section will lead you to compare the approaches of different writers to the same topic. These questions include:

- Where, how, and why do the writers agree and disagree?
- What are the values, **assumptions**, and beliefs that distinguish the positions taken?
- Does each writer imagine the same general audience?

Writing Arguments

Asking questions is the basis for writing as it is for reading. Beginning the process of writing with questions rather than conclusions can also help you solve the problem of starting a writing task. Trying to state your views may seem like a sensible way to start writing, but it assumes that you already know everything you need to know, and that is seldom true. Even though your convictions on a topic are strongly felt, you may still end up staring at an otherwise blank page that looks like this:

I. Introduction
    a.

Such pages tend to remain blank. So don't try to express exactly what you think and feel about a topic until you have explored it fully by going through some other stages of the **writing process**.

The Writing Process: An Overview

You should think of writing as an activity that clarifies issues for yourself as well as for your audience. For most writers, that activity takes time. Remember, clear, well-organized thoughts do not flow out of a writer's mind onto paper as quickly and easily as they flow from the page into the reader's mind.

Many students think that they have "a lot of trouble with writing" because they have false expectations about the writing process: how easy it should be and how long it should take, for example. They believe in the myths about those legendary people for whom writing is a snap and conclude that it should be a snap for everyone. But most people find that they have to go through many stages to get to the final draft of a clear, well-organized, and complete essay. Not everything can be or need be said at once. If you divide up the many tasks involved in completing your essay, you won't have to think about everything at once, and no one stage will seem overwhelming.

In going through some or all of the exercises this section of the book suggests, you will find yourself making use of strategies that have proven successful for millions of beginning writers like yourself. You will find your ideas about your topic becoming more various in content and more forceful in expression. By examining the logic of your argument, you will discover weak points in your reasoning and be able to attend to them before your opponents do. You will discover in many instances how to use qualifiers to keep from stating your case in general or categorical terms that may unnecessarily irritate your reader.

By using the writing process to discover and explore your convictions, you will be doing a service not only to your reader but also to yourself as an educated person. Too often students turn in an unconvincing version of an essay that could have been made into an excellent one if its writer had taken it through a few more stages. Most of the errors teachers note in the margins of student essays could have been discovered and handled by the students themselves, alone or with some help from fellow students or collegiate resource centers. Similarly, matters of poor organization, such as rambling points and confused or missing transitions, are perfectly natural features of a good rough draft but unacceptable in a final draft. Any essay must crawl before it stands up to run. The point is not to turn in the earlier stages of what could eventually be a fine essay, but to go back through the processes that will make your work suitable for public display.

Perhaps the first thing to remember is to start the writing process early enough to go through—or back through—the stages that prove useful or necessary. Some writers will need more time than others on early stages like note taking or the generation of ideas; others will need more time for later stages like revision to tighten and tune the draft. For most essays you should try to have a first draft done at least a week before the due date. Such a schedule will allow you time for extensive revision, even if some of the earlier processes turn out to have taken up more time than you expected when you made your original plan. Remember that *revision* means "seeing again," and since that is what you are asking your audience to do when you address an issue with an argumentative essay, it is only fair that you be willing to look over your own work as many times as necessary. This means not only cleaning up difficulties in mechanical matters like spelling and punctuation but also revising your ideas as you discover more exactly what they entail through the process of putting them in writing.

Stages of the Writing Process

No two people go through exactly the same stages of the writing process, and a given individual may make more or less use of different stages in writing different essays. Your own sense of your strengths and weaknesses will determine how much attention you need to pay to any of the following stages or how often you need to pay conscious attention to the techniques employed in them. If you use them consciously, you may also find that you tend to skip forward to later stages or go back to earlier ones. Don't worry: Use the process the way it works best for you.

FIRST STAGE: GETTING STARTED   For writers of argumentative essays, the beginning of the writing process is usually the discovery of an issue or a problem on which people disagree. You may already have taken sides, or you may think only that you can contribute something to the debate that will clarify the issue or help solve the problem. Sometimes your point of view is already decided at this stage; sometimes it gets its focus later in the process.

Expressive Writing   Expressive writing is talking to yourself on paper. It is useful to keep an idea log or journal as thoughts occur to you. If you have never done this sort of writing before, you will be pleasantly surprised at how much it clarifies your thinking. You needn't make entries every day as you would in an ordinary journal, but you should make entries when thoughts strike you for advancing a possible argument through appeals to character, emotion, or logic. Short entries of a sentence or two will add up to a comforting collection of things to work with as you begin an assignment.

You might do well to keep individual sections of your idea log under some headings commonly found useful for generating an inventory of issues:

- My friends and I tend to argue about . . .
- I think it's wrong that . . .
- I wish people could understand that they should . . .
- X believes . . . ; but I believe . . .
- Our college should definitely do something about . . .
- There ought to be a law that . . .

SECOND STAGE: EXPLORATION AND REHEARSAL This is the stage where you begin to assemble pertinent information on a given topic by recalling and jotting down your own experiences and views or by reading, interviewing, or undertaking other forms of research. At this stage you try to understand not only your own views but also the facts, values, assumptions, and beliefs about life that underlie all sides of the debate. This is the stage for prewriting and note taking or even for a rapidly written set of paragraphs on key points. Getting at least some of your thoughts down on paper, even though they may be revised later, makes you feel you are on your way.

Talking Try talking about ideas with a friend or a small group of classmates. Learning how others think will help turn your sense of an issue from a generalized subject into a collection of more particular views for and against various aspects of the issue. Often you'll find that what you thought could be taken for granted is hotly disputed by others and needs careful explanation on your part. Listen to any objections and try to get a feel for arguments that make sense to your friends on all sides of the issue. Generating ideas and gaining multiple perspectives like this is an especially good way to begin your writing, because it automatically maintains a clear sense of the argumentative essay not as a sermon but as a dialogue between the reader and the writer.

Notes In taking notes on what you read and discuss, get used to putting things under headings like *since* and *because* to form the habit of seeing facts in the explanatory or argumentative patterns you will need in your essay's drafts. The discussion questions and writing assignments will encourage you to get into the questioning habit, but here is some general advice to begin with. Don't worry about where to begin with your notes. You needn't worry at first about organizing your perceptions and thoughts by claim, warrant, and data. Begin anywhere, and one thing will lead to another as you generate material that can be more fully organized or reorganized at a later stage. Use the following checklist for generating notes, along with any other questions a particular subject might suggest:

- Is there really a problem here?
- Would the proposed solution really solve it? Could the problem be solved more simply without disturbing related matters?

- Is the proposed solution really practical? Would there be any un-foreseen consequences?

Once you have some preliminary notes, use the categories of logic for expanding and organizing your material. Get into the habit of sorting out the various claims, warrants, and data in the arguments you read so that you can more readily sort out the notes for your own essays. Like all skills, this analytic sorting may seem awkward at first, and there will be many instances when the proper category for a point is a debatable mat-ter. Whether a statement should be seen as a claim or a warrant, for ex-ample, may depend on your point of view.

THIRD STAGE: WRITING A DISCOVERY DRAFT If you have al-ready begun some writing beyond notes, this stage will blend into the second stage. Discovery drafts are often messy and disorganized. They might seem chaotic to an outside reader, but this draft is meant only for you. Your efforts here should shift from gathering facts and views to put-ting them together. In writing this draft you will discover connections among your ideas, and rereading the draft when you're done will help you see how to reorganize what you have. Rearranging your points in a more effective order is much easier once you have expressed them in sentences and paragraphs, no matter how tentative.

Brainstorming To generate ideas and connections among them, you might try a technique sometimes called speed writing, brainstorming, or free writing. That is, write down sentences as fast as you can without worrying about whether they connect with one another. Keep going for 10 or 15 minutes, even if after the first few minutes you run out of your initial set of ideas. You will soon find that you are writing your way into a problem and discovering new views while you express some you al-ready have.

FOURTH STAGE: REVISION OR "SEEING AGAIN" Discovery drafts may have prompted you to go back to even earlier stages for further information or to rethink some aspect of the problem at hand. Revision is the stage for rethinking, and you may do several rewrites of your dis-covery draft until you are satisfied that you have made all your points, however roughly and awkwardly, and have placed these points in the or-der that seems most effective. As your argument becomes clearer in your own mind, you will begin to imagine your readers' reactions and will look into issues like unity, coherence, and "flow" more carefully. Try to imagine your essay as a conversation rather than a lecture, and you will write more naturally, fluently, and effectively.

Try imagining a classmate who may not agree with you but is well disposed and reasonable. Keeping such an audience clearly in mind will help you decide how much to define or explain and how much to take for granted. These questions are much harder to answer if you imagine yourself high on a podium talking down to a silent, respectful, and completely receptive public. Imagine your classmate as at first agreeable and then dubious, so that you will be better able not only to make your own points but also to meet any counterarguments. Imagine this classmate in class or in some other formal setting for your dialogue rather than in a place like the snackbar. This will help you avoid needless facetiousness or gratuitous remarks, two of the vices opposite but equal to the pomposity that can control your tone of voice when sermonizing from on high. Peer group discussions of your drafts are one of the best ways of making sure you have touched all the bases. Finally, don't be afraid to revise as many times as necessary, but concentrate on important points and leave the matters of detail to the next stage.

Revision Guidelines

- Keep your vocabulary at the natural level of educated readers and writers. Avoid unnecessary specialized words, and imagine your classmate's response when weighing different choices.
- Make sure you have used examples to explain your general or abstract assertions.
- Avoid a belligerent or bossy tone of voice.
- As a rule avoid short paragraphs of one or two sentences. They may seem snappy in a journalistic text, but they suggest superficial or undeveloped thought in serious argument.
- Avoid repeating a point too often. Repetition makes you seem to underestimate your audience's abilities or attention.

FIFTH STAGE: EDITING   At this stage you polish your draft until it shines like an essay. Carefully go over details of grammar and punctuation, and try to tighten up the structure of each sentence to make it as clear and forceful as possible. Avoid using too many sentences of the same form and length. Learn to combine some of your short sentences, and don't begin every sentence with *The*. Variety in sentence structure and length creates flow and pacing in your essay, and a variety of sentence openers will provide opportunities for connection and transition and keep your style from seeming plodding and dull. You can learn different ways to begin a sentence by observing how the professional writers represented here use their sentence openers to make transitions and signal their patterns of reasoning.

Finally, remember that while all these dos and don'ts add up to good general advice, you will learn most about writing by actually writing and by critically reading other writers. When you find yourself admiring any aspect of a writer's method, analyze it and make it part of your own armory of stylistic resources.

Ready to Go

You are now ready to turn the theory you have learned in this Introduction to practical advantage by analyzing the argumentative essays in the rest of the book and writing essays yourself. You may of course come back to this Introduction during the course of your studies to refresh your theoretical knowledge. You will understand better how to take advantage of its advice when you have engaged some of the problems of argument and persuasion yourself.

I *Current Controversies from Three Points of View*

Introduction

In the section that follows, each of 16 controversial issues is addressed by three readings from divergent points of view. This arrangement should discourage any belief that simply choosing sides makes an appropriate method of either analyzing the arguments of others or of forming one's own. Each reading is followed by discussion questions that invite the student to analyze the author's appeals to logic, character, and emotion. In each group of readings a major claim of one argument is analyzed in diagrammatic form according to the Toulmin system of logic. (The *Instructor's Manual* that accompanies the text includes diagrams for all other readings, along with additional material.) Each group ends with "Intertextual Questions" and "Suggestions for Writing" that invite students to move toward forming their own positions. The goal of all the critical apparatus in this part of the book is to make the reading and writing of arguments both easier and richer by encouraging habits of **analysis**—the breaking down of complex matters into simpler ones—and **demonstration**—the provision of reasons and evidence to support assertions.

1 *What Should We Do about Tobacco?*

SMOKING IS BAD FOR EVERYONE SO IT SHOULD BE ILLEGAL

Sally Chen

It breaks my heart to see all the high school kids standing on one foot outside school property and puffing away furtively and defiantly on their cigarettes. They've learned from movies and advertising that smoking makes them more mature and sophisticated. They are more mature in one sense—they're all much further along on their way to horrible deaths and early graves than their friends who have enough sense not to start. And those friends are the ones who are really sophisticated in the true sense of that word. They have a real "knowledge of life and how to live in the world." They know that cigarettes are dangerous and that one of the dangers is how hard it is to stop once you've started.

But none of this fazes the big tobacco corporations like Phillip Morris with their rich executives who make their living by making other people die. And none of this fazes government at any level either. What is more, governments are even more hypocritical than the tobacco companies or the movie big shots who say they are only "portraying the way society really is."

Governments love to "regulate" tobacco through taxes and ineffectual laws that supposedly protect minors. First of all, politicians love to raise taxes of any kind so they can have more money to spend on their favorite programs, which are designed to attract more voters, which allows them to remain in office so that they can raise taxes again. It's a merry-go-round for them and a vicious circle for the rest of us.

But while the voters love programs that benefit them individually, they also hate having their taxes raised generally. Taxing tobacco is the perfect solution: it allows the politicians to feel good about themselves that they are "doing something" about the dangers of smoking. But the

1

taxes on cigarettes are hidden and seem to be a part of the price of the pack, so no one blames the politician. The cigarette smokers themselves are (rightly) too ashamed to protest as they would about a rise in their income taxes that they could see in their paychecks. But what kid ever stopped smoking because it was expensive? That's part of the prestige for them. And those "no one under eighteen" signs—who are they kidding? There is no teenager in the world who can't figure a way around that one.

The only thing to do is to outlaw tobacco entirely. It's an addictive   5
drug that not only harms the user but everyone else through secondary smoke. Since cigarettes are a problem for everyone in this country, cigarettes are a federal problem and we need a constitutional amendment. Petty regulations and more and more taxes have made no dent. We need to stop killing our own citizens and allow everyone the right to life, liberty, and the pursuit of happiness in a world without nicotine.

Questions for Analysis

Logic
1. According to Chen what is the logic of young smokers who wish to be perceived as "sophisticated"? What is the logic of Chen's **refutation** or rebuttal?
2. What is the logic of Chen's opposition to higher taxes as a way of curbing smoking?
3. According to Chen why should smoking be attacked at the constitutional level?

Character
1. What sense of her own character does Chen create in the opening paragraph? Is that sense of character sustained throughout the essay in your view? Explain your answer using evidence.
2. According to Chen how are the character flaws of tobacco companies and politicians alike? How do they differ? Give evidence for your answers.
3. What sense of character in smokers does Chen create in her last paragraph by calling tobacco "an addictive drug"?

Emotion
1. How does Chen use adjectives and adverbs in her first paragraph to create appeals to the emotions of her readers? Account for as many modifiers as you can by explaining their implicit appeals.
2. How does Chen appeal to emotion in her phrase "make their living by making other people die" in paragraph 2?
3. According to Chen, is smoking a sin, a wrong, a crime, or a combination? Explain your answer with examples.

Chen

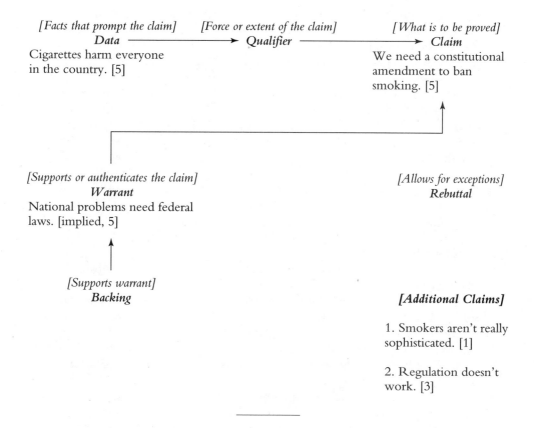

[Facts that prompt the claim]
Data ————————→ *[Force or extent of the claim]* **Qualifier** ————————→ *[What is to be proved]* **Claim**

Cigarettes harm everyone
in the country. [5]

We need a constitutional
amendment to ban
smoking. [5]

[Supports or authenticates the claim]
Warrant
National problems need federal
laws. [implied, 5]

[Allows for exceptions]
Rebuttal

[Supports warrant]
Backing

[Additional Claims]

1. Smokers aren't really
sophisticated. [1]

2. Regulation doesn't
work. [3]

BIG BROTHER'S TWO-MINUTE HATE

Linda Bowles

Eric Fromm, internationally acclaimed social philosopher and psy-   *1*
chologist, viewed the novel *1984* by George Orwell as a warning "that
unless the course of history changes, men all over the world will lose their
most human qualities, will become soulless automatons, and will not
even be aware of it."

George Orwell's story takes place in a futuristic society where the
minds, emotions and bodies of citizens are under the tyrannical control
of Big Brother. One of the techniques of mind management used by this
totalitarian state is to fabricate a loathsome threat to the national well

being—and then have Big Brother step forward to protect the people from it.

Every day, workers are required to gather in groups to participate in a Two-Minute Hate. The face of a hideous enemy, known only as Goldstein, is projected onto a huge screen. Goldstein is the epitome of evil: he is "the primal traitor, the earliest defiler of the Party's purity."

These Two-Minute Hate periods are orgies of screaming emotional outbursts. People curse and rail and throw things at the leering image of Goldstein. Then, at a moment when the rage and fear has reached a climax, Big Brother appears on the screen, speaking words of encouragement and reassurance. His powerful presence wipes away the threat of the enemy.

A typical reaction is that of a woman in the audience who cries   5
aloud, "My savior!" and extends her arms toward the screen. All is well once again. Big Brother has made it so.

Orwell's description of government deceit and manipulation in the future is background for a discussion of government deceit and manipulation in the present.

The subject is tobacco. For purposes of this discussion, substitute "Joe Camel" for Goldstein and "Big Bubba" for Big Brother.

Before continuing, let's get the usual obligatory disclaimers out of the way. Tobacco products are harmful. Those who smoke tobacco should stop. Those who do not smoke should never start. We need to do something to prevent our children from ever lighting up that first cigarette. The people in the tobacco industry who have committed crimes should be indicted and tried.

Having agreed on these points and principles, it's time to talk plainly and think realistically about the implications of our government's approach to solving the problem of smoking.

What we have in view are proposals that have very little to do with   10
curing the ills of tobacco. What we see is a scheme by government autocrats to take over a private industry, plunder its wealth, raise taxes—and look like heroes in the process.

It is a scam. For the scam to work, tobacco executives must be demonized. It must be repeated over and over again that every dirty dollar they own came from selling death-dealing, addictive drugs to hapless adults and innocent children.

These cold-hearted tobacco moguls don't deserve what they have and being stripped of it is pure justice.

It is a format for the advancement of tyranny. Where will Big Bubba next focus our hate? Will it be on those responsible for secondhand exhaust fumes from oversized autos and trucks? Will it be on parents who smoke in homes where children are present? And how about those filthy meat packers, greedy pharmaceutical houses and liquor barons? How about Ronald McDonald as a target?

The opportunities for the government to further intrude into our lives, with our enthusiastic consent, is boundless.

It is frightening that for the scam to work we the people have to view ourselves as victims, needy and powerless, and convinced that the true causes of our problems are out there somewhere, not inside ourselves.   *15*

This sense of helplessness impels us to exchange our freedoms for security. We have given politicians and bureaucrats a mandate to pass laws and institute programs premised upon our helplessness, our dependency and our incompetence.

Eric Fromm wrote a book called *Escape From Freedom,* in which he takes exception to the conventional view that mankind always struggles to be free.

He points out that freedom carries with it the considerable risks and substantial burdens of self-responsibility. Many people, he says, perhaps most, are desperately searching—not for independence but for some person, institution or government willing to take care of them, assume their burdens, make their decisions and give them packaged answers to life's questions.

How lucky we are that Big Bubba stands ready to answer our prayers, assume our burdens and take crib-to-tomb responsibility not only for ourselves but for our children and our parents, as well.

How long will it be before our gratitude is such that at the very sight of the beneficent Big Bubba, we will be unable to resist extending our arms and crying out, "My savior!"   *20*

Questions for Analysis

Logic

1. Bowles argues in part by analogy. Summarize that analogy as concisely as you can. Begin your summary as follows: "Just as in Orwell's *1984. . . .*"
2. According to Bowles in paragraph 13, what is the implied reasoning that could lead to governmental opposition to Ronald McDonald?
3. Bowles begins paragraph 8 by saying "Before continuing, let's get the usual obligatory disclaimers out of the way." In your view, would her overall argument be strengthened or weakened by placing the disclaimers at the end of the essay? Explain your reasoning.

Character

1. Bowles begins by referring to two famous authors. What sense of herself as an author do these literary references tend to create for you?

Would your sense be changed if she had referred only to George Orwell? Explain your answers.

2. Bowles refers to "a feeling of helplessness" as one of the keys to understanding public behavior. Does it seem to you from the manner of her writing that *she* feels helpless? Explain your answer with examples.

3. According to Bowles her opponents encourage hatred of their opponents. How would you characterize the sense Bowles creates of her feelings toward "Big Bubba"? Justify your characterization with evidence from the text.

Emotion

1. In paragraph 4 Bowles characterizes the responses to Goldstein as composed of both rage and fear. According to her, how are the two emotions combined in reactions to the tobacco problem?

2. Bowles calls the proposals of her opponents a "scheme" in paragraph 10 and a "scam" in paragraph 11. What is the emotional appeal made by each word, and how do they differ?

3. The imagined threats of paragraph 13 end with "How about Ronald McDonald as a target?" Name the emotions Bowles invites her readers to feel at this point, and explain how they might be expected to advance her overall argument.

THE TYRANNY OF THE MAJORITY

Walter E. Williams

Whenever Mom told my sister and me to share the last piece of pie or cake, or divide a pot of oatmeal that we both hated, she'd tell one of us to do the cutting or spooning, and the other had the first choice.

That rule gave whoever was the cutter or spooner uncanny incentive to be fair. For example, if I cut the cake unevenly, I'd lose because my sister had first choice and would choose the larger piece of cake (or the smaller bowl of oatmeal). Mom's strategy should be the basis for all societal rules. Good laws (rules) are those written as though our worst enemy had the power to enforce them.

Let's apply this idea to laws about speech and ask: If we seek fairness, what kind of laws should there be about speech? How about a law that says people are permitted to speak freely so long as they don't say something that offends another? Or, how about a law that mandates the nation's official language be English?

Some people might agree, pointing out they would promote sensitivity toward the feelings of others and strengthen the common culture.

But what if your worst enemies win control of Congress and the White House? Then, if you said to a young lady, "Those jeans are really fitting you well," you might be fined or jailed for speech that the majority power deems offensive. If you're for making English the official language, a future majority might make the official language Spanish or French.

We don't have a lot to worry about with speech because the Framers   5
anticipated Mom's rule, saying: "Congress shall make no law . . . abridging the freedom of speech." If there's respect for that rule, even if our worst enemies take over Congress and the White House, no sweat.

There are a bunch of Momlike rules in our Bill of Rights, containing distrustful and highly negative language like: "shall not be infringed," "shall not be violated," "shall not be required," and "nor be deprived."

Mom's rules would never be seen in heaven—they'd be an insulting insinuation that God cannot be trusted with power and that God is not a just God. However, if you are unfortunate enough to end up in the other place, you'd surely want Mom's rules, as you can't trust the Devil to do right.

We Americans have forgotten the warnings of James Madison and Thomas Jefferson about the tyranny of the majority. We think that because there's a majority vote of support, that fact alone confers legitimacy on laws passed by Congress. If you think a majority consensus is fair, how would you like enactment of the following law: Congress shall have the power to ban, regulate or tax out of existence any product found to have no nutritional necessity but [to be] costly to the nation's health-care system?

While most Americans support what Congress is now doing to cigarette smokers, I'd be willing to bet my bank account they wouldn't support those actions as a general rule. For example, there's absolutely no nutritional reason for adding salt to food, or consuming beer, whiskey, butter, potato chips and candy—but consumption of these goods raises health-care costs.

Why would Americans support cigarette control and not a general   10
rule allowing Congress to ban or control consumption of other products deemed harmful to our health? Most of the answer is cigarettes are the other guy's vice, and a majority has the power to be arbitrary. For me, I'll take Mom's rule any day—until I have the power to impose my values on others.

Questions for Analysis

Logic
1. Explain in your own words the reasoning behind "Mom's rule."
2. According to Williams is the rationale of the negative language in the Bill of Rights Momlike?

3. Explain how, according to Williams, the rationale of the hypothetical law proposed in paragraph 8 is *not* Momlike.

Character
1. In the context of the essay as a whole, how do you take Williams's last sentence? As a menacing confession? A joke? Explain.
2. As implied by the beginning of the essay, how does Mom view the characters of her children? Suppose she viewed them differently. Give a rule for cutting the cake that would imply a different assumption about her children's characters.
3. In your view, does Williams present himself as like his mother in the character implied in him as the author of this essay? Does he view the "majority" as she views her children? Explain your answer with evidence.

Emotion
1. What are the usual associations of the words *tyranny* and *majority?* Write some sentences on the topic of government using these words separately. Does the title of Willliams's essay invoke a kind of emotional paradox for you? Explain the emotional appeal of the title as clearly as you can.
2. "Mom and apple pie" is a phrase commonly used to sneer at sentimental appeals to an audience's emotions. Would it be fair to use this phrase to characterize Williams's use of his mother in his argument? Explain your answer with examples.
3. In the last sentence of paragraph 5 Williams is rather casual in his grammar and **dictional** level. What attitudes does this aspect of his style express toward the threats to freedom that are the implied subject of the paragraph? Explain your reasoning.

EXERCISES: WHAT SHOULD WE DO ABOUT TOBACCO?

Intertextual Questions
1. On which aspect of governmental regulation do Chen and Bowles agree? On which do they disagree?
2. Both Bowles and Williams are suspicious of singling out the tobacco industry for regulation. In your view do they come to this common conclusion for the same reasons? Explain your answer with evidence.
3. Which of the other two writers most agrees with the values and assumptions that underlie Williams's "Mom's rule"?

Suggestions for Writing

1. Taking into account the arguments of all three writers, write an essay that argues for your own views on the proper relations of individual and group rights with regard to the problem of tobacco.
2. Taking into account the arguments of all three writers, write an essay that argues for your own views on the propriety of governmental regulation with regard to the problem of tobacco.
3. Both Bowles and Williams are concerned with questions of tyranny that go beyond the issue of tobacco. Write an essay in which you analyze and compare their views of the broader threat of tyranny inherent in the tobacco controversy.

2   Hate Crimes and Justice

HATE CRIME LAWS ARE A BAD IDEA
Charley Reese

Passing "hate crime" laws is a step toward totalitarianism. There are   1
several reasons why such legislation is a bad idea.

First, to make a distinction between crimes based on motive is nonsense and an injustice. People who are victims of violence, vandalism or
arson are equally injured, whether the criminal's motives are greed, general malice or prejudice.

To punish a crime of prejudice more than an otherwise identical
crime of greed or general malice is a slap in the face to the victims of
ordinary criminals.

Second, so-called hate crimes are a minor percentage of crime, and
the government shouldn't be wasting its time trying to make the problem
larger than it is.

Third, hate crime legislation is just laying the groundwork for hate   5
speech legislation, which, indeed, is already on the books in some states.
This is the step toward totalitarianism. This is a direct assault on free
speech and should be vigorously opposed.

The First Amendment of the Constitution was not designed to protect safe or uncontroversial or politically correct speech or government-
approved speech. Such speech needs no protection. You can speak of
trivia and government-approved topics in a government- approved manner in any dictatorship in the world, present or past.

Remember that old Cold War joke, when an American in Moscow
tells a Russian, "Look, I can stand out in front of the White House and
call the president a warmonger and nothing will happen to me. That's
how free my country is."

"So what? So can I," said the Russian, and to prove it, he shouted,
"The American president is a warmonger."

No matter how obnoxious or offensive we find certain speech, we must never consent to allowing the government to police it, for to police speech is to police thought, and that is the essence of the totalitarian philosophy.

And we have plenty of would-be totalitarians who are eager to brand as hate speech any speech that criticizes them or their sacred cows or just meets with their disapproval. In Canada and Germany it is considered hate speech to question even the details of the Holocaust; people in Germany have ended up in prison for doing nothing more than that. Since when does a fact of history need the police power of the state to protect it? No one who values liberty should ever allow a government to make it a crime to be wrong or to question the orthodox version of events.

Truth is often arrived at by argument and debate. Even genuine historians are continuously revising their histories as more information becomes available. As one wag put it, God cannot rewrite history, but historians can and do all the time.

Some people in this country seem to want to enjoy the privileges of the communist party as it was in the Soviet Union—to be completely immune from criticism and to make sure none of their ideas or policies, no matter how cockamamie, are questioned. Hence the eagerness to brand all their critics, legitimate or otherwise, as peddlers of hate speech and to push the government into criminalizing it.

A free society, if it's to remain free, must leave even genuine bigoted speech free to be combatted by reason and education. The alternative is to move toward totalitarianism, in which thinking the wrong thoughts can land you in prison or before a firing squad.

There may not be [a] dime's worth of difference between Republicans and Democrats, but there is a gap light years wide between those who believe in freedom and those who believe in totalitarianism. If you find freedom offensive, perhaps you ought to emigrate.

Questions for Analysis

Logic

1. In paragraph 2 Reese claims that "to make a distinction between crimes based on motive is nonsense." Explain his reasoning on this point in your own words.
2. In the same paragraph Reese also says that the distinction creates an "injustice." Explain his reasoning on this point in your own words.
3. Explain the reasoning behind Reese's claim that the punishment of hate crimes will lead to the punishment of free thought and free speech.

Character
1. What qualities of character does Reese seem to seek to establish by means of the joke in paragraphs 7-8?
2. What qualities of character does Reese attribute to "some people" in paragraph 12?
3. What sense of his own character does Reese seem to seek to establish by his suggestion in the last paragraph that "there may not be [a] dime's worth of difference between Republicans and Democrats"?

Emotion
1. To what emotions does Reese appeal by his use of the phrase "slap in the face" in paragraph 3? Explain the basis of your answers.
2. You have been asked a question about the sense of character established by Reese's Cold War joke in paragraphs 7-8. To what *emotion* or emotions in his reader does this joke seem designed to appeal? Explain your analysis.
3. You have been asked a question about the character Reese seems to seek to establish for "some people" in paragraph 12. To what *emotion* or emotions in his reader does he seem to appeal by his attempt at the characterization of "some people"?

Reese

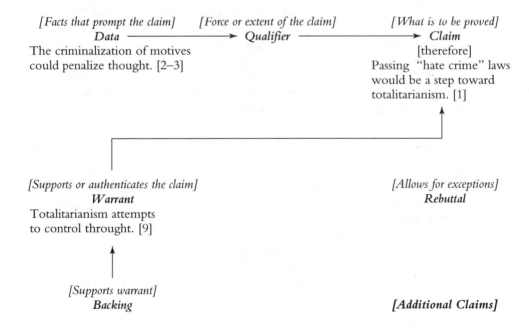

SPECIAL CRIMES NEED SPECIAL LAWS

Helen Dodge

It's over two hundred years since the American Constitution was   *1*
adopted to protect and govern all the people of the thirteen diverse colonies that became the first thirteen states. Yet those people were mostly of
English origin, except for the African slaves who had no protection at all.
As the twenty-first century approaches America is more diverse than ever
before in terms of race, religion, national origin, and sexual orientation.
And great progress has been made over the centuries: Slavery has been
abolished, Eurocentric immigration laws are gone, and people are now
ashamed to admit it publicly if they privately try to keep minorities out
of their clubs and organizations.

Yet hate crimes are on the increase and these crimes strike at the
heart of the American dream itself. They strike at its diversity and the
need for all its people to live in harmony with one another. *E pluribus
unum*—from many one—that is the motto of the United States and it is
a motto that calls for the union not only of state but of people. It calls for
making of one nation out of diverse races, creeds, and sexual orientations.

Those who oppose the goals of the United States are traitors to its
ideals. They attack someone not just to rob him or her and gain money,
they beat people up not just because they are sadistic. No, they do these
things in the case of hate crimes because they hate the victim. They don't
just want money or freaky pleasures; they want to express their hatred as
well. Because there are therefore really two crimes involved, the ordinary
laws against robbery and assault are not enough. We need special hate
crime laws because hate crimes are special and they work to destroy what
is special about America.

Hate crime laws would focus on the hatred behind the crime and
not just on the crime itself. Opponents say that extra laws will not provide
extra protection and for once I agree with them. Those bent on violence
ignore the law and even delight in breaking it all the time. But the law
serves to punish them when they do and in the case of hate crimes it sends
them a message in advance about where we stand as a nation. Special
crimes need special laws and those laws will serve to unite the rest of us
and give public and legal expression to our union. The haters are the only
things worth hating and the rest of us should unite against them. *E pluribus unum!*

Questions for Analysis

Logic

1. Explain in your own words the facts that prompt Dodge's claim in
   paragraph 1 that "great progress has been made."

2. In paragraph 2 Dodge claims that hate crimes "strike at the heart of the American dream itself." Explain her reasoning in your own words.
3. On what basis does Burns attempt to refute those opponents who claim that no special laws are needed for hate crimes?

Character
1. Point to and explain some of the ways in which Dodge attempts to establish a sense of her own character as a patriotic one.
2. What senses of her character besides that of patriotism does the author's knowledge of the Latin motto tend to create?
3. In paragraph 4 Dodge says that in one instance she agrees with her opponents. What sense of character does that acknowledgment tend to create?

Emotion
1. In paragraph 3 Dodge calls those who commit hate crimes "traitors." To what emotions in her reader does she appeal by using this word?
2. In paragraph 3 Dodge attributes the desire for "freaky pleasures" to those who commit hate crimes. To what emotion in her reader does she seek to appeal by using this phrase?
3. To what emotions in her reader does Burns appeal by ending her assignment with the words *E pluribus unum?* Name more than one emotion and explain your answers.

"HATE CRIME" LAWS CHANGE THE LAW

Samuel Francis

The *Economist,* a British-based but globally circulated news magazine of the proper progressive tint, is not exactly a hate-sheet of the racialist right, but even it is having problems with the very concept of "hate crimes." Acknowledging that the murder in Jasper—where three white men, ex-convicts, tied a black man to the bumper of their pickup truck and dragged him to death, dismembering his body—was one of particular "horror," the editorial nevertheless proceeds to argue that "the notion of 'hate crimes' is flawed."

Had the black victim in Jasper, James Byrd, been white and had he been killed in the same way by the same men, the magazine asks, would the crime have been any less a horror? Had the killers been motivated by

perverse sexual drives, by psychopathic delusions, or simply by merce-
nary reasons, to swipe the change in Mr. Byrd's pockets, would the killing
merit the additional punishment that state and federal law reserve only
for crimes motivated by race?

Put in that context, the answer ought to be obvious. Murder is
murder, and to say that some are motivated by "hate" and others aren't
strikes most normal folk as at best a bizarre usage of the word. Sadists
who dismember children for pleasure and jilted husbands who beat their
wives to a pulp are at least as driven by "hate" in any normal usage as
white hoodlums who murder a black man for the fun of it. Yet, the editorial concludes, hate crime laws imply that murders for other motives
are "less awful" than those motivated by race.

It also notes that "Once race—or religion, or gender—is introduced into the equation, this naturally colours the motive for the crime
in the eyes of the criminal justice system." In effect, the law criminalizes
the motives, as it does not do for any other kind of crime.

But the "white supremacist" opinions and the Nazi paraphernalia   *5*
supposedly left at the scene of the crime are not in themselves against the
law. Hence, "The notion of 'hate crime' may be, in effect, an extra penalty imposed on people whose views are offensive, as well as their actions.
Ironically, it makes the justice system pick on them simply because they
are different."

The editorial implies an important point, namely, that hate crime
laws come very close to outlawing certain opinions, ideas and attitudes
simply because they're offensive to most people. On the same grounds,
the law could plausibly penalize perverse sexuality and even jealousy and
greed at least as much as it currently punished "hate."

Yet the editorial could go a bit further. Anglo–American law does
not traditionally criminalize motive, no matter how offensive, and the
distinction between "motive" and "intent" (which is criminalized in law)
used to be quite clear.

If I rob a bank to help my family and my accomplice robs the bank
to pad his pockets, we each have a different motive—but we both had
the same intent: to rob the bank. "In law," found a leading court case on
the issue, People v. Weiss, "there is a clear distinction between" "motive"
and "intent." "'Motive' is the moving power which impels to action for
a definite result. Intent is the purpose to use a particular means to effect
such result."

"Intent," of course, is the element in law that creates the crime
itself. A homicide without intent is not murder but manslaughter, and
carries a lesser penalty. "Motive," on the other hand, is largely irrelevant
to the criminal act and to the punishment the act receives.

No one seems to doubt that the suspects in Jasper "intended" to   *10*
commit murder, and if the prosecution can prove that intent, their road

to the death house will be expedited. But if their crime is tried as one of "hate," not only their intent to kill but also their reasons for killing will have to be proved in court.

That may or may not add to the burdens of the prosecution, but there's no reason to think it will enhance whatever justice is eventually dispensed—and there's every reason to believe that other ideas and the motives they create sooner or later may also become criminal acts.

Questions for Analysis

Logic
1. Beginning in paragraph 5, Francis argues that "hate crime" laws may end up being used to penalize people with views that those in power might find offensive. Explain his reasoning in your own words.
2. Beginning in paragraph 6 Francis argues that "hate crime" laws may end up penalizing other emotions such as jealousy. Explain his reasoning in your own words.
3. Beginning in paragraph 8 Francis addresses the traditional legal distinction between *intent* and *motive*. Explain the logic of his distinction in your own words.

Character
1. Francis begins by emphasizing that *The Economist* is a "progressive" and a foreign publication. What sense of his character does this emphasis seem designed to create?
2. In paragraph 3 Francis uses the phrase "normal folk." What sense of his character does this phrase seem designed to create?
3. According to Francis, what should be the place in criminal prosecution for arguments about the character of the accused? Explain your answer.

Emotion
1. Francis puts the phrase "hate crime" within quotation marks when he uses it for the first time, though later these marks are omitted. What seems to you to be the emotional appeal created by the initial use of quotation marks?
2. Does the word *ex-convicts* in paragraph 1 make an emotional appeal to the reader? If you think it does, explain the appeal and how it works to support the author's argument as a whole. If you think not, explain how you came to your opinion.
3. To what emotions does the example of robbing a bank "to help my family" appeal in paragraph 8? What might be an example of "different motives"? Explain the emotional appeal of the example you invent.

EXERCISES: HATE CRIMES AND JUSTICE

Intertextual Questions

1. Using only four paragraphs Burns write the shortest of the three short arguments here. In your opinion, does her restricted length keep her from addressing all the arguments of the other writers? What if anything do they include that she leaves out?

2. Francis brings up the question of a difference between motive and intent that is not explicitly addressed by the other writers. What do you imagine Dodge and Reese would have to say about this distinction? Explain the reasoning behind your answers.

3. Dodge and Reese both refer to specifically American traditions, while Francis quotes a British magazine. In your opinion, is the issue of hate crimes a particularly American one? Explain your answer.

Suggestions for Writing

1. Francis supports *The Economist*'s position that the legal system must maintain the traditional distinction between motive and intent. Write an essay in which you attack, defend, or modify this position.

2. Dodge claims that the need for hate crime laws is a particularly American one and even that those who commit hate crimes are "traitors." Reese, on the other hand, claims that hate crime laws would be so un-American as to foster totalitarianism. Write an essay in which you argue for or against one or the other view.

3. What are your own views on the need for hate crime laws? Write an essay in which you make your own case, being careful to take into account the views of the writers in this section.

3   Should Blood Alcohol Percentages
for Drunken Driving Be Lowered?

YES!

Judith Lee Stone

Momentum is gaining for enactment of a federal law to lower the   *1*
drunken driving threshold from 0.10 percent Blood Alcohol Content
(BAC) level to 0.08. This effort has support from Republicans and
Democrats, as well as President Clinton, doctors, nurses, police officers,
victims, and more importantly, the general public.

Why? Because every year, more than 17,000 Americans die on our
highways and one million more are injured in alcohol-related crashes.
Every 30 minutes, someone in this country—maybe a neighbor, a friend,
a co-worker or a family member—dies in an alcohol-related crash.

We read about many of those tragic deaths in our hometown newspapers and give thanks that we were spared. But that's not enough. We
need tougher laws to keep drunken drivers off our roads. That is why it
is imperative that Congress pass a 0.08 law.

Under proposed legislation, states will have several years to enact a
0.08 law or lose a portion of their federal highway funds. This approach
is identical to the national Uniform Minimum Drinking Age law signed
by President Reagan in 1984. No state lost money and every state now
has a drinking age of 21. At present, 15 states have 0.08, but it makes no
sense for a driver to be legally drunk in one state but not in another.

Studies show that virtually all driving skills are significantly im-   *5*
paired at 0.08. The average 170-pound male must consume four drinks
in one hour and the average 137-pound female three drinks in one hour
to reach 0.08, according to the U.S. Department of Transportation. Who
would want their child in a car driven by someone who has consumed
three, four or even more beers in an hour? A 0.08 limit is not unreason-

able and lets people have a couple of beers after work or glasses of wine with dinner and still drive home. This is not about stopping drinking. It's about stopping excessive drinking and driving.

A 0.08 law could save your life. A study at Boston University found that 500 to 600 fewer highway deaths would occur annually if all states adopted 0.08. This is the equivalent of preventing three major airline crashes each year. The study compared five states that lowered their BAC to 0.08 from 0.10 with five states that did not. The 0.08 states experienced a 16 percent reduction in the proportion of fatal crashes with a fatally injured driver whose BAC was 0.08 or higher. There was an 18 percent reduction in such crashes with a fatally injured driver whose BAC was .15 or higher.

For years, safety activists have been working to encourage states to lower the BAC limit. They have been stymied by lobbyists of the alcohol and hospitality industries. By using phony statistics and Chicken-Little threats of prohibition, the alcohol industry has stopped many of these bills. Now it's working to block a federal law. These are the same companies that tried to stop the 21 drinking age law, which has saved more than 15,000 lives.

Don't let this industry determine the fate of this law and your family's safety. It's time to adopt 0.08 in every state and make driving safer for everyone.

Questions for Analysis

Logic

1. In paragraph 3 Stone argues that a *federal* law is necessary to achieve her goal. What rationale does she subsequently bring to bear in support of her claim that "it is imperative that Congress pass a 0.08 law"?
2. In paragraph 4 Stone says that "it makes no sense for a driver to be legally drunk in one state but not in another." How might an opponent rationally respond to this claim?
3. In paragraph 5 Stone implies that even a 0.08 BAC is dangerous. Explain how she might make this claim explicit as a logical argument that supports her position.

Character

1. How does the list of supporters in paragraph 1 work to establish Stone's character as an advocate for the rest of the essay?
2. In paragraph 3 Stone speaks of "our hometown newspapers." What sense of her character and its relation to that of her readers does this phrase work to create?
3. Stone concludes paragraph 5 by making some distinctions. What sense of her character does this act and its manner create?

Emotion
1. What is the emotional appeal created by the word *momentum* that begins the essay? How does it invite readers to feel in deciding the issue of a lower BAC?
2. Stone gives several statistics to support her claim. How does she attempt to personalize these statistics, to make them more than cold facts? Give an example and explain how it works.
3. In paragraph 7 "activists" are opposed by "lobbyists." Explain how Stone uses the emotional appeals of these words to advance her argument.

NO!

Rick Berman

Because drunken driving accidents can be unspeakably tragic, the current debate over where to set the drunken driving arrest threshold is fraught with emotion. Unfortunately, emotional reaction is edging out rational thought as we struggle for solutions to this preventable problem.

Rep. Nita Lowey, D-N.Y., and Sen. Frank Lautenberg, D-N.J., want to force every state to lower the drunken driving threshold to 0.08 percent blood-alcohol concentration. For 34 states, that means changing their current 0.10 percent BAC or lose tens of millions of federal highway dollars.

This legislative blackmail has just one hitch: It won't work. It does not address the cause of our nation's drunken driving problem—alcohol abusers who drive.

According to the National Highway Traffic Safety Administration, the average BAC level among fatally injured drinking drivers is 0.18 percent, more than twice the proposed arrest level. Nearly two-thirds of all alcohol-related deaths involve drivers with BACs of 0.14 percent and above.

Worse, not one piece of credible evidence proves that 0.08 percent BAC legislation saves lives. When Department of Transportation Secretary Rodney Slater endorsed the 0.08 percent threshold, he did not cite any DOT research. Instead, he cited a discredited three-page report written by Ralph Hingson, a sociologist with a well-known anti-alcohol bias.

Faced with the reality that 0.08 percent arrest laws do not target the real problem and the lack of evidence attesting to their effectiveness, the rallying cry behind the 0.08 initiative has become "What's the harm?"

Unfortunately, the answer is "Plenty." And that's the reason the restaurant industry is adamantly opposed to this legislation.

According to the NHTSA, if the 0.08 percent BAC arrest threshold becomes law, it will be illegal for a 120-pound woman to drive after drinking just two six-ounce glasses of wine over a two-hour period. When pulled over at a "sobriety checkpoint," she faces arrest, fines, jail, higher insurance rates and license revocation for behavior that today is considered responsible and not part of the drunken driving problem. Meanwhile, the chronic drunken driver goes unaffected by this new "tough" drunken driving law.

In the 15 years since our nation got serious about the war against drunken driving, state legislatures have passed thousands of anti–drunken driving laws. Left to make the decision themselves, 34 states have repeatedly rejected proposals to lower the drunken driving arrest threshold as being ineffective. Of the ten safest states in the nation, eight have a 0.10 percent BAC drunken driving threshold. Obviously, they are doing something right.

Far from being over, the fight against drunken driving becomes 10 more difficult now that the problem is down to alcohol abusers who choose to ignore the existing law. What we need is a logical approach that generates results, not emotional rhetoric that generates headlines.

Questions for Analysis

Logic

1. In paragraph 3 Berman claims that the 0.08 BAC "does not address the cause of the drunken driving problem—alcohol abusers who drive." Explain in your own words how (according to Berman) the statistics of paragraph 4 support this claim.
2. In paragraph 8 Berman implies an error in the rationale of the proposal to lower the BAC. In your own words explain the nature of the error he sees.
3. Explain in your own words the reasoning behind Berman's claim in paragraph 9 that "obviously they are doing something right."

Character

1. Berman's first and last paragraphs deprecate what he calls emotional approaches to the problem of drunken driving. What sense of character does this stance seem designed to create?
2. In paragraph 5 what issue of character does Berman suggest by reporting that the secretary of the DOT cited no DOT research to support his recommendation?

3. In paragraph 9 Berman says that "our nation has got serious about" the problem of drunken driving in the last 15 years. Does Berman himself create a sense of seriousness in his own character? Cite some evidence that supports your view.

Emotion
1. Explain in your own words the argument implied by Berman's use of the word *blackmail* in paragraph 3.
2. What emotions are invited in the reader by putting the words *sobriety check point* and *tough* in quotation marks in paragraph 8? How does the paragraph otherwise support or fail to support the attitudes evoked?
3. In his last paragraph Berman claims that the drunken driving problem is now "down to" one set of people. How does this phrase work to support through emotion the claim of his last sentence?

Berman

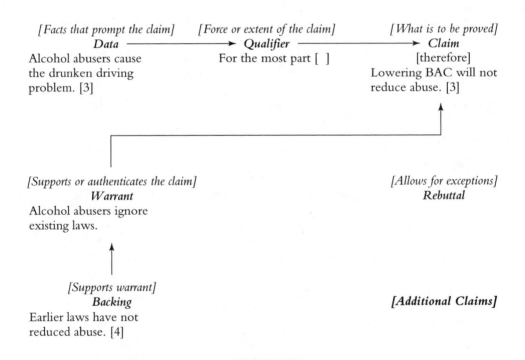

[Facts that prompt the claim]
Data   →
Alcohol abusers cause
the drunken driving
problem. [3]

[Force or extent of the claim]
Qualifier   →
For the most part [ ]

[What is to be proved]
Claim
[therefore]
Lowering BAC will not
reduce abuse. [3]

[Supports or authenticates the claim]
Warrant
Alcohol abusers ignore
existing laws.

[Allows for exceptions]
Rebuttal

[Supports warrant]
Backing
Earlier laws have not
reduced abuse. [4]

[Additional Claims]

ELIMINATE THE MINIMUM DRINKING AGE

Doug Bandow

Every month or so seems to bring another tragic death from binge   1
drinking at a fraternity party. Cries for tougher government action pre-
dictably follow.

But stricter prohibition is no answer. It is illegal in every state for
anyone under 21 to buy alcohol (and in most states to consume it). Unfortunately, observes New York University sociology Professor David
Hanson, "we have driven (drinkers) off campus, so now we have no control over their drinking."

Indeed, the greatest harm occurs from binge drinking, which would
be reduced more through family education than legal sanction, a process
that would be more likely to occur if the drinking age was lower.

Threatened with the cut-off of federal transportation grants, every
state has banned alcohol sales to 18- to 20-year-olds. Some states are tar-
geting enforcement against young adults. Virginia has created a task force
on campus drinking and begun raiding fraternity parties.

Some beach communities arrest kids who try to illegally snatch   5
a drink. Key West, Fla., calls its convict roadside sanitation crew the
"spring break chain gang."

Unfortunately, such measures are not likely to reduce underage
drinking. An incredible 84 percent of college students drink. Nearly
half of college students and one-third of high school seniors say they
binge drink.

There is no evidence that the downward shift in the minimum
drinking age has reduced drinking by young adults.

As former Virginia state Attorney General Richard Cullen observed, "We're failing miserably right now."

A better strategy would be to teach young adults how to drink.
Cullen's successor, Mark Earley, recently observed that Virginia's goal was
not "to prosecute and persecute students," but to "change the culture of
binge drinking on campus." The best way to change that culture would
be to lower the minimum drinking age.

Explains Professor Dwight Heath of Brown University, "The choice   10
is not between control and the absence of control." Rather, the choice is
between formal legal sanctions and informal social pressures "shared by
other members of one's community, and likely to be not only accepted
but highly valued by most people."

In short, most adults will drink before they reach the age of 21, irrespective of the law. The objective, then, should be to encourage them to do so responsibly—for the rest of their lives.

That is most likely to occur by treating drinking as one of many rites of passage to adulthood. Instead of having to violate the law, older teens could drink openly in the company of other responsible users. This would, argues Elizabeth Whelan of the American Council on Science and Health, help those nearing adulthood "learn how to drink gradually, safely and in moderation."

This is the practice in most other countries. Observes Heath: "Where people start to drink at an early age, alcohol is not a mystical, magical thing." People are less likely to "drink to get drunk because they know that's a stupid thing to do."

Only three other nations set the minimum drinking age at 21. Belgium, France, Germany, Italy and Spain all allow 16-year-olds to drink. In some countries there is no age limit for children drinking with their parents.

New Zealand allows kids to drink with their parents in specified   15
establishments. The Liquor Review Advisory Committee is now urging not only that the legal minimum drinking age be reduced from 20 to 18, but that minors be allowed to drink anywhere if accompanied by a parent or guardian.

The panel's goal is to "encourage young people to consume alcohol moderately in safe drinking environments," instead of in situations "where the risks of liquor abuse are very high."

The Committee concluded "that increased legal availability will not make a significant difference to the level of consumption in all age groups, but will bring more young people into controlled drinking environments."

The United States should pursue a similar strategy. Today, kids tend to drink only with other kids. Hanson suggests permitting parents to serve alcohol to their children, even in restaurants, and to stress that responsible drinking, not drinking, is the real sign of maturity.

Family physician Patricia Roy counsels parents to allow their children to learn drinking at home: "Kids should learn how to drink responsibly under the guidance of someone who cares and won't let anything happen to them."

Congress should eliminate the federal minimum drinking age.   20
There's no reason for Washington to set a national standard. In any case, states should cut their drinking age, irrespective of the threatened loss of federal funds.

America has a long and unpleasant history with various forms of prohibition. Instead of prosecuting young adults who drink, families and communities should teach them how to drink responsibly.

Questions for Analysis

Logic

1. Bandow begins his essay by citing some unintended effects of "tougher" antidrinking laws. Explain the logic of the tough argument and why, according to Bandow, that logic is flawed.
2. Why, according to Bandow, do kids tend to drink only with other kids?
3. Explain in your own words the New Zealand argument for allowing children to drink anywhere when accompanied by parents or guardians.

Character

1. Bandow alludes to the experience of other countries in the course of his argument. How do these allusions help to create a sense of his character?
2. Bandow cites several authorities throughout the essay and names them. How does this help to create a sense of his own expertise? Would merely referring to "studies that have been made" have worked as well? Explain your answer.
3. Moderation and self-control are what Bandow claims will make a more mature relationship to alcohol. Do you find moderation and self-control evident in the manner of his argument? Explain your answer with examples.

Emotion

1. What is the effect created by Bandow's relation to the word *cries* in his first paragraph? Would he use the word to describe his own arguments? Why or why not? What does the word suggest about his opponents?
2. Bandow uses the term *binge drinking* several times in the course of his essay but never defines it. What are the emotional implications of the word *binge* and how do they contribute to Bandow's argument?
3. Bandow often refers to "kids" but in his last paragraph he calls the same people "young adults." Explain what he seems to see as the advantages of ending his essay this way.

EXERCISES: SHOULD BLOOD ALCOHOL PERCENTAGES FOR DRUNKEN DRIVING BE LOWERED?

Intertextual Questions

1. In your opinion which writer uses statistics in the most convincing way? Which uses them in the least convincing way? Explain your answer with examples.

2. Find an example in Stone's essay that you think Berman would see as the "emotional rhetoric" he opposes in his last paragraph. Explain your reasoning. Could Stone make a similar case about Berman? Explain.
3. In your view, which of the writers is most realistic about the problems presented by alcohol? Defend your answer with arguments and examples.

Suggestions for Writing
1. Taking account of the arguments in all three readings, write an essay on the direction that you think national alcohol policy should take.
2. Do you agree with David Hanson (in paragraph 2 of Bandow's essay) that college regulations only displace the alcohol problem? Write an essay in which you advocate and defend a sensible drinking policy for colleges and universities.
3. Bandow does not directly address the problem of drunken driving. Write an essay in which you argue that his proposals will or will not help solve the problem.

4   Giving Computers the Boot

ALONE WITH MY E-MAIL

David Pellicane

After college, our fraternity e-mail became an extension of room   *1*
301, the hangout with two TVs and four to twelve people sharing scut-
tlebutt and taunting each other for various infractions—not drinking
enough, hanging around with girls, getting fat, working out too much,
and so on.

For the first two years the e-mail was entertaining. The content
consisted of drinking and dating stories (old and new), would-be witty
comments about mothers and girlfriends, and the occasional book or
movie review. Practical and engaging.

Now it's five years after college and those common memories are
starting to dissolve—how much can you write about throwing up in a
bucket? As people go further back and try to find common memories
from before we knew each other, the results read like an eighties home
page ("Remember when all you needed was a Rubik's cube to be happy
and Mom would bring you a Chocodile while you watched Captain
Caveman?") The last batch of e-mail I browsed through was about favorite toys and TV shows from the seventies.

I don't blame my fraternity brothers for choosing this road; it's supposed to be the lingua franca between the mediated generation and the
media. But it disturbs me when the people I've known for years are discussing slot cars and Punky Brewster. There is something insidious about
actively searching for a shared identity in the first place, but when the
trek starts with Rick Springfield and hackey sacks I get the shakes. Just
because it existed while we were growing up doesn't mean it deserves
discussion. Just because our generation wasn't thinned by an unwinnable
war or galvanized by a mustachioed madman or harmonized by a mongo
concert doesn't mean that I have to talk about Etch-a-Sketch to relate.

The truth is, I don't really remember watching the Brady Bunch. I 5
remember the Brady Bunch being on while I wrestled with my brother
until my mother had to whack us with her wooden spoon. I remember
finally beating up that bus stop bully Mark Gorganza, and Justin Merrill
beating me up. I remember when my cousin Brian got killed in a car
accident and he looked like Dracula at the wake.

These are pretty boring as memories go, not as enthralling as a fire-
fight in Da Nang or a wintry march through Siberia or seeing Jimi Hen-
drix with two million stoned people. The only time I mention them is
when they directly pertain to the conversation I'm in, and even then I
spruce them up, embellish them, or add a funny moral.

The problem with the Internet is that there are no censors. In the
real-time version of room 301 there were always five or six censors
around. When things got boring or maudlin or tangential the censors said
so—loudly, clearly, and instantly. In the virtual version of room 301 the
censorship is delayed. There's nobody hovering over you when you write
e-mail, shouting "BOR-ING!"

The really disturbing part is that this mental onanism doesn't even
lead back to real memories, but instead to media and products. This
search for shared memory is dangerous for a number of reasons. It creates
a specious history that demeans your real life story; it gives corporations
exactly the self-reflexive power they want. And finally, to use an eighties
phrase, idolizing pop culture that we didn't even create is just lame.

Imagine an Internet many times bigger than the one we have now.
Faster too, and with enough memory to store high-resolution versions
of every Jenny McCarthy JPEG. Some 3 billion of the 6 billion people
on earth have access to the Web, and 1.5 billion people have their own
pages—with top ten lists, favorite movies, lyrics to Weezer songs, links,
Yes album covers, all the stuff that makes Web pages rich. That leaves one
reader for every Web page. And since nobody has the time or chutzpah
to read, let alone browse the Web, that leaves no readers for most of the
text that exists on earth. Complete, unchecked onanism. No interaction,
no breeding of ideas, no dynamic between reader and audience. The
exact opposite of a community.

In other words, about what we have now. If the Web has achieved 10
nothing else, it's shown how superfluous locks on diaries always were.
Nobody reads because nobody cares, and they doubly don't care when
your only known connection to the outside world is knowing Apu's last
name. The important stuff in our lives happened while we weren't paying
attention to TV. Not every prefabbed generational bond is worth exploring. I'd rather think I have nothing in common with someone my age,
except what community we make ourselves.

Questions for Analysis

Logic

1. Explain in your own words the author's reasoning about the role of "censors" in college discussions.
2. The author is suspicious of "popular culture" as a basis for generational solidarity. Using an example from the text, explain how the author argues on this theme.
3. The author is suspicious of "corporations" and their relation to "specious" history. Explain his arguments on this theme.

Character

1. Waiving the issue of what college fraternities mean to you, explain with examples the sense of the character created for the author as a fraternity member.
2. Does the author create a sense of change in his character from the time he was in college? If you think so, describe the change and explain how your sense of change is created through the author's use of language. If you think not, show how the author uses language to create a sense of continuity in his character.
3. What qualities of character does the author attribute to home page creators in general? What language does he use to create a sense of these qualities for the reader?

Emotion

1. *Fraternity* and *generation* are terms that appeal to feelings of solidarity. In addition to his use of these individual words, what techniques does the author employ to appeal to his readers for the value of solidarity? Does he attempt to create a sense of solidarity with his reader? Explain your answer.
2. The word *alone* in the title has emotional connotations opposite to those of *fraternity* and *generation*. What uses of those opposite connotations does the author make in his argument through emotional appeal? Point to some examples.
3. At the end of the essay the author's "tone of voice" is far from that of the happy-go-lucky persona we hear early on. To what emotions in his reader does this change appeal? Does the change contribute to the argument as a whole? Explain your answer.

Pellicane

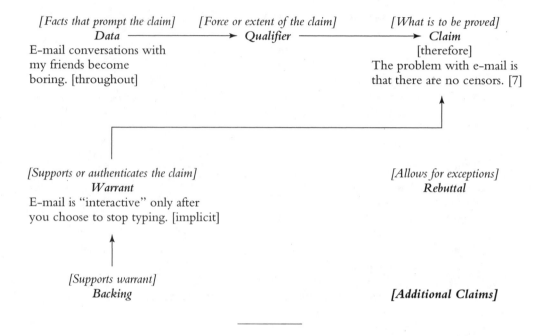

BAD ASSOCIATIONS

Papia Bhattacharyya

If you could go back in time ten years to my high school and ask   *1*
me, "What is 'RAM'?" I would have probably told you that it was a male
sheep. If you had asked my peers what a "hard drive" was, they quite
likely would have confused it with "overdrive." If you had, out of frustration due to our ignorance of technology, approached our teachers and
asked them what a CPU was, I guarantee that you would have received
many blank looks except perhaps for Ms. Stolfi, who in her determina-
tion to convince us of her omniscience, would have told you that it was
a small remote university in Delaware.

If you could go back five years and ask my brother and his peers the
same questions, they would surprise you with not only a definition of
each, but probably specifics about the most innovated items on the cur-

rent market. They could all tell you how many megahertz their processors in their home computers were, how many megabytes of RAM they had and how large their hard drive was.

Technology has bounded onto the center stage in the last few years, hogging the spotlight and forcing us to watch it engorge itself with power, growing ever strong and more prominent. This has impacted our society in one way by the creation of two classes of people, those who know computers (the "literate") and those who don't. There is no middle class. I am a lover of reading and writing, and I hate the thought of books and journals being obliterated by electronics, so herein we will refer to the "literate" as the "knowers," reserving the former term for its original meaning. Sure, the degree of computer knowledge varies from individual to individual, but this distinction is more of a social one than an educational one. In high school, you are either "in" or you are not. You cannot be sort of "in." You are either a knower or you are not. Knowers are the ones who get the most prestige and money these days. They are climbing the powerful social ladder, inducing an awe and respect from the rest of society not unlike that which was bestowed by mere mortals upon the mythological Greek oracles, who imparted to them the knowledge of the gods.

Everyone wants to, and may perhaps eventually have to be a knower to survive. Most people have computers in their homes now. Every day there seems to be newer, faster, and more advanced hardware and software available to us, requiring us to keep upgrading to be able to use our computers effectively in today's world. Yesterday's technology today is like the library card catalogue. This recent exponential growth in technology has suddenly put a lot of power at our fingertips, and I don't know if we are ready to handle it.

I think that this power is adversely affecting both classes of people, the knowers and the rest. I used to be the one of the rest. About two years ago, I was sitting in my study, checking out my recent purchase, the newest operating system on the market at the time, Windows 95. I decided that I would try to organize my files and bring some structure into my otherwise chaotic existence. I moved the pointer to the File Manager icon, and clicked the button on my cute little white mouse. I was happily seeking out old files and putting them into categorized folders, when I accidentally chose "Associate" from the menu instead of "Find." A harmless looking window appeared, and I clicked "Okay," not realizing that I should have clicked "Cancel." I was getting hungry, so I closed the programs and shut down my computer.

The next day, when I turned my computer on to finish my filing job, none of the icons were working. Confusion began to stir within me. The programs refused to open. My hands started to feel weak and hot.

Even my favorite game, "Hearts," rejected me. After about fifteen minutes of failed attempts I started to grow frantic, and I decided that I must use the universal solution of the non-knowers: I turned off the computer and turned it back on. This time I think that I actually jumped out of my chair in disbelief. Windows 95 did not even work now, instead a taunting black and white screen stood in its usually colorful place. Where were my cute icons? What the heck happened to "user-friendly"? Realizing that I was in over my head, I called the technical support number for Micron, the company that made my computer. It took them almost four hours' worth of phone conversation with me, over the course of three days, to get things back to normal. Well, almost normal. I had to reinstall Windows 95, and I lost a bunch of fairly important files that I had been trying to organize, including most of my financial records, which I had computerized in an effort to be more efficient. Paying my bills was not at all fun at the end of that month. Tech support never did figure out what went wrong exactly, all they could tell me was that I must have associated a bunch of files with something they shouldn't have been associated with.

One click. That's all it took to create this mess. The computer industry is growing up so fast that although we feel that we should buy the most up-to-date technology, we don't know how to use it. We aren't given the opportunity; by the time we learn to use the latest hardware or software, it is already passé. We however, have no one to blame but ourselves. As a money-driven society we, both knowers and non-knowers, are working hard to increase the power of this business. Unfortunately, my family is not exempt from this. Two of my cousins are computer engineers at two different successful and famous companies. They entered the industry because they wanted prestigious and lucrative careers. Now, they often have to go to work at seven a.m., and come home after ten at night. They almost always work one weekend day, sometimes two. They don't have time for their families or even themselves. They are miserable, and seem to have aged about ten years in the past five, a rate comparable to that at which the technological industry is aging—in terms of power, that is.

Two years ago, one click screwed up my PC. Two years from now, or maybe less (that's about four in computer years), I can't help but wonder what some unsuspecting but well-meaning person, one who perhaps is just trying to keep up with the times, might unleash upon us with that innocuous CLICK. Even scarier is the magnitude of harm that someone with malicious intentions may be able to cause now, or will soon be able to cause, because of computers. Privacy may very well become a luxury of the past, and personal safety will be nothing but an old and dusty cobweb around each of us, merely a foolish notion that we will cling to out of nostalgia. McNichol puts it best in "In the Blink of a Screen":

Computers have made us more productive, but at the cost of making us more vulnerable. . . . If an enemy really wants to bring America to its knees, it will fire off an enormous electromagnetic pulse that erases every hard drive in the country. In two weeks we'll all be wearing animal pelts and huddling in caves for warmth.

Questions for Analysis

Logic

1. Explain in your own words the author's reasons for arguing that a growing gap between "knowers" and "non-knowers" not only exists but is of crucial importance.
2. The author's essay is organized in part by a movement from an image of personal helplessness to an image of national helplessness. In what ways does that organization support her general argument? Suppose, for example, that the movement of the essay had been reversed.
3. Explain in your own words the facts that prompt the author's claim that two years is really four computer years.

Character

1. The author is in a difficult position because she has to convince the reader that she knows enough about computers to be in a position where not knowing more is dangerous. Identify and analyze some of the techniques of writing by which she establishes her level of expertise.
2. What general qualities of character does the author attribute to those she calls "knowers"? Identify and analyze some examples of the author's uses of language to establish these qualities.
3. What additional qualities of character does the author create for her cousins? How do these additional qualities support her general argument?

Emotion

1. The essay's title certainly points to the immediate cause of the author's disaster. What other aspects of the essay does its title "entitle," and what emotional appeals does the title phrase make in each case?
2. When the disaster first occurred, what emotions did the author experience, and how does she create a sense of them through her uses of language? What are the emotions of the next day, and how are they created?
3. To what emotions in her reader does the author appeal in the example of her cousins? Do these appeals support the essay's main argument? Explain your answer.

IF YOU WISH TO SPEAK WITH A COMPUTER, PLEASE CHOOSE FROM THE FOLLOWING LEVELS OF FRUSTRATION

Greg Tuculescu

For those as yet unfamiliar with the terms *Voice Messaging System* or *Touch-Tone Response System,* they refer to those irritating and impersonal menu options one receives with a call to almost any toll-free number and an increasing number of institutions. You know the ones, ". . . for the option even minutely resembling your inquiry, press 73." As annoyingly comic as these systems may seem, they are representative of a dangerous trend in the reduction of basic human interaction under the guise of efficiency and progress.

Under the banner of efficiency, many institutions and corporations implement Voice Messaging or Touch-Tone Response Systems without realizing (or perhaps caring about) the frustration they cause the consumer. It used to be that these menus were used as an intermediary step to contacting a sales representative, or some sentient being that would help you with your needs. However, it is now commonplace to filter through menu after menu, option after option and conclude your phone call having never spoken with a living, breathing human being.

Perhaps these systems are efficient to the extent that they conserve manpower and money in the all-important endeavor to maximize profit, but they are pedaling the consumer/clerk rapport into extinction.

Many will contend that this is one of the unfortunate effects of progress, or that in a society where one can have their hearts' content with a computer, a phone jack, and a credit card certain sacrifices (like the consumer/clerk relationship) must be made to allow for such tremendous convenience.

Such arguments, however, are skirting the issue by comparing apples and oranges. Sitting in front of a computer to do your shopping or to find the answer to a question is quite different from picking up a telephone to achieve the same ends. As sad as it is that some people are willing to sit in their homes in front of an inanimate object rather than go outside and interact on a social level, that is a choice they are making. If I sit down to my computer to order a book off the Internet, I am choosing the sterile machine interaction over the active social action of going to my neighborhood bookstore and dealing with a salesperson. When I pick up the phone, on the other hand, I'm using a medium that has, since its inception, fostered human interaction. On the telephone, I expect to interact with someone. When I dial a toll-free number, I want to speak with someone who will be able to help me with what I want, answer whatever questions I may have, and maybe even joke around a little in the process, yet when the voice on the other end is not a real human, I can do none of these.

You can't ask a Touch-Tone Response System questions. You may chose from a list of specially tailored questions that may or may not cover what you want to know, but it is not the active question and answer you would have with a person. Rarely if ever do I have a question or concern that is specifically addressed by one menu option. It is usually necessary to press numerous vague options to arrive at a solution that only partially answers my question.

Suppose I have a specific problem that requires immediate attention. I'm not going to get immediate attention from a machine, because it doesn't care whether or not I'm pressed for time. It doesn't care about my problem, and it certainly doesn't care about me.

I could roll into an emergency room in critical condition and in desperate need of a highly specialized operation. Of course the doctor would have to find out if my insurance plan covers such an operation, and while he filters through the infinite maze of menu options, my ruptured organ is slowly killing me. When I'm finally dead, the patient doctor will still be listening to, "for killer bee coverage, press 13."

Ultimately these systems are a depressingly passive, and a laborious means of getting what you need. In fact, I would consider them highly inefficient. Fortunately, several companies have caught onto this sentiment. The other day I heard a commercial that went out of its way to assure the consumer that if they called they would not hear a machine, but rather a helpful customer service representative. Perhaps this reflects the fact that people are speaking out in an attempt to stop the dangerous trend, that if left unchecked could have you hearing ". . . please choose from the following list of options. . ." the next time you dial 911.

Questions for Analysis

Logic
1. In paragraph 1 the author claims that the trend marked by Voice Messaging Systems is a "dangerous" one. List the data that prompt this claim.
2. In paragraph 2 the author implies that the systems promote a false efficiency. What is the rationale of efficiency as far as his opponents, the believers in the systems, are concerned?
3. In the last paragraph the author claims that the systems are highly inefficient. Explain his rationale in your own words.

Character
1. The author begins by giving common systems their technical names. What sense of character does this help to create for him?
2. In paragraph 3 the author speaks of "the all–important endeavor to maximize profit." Do you take him to be ironic here? What evidence has led you to your answer? What difference does the issue make for the sense of character that the author creates for himself?
3. The author presents himself as one who values human interaction. Point to one example where he dramatizes (rather than simply asserts) this claim for his reader. That is, find an example in which he seems to value your reaction to his essay and explain how he creates this sense.

Emotion
1. In the first paragraph the author gives the number 73 as an example, and in paragraph 8 he offers 13. Explain the emotional appeals made by his examples in each instance.
2. The author frequently speaks of frustration. Pick an example and describe the techniques of writing by which he seeks to create for you a sense of that emotion.
3. Circle the author's uses of the word *human* in the essay and describe the appeals to emotion that the author makes by his use of this word.

EXERCISES: GIVING COMPUTERS THE BOOT

Intertextual Questions
1. Pellicane's title emphasizes the alienation from others created for him by computers, and the other two writers also speak of feelings of isolation. In your opinion, do computers foster or prevent communication in the modern world on the whole? Explain your answer with examples and reasons.
2. Each author finds something wrong with the *form* of communication that computers dictate. Do their complaints have a common source (beyond the isolation discussed above), or does each report a distinct problem? Provide examples from the essays in making your response.
3. Bhattacharyya quotes the writer Tom McNichol at the end of her essay to the effect that if American computers all failed, we'd soon be wearing animal skins. Is this just a joke? Given what you know about the roles of computers in your life, discuss your response to McNichol's proposition.

Suggestions for Writing
1. Do you have a complaint or a horror story about your relations with computers? If so, write an essay in which you not only complain but

also argue that you now understand the general cause of your complaint or disaster.

2. In her essay Bhattacharyya argues that there is a growing gap between "knowers" and "non-knowers" caused by the rapid rate of change in computer technology. In which camp would you place yourself? Write an essay in which you reason with a member of the other camp and defend your own status.

3. Which of the authors shows the most respect for what he or she opposes? Write an essay in which you exemplify and analyze the techniques by which that writer does justice to what he or she opposes.

5 Affirmative Action in College and Business

THE QUOTA BASHERS COME IN FROM THE COLD

Brent Staples

California's decision to outlaw the use of race in public college admissions was widely viewed as a death sentence for affirmative action. But Proposition 209 may actually have saved its life. The abruptly diminished black and Latino enrollment in California has raised the specter of "white-outs" not just on campus but in the professions and in the next generation of state leadership. Californians are looking for ways to undo the mess and other states have been frightened into slowing down. A recent survey by *The Chronicle of Higher Education* finds legislatures from South Carolina to South Dakota back-pedaling furiously from California-style proposals. Texas has ordered its university to accept any student who finishes in the top 10 percent of a public high school.

The emerging consensus is that special admissions measures must remain intact until urban schools do better by black and brown students, who currently have little chance of first-rate preparation for college. This realization has taken root even among the neoconservatives who started the war against affirmative action 20 years ago. The change was on display in the March issue of *Commentary*, which devoted much of the issue to affirmative action and carried several articles by writers who reluctantly supported measures that increase minority participation.

Some neocons now argue that race should be taken into account in undergraduate admissions, but not beyond. The distinguished hard-liner James Q. Wilson grudgingly accepts affirmative action at public colleges, but proselytizes for it in police and fire departments, arguing that these agencies must be racially representative to work.

The sociologist Nathan Glazer has had a startling change of heart. His 1975 book "Affirmative Discrimination" served as the bible of neo-conservative thought on the subject. Twenty years ago, Mr. Glazer argued that taking race into account in hiring and college admissions was morally wrong and socially corrosive. But his most recent book, "We Are All Multiculturalists Now," and subsequent essays in *Commentary* and The New Republic find this price of the intellectual right transformed. He now argues that failure to integrate institutions that have become the gateways to wealth and power would "undermine the legitimacy of American Democracy." This was clear enough to the rest of the country 20 years ago. But Mr. Glazer says he accepted the idea only when the presumption that African-Americans would soon be absorbed by the mainstream—and afforded equal opportunity at school—proved false.

Mr. Glazer has changed his mind on affirmative action, but clings   5
to the rhetorical tics that poisoned the debate in the first place. He insists on speaking of it as a form of discrimination rather than as a measure that enhances minority access and the health of the body politic. Californians killed affirmative action only because it was pitched to them as discrimination. But the whitening of the university has revealed this as a bankrupt formulation.

Mr. Glazer's insistence that Americans on the whole are massively hostile to affirmative action is clearly overstated. Women—who make up a slight majority of the electorate and benefit heavily from Federal set-asides—like it a great deal.

In truth, most Americans prefer multicultural environments, including schools, workplaces, movies and television shows. Elite universities have made diversity a prominent selling point and are unlikely to give it up, no matter what the public colleges do. The same impulse is thriving even at Commentary, whose recent issue featured more black writers than once would have appeared in the course of a dozen issues.

Mr. Glazer's change of heart has created fissures among the neocon-servatives. No doubt the most zealous of them will shake their canes at affirmative action even unto the grave. But the most striking feature of the debate is that the impulse toward diversity—and by extension, toward affirmative action—is a mainstream impulse, endorsed in varying degrees even by conservatives who once saw it as the embodiment of evil.

Questions for Analysis

Logic
1. Summarize in your own words the rationale of Staples's claim that Proposition 209 has saved the life of affirmative action.
2. Nathan Glazer's reasoning is reported beginning in paragraph 4.

According to this report what led him to change his views of affirmative action?

3. In paragraph 6 Staples claims that women like affirmative action "a great deal." What reasoning on their part is implied by Staples? Is this the same reasoning he attributes to racial minorities? Explain your answer with examples.

Character

1. Staples refers to several different publications in the course of the assignment. List them and then explain what sense of his character is created by the evidence of his reading.

2. In paragraph 4 Staples refers to "a startling change of heart" on the part of Nathan Glazer. What sense of Staples' character is suggested by his professing to be startled?

3. What sense of Nathan Glazer's character does Staples suggest in paragraph 4 when he says: "This was clear enough to the rest of the country 20 years ago"?

Emotion

1. What does the essay's title imply about the natures of those characterized as "Quota Bashers" by describing them as having "Come in from the Cold"?

2. What general argument is suggested by emotional appeal in paragraph 4 where Nathan Glazer is said to have experienced a "change of heart" rather than, say, a change of mind?

3. What emotional appeal does Staples make in paragraph 8 when he says: "No doubt the most zealous of them will shake their canes at affirmative action even unto the grave"?

"RAINBOW, INC." 2

Michael Lewis

One summer many years ago, I went to work for a company that   *1*
sold municipal bonds. The firm was made up entirely of white men
whose views on race could never be printed in this newspaper [*The New
York Times*]. Our essential business was to curry favor with high-ranking
city and state officials, many of whom were suddenly black. Any fool
could see in about three minutes that we were doomed.

The competing firm of white males down the street had hired a
couple of black males to represent them in discussions with black state

and city officials. (Back then, there wasn't anything as radical as local minority-owned municipal-bond firms; that was for the next generation.) Our white males could no longer get their feet in the door. But then one day, the white male owner of the firm I worked for arrived with a big smile on his face. To the astonishment of all, he announced, "I just went out and hired me one of the brothers." Our white males rose as one and cheered.

The Texaco case is misleading in a couple of important ways, and not only because the most sensational of the original accusations made against the company—that a Texaco executive, in a discussion of black employees he was having with other executives, used the word "nigger"—turned out to be false. The case is obscuring the fact that affirmative action is more fully embraced in corporate America than it is in political America. "Quotas," of course, is a dirty word even in corporate America, but that is more or less what a lot of American companies use to increase their racial and gender diversity and why, for instance, a lot of California C.E.O.'s wanted no part of the state's anti-affirmative-action ballot last month. All sorts of big firms—General Motors, Federal Express, Xerox, McDonald's—now routinely boast of employing representative numbers of blacks.

"We believe that no particular background . . . enjoys inherent advantages or possesses the secret to success," says the I.B.M. employment brochure before explaining how far the company has come in its hiring of minorities. And it has! In 1962, I.B.M. employed 1,250 minorities and women, or 1.5 percent of its work force. In 1995, I.B.M. employed 19,400 minorities and women, constituting 18.2 percent of its work force. Of its managers, 3,500 are now women and 2,000 are minorities.

Corporations like the Army are perfectly designed for social engineering. The same arbitrary authority that once enabled I.B.M. to favor a white job applicant over a black one for extracommercial reasons now enables it to favor a black job applicant over a white. But the operative question clearly is no longer: Why is corporate America so conservative? It is: Why is corporate America so liberal?

Occasionally you hear the argument that diversity actually pays— or at least that you pay a price when you cut yourself off arbitrarily from the talents of minorities and women. The chairman and C.E.O. of AT&T, Robert Allen, has said he views his company's "diversity strategy" as a "competitive advantage." Even liberal activists who have devoted their careers to increasing minorities in corporate America on grounds of fairness often suggest that their activism boosts corporate profits. And who knows, maybe it's true. What is surely true is that it is impossible to disentangle "the market" from the society in which it operates. Whether or not diversity pays in and of itself, it clearly pays to avoid the public perception that you lack it. Interestingly, one of Texaco's first moves after settling its discrimination suit has been to hire a "black" advertising firm (hilariously named Uniworld). Even more interesting, the biggest problem it had in doing this was finding a black advertising firm that wasn't already working for a major oil company.

And maybe the strangest twist of the Texaco case is the speed with which the company's new understanding is coursing through the rest of corporate America. "At a board meeting Wednesday," *The Wall Street Journal* reported last month, "Columbia Gas System Inc. directors urged executives to speed their planned introduction of a diversity program." On Nov. 19, the Chase Manhattan Corporation board discussed, apparently for the first time ever, the possibility that the bank was slow to promote minorities and women. As Robert J. Brown, a director of Duke Power Company, First Union Corporation and Sonoco Products, explained to The Journal: "Diversity has become a bottom-line issue. Before Texaco it was not."

It is no accident that the companies that practice affirmative action most conspicuously—McDonald's, Fedex, General Motors—are precisely those companies selling a product to consumers in the retail marketplace. Corporations are not inherently ideological; they are inherently greedy: if you will buy a product or service more readily from a minority, they will hire minorities to pitch or sell their products. Moreover, all corporations are inherently afraid of any sort of controversy. That is why Jesse Jackson finds them so easy to terrorize. To change the behavior of an American company you don't need to change the attitudes of the people at the top; you don't even need to persuade the company of the righteousness of your argument. All you need to do is generate a noise loud enough that their customers hear it.

People are forever complaining about the power of business leaders. But how powerful can the man be if to scare the hell out of him all you need do is to call him up and ask how many blacks sit on his board?

Questions for Analysis

Logic

1. In paragraph 4 what is the expressed reasoning of IBM in justifying its diversity program? Does Lewis endorse the same reasoning in his essay as a whole?

2. What is the reasoning behind Lewis's claim in paragraph 5 that "Corporations like the Army are perfectly designed for social engineering"?

3. What is the reasoning behind Lewis's claim in paragraph 8 that corporations that sell retail goods to consumers are particularly responsive to diversity plans?

Character

1. What sense of Lewis's character is created in paragraph 1 by his use of the phrase "curry favor"? What sense of his view of his coworkers' characters is created by the phrase? Explain the rationale of any difference you see in the application of the term.
2. What sense of his view of the character of liberal activists does Lewis express in paragraph 6 by his use of the word *even* in the phrase "Even liberal activists . . . "?
3. According to Lewis what is the inherent nature of the character of corporations? Explain your answer with evidence.

Emotion

1. At the end of paragraph 2, what emotional appeal in the word *brothers* seems intended by the owner? Does it, for example, invite his hearers to consider all men "brothers under the skin"?
2. At the end of paragraph 2, what emotions are expressed by the cheer? Explain some of the ways in which Lewis has helped you to understand these emotions by this point.
3. What is the emotional appeal of the company name *Uniworld* in paragraph 6? Why does Lewis find the name "hilarious"?

Does he go far enough in suggesting a solution?

A WORLD OF VIRTUAL REALITY

Thomas Sowell

Domestically, such issues as affirmative action have festered amid   *1*
bitter controversy for decades, partly because the reality could not even
be discussed in many places, including the federal courts. Both have been
discussed in terms of a virtual reality created by pious rhetoric and weasel-
worded evasions.

Those defending affirmative action are quick to point out the historic wrongs done to blacks—but blacks are not even half the people
covered by affirmative action. In the real world, white women are the
biggest beneficiaries. Explain why the enslavement of blacks justifies
giving preferential treatment to white women. Explain why a computer
manufacturer who just arrived from India is entitled to affirmative action
because of what was done to the ancestors of blacks.

Only in the world of virtual reality do such justifications seem to
make sense.

Even in the case of blacks, it is by no means clear that various
"under-representations" can be traced to historic wrongs. The greatest
triumph of virtual reality is the blindly accepted dogma that everyone

would be evenly distributed in occupations, institutions, industries and income levels if it were not for discrimination.

First of all, the many different groups of whites have never been evenly represented. To this day, people of German ancestry and people of Irish ancestry are distributed in different geographical patterns across this country—as they are in Australia and Brazil. Historically, each has been concentrated in different industries and occupations. Moreover these are the same industries for each in other countries around the world—the Germans being over-represented in optics, piano manufacturing and beer brewing, for example, and the Irish in politics, law and writing.

The same kinds of statistical disparities can be found if you trace the history of Jews and Gentiles, Slavs and Scandinavians, or northern and southern Italians. Not only have the adults in these groups differed, the children raised by those adults have performed very differently in school.

While disparities in the United States are discussed in terms of blacks and whites, the same kinds and magnitudes of disparities have been common among different groups in Asia, Africa, Latin America and the Middle East.

Huge controversies have raged over the fact that different groups have different IQ levels. Again, this is discussed as if it were a black-white thing, when in fact all sorts of groups all around the world score differently on IQ tests, whatever color they might be. Even illiterates from different groups score differently—some by greater amounts than the black-white IQ differences—in countries around the world.

Only in virtual reality is there this wonderful sameness which we take as a starting point for measuring the sins of American society. If our educational system taught people history and geography, it would become obvious why there was never any serious likelihood that various groups would be evenly represented anywhere. Geography especially has not been an equal-opportunity factor.

But to expect our education system to study serious subjects like these, when there are so many fun projects, and so much political correctness to indoctrinate the children with, is to go beyond virtual reality to utopian fantasy.

Questions for Analysis

Logic

1. According to Sowell, what is wrong logically with the defense of affirmative action in general? Explain his critique in your own words, but be sure to address Sowell's examples.
2. According to Sowell, what is wrong logically with the defense of affirmative action as it affects blacks? Explain his critique in your own words, but address Sowell's examples.

3. In paragraph 9 Sowell suggests the possibility for a different "starting point for measuring the sins of American society." According to Sowell what would be the logical consequences of choosing his alternative?

Character

1. In his first paragraph, Sowell scorns "pious rhetoric and weasel-worded evasions." Does his essay display for you a character free of those faults? Explain your answer with examples.
2. In paragraph 4, Sowell refers to "blindly accepted dogma." Does his essay display for you a character free from that fault? Explain your answer with examples.
3. Toward the end of his essay, Sowell says the education system is partly responsible for the errors of reasoning he sees. How does he create a sense of himself as a better-educated person?

Sowell

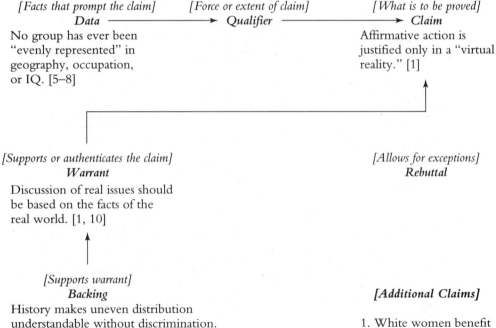

[Facts that prompt the claim]
Data ⟶

[Force or extent of claim]
Qualifier ⟶

[What is to be proved]
Claim

No group has ever been "evenly represented" in geography, occupation, or IQ. [5–8]

Affirmative action is justified only in a "virtual reality." [1]

[Supports or authenticates the claim]
Warrant

Discussion of real issues should be based on the facts of the real world. [1, 10]

[Allows for exceptions]
Rebuttal

[Supports warrant]
Backing

History makes uneven distribution understandable without discrimination.

[Additional Claims]

1. White women benefit most from affirmative action.

2. It is unclear even for blacks that uneven representation is traceable to historic wrongs. [4]

Emotion

1. In the context of the essay as a whole, explain the ways in which the title of the argument itself makes an argument by appealing to the reader's emotions.
2. Sowell ends paragraph 2 with **rhetorical questions**. What is the tone in which you hear these questions asked? What emotions in Sowell does that tone imply? What emotions does he invite his reader to feel by means of the rhetorical questions? Explain your answer.
3. Sowell's voice in paragraph 10 drips with **irony**. Explain what the irony means and the implicit argument it makes by appeal to the reader's emotions.

EXERCISES: AFFIRMATIVE ACTION IN COLLEGE AND BUSINESS

Intertextual Questions

1. In the current terms of racial classification Staples and Sowell are "black" or "African American" while Lewis is "white." Could you have deduced these identities from their writings alone without biographical knowledge? Explain the reasoning and evidence behind your decision.
2. All three writers seem annoyed at one point or another by the vocabularies employed by those they oppose. Discuss the ways in which each operates similarly in this regard. If you think they differ, discuss the ways in which they do.
3. All three writers seem to consider themselves realists who understand the nature of reality. Discuss some of the ways in which each differs in his sense of the reality of contemporary America.

Suggestions for Writing

1. What are your own views on affirmative action? Write an essay in which you argue for those views, being sure to attempt the refutation of any opposing arguments raised by any of the writers in the section.
2. Affirmative action is an emotionally charged issue. Without regard to your own views on the topic as a whole, which writer would you say best copes with the emotional aspects of the issue in his writing? Write an essay in which you analyze the techniques of writing you would praise in this regard.
3. Both Staples and Sowell make an extensive use of irony in their arguments. Write an essay in which you compare their use of irony as an argumentative tool.

6 Should We Take a Chance on Gambling?

GAMBLING WITH OUR NATIONAL CHARACTER

George F. Will

If life is, as a poet said, a sum of habits disturbed by a few   1
thoughts, we should think clearly about those habits we deliberately develop. Consider the rapid spread of legal gambling.

Until 1989, just two states, Nevada and New Jersey, had casino
gambling. Then such gambling returned to Deadwood, S.D., where in
1876 Wild Bill Hickok was shot in the back while holding a poker hand.
Since then 11 more states have legalized some casinos. Staid Minnesota
today has more than New Jersey.

Lotteries helped to finance Jamestown, the Continental Army, Dart-
mouth, Harvard, Princeton and many public works. Today 32 states and
the District of Columbia have government-run lotteries which in 1991
siphoned up $17 billion. Forty-seven states participate in some form of
gambling.

Fifty-two Indian tribes in 17 states (so far), exploiting a Supreme
Court ruling that states do not have regulatory powers over tribes, are
operating casinos and bingo operations grossing $6 billion annually. States
cannot tax Indian casinos, but can profit from them. For example, a Connecticut tribe—whose casino, a three-hour drive from New York City,
soon will employ 10,000—has struck a bargain with their state: The
tribe will give a projected $100 million annually to Connecticut as long
as not even a single slot machine is legalized off the reservation. Around
the nation some cities are contemplating ceding parcels of land to Indi-
ans as "reservations" where gambling would be legal and the cities would
get a cut.

In Tunica County, Miss., America's fourth-poorest county in the   5
1990 census, unemployment has been halved, largely because of a riverboat casino. (Four other states also have riverboat casinos.) It may net the
county $2 million annually, a sum about the size of the county's current
budget.

Five states operate keno and two others are flirting with it. Maryland hopes to raise $100 million this year from keno gambling. Maryland
keno is a high-speed video lottery offering bets every five minutes on
monitors in 1,800 bars and other places. Supporters of this say to critics:
If you object to this windfall from the behavior of consenting adults,
what taxes do you propose to use to compel a similar sum from reluctant
citizens?

In 1991 gross revenues from legal gambling nationwide were $26.7
billion, more than five times the box office of the domestic movie industry. States received only 2.4 percent of their revenues from lotteries, but
this sum—$7.5 billion net—was not trivial.

Are there social costs from all this? Lots, beginning with the ruin-
ous—to health, work and families—excesses of compulsive gamblers.
These are people susceptible, perhaps for psychological or even physio-
logical reasons, to what the American Psychiatric Association calls "a dis-
order of impulse control."

Now, classifying such destructive behavior as a "disease" can be a
tactic for attaining access to government and insurance money, and can
further attenuate the notion of individual responsibility. And calling
a behavior "addictive" is problematic. But research suggests that some
compulsive gamblers are peculiarly prone to a "high," like a drug user's,
from abnormally elevated levels of endorphins in the blood when they
are excited by gambling. For such people, gambling truly is "suicide
without death."

Furthermore, state-sponsored and advertised and hyped lotteries are   10
exploitative. Per capita sales of lottery tickets are higher in poor inner-
city neighborhoods than in suburbs, and the disparity is even larger when
lottery spending is compared as a percentage of household income.

Michael Berberich, writing in Notre Dame magazine, recalls with
appropriate disgust an Illinois lottery billboard in a Chicago ghetto: "This
could be your ticket out." Thus does government peddle a spurious but
tantalizing hope to people particularly vulnerable to delusive promises.

Gambling can be a benign entertainment, but it can become, for
individuals and perhaps for a society, a way of attempting to evade the
stern fact that (as Henry James said) "life is effort, unremittingly repeated." Gambling inflames the lust for wealth without work, weakening
a perishable American belief—that the moral worth of a person is gauged
not by how much money he makes but by how he makes his money.

By institutionalizing a few highly publicized bonanzas, government foments, for its benefit, mass irrationality. It also deepens "the fatalism of the multitude," the belief that life's benefits are allocated randomly.

Joseph Epstein, the essayist, notes that "to have come to America in the first place was to take a serious gamble. To advance with the country's frontier was another gamble." Nowadays, when life for most Americans is without routine risk, gambling may be a way of infusing life with stimulating uncertainty.

But by now, with a deepening dependency of individuals and gov-   15
ernments on gambling, we are gambling with our national character, forgetting that character is destiny.

———————

Questions for Analysis

Logic
1. In your opinion, does Will consider gambling a sin, a wrong, or a crime? How does his implicit definition of harm affect his reasoning, especially the ways in which he meets the arguments of gambling's supporters?
2. Explain the logic of supporters of legalized gambling in paragraph 6. Do you think Will answers this reasoning in his essay? Explain your answer with evidence.
3. What are Will's objections to the logic of gambling as a "disease" (8–9)? Where in the logical process are the objections located?

Character
1. According to Will, what are some of the aspects of our national character that we are gambling with?
2. What risks to the national character does Will suggest we run by legalized gambling?
3. Find a moment or a sequence of moments in Will's writing where he creates for you a sense of his own character. Briefly describe that sense and explain how it is created through language.

Emotion
1. Will's essay seems to begin rather calmly. Rewrite his first paragraph in a tone of greater intensity to see by contrast how that calm is achieved.
2. Will's tone becomes more emotionally charged as the essay proceeds. Pick a later moment and show how his language creates a sense of his emotions.
3. According to Will, what is the emotional attraction of gambling for the gambler? What is the emotional attraction for governments of legalized gambling?

Will

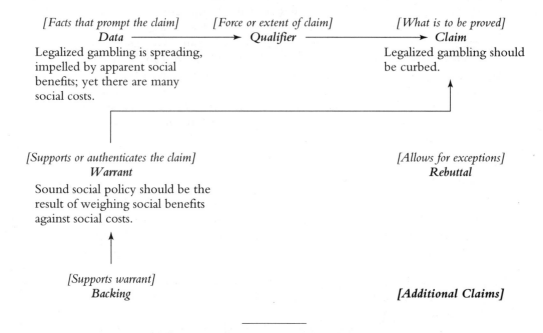

HOW TO WIN EVERY TIME

Marnie Moniere

I like to gamble—always have—but now I've learned how to play   1
with the odds instead of against them. In fact, I'm onto a sure thing. I'll
let you in on it. Here's my system.

I'm still a college student, but since high school I've always worked:
part-time in the school year and full-time in the summers. Waitressing,
data entry, phone banks—you name it—I'm not proud. And I need the
money. I live at home and commute to school. My mother pays my tu-
ition and feeds me. That's it. Anything else I want, it's up to me.

And I want! I want! I still don't know what I'm going to do with an
English degree after college, but I do know it won't make me rich. Now
this may sound strange, but I'd *like* to be rich! I can imagine just how I'd
spend my money—not wisely but too well. I have put quite a bit of time
into mental exercises along this line.

Since I always thought of myself as a logical person and knew I could never get rich by working, I logically decided that gambling was the only way. Besides I like the rush of gambling, the thrill of the action. It's like no other thrill, and the bigger the stakes the better I like it.

I started out with lottery tickets and used up all the combinations   5
of lucky numbers and premonitions—license plate numbers on expensive cars always seemed to be trying to tell me something. But the lottery got old pretty quickly. You have to wait a week for the big one, and the take on the daily numbers didn't do anything for me—not that I ever won any. Then I discovered free trips to Atlantic City. You pay up front for the bus ticket, but they give you more than that in casino chips when you get there. You're already ahead before you start!

I went for a whole semester every weekend and sometimes during the week. At some point in almost every session I'd be ahead, but at some other point I would visit my friendly MAC machine. As a working woman I naturally had my own credit cards—five of them in fact. Guess what. At the end of the term, I was $2,473.35 into my credit cards, almost all of it from gambling. As I slipped away into debt, I got more and more frantic and started doubling up stupid bets and so on and so forth. I didn't want to work for nothing—just to pay back the debt, so I logically got deeper and deeper in the hole. I have worked for the last year, spending practically nothing on myself, and I'm still not clean. I figure I had to work to pay about $400 in interest alone. Some rush.

Here's my system. I went cold turkey on New Year's Eve and started dealing with my temptations by playing blackjack on the computer and writing down lottery numbers in a sealed envelope. Not very thrilling, but I am at this very moment $3,526.00 ahead by not having to pay what I've lost to myself. That is, I still lose most of the time, but I don't have to pay the computer or the man at the convenience store.

Questions for Analysis

Logic
1. Moniere claims to be a logical person. Explain the logic of her behavior when she was a gambler.
2. Explain Moniere's logic in giving up gambling.
3. Explain the logic of her substitution for real gambling.

Character
1. The writer seems a friendly person in the beginning of the essay. Explain how this sense of relation to her audience is achieved.
2. In your opinion, does Moniere see her difficulties with gambling as difficulties of character? Explain your answer.
3. What sense of her character, its strengths and weaknesses, is created for you by the new "system" Moniere has come to employ?

Emotion
1. To what emotions in her reader does Moniere appeal with her repeated insistence on the pleasures of gambling?
2. With the transitional word *besides* in paragraph 4, the writer seems to distinguish between logic and emotion. Do you find the distinction a valid one? Explain your answer.
3. At the end of the essay, how would you describe the writer's tone and the emotions it implies? Rueful? Resigned? Cheery? Describe the emotions you find expressed and describe how they are created through language.

RAKING IT IN

Peter Alson

Last month, the Brooklyn District Attorney, Charles Hynes, led an 1
investigative team that busted the first computerized bookmaking ring ever uncovered in the metropolitan area. Last week, the New York State Lottery introduced a new legal gambling game, Quick Draw, a video version of Keno that is available in bars and restaurants and features nearly instant results. What is going on here?

Mr. Hynes's ongoing crackdown has him pursuing offenders outside his own borough and calling for legislation that would target bettors. In a city open to games like Quick Draw, his preoccupation seems odd to say the least. It's not as if there aren't more serious crimes to wage war against.

I must admit to having an unusual perspective: for about a year, I worked in a Manhattan bookmaking office, which was one of those raided by Mr. Hynes's task force. The bust, last October, was regarded primarily as an inconvenience. We spent the night in the Brooklyn House of Detention, paid our fines and were back in business the next day, shaking our heads at the hypocrisy of the law.

Why, after all, should sports betting be seen in a different light than lotteries, OTB parlors or casino gambling? It defies common sense to suggest that betting on the outcome of a football or basketball game is more pernicious than betting on a horse race.

While Charles Hynes can be defended on the grounds that he is 5
simply doing his job, his fixation helps highlight the national hypocrisy surrounding gambling. New York judges appear to be sensitive to that hypocrisy, since stiff sentences are rarely handed down for illegal gambling. One of the guys I worked with had been arrested on 12 different occasions, but he never served time.

In Britain, bookmaking parlors are legal—licensed, not run, by the government, and the results are quite lucrative for everyone involved (except the bettors). Here, casinos operate much the same way. And the lotteries, including Quick Draw, which offer the worst odds of winning, are the most widely accepted and profitable ventures of all.

Charles Hynes has justified his crusade, in part, by saying that "sports betting is organized crime's cash cow." This may or may not be true. Bob, a bookmaker in his twenties who heads up a medium-sized operation in Manhattan, told me that such assertions were "wildly exaggerated." Bob's office was also busted by the Hynes team last October, and afterward a task force spokesman boasted to the newspapers that Bob's outfit had links to the Gambino and Columbo crime families. "The fact is," says Bob, who is Jewish, "the only Columbo I know is the one from the old TV show."

Even assuming there is mob involvement in many bookmaking operations, this would be just one more reason to make bookmaking legal—so it can be regulated and taxed. The Mafia no doubt wants to keep sports betting illegal, and therefore more profitable (as might Donald Trump, who has thus far been unsuccessful in lobbying to block unwanted competition from Quick Draw). But while keeping bookmaking illegal may profit some, it certainly doesn't benefit the public, whose tax dollars are being spent on a losing proposition.

Questions for Analysis

Logic
1. What according to Alson seems "odd" about the logic of the district attorney? Explain with examples.
2. In your opinion, does Alson's having been arrested serve in any way as a "warrant" for any of his arguments? Explain your answer.
3. Explain the logic of Alson's argument that legalized gambling would have a good effect for society as far as organized crime is concerned.

Character
1. According to Alson, what is the principle feature of character expressed by the district attorney's policy? Explain your answer.
2. What sense of his own character do you find expressed by Alson? What role is played within that sense by his admitting to having been arrested as a bookie?
3. Along with his admitted self-interest, does Alson ever create a sense of being public-spirited? Explain the evidence for your answer.

Emotion
1. To what emotions in his audience does Alson appeal by the "paradox" of his first paragraph?

2. What emotions does Alson implicitly claim he felt in jail? How is your sense of those emotions created?
3. To what emotions in his audience does Alson appeal in his argument about organized crime? Explain your answer.

EXERCISES: SHOULD WE TAKE A CHANCE ON GAMBLING?

Intertextual Questions
1. Compare the views of the three authors on the moral issues of gambling. What are the differences in viewpoint, and what if anything do the writers share in this regard?
2. Compare the views of governmental support for legalized gambling taken by Will and Alson.
3. Which writer seems most in line with your views on the issue of gambling? Which of your views does the writer include, and which does the writer leave out?

Suggestions for Writing
1. Write an essay that makes the arguments you think Will would use against Alson.
2. Write an essay that makes the arguments you think Alson would use against Will.
3. What role or roles do you think it proper for government to play in gambling? Write an essay that advances your views, being sure to take into account the various arguments made by the three writers.

7 Animal Testing

THE TRIALS OF ANIMALS

Cleveland Amory

Ask an experimenter about the animals in his laboratory. Nine
times out of ten he will tell you that they are well cared for and that he
abides by the Animal Welfare Act passed by Congress in 1966.

What he will not say is that both he and his colleagues fought the
act and the amendments to it every step of the way; that, under the act,
his laboratory is inspected at most (if at all) once a year; that when his
animals are under experimentation, the act doesn't apply. Nor will he
say that many laboratories ignore the act's most important amendment,
passed in 1986, which mandates that at least one member of the public
vote on the laboratory's animal-care committee.

Your experimenter is not a scofflaw. Having been for so long sole
judge and jury of what he does, he believes that he is above the law. A
prime example is that of the monkeys in Silver Spring, Maryland.

The monkeys were used in experiments in which, first, nerves in
their limbs were removed and then stimuli—including electrical shocks
and flames—were applied to see if they could still use their appendages.

Dr. Edward Taub, who ran the laboratory, was eventually tried and
found guilty, not of cruelty to animals but of maintaining a filthy lab.
Maryland is one of many states that exempts federally funded experiments from cruelty charges.

Dr. Taub is today a free man. His monkeys, however, are not. They
are still in a laboratory under the jurisdiction of the National Institutes
of Health, which first funded these cruel experiments. Three hundred
members of Congress have asked the NIH to release the monkeys; the
NIH says it does not want them; two animal sanctuaries have offered to
take them. Why can't they live what remains of their lives receiving the
first evidence of human kindness they have ever known?

In the overcrowded field of cat experimentation, researchers at

Louisiana State University, under an eight-year, $2 million Department of Defense contract, put cats in vises, remove part of their skulls, and then shoot them in the head.

More than two hundred doctors and Senator Daniel Inouye, chairman of the Defense Appropriations Subcommittee, have protested this cruelty. The experimenters say that their purpose is to find a way to return brain-wounded soldiers to active duty.

"Basic training for an Army infantryman costs $9,000," one experimenter argued. "If our research allows only 170 additional men to return to active duty . . . it will have paid for itself." But Dr. Donald Doll of Truman Veterans Hospital in Columbia, Missouri, said of these experiments: "I can find nothing which supports applying any of this data to humans."

At the University of Oregon, under a seventeen-year, $1.5 million grant, psychologists surgically rotated the eyes of kittens, implanted electrodes in their brains, and forced them to jump onto a block in a pan of water to test their equilibrium. These experiments resulted in a famous laboratory break-in in 1986, and the subsequent trial and conviction of one of the animals' liberators.

10

During the trial, experimenters were unable to cite a single case in which their research had benefited humans. Additional testimony revealed instances of cats being inadequately anesthetized while having their eye muscles cut, untrained and unlicensed personnel performing the surgery, and mother cats suffering such stress that they ate their babies.

The trial judge, Edwin Allen, stated that the testimony was "disturbing to me as a citizen of this state and as a graduate of the University of Oregon. It would be highly appropriate to have these facilities opened to the public."

It would, indeed—and a judge is just what is needed. A judge first, then a jury. The experimenters have been both long enough.

Questions for Analysis

Logic
1. Is there anything puzzling to you about the logic of paragraph 6? Give an example of some facts or reasons that could be added to the paragraph to help clear up any problems or sharpen the reasoning there.
2. Two acknowledged experts testify in paragraph 9. In what ways does Amory work here and in the surrounding paragraphs to influence your view of the testimonies?
3. Throughout the essay Amory supports public scrutiny, and his own essay may be seen as a means toward allowing that scrutiny. Explain in your own words Amory's apparent reasoning on the benefits of greater public scrutiny.

Character

1. What qualities of character does the beginning of the essay seek to establish in its author? How do the implications about the element of character in his opponents' arguments contribute here to your sense of Amory's own character?
2. Some of the people who figure in the essay are named and some are not. What differences of effect does Amory's choice in naming create for your sense of the characters involved?
3. Amory uses selected and edited quotations in his essay. In what differing ways do the differences among the quotations contribute to your senses of their speakers? How for example does the emphasis on costs in the content of paragraph 9 affect your sense of the speaker?

Emotion

1. After you have read the essay, what two senses does the word *trials* in the essay's title come to have for you? Briefly describe the emotional appeal made in the essay by each sense of the word.
2. Two legal trials resulting in convictions are described in the course of the essay [5–6; 10]. What emotional appeals does Amory make in each case?
3. How would you describe the general tone of voice that Amory uses in the essay? Formal and scholarly? Breezy and amused? Controlled outrage? Point to some examples and show how particular uses of language create the tone you hear.

A SCIENTIST: "I AM THE ENEMY"

Ron Kline

I am the enemy! One of those vilified, inhumane physician-scientists involved in animal research. How strange, for I have never thought of myself as an evil person. I became a pediatrician because of my love for children and my desire to keep them healthy. During medical school and residency, however, I saw many children die of leukemia, prematurity and traumatic injury—circumstances against which medicine has made tremendous progress, but still has far to go. More important, I also saw children, alive and healthy, thanks to advances in medical science such as infant respirators, potent antibiotics, new surgical techniques and the entire field of organ transplantation. My desire to tip the scales in favor of the healthy, happy children drew me to medical research.

My accusers claim that I inflict torture on animals for the sole purpose of career advancement. My experiments supposedly have no relevance to medicine and are easily replaced by computer simulation. Meanwhile, an apathetic public barely watches, convinced that the issue has no significance, and publicity-conscious politicians increasingly give way to the demands of the activists.

We in medical research have also been unconscionably apathetic. We have allowed the most extreme animal-rights protesters to seize the initiative and frame the issue as one of "animal fraud." We have been complacent in our belief that a knowledgeable public would sense the importance of animal research to the public health. Perhaps we have been mistaken in not responding to the emotional tone of the argument created by those sad posters of animals by waving equally sad posters of children dying of leukemia or cystic fibrosis.

Much is made of the pain inflicted on these animals in the name of medical science. The animal-rights activists contend that this is evidence of our malevolent and sadistic nature. A more reasonable argument, however, can be advanced in our defense. Life is often cruel, both to animals and human beings. Teenagers get thrown from the back of a pickup truck and suffer severe head injuries. Toddlers, barely able to walk, find themselves at the bottom of a swimming pool while a parent checks the mail. Physicians hoping to alleviate the pain and suffering these tragedies cause have but three choices: create an animal model of the injury or disease and use that model to understand the process and test new therapies; experiment on human beings—some experiments will succeed, most will fail—or finally, leave medical knowledge static, hoping that accidental discoveries will lead us to the advances.

Some animal-rights activists would suggest a fourth choice, claiming that computer models can simulate animal experiments, thus making the actual experiments unnecessary. Computers can simulate, reasonably well, the effects of well-understood principles on complex systems, as in the application of the laws of physics to airplane and automobile design. However, when the principles themselves are in question, as is the case with the complex biological systems under study, computer modeling alone is of little value.

One of the terrifying effects of the effort to restrict the use of animals in medical research is that the impact will not be felt for years and decades: drugs that might have been discovered will not be; surgical techniques that might have been developed will not be, and fundamental biological processes that might have been understood will remain mysteries. There is the danger that politically expedient solutions will be found to placate a vocal minority, while the consequences of those decisions will not be apparent until long after the decisions are made and the decision making forgotten.

Fortunately, most of us enjoy good health, and the trauma of watching one's child die has become a rare experience. Yet our good fortune should not make us unappreciative of the health we enjoy or the advances that make it possible. Vaccines, antibiotics, insulin and drugs to treat heart disease, hypertension and stroke are all based on animal research. Most complex surgical procedures, such as coronary-artery bypass and organ transplantation, are initially developed in animals. Presently undergoing animal studies are techniques to insert genes in humans in order to replace the defective ones found to be the cause of so much disease. These studies will effectively end if animal research is severely restricted.

In America today, death has become an event isolated from our daily existence—out of the sight and thoughts of most of us. As a doctor who has watched many children die, and their parents grieve, I am particularly angered by people capable of so much compassion for a dog or a cat, but with seemingly so little for a dying human being. These people seem so insulated from the reality of human life and death and what it means.

Make no mistake, however: I am not advocating the needlessly cruel treatment of animals. To the extent that the animal-rights movement has made us more aware of the needs of these animals, and made us search harder for suitable alternatives, they have made a significant contribution. But if the more radical members of this movement are successful in limiting further research, their efforts will bring about a tragedy that will cost many lives. The real question is whether an apathetic majority can be aroused to protect its future against a vocal, but misdirected, minority.

Questions for Analysis

Logic

1. How does the metaphor of "scales" in paragraph 1 represent the reasoning as a whole in Kline's support for animal experimentation?
2. In paragraphs 4 and 5 Kline lists the choices he sees as available on the issue of experiment and medical advance. In your own words explain the implied logic of the support these paragraphs create for his own choice.
3. In what ways during the essay does the author acknowledge and concede well-made points of argument to his opponents?

Character

1. How does the essay as a whole work to refute the self-styled negative characterization of Kline's first two sentences?
2. How does Kline establish a sense of character that includes compassion? Does his compassion extend to the **point of view** that his essay opposes? Explain.
3. Kline attributes apathy on the issue of experimentation to the general

public. Does he seem to include his readers in that characterization? Explain. How does he work to overcome apathy in the essay?

Emotion

1. Kline is a pediatrician, and his examples focus on children. Explain the operation of the emotional appeal created by that focus.
2. In paragraph 4 Kline examines some emotional appeals of his opponents and makes some emotional appeals of his own. Explain why he thinks his own arguments in this regard "more reasonable."
3. What is the emotional appeal of the "computer model" discussed in paragraph 5? In what ways does Kline seek to refute this emotional appeal?

Kline

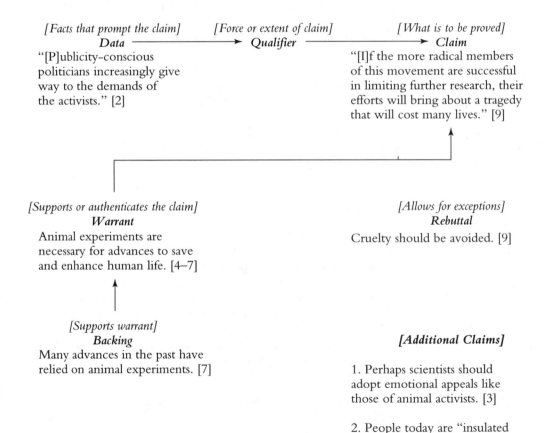

[Facts that prompt the claim]
Data
"[P]ublicity-conscious politicians increasingly give way to the demands of the activists." [2]

[Force or extent of claim]
Qualifier

[What is to be proved]
Claim
"[I]f the more radical members of this movement are successful in limiting further research, their efforts will bring about a tragedy that will cost many lives." [9]

[Supports or authenticates the claim]
Warrant
Animal experiments are necessary for advances to save and enhance human life. [4–7]

[Allows for exceptions]
Rebuttal
Cruelty should be avoided. [9]

[Supports warrant]
Backing
Many advances in the past have relied on animal experiments. [7]

[Additional Claims]

1. Perhaps scientists should adopt emotional appeals like those of animal activists. [3]

2. People today are "insulated from the reality of human life and death...." [8]

IN DEFENSE OF THE ANIMALS
Meg Greenfield

I might as well come right out with it: Contrary to some of my   1
most cherished prejudices, the animal-rights people have begun to get to
me. I think that in some part of what they say they are right.

I never thought it would come to this. As distinct from the old-style
animal rescue, protection, and shelter organizations, the more aggressive
newcomers, with their "liberation" of laboratory animals and periodic
championship of the claims of animal well-being over human well-being
when a choice must be made, have earned a reputation in the world I live
in as fanatics and just plain kooks. And even with my own recently (relatively) raised consciousness, there remains a good deal in both their critique and their prescription for the virtuous life that I reject, being not
just a practicing carnivore, a wearer of shoe leather, and so forth, but also
a supporter of certain indisputably agonizing procedures visited upon innocent animals in the furtherance of human welfare, especially experiments undertaken to improve human health.

So, viewed from the pure position, I am probably only marginally
better than the worst of my kind, if that: I don't buy the complete "spe-
ciesist" analysis or even the fundamental language of animal "rights" and
continue to find a large part of what is done in the name of that cause
harmful and extreme. But I also think, patronizing as it must sound, that
the zealots are required early on in any movement if it is to succeed in
altering the sensibility of the leaden masses, such as me. Eventually they
get your attention. And eventually you at least feel obliged to weigh their
arguments and think about whether there may not be something there.

It is true that this end has often been achieved—as in my case—by
means of vivid, cringe-inducing photographs, not by an appeal to reason
or values so much as by an assault on squeamishness. From the famous
1970s photo of the newly skinned baby seal to the videos of animals being
raised in the most dark, miserable, stunting environment as they are read-
ied for their life's sole fulfillment as frozen patties and cutlets, these sights
have had their effect. But we live in a world where the animal protein we
eat comes discreetly prebutchered and prepacked so the original beast
and his slaughtering are remote from our consideration, just as our furs
come on coat hangers in salons, not on their original proprietors; and I
see nothing wrong with our having to contemplate the often unsettling
reality of how we came by the animal products we make use of. Then we
can choose what we want to do.

The objection to our being confronted with these dramatic, dis-   5
turbing pictures is first that they tend to provoke a misplaced, uncritical,
and highly emotional concern for animal life at the direct expense of a

more suitable concern for human suffering. What goes into the animals' account, the reasoning goes, necessarily comes out of ours. But I think it is possible to remain stalwart in your view that the human claim comes first and in your acceptance of the use of animals for human betterment and *still* to believe that there are some human interests that should not take precedence. For we have become far too self-indulgent, hardened, careless, and cruel in the pain we routinely inflict upon these creatures for the most frivolous, unworthy purposes. And I also think that the more justifiable purposes, such as medical research, are shamelessly used as cover for other activities that are wanton.

For instance, not all of the painful and crippling experimentation that is undertaken in the lab is being conducted for the sake of medical knowledge or other purposes related to basic human well-being and health. Much of it is being conducted for the sake of superrefinements in the cosmetic and other frill industries, the noble goal being to contrive yet another fragrance or hair tint or commercially competitive variation on all the daft, fizzy, multicolored "personal care" products for the medicine cabinet and dressing table, a firmer-holding hair spray, that sort of thing. In other words, the conscripted, immobilized rabbits and other terrified creatures, who have been locked in boxes from the neck down, only their heads on view, are being sprayed in the eyes with different burning, stinging substances for the sake of adding to our already obscene store of luxuries and utterly superfluous vanity items.

PHONY KINSHIP

Oddly, we tend to be very sentimental about animals in their idealized, fictional form and largely indifferent to them in realms where our lives actually touch. From time immemorial, humans have romantically attributed to animals their own sensibilities—from Balaam's biblical ass who providently could speak and who got his owner out of harm's way right down to Lassie and the other Hollywood pups who would invariably tip off the good guys that the bad guys were up to something. So we simulate phony cross-species kinship, pretty well drown in the cuteness of it all—Mickey and Minnie and Porky—and ignore, if we don't actually countenance, the brutish things done in the name of Almighty Hair Spray.

This strikes me as decadent. My problem is that it also causes me to reach a position that is, on its face, philosophically vulnerable, if not absurd—the muddled, middling, inconsistent place where finally you are saying it's all right to kill them for some purposes, but not to hurt them gratuitously in doing it or to make them suffer horribly for one's own trivial whims.

I would feel more humiliated to have fetched up on this exposed rock, if I didn't suspect I had so much company. When you see pictures of people laboriously trying to clean the Exxon gunk off of sea otters even knowing that they will only be able to help out a very few, you see this same outlook in action. And I think it *can* be defended. For to me the biggest cop-out is the one that says that if you don't buy the whole absolutist, extreme position it is pointless and even hypocritical to concern yourself with lesser mercies and ameliorations. The pressure of the animal-protection groups has already had some impact in improving the way various creatures are treated by researchers, trainers, and food producers. There is much more in this vein to be done. We are talking about rejecting wanton, pointless cruelty here. The position may be philosophically absurd, but the outcome is the right one.

Questions for Analysis

Logic

1. In paragraph 4 Greenfield says that the ends of animal-rights activists have "often been achieved—as in my case—by means of vivid, cringe-inducing photographs, not by an appeal to reason or values so much as by an assault on squeamishness." In your view, have the nonlogical means by which Greenfield herself has been persuaded affected the logic of her argument? Explain.

2. In your view, have the nonlogical means of Greenfield's own persuasion affected the organization of her argument?

3. On what basis does Greenfield fault the "philosophical" logic of her own position? Explain in your own words with examples.

Character

1. What aspects of her character does Greenfield seek to establish in paragraph 1? Pick another moment in the essay where she also seeks to establish similar qualities and analyze the ways in which she does so.

2. In paragraph 2 Greenfield says that she rejects "a good deal" of the animal-rights activists' "prescription for the virtuous life." What elements in her own implied definition of the virtuous life does she seek to establish by this rejection?

3. What does Greenfield define in her last paragraph as "the biggest cop-out"? What elements of her own character does she seek to establish by her definition here?

Emotion

1. Greenfield says she is embarrassed by her new position on the issue. In your own words explain (a) the source of her embarrassment and (b) the ways in which she uses this embarrassment as an emotional appeal to her reader.

2. In paragraph 6 Greenfield argues against experiments for purposes

other than those related to "basic human well-being and health." In your own words, analyze the ways in which she creates her emotional appeal within this paragraph.

3. In paragraph 7 Greenfield argues against human sentimentality about animals. In your own words analyze the ways in which she creates her emotional appeal in this paragraph.

EXERCISES: ANIMAL TESTING

Intertextual Questions

1. All the authors may be said to oppose "needless" cruelty. Compare the differing ways in which you understand each author to define implicitly or explicitly this key term.

2. In your view, which of the writers best counters the position of those opposed to the writer's own opinions? Explain your answer using particular examples.

3. Another writer has said: "All other animals are always cruel. Human beings are the only animals who *don't* treat animals like animals." Discuss the ways in which you think each of the three authors would respond to this statement.

Suggestions for Writing

1. In your opinion, which argument makes the most effective emotional appeal, whether or not you agree with its conclusion? Write an essay in which you analyze the strength of the essay's emotional appeal by comparing it to the emotional appeals of the other essays.

2. Another writer has said: "The sufferings of animals take place in the present, while the benefits to human beings are only imagined for the future—this is the strength of the claims to animal rights." Write an essay on animal experimentation in which you examine and discuss the theme of time as it affects differing points of view on the topic.

3. Another writer has said: "Almost all animals used in experiments are bred only for that purpose. If life is a good, they are rewarded by existence. If their lives include suffering and end in death, they are no different from other lives." Write an essay that begins with your response to this proposition and goes on to argue for your further views on animal experimentation.

8   Should Flag Burning Be Made Unconstitutional?

BURNED UP OVER FLAG BURNING

Cal Thomas

Watching the Fourth of July festivities in Washington (and around   1
the country on television) showed the depth of love most Americans have
for this country. That is why a constitutional amendment to ban the
burning of the American flag is so silly, stupid and unnecessary.

No one forced the millions of people waving flags—who respect
and honor the republic for which it stands—to love America. They ex-
hibited a spontaneity no law can impose.

When the House last month passed a constitutional amendment
that would, should the Senate and states concur, outlaw flag burning, it
continued a game politicians have been playing with public school prayer.
The rules of the game are that the social problems confronting America
can be fixed from the top—a kind of "trickle-down" morality.

Politicians love this because they have done much to promote such
a view, which advances their careers and preserves their jobs. Many others
hold this belief because it absolves them of responsibility for fixing what
is wrong with their own priorities and transfers it to government. And
when government increasingly reveals its inability to repair social damage, we blame not ourselves but government and politicians, deepening
the cynicism against institutions and those who work in them.

There hasn't been a lot of flag burning since the Vietnam War. Sen.   5
Howell Heflin (D-Ala.) says that's why now, when the heat of passion is
reduced, is the best time to ban it.

But any time is a bad time for such a ban. First, what constitutes a
"flag"? Is it only the cloth that waves from a flagpole or can be stapled to

a wooden stick and held in the hand? Is the reproduction of the Stars and Stripes on a napkin, patch or coffee cup considered a flag? Some flags are made in Taiwan or in other nations. Would they count as American flags? I saw a chair upholstered in a flag. If the chair was thrown on a bonfire during a protest rally, would that violate the proposed constitutional amendment? And why is burning being singled out for prohibition? Isn't stomping, spitting or pouring paint on the flag also desecration?

Those who would ban flag burning have placed the American flag in a category and context that is idolatrous. Idolatry is defined as "the worship of a physical object as a god; immoderate attachment or devotion to something." While we don't worship or devote ourselves to the flag as we might a religious symbol or being, the attachment some would force on the rest of us comes pretty close to resembling that definition.

The Fourth of July overwhelms us all with the number of displayed and waved American flags. As with speech, the best way to overcome the ugly variety is with more and more beautiful speech, along with a common rejection of the ugly speaker and his words. When a flag is burned, it is the protester, not the flag, who is demeaned. He reveals his base ingratitude when he burns a symbol of a nation great enough even to allow him to indulge in moronic behavior.

Banning flag burning will increase the probability flags will be burned. Allowing it removes the political stinger.

Questions for Analysis

Logic
1. Thomas says in his first paragraph that an amendment is "silly, stupid and unnecessary." In your opinion, does the logic of his essay address all three criteria? Explain your answer with examples.
2. Explain Thomas's reasoning when he claims in paragraph 4 that "politicians" love what he calls in paragraph 3 "trickle-down" morality.
3. Explain Thomas's reasoning in his last paragraph. Do you think he logically connects politicians and flag burners earlier in ways sufficient to earn this claim? Explain your answer.

Character
1. Describe the ways in which Thomas attempts to establish his character as containing "patriotism."
2. Describe the ways in which Thomas attempts to establish his character as containing "objectivity."
3. Describe the ways in which Thomas attempts to establish the characters of his opponents as "silly."

Emotion
1. Thomas's title claims he is "burned up." What is he burned up over, and how does he attempt to convince you he feels that emotion?
2. Explain the appeal to emotion used by Senator Howell as reported in paragraph 5.
3. How does the word *desecration,* which ends paragraph 6 serve as a transition to the theme of paragraph 7?

MY FLAG—BURN IT AND BURN

Maria Hernandez

If anyone is ever foolish enough to try to sexually harrass me at work, he (or she) will be out of a job in a hurry. If anybody insults me in print, I'll make sure he (or she) is hit with a libel suit right away. If anyone trys to trash my home, I'll call the police and have him (or her) sent directly to jail without stopping to pass go. Put some graffiti on my car, and it's bye bye birdbrain.

Every individual in this great country has the same rights I do because so many people have fought and struggled for those rights in battle and through representative democracy. Our flag is the great symbol of this struggle, and it belongs to each and every American. Now why in God's name shouldn't each of us have our flag protected just as we are protected by law in every other way?

Some people say that the Constitution guarantees free speech in the First Amendment of the Bill of Rights and that everyone should have the right to protest government by burning or otherwise desecrating our flag. What nonsense! Everyone agrees that sexual harrassment and libel aren't free speech, that trashing my house is not the way to disagree with me, and that graffiti is not only ugly and insulting but illegal. If you want to protest the government's actions, write to your representatives or senators or the president—you elected them. You are the government. If the representatives and senators or president don't do anything, talk to your neighbors or anyone who will listen about electing people who will. That's real free speech and real democracy.

All this is so obvious that we have never had to have a particular law before to protect the flag that is our common property and common dignity. It's too bad that nowadays there are some who take advantage of this loophole to show off by trashing everyone's flag without fear of being punished. But luckily since we live in a democracy there is something we can do about those cowards who insult the brave soldiers who died for the flag and the rest of us as well. We need to pass a constitutional amendment to ban the desecration of our flag so that we all can be protected against common insults just as we are already protected against individual insults.

Questions for Analysis

Logic

1. The writer makes several analogies in the first paragraph. How does the logic of each of these analogies serve as an attempt to refute the logic of the "free speech" argument of her opponents in paragraph 3?

2. Hernandez sees both "battle" and "representative democracy" as parts of the same "struggle." Explain the logic by which she attempts to connect acts of war and acts of peace.

3. In her last paragraph, Hernandez speaks of a "loophole," but her own claim is that no law protecting the flag exists. How could there be a loophole in a law when there is no law? How do you imagine she would respond to this objection to her logic?

Character

1. What are the principal features of character that the writer seeks to create through her writing? In what ways does each feature act to further her argument? Explain with examples.

2. What are the principal features of character that the writer appeals to in her audience? Are they necessarily the same as those she projects? Explain your answer.

3. What are the principal features of character with which the writer seeks to create a sense of her opponents? Explain with examples.

Emotion

1. In what ways, if any, do the analogies of the first paragraph appeal to the same emotions in the audience? In what ways, if any, does each analogy appeal to a different emotion? Explain your answer.

2. Would it be fair to say that Hernandez appeals to her audience to respect its government? Explain your answer.

3. In her last paragraph Hernandez asserts that the flag is our "common dignity." Where else in the essay do you find the issue of dignity as a theme?

Hernandez

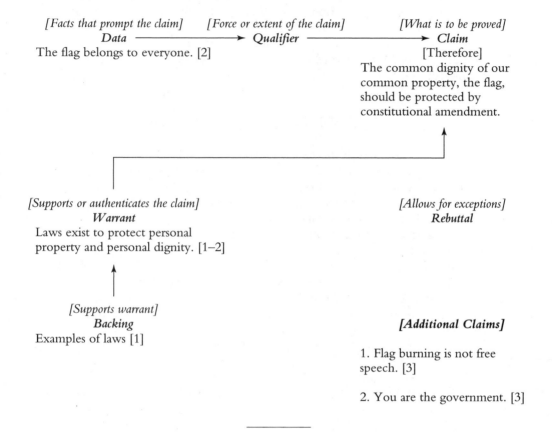

[Facts that prompt the claim]
Data ⟶ *[Force or extent of the claim]* Qualifier ⟶ *[What is to be proved]* Claim
The flag belongs to everyone. [2]

[Therefore]
The common dignity of our common property, the flag, should be protected by constitutional amendment.

[Supports or authenticates the claim]
Warrant
Laws exist to protect personal property and personal dignity. [1–2]

[Allows for exceptions]
Rebuttal

[Supports warrant]
Backing
Examples of laws [1]

[Additional Claims]

1. Flag burning is not free speech. [3]

2. You are the government. [3]

AN AMENDMENT IS NOT THE WAY TO HONOR THE FLAG

Don Feder

Concerning the constitutional amendment to ban flag desecration, *1* which passed in the House of Representatives by a resounding 312–120 vote last week, my heart tells me to go one way, my head the other.

My heart says, "Yeah, punish the bastards. The flag is our highest national symbol, and symbols deserve protection."

My heart swells at the words of Rep. Henry Hyde (R-Ill.), chairman of the House Judiciary Committee, who told his colleagues during the floor debate: "Too many men have marched behind the flag, too many have returned in a wooden box with the flag as their only blanket . . . not to honor and revere that flag."

And I do, believe me, I do. I understand what a blessing America has been in a benighted world, how much that star-spangled banner represents our yearnings and all we hold dear—freedom, compassion, virtue and brotherhood. Even its devices, the stars of heaven's field, allude to the eternal.

For me, the flag provokes a thousand unspoken emotions—all of them poignant. 5

If I only listened to my heart, I would be in the vanguard of proponents of this amendment. But my head says: "Hold on a minute. Vile and reprehensible as flag burning is, it's also an authentic form of political expression. Do we want to start limiting the First Amendment?"

Now, I happen to be an iconoclast of First Amendment law. Much of what the Supreme Court has said regarding the Bill of Rights in the past 50 years is the most pluperfect nonsense.

In rulings on the First Amendment's free-speech clause, the words of the founding fathers have been perverted beyond recognition. Not in their wildest imagining did those gentlemen ever suppose the amendment would be used to protect porn shops, obscenities on T-shirts or the lewd gyrations of exotic dancers.

The First Amendment was intended to shield political dissent, period—including protest of every shape and hue. Sadly, flag burning falls within these very broad parameters.

In its 1989 case, the Supreme Court asked if flag burning is intended 10
to convey a message and if there is a likelihood that the communication would be understood. To both, they answered in the affirmative.

The message of flag burners is utter contempt for our nation and its institutions. That's the intent; that's the interpretation. "America, the red, white and blue, we spit on you," chanted the scummy savages in the Texas case that prompted the 1989 decision.

Disgusting? Yes. But it was just such disgusting, obnoxious, loathsome advocacy (words repellent to the majority) that James Madison and his associates had in mind when they erected the great bar to governmental infringement of political speech.

After all of the Fourth of July rhetoric is done, the anti-flag-burning amendment is really about safeguarding the sensibilities of veterans and other patriotic Americans.

But isn't this exactly what the politically correct crowd is doing on the college campuses with their totalitarian speech codes, which punish people for "hurtful words" and aggravate and agitate various minorities? How ironic that conservatives have fallen into their own form of political correctness.

Once we begin limiting symbolic speech that causes emotional   15
trauma, where do we stop? When a Holocaust survivor sees a swastika arm band, does he feel more or less psychic pain than the war veteran at a flag burning? Should we ban Nazi paraphernalia?

African Americans are outraged by cross-burnings. How many of their people have been beaten or lynched by the diabolical light of the Ku Klux Klan's satanic emblem? Ban them too?

It hurts me to see my nation's flag dishonored. But the flag itself feels no pain, unlike the 1.5 million unborn children grimly reaped in our annual abortion harvest. The child in the womb is in far greater need of protection than a piece of cloth, however splendid the ideals it represents.

Our national government is sorely in need of reform. A balanced-budget amendment would avert the looming debt crisis. A term-limitation amendment would save the republic from the cancerous growth of career politics by re-establishing a citizen legislature.

An anti-flag-burning amendment would achieve nothing substantive. Given the mind-set of the Kunstler clients who engage in such odious acts, it will do little to stop flag desecration. Its sole effect will be to comfort the majority (with the knowledge that flag-burners can be punished) and, in the process, compromise free-speech rights.

Perhaps the best rebuke to flag burners is for those of us who love   20
America to respect the flag more—to honor it by our devotion instead of passing laws that give inane protesters the attention they so desperately crave.

Questions for Analysis

Logic

1. Feder argues in general that with regard to the proposed amendment his head is more important than his heart. In your opinion, does Feder make a logical case for this preference or is his argument basically an appeal to the assumption that we should be cautious of emotion? Explain your answer.
2. Explain Feder's reasoning on the "perversion" of the First Amendment (7–12).
3. Explain the parallels Feder draws between the logic of the amendment's proposers and the logic of "political correctness" (13–16).

Character
1. Describe the ways in which Feder works to establish patriotism as part of his character.
2. Describe how Feder works to establish "feeling" as a part of his character. In other words, how does he come to seem more than a cold-hearted rationalist?
3. What aspect of character does Feder attempt to express by his attack on and support of flag burners (11–12)?

Emotion
1. In paragraph 2 do you find "yeah" a more or less appropriate expression than "yes"? Explain your answer.
2. In paragraph 5 Feder says that "the flag provokes a thousand unspoken emotions." What are some emotions that are expressed verbally in the essay? Name some and explain how they are expressed through language.
3. Compare the emotional temperature of paragraphs 10 and 11. In a way they make the same point. Explain how the difference in emotion is achieved, paying particular attention to the cooler tone of paragraph 10.

EXERCISES: SHOULD FLAG BURNING BE CONSTITUTIONAL?

Intertextual Questions
1. In your opinion, who in the section makes the strongest logical case? Support your answer by explaining the strengths of your choice and the weaknesses of the other essays with regard to logic.
2. In your opinion, who in the section makes the strongest appeal to emotion? Support your answer by explaining the strengths of your choice and the weaknesses of the other essays in their appeals to emotion.
3. Representatives of government are mentioned in each essay. Which writer seems to have the most respect for his or her political representatives and which the least? Explain your answer with examples.

Suggestions for Writing
1. Feder suggests that banning flag burning would lead to attempts to ban an impossibly long and disputed series of symbols. Do you agree? Write an essay in which you address the unintended consequences of the proposed amendment, whether or not you find them serious.
2. All the writers use religious terms at some point, terms like *desecrate* and *idolatry*. Write an essay in which you attack or support the

proposition that the dispute over flag burning is essentially a religious dispute. Be sure in your essay to take a position on the proposed amendment.

3. All the writers appeal to the emotion of patriotism. In your opinion who does the best job in this regard? Write an essay in which you support your answer using examples from all three essays.

9 Multiculturalism and the College Curriculum

RADICAL ENGLISH

George F. Will

At the University of Texas in Austin, as on campuses across the country, freshmen are hooking up their stereos and buckling down to the business of learning what they should have learned in high school—particularly English composition. Thousands of young Texans will take English 306, the only required course on composition. The simmering controversy about that course illustrates the political tensions that complicate, dilute, and sometimes defeat higher education today.

Last summer an attempt was made to give a uniform political topic and text to all sections of E306. It was decided that all sections would read *Racism and Sexism,* an anthology of writings with a pronounced left-wing slant.

The text explains that a nonwhite "may discriminate against white people or even hate them" but cannot be called "racist." The book's editor, a New Jersey sociologist, sends her students to make "class analysis of shopping malls." "They go to a boutiquey mall and a mall for the masses. I have them count how many public toilets are in each and bring back samples of the toilet paper. It makes class distinctions visible."

After some faculty members protested the subordination of instruction to political indoctrination, that text was dropped and the decision about recasting E306 was postponed until next year. But the pressure is on for political content, thinly disguised under some antiseptic course title such as "Writing about Difference—Race and Gender."

Such skirmishes in the curricula wars occur because campuses have become refuges for radicals who want universities to be as thoroughly politicized as they are. Like broken records stashed in the nation's attic in 1968, these politicized professors say:

America is oppressive, imposing subservience on various victim groups. The culture is permeated with racism, sexism, heterosexism, classism (oppression of the working class), so the first task of universities is "consciousness-raising." This is done with "diversity education," which often is an attempt to produce intellectual uniformity by promulgating political orthodoxy.

Such "value clarification" aims at the moral reformation of young people who are presumed to be burdened with "false consciousness" as a result of being raised within the "hegemony" of America's "self-perpetuating power structure."

The universities' imprimatur is implicitly bestowed on a particular view of American history, a political agenda, and specific groups deemed authoritative regarding race, sex, class, etc.

This orthodoxy is reinforced—and enforced—by codes of conduct called "anti-harassment" codes, under which designated groups of victims are protected from whatever they decide offends them. To cure the offensiveness of others, therapists and thought police are proliferating on campuses, conducting "racial awareness seminars" and other "sensitivity training."

These moral tutors have a professional interest in the exacerbation of group tensions, to which university administrations contribute by allowing, even encouraging, the Balkanization of campus life. This is done by encouraging group identities—black dorms, women's centers, gay studies, etc.

The status of victim is coveted as a source of moral dignity and political power, so nerves are rubbed raw by the competitive cultivation of grievances. The more brittle campus relations become, the more aggressive moral therapy becomes, making matters worse.

The attempt to pump E306 full of politics is a manifestation of a notion common on campuses: Every academic activity must have an ameliorative dimension, reforming society and assuaging this or that group's grievance. From that idea, it is but a short step down the slippery slope to this idea: All education, all culture, is political, so it should be explicitly so.

And any academic purpose is secondary to political consciousness-raising. The classroom is an "arena of struggle" and teaching should be grounded in the understanding that even teaching English composition is a political activity.

Recently at the University of Michigan, a teacher's description of a freshman composition course said that writing skills should be learned "in connection to social and political contexts" so "all of the readings I have selected focus on Latin America, with the emphasis on the U.S. government's usually detrimental role in Latin American politics . . . damning commentary on the real meaning of U.S. ideology . . . responsibility for 'our' government's often brutal treatment of. . . ." And so on.

This, remember, for a course on composition. But, then, the

10

15

teacher is candid about sacrificing writing skills to indoctrination: "Lots of reading . . . Consequently, I will assign considerable (sic) less writing than one would normally expect . . ."

On other campuses, writing requirements are reduced to the mere writing of a journal, a virtually standardless exercise in "self-expression" that "empowers" students. This is regarded as political liberation because rules of grammar and elements of style are "political" stratagems reinforcing the class structure to the disadvantage of the underclass, which has its own rich and authentic modes of expression from the streets.

So it goes on many campuses. The troubles at Texas are, as yet, mild. But the trajectory is visible: down. So is the destination: political indoctrination supplanting education.

Questions for Analysis

Logic

1. Would you agree that the warrant for Will's main claim is to the effect that politics can be separated from education? If you think so, show where and how you understand him to express or imply that warrant. If you think not, explain and exemplify his warrant as you understand it.
2. Explain in your own words Will's reasoning about the "slippery slope" in paragraph 12.
3. Explain Will's reasoning in objecting to the course that required fewer writing assignments [14–15]. In your view, is his reasoning here logically compatible with his assertion that students should have learned composition in high school? Explain.

Character

1. Does Will seem to characterize the arguments of his opponents in a fair-minded way? Explain your answer by pointing to particular examples.
2. Consider Will's remarks about "the status of victim" in and around paragraph 11. In your view, does he seem to make an appeal to his audience to consider himself and his supporters "in the status of victim"? Explain your answer.
3. When, where, and how does Will use irony in the essay? Pick one example and explain the appeal to character that it expresses.

Emotion

1. Explain the emotional appeal Will implicitly makes in paragraph 3 on the subject of the textbook he mentions. Note that its author, Paula Rothenberg, replies to Will and others in the next essay.
2. How does Will use quotation marks to make emotional appeals in the essay? Pick a paragraph that uses words or phrases within quotation marks and explain how and why the author does so.

3. Explain the emotional appeal of the phrase "moral tutors" as Will uses it in paragraph 10.

———————

CRITICS OF ATTEMPTS TO DEMOCRATIZE THE CURRICULUM ARE WAGING A CAMPAIGN TO MISREPRESENT THE WORK OF RESPONSIBLE PROFESSORS

Paula Rothenberg

I remember watching hearings of the House Un-American Activi- [1] ties Committee on television as a very young girl, sharing my mother's horror at the way in which Wisconsin Senator Joseph McCarthy trampled on the Bill of Rights. I knew kids whose parents were public-school teachers who had hidden books away in the cellar or destroyed them for fear of being accused wrongly of some amorphous crime and losing their jobs.

Later, I was moved to tears by Eric Bentley's dramatization of the hearings, which I heard on the radio. I have read endless accounts of that terrible time of redbaiting and blacklisting, ranging from the much-publicized stories of Lillian Hellman and Dashiell Hammett to the recent article in *The New York Times Magazine* by television producer Mark Goodson, father of a childhood friend and classmate. Each one chills my soul.

Imagine my feeling then, when I picked up the December 24 issue of *Newsweek* and found the cover story on integrating issues of race and gender into college curricula asking the question, "Is This the New Enlightenment—or the New McCarthyism?" and referring to my own book, *Racism and Sexism: An Integrated Study* (St. Martin's Press, 1988) as the "primer of politically correct thought." In fact, rather than trying to direct thought into approved channels, the book is an interdisciplinary text designed to allow students and teachers to examine the comprehensive and interconnected nature of racism, sexism, and class privilege within the United States. It employs scholarly writings from the humanities and social sciences, Supreme Court decisions and other historical documents, newspaper and magazine articles, poetry, and fiction.

But I suppose I should not have been surprised by the headline. Three months earlier George Will, in a nationally syndicated column, had announced "Political Indoctrination Supplants Education in Nation's

Universities," referring to me (mistakenly) as a "New Jersey sociologist" (my graduate training was in philosophy) and describing some of my work in terms so ludicrous they would have been funny were the man not so widely read or his conclusions so dangerous.

Earlier, *The New York Times,* as well as *The Chronicle,* had reported on the decision at the University of Texas at Austin to use my book as the primary text in its required composition course—and the subsequent retraction of that decision in response to political pressure from inside and outside the university. Since that time, a steady stream of articles on "politically correct" thought have appeared in countless national, regional, and local publications. None of them, whether news stories or opinion pieces, makes even a pretense of presenting a fair and balanced account of the issues; each of them seems content to repeat the same set of half-truths and distortions being circulated by the National Association of Scholars, a Princeton-based organization of academics seemingly committed to curricula based on the Orwellian slogans: *War Is Peace, Freedom Is Slavery,* and *Ignorance Is Strength.*

For example, the writer of an article in *The New Republic* reduced the comments I had made during a lengthy telephone interview to a single sentence that misrepresented what I had said. The article reported that I couldn't name a single book that was so racist and sexist that it should be dropped from the canon. In fact, when asked to specify such works during the interview, I had refused on the grounds that transforming the college curriculum was not about banning books. I had added that other teachers might use very effectively books that I might find objectionable. Needless to say, this comment did not appear in the article.

In response to a curriculum-reform movement that seeks to expand the horizons of students' learning to include all peoples and all places, the N.A.S. and other opponents of a multicultural, gender-balanced curriculum propose the continued silencing of all but a tiny fraction of the world's population. They have so little faith in this nation's potential to realize the democratic values we have so long espoused that they mistakenly believe that identifying the racism and sexism in our past and present will weaken this nation rather than strengthen it. They have even managed to persuade some people that those who seek to decrease the violence of our language and our behavior somehow seek to limit the Bill of Rights rather than to extend its protections to all.

Recoiling in horror from those who advocate a critical reading of Shakespeare or Milton (I thought scholarship was about critical readings), they show no equivalent concern for the peoples and cultures rendered invisible by the traditional curriculum. At another time in history opponents' attempts to misrepresent so completely the goals of curriculum reform might well have attracted little serious attention; at this moment they have gained a hearing because they express the collective fears of a

5

small but still dominant group within the academy that sees its continued power and privilege in jeopardy. What exactly is the critique of the traditional curriculum they have tried so hard to silence—and failing that— to misrepresent? How does the traditional curriculum serve their interests and perpetuate their power?

The traditional curriculum teaches all of us to see the world through the eyes of privileged, white, European males and to adopt their interests and perspectives as our own. It calls books by middle-class, white, male writers "literature" and honors them as timeless and universal, while treating the literature produced by everyone else as idiosyncratic and transitory. The traditional curriculum introduces the (mythical) white, middle-class, patriarchal, heterosexual family and its values and calls it "Introduction to Psychology." It teaches the values of white men of property and position and calls it "Introduction to Ethics." It reduces the true *majority* of people in this society to "women and minorities" and calls it "political science." It teaches the art produced by privileged white men in the West and calls it "art history."

The curriculum effectively defines this point of view as "reality" *10* rather than as a point of view itself, and then assures us that it and it alone is "neutral" and "objective." It teaches all of us to use white male values and culture as the standard by which everyone and everything else is to be measured and found wanting. It defines "difference" as "deficiency" (deviance, pathology). By building racism, sexism, heterosexism, and class privilege into its very definition of "reality," it implies that the current distribution of wealth and power in the society, as well as the current distribution of time and space in the traditional curriculum, reflects the natural order of things.

In this curriculum, women of all colors, men of color, and working people are rarely if ever subjects or agents. They appear throughout history at worst as objects, at best as victims. According to this curriculum, only people of color have a race and only women have a gender, only lesbians and gays have a sexual orientation—everyone else is a human being. This curriculum values the work of killing and conquest over the production and reproduction of life. It offers abstract, oppositional thinking as the paradigm for intellectual rigor.

The traditional curriculum is too narrow. It leaves out too much. Its narrow approach to defining knowledge implies that people who look different, talk differently, and embrace different cultural practices are not studied because they have nothing to teach "us."

Not content to debate curriculum reform in a straightforward and intellectually honest fashion, the opponents of such reform are mounting a nationwide campaign to smear and misrepresent the work of responsible teachers and scholars all across the country who are committed to democratizing the curriculum. After serving as "thought police" for generations, effectively silencing the voices and issues of all but a few, they now attempt to foist that label on the very forces in the university seeking to expand, rather than to contract, the discourse. The opponents of curriculum reform seek to effectively ban books like my own that, among other things, survey U.S. history by asking students to read our Constitution, Supreme Court decisions, and other public documents so that the "founding fathers" and their descendants can speak for themselves. Perhaps their fear is justified. I read the *Dred Scott* decision in ninth grade and have never been the same since.

And what of white males' scholarship and perspectives in this new and evolving curriculum? Will there be a place for them? The question is absurd, and the need to answer it reflects how far the misrepresentations have gone. The perspectives and contributions of that group are valid and valuable: there is much to be learned from them. The difficulty is not with their inclusion but with the exclusion of everyone else. The difficulty is with universalizing that experience and those interests.

Yes, *Newsweek,* there may well be a new McCarthyism. If so, it is   15
coming directly from the irresponsible right and its fellow travelers. How ironic that those who actively attempt to dictate what books students will and will not read portray themselves as defenders of academic freedom. How ironic that those of us seeking to make the curriculum and campus climate *less* racist, *less* sexist, and *less* heterosexist are portrayed as threats to democratic freedoms rather than their champions. But in the end, war is *not* peace, slavery is *not* freedom, and no matter what the N.A.S. may believe, ignorance is *not* strength.

Questions for Analysis

Logic
1. How does Rothenberg use autobiography as an organizational device throughout the essay?
2. Explain in your own words the author's reasoning when she claims that the traditional curriculum falsely claims to represent "reality."
3. Explain in your own words the author's reasoning when she claims that a multicultural curriculum would truly represent "reality."

Character
1. Explain the sense of her character that you see Rothenberg attempting to create in the autobiographical account of the first two paragraphs.
2. Explain the sense of her character that you see Rothenberg attempting to create through her claim in paragraph 6 to have been misrepresented.
3. Where and how does Rothenberg use irony in the essay? Pick one example and explain the appeal to character it expresses.

Emotion

1. Describe the emotions that the author expresses and those that she appeals to by referring to McCarthy and Orwell in the essay.
2. How does Rothenberg use quotation marks to make emotional appeals in the essay? Pick a paragraph that uses words or phrases within quotation marks and explain how and why the author does so.
3. Explain the operation of the author's emotional appeal on the theme of "thought police" at the end of the essay.

Rothenberg

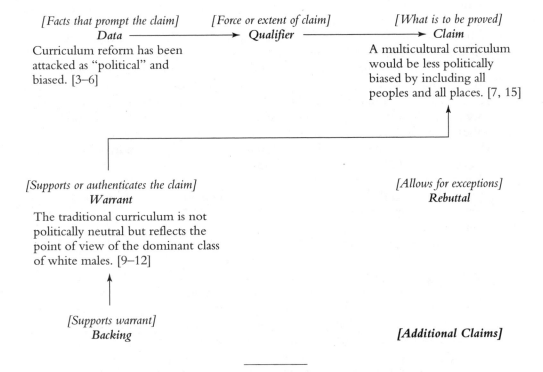

[Facts that prompt the claim]
Data → [Force or extent of claim] **Qualifier** → [What is to be proved] **Claim**

Curriculum reform has been attacked as "political" and biased. [3–6]

A multicultural curriculum would be less politically biased by including all peoples and all places. [7, 15]

[Supports or authenticates the claim]
Warrant

The traditional curriculum is not politically neutral but reflects the point of view of the dominant class of white males. [9–12]

[Allows for exceptions]
Rebuttal

[Supports warrant]
Backing

[Additional Claims]

ETHNIC STUDIES ARE A DELUSION

Jeffrey Hart

I read recently that in the American Southwest there is a growing movement to celebrate the Spanish contribution to American history. There apparently is much Latino resentment over the fact that the Mayflower and Jamestown are taught in the schools, while the earlier Spanish settlements are not—or not so much, at least.

There is some merit to such complaints. The early Spanish presence in what is now the United States is in itself an interesting and heroic story. Such names as "San Francisco," "Los Angeles" and "San Diego" remind us of that presence.

American schoolchildren presumably are taught today about the great exploits of the 15th century navigators and explorers, including the Spaniards. But the truth is that historically, the early Spanish settlements in the Southwest amounted to little or nothing, and Spanish influence was largely obliterated, while the future belonged to the Plymouth Bay Colony and to Jamestown.

French influence, which remained a contender for about a century, came to an end for all practical purposes when the French were defeated by the English in what we call "The French and Indian War."

The truth is that our language, our political system of representa-   *5*
tive democracy, our legal tradition and even our tradition of good manners come from England and from nowhere else. That is why American schoolchildren hear more about Plymouth and Jamestown than they do about the vestigial Spanish settlements.

And it certainly is a fortunate thing that our political tradition and our cultural tradition came from England and not from the Spain of Ferdinand and Isabella or Philip II. If you want an idea of the Spanish political tradition, consider Latin America, which only today is struggling with any success toward a version of the English system of representative democracy.

Indeed, representative democracy, with its roots in England, is becoming the only legitimate system in the modern world. Even China is struggling to approach it, now holding genuine elections at the local level.

In the universities today there is considerable agitation for ethnic studies courses and programs: Caribbean studies, Latino studies and so forth. I am not aware that in the past we saw anything much resembling the current demand for ethnic studies in education.

American history is part of the narrative of European history, with England very much in the foreground. Urges to celebrate Caribbean history and so on can scarcely change that. And anyway, what reasonable person would want to celebrate the culture of Haiti, Guinea or Paraguay? People flee such cultures.

It is sometimes said that we are all members of ethnic groups, but   *10*
I don't feel that I am. I feel undilutedly American.

My maternal ancestors were mostly German, from the Black Forest region, and my paternal ancestors were mostly Irish. But all of that was a long time ago.

Both my grandfathers were wholly 19th century types, self-made, successful businessmen in New York. Behind that there was an artillery colonel in the Union army and a successful artist from the Civil War period. But about Ireland and Germany as part of my heritage I care less than nothing.

In fact, I never feel more solidly American than when I am in Germany or Ireland. As G.K. Chesteron said, "Travel narrows the mind."

The history of both Germany and Ireland is ludicrous and tragic. German science, philosophy and music are remarkable; but Germany, for all its attitudes of superiority, managed the singular feat of losing two world wars in this century. The Irish have produced wonderful literature; but they have been killing each other for no apparent reason for about seven decades.

I suppose that if I were of recent Spanish descent I might well be   15
inclined to study Spanish history. But I would concentrate on Cervantes, Goya, Velasquez and such figures, thank you very much, and not stress Spanish achievements in the art of government, or the Spanish legal and religious traditions.

The celebration of "roots" is fine, I suppose. But we should be clear-sighted.

Ethnic studies in American colleges are a pathetic delusion and a pitiful snare.

Questions for Analysis

Logic
1. Explain in your own words Hart's reasoning in the beginning of his essay for his claim that it is more important to study English colonies than Spanish ones.
2. Explain in your own words Hart's reasoning for his claim in paragraph 6 that "it certainly is a fortunate thing that our political tradition and our cultural tradition came from England and not from the Spain of Ferdinand and Isabella or Philip II."
3. Explain in your own words Hart's reasoning beginning in paragraph 10 for his denial of interest in his own "ethnicity."

Character
1. How would you characterize the general manner and tone of voice in which Hart conducts his argument? Contrast his manner and tone with those of the other writers in the section to refine your sense of his general appeal through character.
2. What aspects of character does Hart attribute to his opponents through his choice of the word *delusion* in his title? Again, it may be helpful to review the other essays.
3. Hart advocates the study of the English tradition but seems to know

about the traditions of many other countries. What sense of his character as an advocate does this fact create? Hypocritical? Well educated? Something else? Explain and defend your answer.

Emotion
1. *Heritage* is a word much used in discussions of ethnicity and Hart uses it himself in paragraph 12. What is the emotional appeal of this metaphor? Why do you imagine it is used more than, say, *gene pool?*
2. At the end of his essay Hart claims that "Ethnic studies are a pathetic delusion and a pitiful snare." Where in his essay does he point out the "pathetic" nature of what he sees as a delusion? What does pathetic mean in context?
3. Where in his essay does Hart point to ethnic studies as a "pitiful snare"? In what ways is the reader invited to feel that the attempt at ensnarement is "pitiful"?

EXERCISES: MULTICULTURALISM AND THE COLLEGE CURRICULUM

Intertextual Questions
1. Do you find Will and Hart to be fair in their representations of advocates of a multicultural curriculum as exemplified by Rothenberg? Explain your answer with examples.
2. Do you find Rothenberg to be fair in her representation of opponents of a multicultural curriculum as exemplified by Will and Hart? Explain your answer with examples.
3. Which author's arguments do you find most convincing overall on the issue of a multicultural curriculum? Explain and exemplify your answer.

Suggestions for Writing
1. In your view, which author most effectively employs the appeal to reason? Write an essay in which you explain your judgment through comparison and contrast.
2. In your view, which author most effectively employs the appeal to emotion? Write an essay in which you explain your judgment.
3. Write an essay that argues in favor of your own views for or against a multicultural curriculum.

10   *Global Warming*

MEETING THE CHALLENGE OF GLOBAL WARMING
Remarks at the UN Committee on Climate Change Conference of the Parties, Kyoto, Japan

Albert Gore

Thank you. Prime Minister Hashimoto and President Figueres,   1
President Kinza Clodumar, other distinguished heads of state, distinguished delegates, ladies and gentlemen: It is an honor to be here at this
historic gathering, in this ancient capital of such beauty and grace. On
behalf of President Clinton and the American people and our U.S. negotiator, Ambassador Stu Eizenstat, I salute our Japanese hosts for their
gracious hospitality and offer a special thank you to Prime Minister Hashimoto and to our chairs—Minister Ohki and Ambassador Estrada—for
their hard work and leadership.

Since we gathered at the Rio Conference in 1992, both scientific
consensus and political will have come a long way. If we pause for a moment and look around us, we can see how extraordinary this gathering
really is.

We have reached a fundamentally new stage in the development of
human civilization in which it is necessary to take responsibility for a
recent but profound alteration in the relationship between our species
and our planet. Because of our new technological power and our growing
numbers, we now must pay careful attention to the consequences of what
we are doing to the Earth—especially to the atmosphere.

There are other parts of the Earth's ecological system that are also
threatened by the increasingly harsh impact of thoughtless behavior:
the poisoning of too many places where people, especially poor people,

live and the deaths of too many children, especially poor children, from polluted water and dirty air; the dangerous and unsustainable depletion of ocean fisheries; and the rapid destruction of critical habitats—rainforests, temperate forests, borial forests, wetlands, coral reefs, and other precious wellsprings of genetic variety upon which the future of humankind depends.

But the most vulnerable part of the Earth's environment is the very   5 thin layer of air clinging near the surface of the planet that we are now so carelessly filling with gaseous wastes that are actually altering the relationship between the Earth and the sun by trapping more solar radiation under this growing blanket of pollution that envelops the entire world. The extra heat, which cannot escape, is beginning to change the global patterns of climate to which we are accustomed—and to which we have adapted over the last 10,000 years.

Last week we learned from scientists that this year—1997, with only three weeks remaining—will be the hottest year since records have been kept. Indeed, 9 of the 10 hottest years since the measurements began have come in the last 10 years. The trend is clear. The human consequences—and the economic costs—of failing to act are unthinkable: more record floods and droughts; diseases and pests spreading to new areas; crop failures and famines; melting glaciers; stronger storms; and rising seas.

Our fundamental challenge now is to find out whether and how we can change the behaviors that are causing the problem. To do so requires humility, because the spiritual roots of our crisis are pridefulness and a failure to understand and respect our connections to God's Earth and to each other.

Each of the 160 nations here has brought unique perspectives to the table, but we all understand that our work in Kyoto is only a beginning. None of the proposals being debated here will solve the problem completely by itself. But if we get off to the right start here, we can quickly build momentum as we learn together how to meet this challenge.

Our first step should be to set realistic and achievable, binding emissions limits, which will create new markets for new technologies and new ideas that will, in turn, expand the boundaries of the possible and create new hope. Other steps will then follow. And then, ultimately, we will achieve a safe overall concentration level for greenhouse gases in the Earth's atmosphere. This is the step-by-step approach we took in Montreal 10 years ago to address the problem of ozone depletion, and it is working.

This time, success will require first and foremost that we heal the divisions among us. The first and most important task for developed countries is to hear the immediate needs of the developing world. And let me say, the United States has listened, and we have learned. We understand that your first priority is to lift your citizens from the poverty so many endure and build strong economies that will assure a better future. This is your right; it will not be denied.

And let me be clear in our answer to you: We do not want to founder on a false divide. Reducing poverty and protecting the Earth's environment are both critical components of truly sustainable development. We want to forge a lasting partnership to achieve a better future. One key is mobilizing new investment in your countries to ensure that you have higher standards of living, with modern, clean, and efficient technologies.

That is what our proposals for emissions trading and joint implementation strive to do. To our partners in the developed world, let me say that we have listened and learned from you as well. We understand that while we share a common goal, each of us faces unique challenges.

You have shown leadership here, and for that we are grateful. We came to Kyoto to find new ways to bridge our differences. In doing so, however, we must not waiver in our resolve. For our part, the United States remains firmly committed to a strong, binding target that will reduce our own emissions by nearly 30 percent from what they would otherwise be, to a commitment as strong, or stronger, than any we have heard here from any country. The imperative here is to do what we promise, rather than to promise what we cannot do.

All of us, of course, must reject the advice of those who ask us to believe there really is no problem at all. We know their arguments; we have heard others like them throughout history. For example, in my country, we remember the tobacco company spokesmen who insisted for so long that smoking did no harm. To those who seek to obfuscate and obstruct, we say: We will not allow you to put narrow special interests above the interests of all humankind. So what does the United States propose that we do?

The first measure of any proposal must be its environmental merit, and ours is environmentally solid and sound. It is strong and comprehensive, covering all six significant greenhouse gases. It recognizes the link between the air and the land, including both sources and sinks. It provides the tools to ensure that targets can be met—offering emissions trading, joint implementation, and research as powerful engines of technology development, and transfer. It further reduces emissions—below 1990 levels—in the years 2012 and beyond. it provides the means to ensure that all nations can join us on their own terms in meeting this common challenge. It is also economically sound. And, with strict monitoring and accountability, it ensures that we will keep our bond with one another.

Whether or not agreement is reached here, we will take concrete steps to help meet this challenge. President Clinton and I understand that our first obligation is to address this issue at home. I commit to you today that the United States is prepared to act—and will act.

For my part, I have come here to Kyoto because I am both determined and optimistic that we can succeed. I believe that by our coming together in Kyoto, we have already achieved a major victory—one both of substance and of spirit. I have no doubt that the process we have started here inevitably will lead to a solution in the days or years ahead.

Some of you here have, perhaps, heard from your home capitals that President Clinton and I have been burning up the phone lines, consulting and sharing new ideas. Today let me add this: After talking with our negotiators this morning and after speaking on the telephone from here a short time ago with President Clinton, I am instructing our delegation right now to show increased negotiating flexibility if a comprehensive plan can be put in place—one with realistic targets and timetables, market mechanisms, and the meaningful participation of key developing countries.

Earlier this century, the Scottish mountain climber W. H. Murray wrote:

> Until one is committed there is hesitancy, the chance to draw back, always ineffectiveness. Concerning all acts of initiative . . . there is one elementary truth, the ignorance of which kills countless ideas and splendid plans: that the moment one definitely commits oneself, providence moves, too.

So let us press forward. Let us resolve to conduct ourselves in such a way that our children's children will read about the "Spirit of Kyoto," and remember well the place and the time where humankind first chose to embark together on a long-term sustainable relationship between our civilization and the Earth's environment.

In that spirit, let us transcend our differences and commit to secure our common destiny: a planet whole and healthy; whose nations are at peace, prosperous, and free; and whose people everywhere are able to reach for their God-given potential. Thank you.

20

Questions for Analysis

Logic

1. Explain in your own words Vice President Gore's rationale for claiming in paragraph 3 that "We have reached a fundamentally new stage in the development of human civilization." You need not limit your evidence to the paragraph itself.

2. In your opinion, would the basic logic of the argument in paragraph 6 have been destroyed had 1997 *not* turned out to be "the hottest year since records have been kept"? Explain your answer.

3. In paragraph 13 Vice President Gore makes an argument by analogy. He attempts to refute his opponents by referring to arguments he says were made by the tobacco industry. How might an opponent counter his logic here?

Character

1. What sense of character is created by Vice President Gore through his repeated emphasis on poor people in paragraph 4?

2. What sense of character is created for the vice president in paragraph 17 by the report that "President Clinton and I have been burning up the phone lines consulting and sharing new ideas"?

3. What sense of his own character does Vice President Gore create in paragraph 18 by asking his audience to find inspiration in a quotation from a mountain climber? Would the same ideas expressed by, say, an industrialist or a general have created the same effect? Explain your answer.

Emotion

1. Consider the effect of Vice President Gore's repeated references to time in paragraph 6. What emotions does he invite or expect his audience to feel as the numbers proceed?

2. In paragraph 8 Vice President Gore begins to describe his plan. Circle some words that seem designed to invite feelings of confidence in that plan and briefly explain their emotional implications. For example, *realistic* invites a feeling of confidence through the implication that the limits will not be overly ambitious or impossible to achieve.

3. Paragraph 10 begins with *And*. Suppose it had begun with *But*. Would the emotional appeal of the paragraph have changed for you? Explain why or why not.

Gore

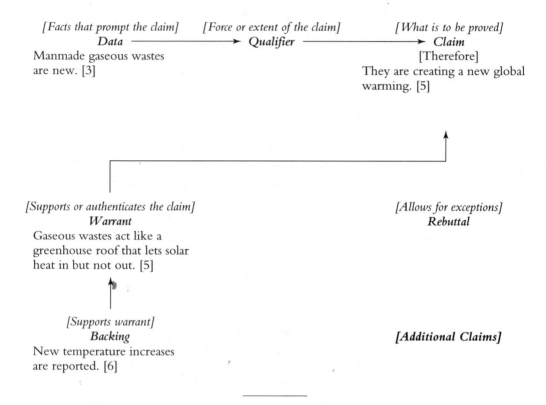

[Facts that prompt the claim]
Data
Manmade gaseous wastes
are new. [3]

[Force or extent of the claim]
Qualifier

[What is to be proved]
Claim
[Therefore]
They are creating a new global
warming. [5]

[Supports or authenticates the claim]
Warrant
Gaseous wastes act like a
greenhouse roof that lets solar
heat in but not out. [5]

[Allows for exceptions]
Rebuttal

[Supports warrant]
Backing
New temperature increases
are reported. [6]

[Additional Claims]

CLINTON MAY GET TOASTED BY GLOBAL WARMING

Phyllis Schlafly

The confrontation with Iraq is tending to conceal an impending   *1*
policy defeat for President Clinton that may dwarf his embarrassments
over losing fast track and the appropriations for back U.N. dues. Clinton
is planning on going to Kyoto, Japan, in early December to sign a United
Nations treaty called the Climate Change Protocol.

Administration fears of impending embarrassment are reflected in
the gag order that Clinton's lead negotiator in the global-warming talks,
Undersecretary of State Timothy Wirth, is trying to impose on the dele-

gates to Kyoto. He told the 16 Republican and Democratic delegates to keep their mouths shut and not criticize the administration's position.

When then-Colorado Sen. Wirth was an observer at the 1992 Earth Summit in Rio de Janeiro, Brazil, he had no reluctance about blasting then-President George Bush. He accused Bush of "adolescent politics" and of looking "silly" for not signing the Biodiversity Treaty that the Rio summit produced. It's going to be payback time in Kyoto.

Another attempt to intimidate those opposed to global-warming dogma was uttered by Interior Secretary Bruce Babbitt, who now has his own credibility problems. Babbitt labeled anyone who opposes the treaty "un-American."

The treaty would legally bind us to reduce our energy emissions to 20 percent below our 1990 levels, and would set 2005 as the year when this goal is to be reached. This would reduce our gross domestic product by $200 billion annually, cost us more than 1 million jobs and cause massive disruption in the American economy.

These drastic cutbacks would be enforced by the typical liberal "solutions": taxes and regulations. The federal government would impose a massive energy tax that would drive up the cost of home heating and electricity by 30 percent to 40 percent and put an additional tax of at least 60 cents on every gallon of gasoline.

Every product produced with the use of energy, including food, would increase in price, and major industries (such as paper, steel, petroleum refining, chemicals, aluminum and cement) would be crippled. The average family would pay $1,600 to $4,000 per year in increased energy costs.

The rationale behind this treaty is the claim that America's high standard of living, based on our large consumption of energy produced by burning oil, gas and coal, causes carbon dioxide emissions which in turn produce a worrisome warming of the global atmosphere called the greenhouse effect. The evidence to support this theory is so unclear, inconclusive and contradictory that it cannot be dignified by the term science.

Clinton's predictions of global warming rely on a 1996 U.N. report. But before releasing it, the U.N. bureaucrats deleted two key paragraphs written by the scientists who made the analysis.

The omitted passages state: 1) "None of the studies cited above has shown clear evidence that we can attribute the observed climate changes to increases in greenhouse gases," and 2) "No study to date has positively attributed all or part of the climate change to man-made causes."

The only thing that we know for sure is that temperature fluctuations occur. Many observers think that global warming, if indeed it is taking place, would be a good thing and would generate net benefits and savings to the United States.

5

10

Science Times suggests that, if our planet is heating up, the cause may be the sun, over which we have no control. Almost all the demonstrable global warming occurred before 1940, and so it can't be blamed on the widespread use of the automobile.

The Illinois State Climatologist Office released a report Oct. 22 stating that projections from several new international climate models indicate that parts of the United States will "cool by several degrees Fahrenheit through the year 2050." This report states that current climate models are now "more realistic," and predict "cooler, wetter weather for the central United States rather than the warmer and drier predictions of earlier models."

The Kyoto treaty is manifestly unfair to the United States because Third World nations, including Mexico, China, Indonesia, India and Brazil, would not be subject to the emissions restrictions imposed on us. That would accelerate the flight of U.S. industries and jobs to those countries.

In the face of the horrendous costs of this proposed treaty, Clinton will try to wiggle out of the box that he is in. But all his fall-back positions are bad, too.

One option being discussed is "emissions trading," i.e., to allow industries that find the emissions limits prohibitively expensive to buy emissions permits from the Third World. That's just a devious type of foreign giveaway and would redistribute U.S. wealth to other countries (which is probably the real purpose of the treaty anyway).

Another option is to force the taxpayers to finance exotic alternative energy sources such as solar and wind energy, and automobiles that run 70 miles to the gallon. Those are just more expensive government boondoggles.

Clinton can't control global climate any more than King Canute could hold back the tides. But the Kyoto treaty can change the temperature in your home if you can't afford the high energy taxes to keep it warm in the winter and cool in the summer.

15

Questions for Analysis

Logic

1. Under the constitution the Senate must *ratify* treaties for them to take effect. Explain how this fact underlies the logic of Schlafly's claim that supporters of the treaty about to be *signed* may face embarrassment.
2. In paragraph 5 Schlafly places the word *solutions* in quotation marks. What does she imply is so wrong with the logic of her opponents that she must qualify this common word in that way?
3. Schlafly obviously sees the treaty as a mistake. List the different kinds of data in Toulmin's terms that might be said to support the language of this claim.

Character
1. In paragraph 7 Schlafly says of the theory supporting the treaty that "it cannot be dignified by the term science." What does her assertion imply about her own character and expertise with regard to science?
2. In paragraph 8 what does Schlafly imply about the characters of her opponents when she claims that two key paragraphs were deleted from the report?
3. In paragraph 9 what is implied about Schlafly's own character and by her ability to quote the deleted paragraphs? Is the issue here one of honesty or expertise? Explain your answer.

Emotion
1. In paragraph 3 what emotions does Schlafly invite her audience to feel about the tactics she attributes to Bruce Babbitt? Do you think that placing this accusation of a "gag order" *last* is emotionally effective? Explain.
2. In paragraph 13 Schlafly raises the issue of jobs. What emotions does she invite in her audience at this point, and how might they be expected to make her general argument a convincing one?
3. King Canute was a legendary figure so convinced of his royal power that he *ordered* the ocean tide to stop advancing on him. Explain the emotional appeal made by Schlafly's analogy and how it supports her general argument.

"GLOBAL WARMING" IS A GRAB FOR POWER

Thomas Sowell

"Pact to Slow Global Warming" said the headline.

Hold it! Who said the globe is warming? By sheer repetition, we have been conditioned to respond to the phrase "global warming" the way Pavlov's dog was conditioned to salivate when a bell rang.

With all the hot air about global warming, have you ever heard how much it has actually warmed? Or where? Or since when? Probably not, because most of the orchestrated hysteria about global warming comes from computer models about greenhouse gasses, rather than from actual temperature readings.

Computer models are no better than the assumptions and theories that go into them: "Garbage in, garbage out." Back in the 1970s, computer models were predicting economic disaster on the way. Since then, there has been one of the longest periods of economic prosperity on record.

Incidentally, there were also predictions of global cooling back in the 1970s—a "new ice age" was on the way. Before you start planting palm trees in Minnesota, you might want to wait for some hard evidence of global warming, rather than depend on computer models.

Temperatures go up and down like the stock market. Moreover, some particular places are getting colder while other places are getting warmer. For some places we have statistical data going way back and for other places we don't. This is very iffy stuff.

Temperatures have been collected in cities for a long time but this can be very deceptive because cities are generally warmer than the surrounding countryside and cities have been growing in size over time, with concrete structures and paved streets replacing wooden structures and dirt paths. In short, places and structures that hold heat are growing.

Weather balloons that circle the earth give a much more balanced picture of what is happening to temperatures on the planet as a whole. Data from these balloons do not show the "global warming" that politicians, environmentalists and the media are hyping. Some experts say that global temperatures have actually gotten a little cooler, in fact.

A lot depends on the years you pick as "before" and "after." Global data show the earth's temperature the same in 1990 as in 1980. However, the temperature went up and down in between. Pick a low point on these oscillations and the temperature has been rising since then. Pick a high point and the temperature has been falling.

Before we get too carried away with all the big talk about "science" and "experts," let's not forget that we are talking about a field that has trouble predicting whether or not it will be raining tomorrow. Yet we are expected to pile staggering costs onto the American consumers and taxpayers because of speculative theories turned into computer models.

Some weather scientists may read the data differently from others, as has happened many times in the past and will undoubtedly happen many times in the future. Unfortunately, there are strong pressures at work to cause those scientists who proclaim "global warming" to come forward and for those scientists who think it is a crock to keep quiet.

Huge research grants are far more likely to go to those scientists who can scare money out of Congress than to those who say that there is nothing to go crazy over.

Moreover, imagine yourself a skeptic in an academic department that is getting big bucks from Washington to study "global warming" and come up with "solutions." What's in it for you to publicly contradict your colleagues who are raking in big bucks for the whole department, some of which may be paying your salary? If you are a junior faculty member, you may never get to be a senior faculty member if you rock the boat.

One tip-off on the shakiness of the evidence behind this latest drive to expand big government controls in the name of "global warming" is that its advocates are saying "we can't wait" to be sure. That argument proves too much. Why couldn't we wait to be sure when global cooling was the hysteria of the day back in the 1970s?

If we are going to let Washington grab more of our money and   *15* expand their power over our lives every time they can throw a scare into us, then look for a lot of people to be saying "Boo!" about a lot of things.

———

Questions for Analysis

Logic

1. Explain the rationale behind Sowell's claim at the beginning of his essay that "we have been conditioned." How is this supposed to have occurred, why is it supposed to work, and so on?
2. Explain in your own words the logic behind Sowell's phrase "garbage in, garbage out" in paragraph 4. How does he use this logic to oppose the claims for global warming?
3. Explain in your own words the logic of Sowell's argument in paragraph 10 against overvaluing the terms *science* and *experts* in the case of "global warming."

Character

1. In paragraph 3 Sowell refers to "orchestrated hysteria." In the essay as a whole what evidence does he present to support the sense that his own character is *not* hysterical? Pick an example and discuss its implications.
2. Sowell opens paragraph 5 with the word *incidentally.* What impression of his status as a person who knows the issue at hand does this word tend to create? Explain.
3. What sense of Sowell's character does his choice of the word *boo* create at the end of the essay? Is he childish? Does he possess confidence? Courage? Characterize your own impression and explain your reasoning.

Emotion

1. Sowell begins paragraph 2 with "Hold it!" What emotions does this phrase imply that he feels, and what emotions does it invite his readers to feel?
2. What emotions does Sowell attribute to academic scientists by implication in paragraph 13? Name them and explain your reasoning.
3. According to Sowell what emotions does the "we can't wait" argu-

ment invite in the American public? Explain what he means by saying "This argument proves too much."

EXERCISES: GLOBAL WARMING

Intertextual Questions
1. In all the essays, which claim to scientific fact would you most wish to see footnoted so that you might judge its argumentative weight for yourself? Discuss the reasons for your choice.
2. In his paragraph 9, Sowell gives an example of how temperatures might truly be seen as either rising or falling during the decade of the 1980s. Would this analysis or one like it apply to any part of Vice President Gore's factual basis for his argument? Explain your reasoning.
3. Both Schlafly and Sowell are highly skeptical of scientific claims for global warming. How does Vice President Gore attempt to counter such skepticism? Is he successful in your opinion? Explain your answer.

Suggestions for Writing
1. What do you think of the "we can't wait to be sure" argument alluded to by Sowell in his paragraph 14 and implied by Vice President Gore at several points during his remarks? Write an essay in which you attempt either to support or refute this argument for taking action on the claims for global warming.
2. Vice President Gore originally delivered his remarks as a speech. Waiving your agreement or disagreement with his position, do you think it a well-written speech? Write an essay in which you analyze the strengths and weaknesses of his remarks with regard to the form and occasion of their presentation.
3. Sowell claims that Washington wants to scare the population about global warming to raise a clamor for salvation from this menace that only governmental expansion can provide. Write an essay in which you attack, modify, or defend his view of governmental motives in the case of global warming.

DOWNSIZING THE MIDDLE CLASS

Rhonda Burns

It used to be that people were proud to work for the same company
for the whole of their working lives. They'd get a gold watch at the end
of their productive years and a dinner featuring speeches by their bosses
praising their loyalty. But today's rich capitalists have regressed to the
"survival of the fittest" ideas of the nineteenth-century Robber Barons
and their loyalty extends not to their workers or even to their stockhold-
ers but only to themselves. Instead of giving out gold watches worth a
hundred or so dollars for forty or so years of work, they give themselves
"golden parachutes" worth tens and even hundreds of million dollars
as they sell down the river the company they may have been with for
only a few years. Some other corporation is the purchaser and this new
"player" (other people's lives are only a game to them) immediately announces new profits and "growth" to be had through downsizing (i.e.,
firing the people whose loyalty created the company's worth at time of
sale) and outsourcing (i.e., shipping the jobs of loyal Americans overseas
to low-paid foreigners).

The new rich selfishly act on their own to unfairly grab the wealth
that the country as a whole has produced. The top 1 percent of the population now has wealth equal to the whole bottom 95 percent and they
want more. Their selfishness is most shamelessly expressed in downsizing and outsourcing because these business maneuvers don't act to create
new jobs as the founders of new industries used to do, but only to cut
out jobs while keeping the money value of what those jobs produced for
themselves.

To keep the money machine working smoothly the rich have bought
all the politicians from the top down. The president himself is constantly
leaving Washington and the business of the nation because he is sum-

moned to "fundraising dinners" where fat cats pay a thousand or so dollars a plate to worm their way into government not through service but through donations of vast amounts of money. Once on the inside they have both political parties busily tearing up all the regulations that protect the rest of us from the greed of the rich—regulations that took the whole of the twentieth century to create and that are now being destroyed overnight.

The middle class used to be loyal to the free enterprise system and throughout the Cold War with Russia it had nothing but laughter to give in response to Communist propaganda that urged it to hate the rich. In those days the people of the middle class mostly thought they'd be rich themselves someday or have a good shot at becoming rich, so why poison the well? But nowadays income is being distributed more and more unevenly and corporate loyalty is a thing of the past. The middle class may also wake up to forget its loyalty to the so-called free enterprise system altogether and the government which governs only the rest of us while letting the corporations do what they please with our jobs. As things stand, if somebody doesn't wake up, the middle class is on a path to being downsized all the way to the bottom of society.

Questions for Analysis

Logic
1. Burns argues that politicians are "bought." What evidence does she bring in support of this claim? Explain your judgment of the importance of evidence in this and similar instances.
2. According to Burns, what was the reasoning of the middle class with regard to the rich throughout the Cold War? What does she suggest may be the new middle-class reasoning with regard to the rich?
3. Burns claims that the rich are loyal only to themselves. What evidence or data does she bring in support of this claim?

Character
1. In the course of her argument Burns speaks of the past, the present, and the future. How old do you imagine her to be, and what aspects of her writing work toward creating a sense of her character as a woman of experience?
2. How would you characterize the tone of voice in which Burns makes her points? Aggrieved? Offended? Outraged? Describe her tone as clearly as you can, and point to some of the ways in which her use of language works to create it.
3. Burns seems to have a low opinion not only of business leaders but also of politicians. Point to some of the ways in which she works

to create a sense of the character of politicians through her uses of language.

Emotion

1. Throughout her argument Burns values loyalty as a means of creating social cohesion. Make a list of the actions that seem to her to define acts of *disloyalty* and explain how their presentation is designed to appeal to the reader's emotions.
2. In paragraph 1 Burns redefines several terms in her own way. Pick two of these terms and explain how the redefinitions appeal to the reader's emotions.
3. Burns uses the term *downsizing* in her last sentence in a different sense from the one she employs earlier in the essay. Explain what is added to the negative emotional appeal of the term by this new twist.

THE POOR HAVE ENSLAVED THE RICH

Paul Craig Roberts

The two greatest myths of our time are: "Bill Clinton cares" and "the rich don't pay taxes." Even more people believe the latter than the former, and it is no less untrue.

According to the latest information released by the Internal Revenue Service, the top 1 percent of income earners in the United States paid 30.4 percent of the personal income tax revenues collected in 1995, the latest year for which the information is available. The top 5 percent of income earners paid almost 50 percent of the income tax collected, and the top 25 percent paid over 80 percent. The top half of income earners paid over 95 percent of the income tax, leaving the bottom 50 percent to bear less than 5 percent of the tax burden.

If that's not the rich paying taxes, I don't know what is.

Is it fair? Absolutely not. Anyone in the top 1 percent is paying the government amounts ranging from hundreds of thousands to millions of dollars annually. In exchange, they are permitted to stay out of prison but get very little else for their money. They don't use public housing, food stamps, Medicaid, subsidized public transportation or public schools. In the United States today, the rich are the equivalent of slaves in the 19th century. The only real difference is that they are owned by the government instead of by private owners.

In a democracy, the people are the government, and what we have done is to put the rich in chains and make them work for the rest of us. They are publicly owned slaves. This system works because our slaves are such productive people that governments at all levels can take away more than half of their incomes and they are still rich after-tax. But nonetheless slaves.

Once we perverted our democracy in 1913 with a constitutional amendment permitting an income tax, we set about enslaving our most productive citizens. Historically, slaves were exploited to the extent of about half of their labor. The other half was necessary to support their own lives and reproduction. In the United States today, only about the top 2 percent of income earners meet the historical definition of a slave, but many of the rest of us are partial slaves. With the top half of income earners paying more than 95 percent of the income tax, they are at least the partial property of the other half and of the governments that run the plantation.

Many Americans do not understand their slave status. They think they are free because they travel to and from work, change jobs and generally move about impeded only by traffic in contrast to their 19th century counterparts, who labored directly on the property of their owners. If 19th century slave owners had possessed the equivalent of the IRS, social security numbers and payroll withholding, their slaves could have been put out to work for wages instead of toiling directly in the fields. Indeed, some slaves did work for wages, which they shared with their owners. Some even saved enough from their earnings to purchase their freedom, something we cannot do from the IRS.

Any American who imagines he is free can put it to a test by trying to hold on to all of his income. The jerk on the chain from the IRS will quickly cure the illusion.

Income tax apologists try to muddy the issue by claiming (falsely) that whereas the rich pay 30 percent of the taxes, they receive 30 percent or more of the income, so there is no disproportion. According to the IRS, this is definitely not the case. In 1995 the rich paid over 30 percent of the total income tax but earned less than 15 percent of the total income. The top 5 percent paid almost half of the income tax but earned only 28 percent of the total income.

Thus, extreme disproportion does exist. Like 19th century slaves, the rich own no more than half of their own labor. The rest of their labor pays for the upkeep of others. The only difference between the income tax and prior forms of slavery is that the poor have enslaved the rich rather than vice versa.

This is not what our country was supposed to be. Unless we get rid of the income tax, we won't return to the path of freedom on which citizens receive the full fruit of their labors and are responsible for themselves and their families.

Questions for Analysis

Logic

1. Explain in your own words the reasoning that Roberts brings to justify his title.
2. In paragraph 8 Roberts expands his argument to include "any American." Explain why, according to Roberts, any American is like the rich.
3. In paragraph 9 Roberts refutes what he sees as the false reasoning of "income tax apologists." According to him, what is that reasoning, and why is it false?

Character

1. *Slavery* is a highly charged emotional word. What sense of Roberts's character is created for you by the way in which he uses that term strictly as an economic one, as opposed to, say, a moral or a racial one?
2. In paragraph 4 Roberts speaks of fairness. In the essay as a whole, does he present himself in your view as possessing the quality of fairness in his character? Explain your answer with evidence.
3. In paragraph 5 Roberts speaks of "the rest of us" in contrast to the rich. Explain the sense of his character created by claiming to argue as he does from such a position in society.

Emotion

1. Roberts begins by speaking of "myths" and acts throughout as a demythologizer of conventional wisdom. To what emotions in his audience does a demythologizer attempt to appeal? What response does he risk? Explain your answers.
2. In paragraph 8 Roberts speaks of a "jerk on the chain." Make a list of other images of slavery used throughout the essay to create emotional appeals.
3. What is the emotional appeal of "the path of freedom" in paragraph 11? Is the reference here purely an economic one? Explain your answer.

KING'S RANSOM

Dan Moran

The Doctor tells Stephen King he has six months to live. King *1* says "I want a second opinion." Doctor: "Alright, you're the King of Horror."

Complaining about celebrity salaries has become such a national pastime that Stephen King's decision last week to end his 20-year relationship with Viking Books seemed like, well, if not the World Series, at least Scott Hamilton's triumphant return to the ice.

There is certainly plenty to complain about in the notion of King, whose multimedia and licensing deals constitute an empire as vast and sprawling as Diamond Jim Brady's, turning up his nose at his longtime publisher's offer of "almost" $15 million. When you consider that an M.A.-equipped entry-level Viking editor makes $18,000 a year, the discrepancy between Barry Bonds' salary and the peanut vendor's begins to look as equitable as communism by comparison.

Right now, King is "shopping around" different publishing houses to see who gets to release his latest novel, *Bag of Bones*. And how can he lose? He is a writer so popular that he can release two 800 page books on the same day (last year's *The Regulators* and *Desperation*)—retailing in the neighborhood of $25 each—and see both make it to the top of the bestseller list (the "Richard Bachman" alias he used on *Regulators* was originally intended to help King avoid flooding the market—but it's now mainly a marketing gimmick). It's a wonder they don't call him the Hughes of Horror instead.

Writer? And money? For shame! Isn't it offensive enough that we   *5* live in a nation where John Grisham is now contractually entitled to have his name included in all future film adaptations of his books (e.g., "John Grisham's The Pesky Prosecutor") while not one of Charles Portis' books is in print, and Thomas Berger (or even Joseph Hergesheimer) is remembered mainly for being forgotten? Where American poetry is long dead, and the short story is limited to a few column inches in the *New Yorker* and a few other literary petri dishes? We should be wounded to the heart that *The Dead Zone* outsells *Moby Dick,* and more people have seen *Maximum Overdrive* than Branagh's *Hamlet*. King's empire, you could argue, is everything that's wrong with publishing as well as the reading public.

Well, you have to agree with some of this, and as an English teacher, I know that at least part of my job is to loiter in the school library and make sure the kids are reading *Ivanhoe* or *Two Years before the Mast* instead of *Salem's Lot* or *The Stand*. I'm supposed to tell students that their time would be better spent reading Franklin's autobiography than *Christine*. And if a kid tries to tell me how much he liked reading *The Shining,* I may be patient, and even encouraging (this is almost the twenty-first century, after all), but must always remind him that if he doesn't move on to deciphering the courtly double entendres in *Love's Labour's Lost* he will end up wearing a name tag and hairnet for his entire working life.

But if we assume that getting people to read is a worthy end, it's hard to see the King of Horror's empire as anything other than a good thing. In fact, I'll stake my reputation as a fuddy-duddy and say that reading his first eight or nine books were instrumental in making me a dedicated reader.

I can already hear my audience muttering, "Who cares about this guy's reputation? Who the hell is he?" The answer is, of course, nobody—just another fan who's full of beans. But I've seen too many kids introduced to nose-in-the-book reading because they were wowed by the history of the Overlook Hotel, or the flat-out coolness of Trashcan Man's blowing up oil tanks to be completely appalled at King's imperial delusions. If you ever went through your King period, you'll know there's nothing as drop-dead scary (at the time, anyway) as Barlow, the vampire (or should I say "vampyre"?), floating in front of kids' windows, or as satisfying as Carrie's dropping a psychic neutron bomb on the bullies who have doused her in pig's blood! Nothing comes close. And if you get hooked on these things it matters little if, in ten years, you grow tired of reading parenthetical remarks in midsentence, or realize that Kubrick's movie of *The Shining* is better and smarter than the book. No—the point is that this goofy literary industrialist manipulated you into loving books—and who can fault him for that?

And if he gets rich as King Farouq for doing it, why do we complain? It's part of our old mistrustful love affairs with both money and learning. We lament the nation's preference for smart bombs to smart children, then object when a writer gets rich by actually getting kids to read. We tuttut at the still mostly male literary world, then sneer at the writers (most of them women) whose careers have soared after having their books chosen for Oprah's Book Club.

With King, there is the added benefit that he is, by any reasonable   10
standard, a good writer. His companions in the club of most-read fiction authors include the objectionable Grisham, turgid weapons pornographer Tom Clancy (whose books are popular with male adolescents aged 25 to 55), masters of false elegance like Nicholas Evans and David Guterson, "H Is for Heebyjeebies" assembly line Sue Grafton, and so on. Stephen King looks like Dickens in this company, and his recent elevation to Author of Literature status (signified by a glowing Roger Angell review and the inevitable appearance in the *New Yorker*) justifies his lifelong devotion to superbly purple prose and detailed (if often shockingly lazy) plot construction.

Whether you think the Maine book machine has given a false brilliance to the bestseller list or contributed to the delinquency of American letters, don't ignore the testimony of 12-year-old andrew__c__d@ hotmail.com, who posted a review to Amazon that called *Desperation* "an awesome book," and one of his "favorite books of all time."

Maybe Andrew is the kind of geek who would have become a book junky even without Stephen King's assistance. But this year, thousands of kids will read *Bag of Bones* and tell themselves that it is The Best Book Ever. With any luck, 0.05% of them may go on to chuckle at the trilingual puns in *Ulysses,* or just to better books generally. Perhaps they'll even grow up to be misshapen bookworms like me. Whatever happens, they'll most likely grow up, like all of us, to be serfs. And like all serfs, they'll be secretly happy to know their King is rich.

Questions for Analysis

Logic

1. In paragraph 3 Moran claims that "there is certainly plenty to complain about" with regard to King's refusal of a $15 million contract. Explain in your own words the rationale behind Moran's complaint.
2. In paragraph 5 Moran says that "King's empire, you could argue, is everything that's wrong with publishing as well as the reading public." What *are* the arguments for what's wrong? Does Moran himself make or imply them? Give evidence in support of your answers.
3. In paragraph 7 Moran argues for seeing King's "empire" as a good thing. Explain the rationale of this argument, and point to the language of the text that supports it.

Character

1. In paragraph 6 Moran jokes about the different career paths open to those who read Shakespeare and those who don't. What aspects of character are created for Moran by the joke? What for the hypothetical student? Explain in your own words how these aspects are suggested by Moran's writing.
2. In paragraph 7 Moran offers to "stake my reputation as a fuddy-duddy." Does the character he creates for himself through his writing in general seem to you like that of a fuddy-duddy? Support your answer with evidence.
3. Throughout the essay Moran puns on King's name and calls him by other titles such as "the Maine book machine" in paragraph 11. How do these mock-heroic titles work to create a sense of Moran's estimation of King's character as a writer?

Emotion

1. In paragraph 2, what are the emotions that Moran suggests are involved in "complaining about celebrity salaries"? What is the effect of his implied comparison of King with baseball players in qualifying these emotions? Does the comparison invite a stronger feeling about King or a weaker one? Explain.
2. Paragraph 5 introduces the issue of "shame." According to Moran, who should feel shame and why? Even if you see the phrase "for shame" as a joke, try to explain the values and assumptions that make the emotional basis of the joke.
3. At the end of his essay Moran suggests that "serfs" are "secretly happy

to know that their King is rich." In what does Moran imply that the happiness is assumed to reside, and why is it secret? If you agree with him, further explain the basis of your own feelings. If you disagree, explain the emotions you do feel and explain their bases.

Moran

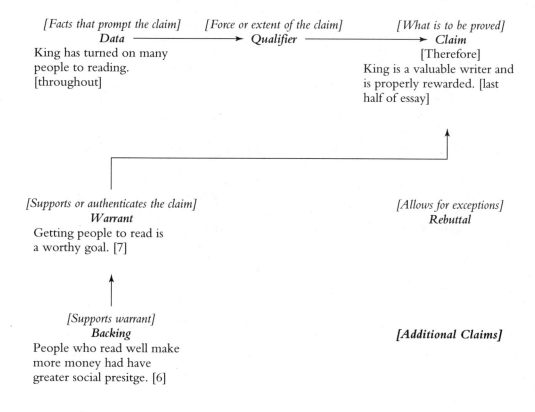

[Facts that prompt the claim]
Data
King has turned on many
people to reading.
[throughout]

[Force or extent of the claim]
Qualifier

[What is to be proved]
Claim
[Therefore]
King is a valuable writer and
is properly rewarded. [last
half of essay]

[Supports or authenticates the claim]
Warrant
Getting people to read is
a worthy goal. [7]

[Allows for exceptions]
Rebuttal

[Supports warrant]
Backing
People who read well make
more money had have
greater social presitge. [6]

[Additional Claims]

EXERCISES: THE RICH—SAINTS OR SINNERS?

Intertextual Questions

1. The management theorist P. Owen Hatteras has written that "those excluded from the great American pastime of wealth like to speak of "fairness" because that magic word—like abracadabra or Open, Sesame!—instantly transforms the speaker from humble spectator to all-powerful umpire." In your view where does each writer stand on the issue of "fairness" with regard to money? Would any of them agree with Hatteras? Disagree? Explain your judgments.

2. Burns and Roberts use similar statistics to reach opposite conclusions. Explain the differing ways in which each interprets the numbers.
3. The topic of money can raise powerful emotions, including envy and greed. In what differing ways do the authors in this chapter take account of those emotions in themselves and in their readers? First, identify some particular uses of language that seem to you to express or invite greed or envy; then show how the language works emotionally.

Suggestions for Writing
1. *Rich, middle class, poor, serfs,* and *slaves* are some of the emotion-laden terms of economic status used by the writers in this section, but how are they defined? Pick any one of the key terms used by two writers and write an essay showing how each works to define it.
2. Waiving the issue of their definition, which of the writers in your view best uses the emotion-laden terms of economic status to advance his or her argument through appeals to emotion? Write an essay that analyzes the methods of the writer of your choice.
3. Which of the writers in the chapter best represents your views on "the rich"? Write an essay in which you advance and defend your views, taking account of those expressed by the writers here.

12   *Toys for Tots*

WHAT BARBIE REALLY TAUGHT ME
Lessons from the Playroom, Both Naughty and Nice

Yona Zeldis McDonough

Now that my son is 6 and inextricably linked to the grade-school   *1*
social circuit, he gets invited to birthday parties. Whenever I telephone
to say he is coming, I ask about gifts. And whenever the child is a girl, I
secretly hope the answer will be the dirty little word I am longing to hear.
The word is Barbie.

No such luck. In our Park Slope, Brooklyn, neighborhood, there is
a bias against the doll. "My daughter loves her, but I can't stand her,"
laments one mother. "I won't let her in the house," asserts another. "Oh,
please!" sniffs a third.

But I love Barbie. I loved her in 1963, when she made her entrance
into my life. She had a Jackie Kennedy bouffant hairdo. Her pouty mouth
gave her a look both knowing and sullen. She belonged to a grown-up
world of cocktail dresses, cigarette smoke and perfume. I loved her in the
years that followed, too, when she developed bendable joints, a twist-'n'-
turn waist, long, ash-blond hair and lifelike lashes.

I've heard all the arguments against Barbie: she's an airhead, she's an
insatiable consumer—of tarty clothes, a dream house filled with pink
furniture, a Barbie-mobile—who teaches girls there is nothing in life
quite so exciting as shopping. Her body, with its no-way-in-the-world
breasts, wasp waist and endless legs, defies all human proportion. But at
6, I inchoately understood Barbie's appeal: pure sex. My other dolls were
either babies or little girls, with flat chests and chubby legs. Even the
other so-called fashion dolls—Tammy, in her aqua and white playsuit,
and Tressy, with that useless hank of hair—couldn't compete. Barbie was
clearly a woman, and a woman was what I longed to be.

When I was 8 and had just learned about menstruation, I fashioned   5
a small sanitary napkin for Barbie out of neatly folded tissues. Rubber
bands held it in place. "Look," said my bemused mother, "Barbie's got
her little period. Now she can have a baby." I was disappointed, but my
girlfriends snickered in a way that satisfied me. You see, we all wanted
Barbie to be, well, dirty.

Our Barbies had sex, at least our childish version of it. They hugged
and kissed the few available boy dolls we had—clean-cut and oh-so-
square Ken, the more relaxed and sexy Allan. Our Barbies also danced,
pranced and strutted, but mostly they stripped. An adult friend tells me
how she used to put her Barbie's low-backed bathing suit on backward,
so the doll's breasts were exposed. I dressed mine in her candy-striped
baby-sitter's apron—and nothing else. Girls respond intuitively to the
doll's sexuality, and it lets them play out those roles in an endlessly com-
pelling and yet ultimately safe manner.

I've also heard that Barbie is a poor role model. Is there such widespread contempt for the intelligence of children that we really imagine
they are stupid enough to be shaped by a doll? Girls learn how to be
women from the women around them. Most often this means Mom.
Mine eschewed beauty parlors. She was a painter who wore her long,
black hair loose, her earrings big and dangling and her lipstick dark. She
made me a Paris bistro birthday party, with candles stuck in old wine
bottles. Instead of games, she read T. S. Eliot to the group of enchanted
10-year-olds. My mother, not an 11½-inch doll, was the most powerful
female role model in my life. What she thought of Barbie I really don't
know, but she had the good sense to back off and let me use the doll my
own way.

Barbie now exists in a variety of "serious" incarnations: teacher,
Olympic athlete, dentist. And later this year we'll even get to see the
Really Rad Barbie, a doll whose breasts and hips will be smaller and
whose waist will be thicker, thus reflecting a more real (as if children
want their toys to be real) female body. I personally don't think any of
this matters one iota. Girls will still know the reason they love her, a
reason that has nothing to do with new professions or a subtly amended
figure.

Fortunately, my Barbie love will no longer have to content itself
with buying gifts for my son's female friends. I have a daughter now, and
although she is just 2, she already has a half-dozen Barbies. They are,
along with various articles of clothing, furniture and other accouter-
ments, packed away like so many sleeping princesses in translucent pink
plastic boxes that line my basement shelves. The magic for which they
wait is not the prince's gentle kiss. It is the heart and mind of my little girl
as she picks them up and begins to play.

Questions for Analysis

Logic

1. On the basis of the essay as a whole, fill out more completely the implied logic of "the arguments against Barbie" in paragraph 4.
2. Explain in your own words the ways in which McDonough explicitly and implicitly answers the objections of the opponents of Barbie.
3. Explain McDonough's reasoning in paragraph 7 about the role of role models.

Character

1. McDonough claims that there was a serious side to her playing with dolls. Does her character as a writer display both seriousness and playfulness? Explain your answer with evidence.
2. What qualities of character does the author attribute to Barbie's opponents? How does she create for her reader her sense of these qualities? Analyze some examples.
3. What are the qualities of Barbie attributed to the doll by her opponents? What aspects of her "style" are said to create those qualities? In what ways has Barbie's remake addressed those criticisms?

Emotion

1. To what emotion does the word *dirty* in paragraph 1 seem to appeal? How is that appeal modified or changed by the writer's choice of the word *bias* in paragraph 2. What sense does the word *dirty* have for the reader of the essay as a whole?
2. What emotions and emotional attitudes are created for the reader by the narrative attributions of *laments, asserts,* and *sniffs* in paragraph 2?
3. To what emotions in her reader does McDonough appeal in her last paragraph? In what ways might these appeals, if successful, be expected to support her argument as a whole?

McDonough

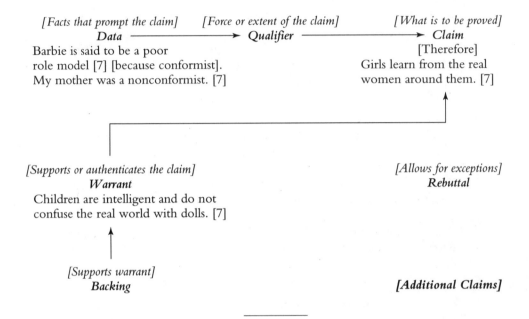

A MEDITATION ON BARBIE DOLLS

Robert Atwan

> *When nature has work to be done, she creates a genius to do it.*
> Ralph Waldo Emerson

Our daughter has always displayed an aversion to dolls. This never   1
bothered me, but it disappointed my wife who for years kept trying to
interest Emily in an endless parade of Barbies, with their cute costumes
and flashy accessories. I recently found the Barbies, about forty of them,
stuffed into a plastic laundry basket in the basement. The dolls had been
violently ripped apart, their arms and legs detached from their nubile
torsos, strands of shiny hair scissored off, smiling heads removed. Their
little skirts and jackets and shoes had disappeared. Emily hadn't been playing with her Barbies over the years, she had been submitting them to
torture. No wonder she never watched Sesame Street.

As I carted the mutilated dolls to the town dumpster, along with what was left of an expensive, two-story doll house my wife had also optimistically purchased, I amused myself by reflecting on one of today's favorite "issues": toys and gender. Are boys and girls inherently different, or do we shape their development to encourage certain masculine and feminine characteristics? Do girls play with dolls because they are gentle, nurturing creatures or simply because they have been taught— or, as some would say, "conditioned"—to prefer dolls. Do boys go gun-crazy because they're naturally violent predators or because our culture encourages them to relish gun play?

I realized right off that my daughter's case raises a problem, what philosophers would call a "counterexample." If girls are instinctively drawn to dolls, then how do I explain Emily's apparent rage against the Barbies? If a preference for dolls is really a result of exposure and environment, then why didn't she simply learn to appreciate the dolls lavished upon her? Something was wrong with the equation. Emily's antidoll behavior could not be the result of Na (Nature) or Nu (Nurture), nor even Na + Nu. What was missing? Was my ten-year-old daughter a complete anomaly? Should I worry about a little girl who savaged her Barbie dolls? Should I be concerned that she harbors in her room a water gun the size of an AK 47 and that her favorite video—the one she knows by heart— is *The Great Escape?*

When I got to the dump, I tossed out the doll house first. It was hard to tell what she had done with it, but the wood was cracked in so many places that it looked like it had been used as a climbing toy—which is probably what she had wanted in the first place. I then reached for the dolls. Emily herself had—being told to clean her closet—thrown all the butchered Barbies into the laundry basket. Arms and legs stuck out all over. I worried that a neighbor might see the Barbies and think I was responsible for the carnage.

The stuffed basket mesmerized me. It was shocking, almost por- 5 nographic, but at the same time comical. I imagined that if I surreptitiously piled the dolls into a corner of an art museum the grotesque assemblage could very easily be accepted as a work of contemporary art, most likely profeminist. "*Nature v. Nurture,* Emily Atwan 1996"

As I stared in fascination at the Barbies, the answer to my question slowly edged its way forward. The truth is we're all counter examples in one way or another, every one of us, all of the time. Variation rules; not predictability. This heap of massacred dolls represented neither Nature nor Nurture—what could be more artificial than these capitalized dichotomies?—but something else, something not so easily labeled and polarized for discussion groups or news magazine cover stories. Emily isn't a bundle of instincts nor a sponge prepared to absorb whatever messages "society" or "culture" sends her. Like any of us, her behavior can't be explained by genes or environment, or some convenient combination of both. There's another powerful factor at play—the unique, complex, independent, emerging consciousness that is Emily and Emily alone. We are shaped, to be sure, by what we inherit and by the world around us. But that's not the sum of the human story. We also do a lion's share of the shaping—or, in some cases, the unshaping. And the messages travel both ways. Emily's message was loud and clear. It read: "Watch out, world!"

She saw those Barbies and *chose* to destroy them. "A perfectly rational response," I thought, as I tossed her artistic creation into the dumpster and watched the ravenous gulls circle overhead.

Questions for Analysis

Logic
1. According to Atwan, what is the logic of the claims made by the "nature" side of the debate over toys and gender?
2. According to Atwan, what is the logic of the claims made by the "nurture" side of the debate over toys and gender?
3. In the context of the essay as a whole, explain the rationale of the "perfectly rational response" mentioned in the last paragraph.

Character
1. As you begin the essay, what sense of the writer's character is created for you by his choice of an epigraph from Emerson?
2. After reading the essay as a whole, what aspects of character in the writer are created for you by his having chosen the epigraph by Emerson?
3. What senses of character in father and in daughter are suggested by the image of the gulls at the end of the essay?

Emotion
1. In paragraph 2, what is the difference between the emotional appeals of the words *taught* and *conditioned?* What sense of human nature does each imply?
2. *Destruction* and *creation* are words with very different emotional appeals. What appeals to the reader's emotions does Atwan create by describing a destruction as a creation in paragraph 5 and again at the end of the essay? Do you think the paradox supports Atwan's argument as a whole? Explain your answer.
3. What emotions in Emily are suggested by her implied "message" to the world in the next-to-last paragraph? What does Emily seem to warn the world about?

THE Q GENE

Sara Bird

I suppose the moment of maximum political incorrectness came last   *1*
Saturday at that commercial shrine to all that is right-thinking and green,
the Nature Company, when my 4-year-old son, Gabriel, strafed the baby
dolphins in the computer-generated video with his toy Uzi.

A woman standing behind us pulled her own children away as the
frolicking Flippers ate hot lead. I imagine that this woman was probably
the sort of mother who had a bumper sticker like the one I had scraped
off the back of my own car when Gabriel was 18 months old: "Don't
Encourage Violence. Don't Buy War Toys." I imagine that she was the
sort of mother who had successfully banned all implements of destruction
from her house. You know the sort of mother I mean. The mother of
daughters. Or the mother of a son who obsesses about Thomas the Tank
Engine rather than battle-axes, nunchuks, hand grenades and catapults.

My boy, however, came hard-wired for weaponry. His first two-
syllable word, right after momma, dadda and backhoe, was scabbard.
Scabbard at 18 months? Why did I ever bother resisting?

Why? Because in college, in the sixties, I started Damsels in Dissent,
which counseled draft candidates to eat balls of tinfoil and put laundry
soap in their armpits to fool induction center doctors. Because I believed
that wars were a manifestation of testosterone run amok, much like the
purchase of bad toupees and red Miata convertibles. Because I believed
that white sugar, commercial television and guns were afflictions of a sick
society and that any child could be immunized against them *if only he had
the right mother* to pass along her more highly evolved antibodies.

Parents do not, indeed, live by bread alone. We feast daily on ban-   *5*
quets of our own words. My child has never seen an adult touch another
adult in anger; he has never been spanked; he has never even watched a
Ninja Turtle cartoon—yet he is as bloodthirsty as Quentin Tarantino.

In his toy bin are half a dozen Ninja Silent Warrior Assassin Swords,
two scimitars, three buccaneer blades, two six-shooters, four Laser Fazer
stun guns, a Captain Hook flintlock, the aforementioned Uzi and a silo
full of items he manufactures himself. This inventory is by no means
complete. I have lost friends over this arsenal. They cannot allow their
children to be exposed to such untrammeled barbarism. Friends? I have
lost an entire self-image and my deep Jeffersonian faith in the infinite
perfectibility of man.

I resisted at first, certain that if only I stayed the course I would
end up with a gentle little boy who named his stuffed animals and found

Beatrix Potter a bit brutish. And I was holding the line rather well, too, till he started sleeping with a shoe. Though never one to question too closely anything that encourages slumber, I did finally ask, why a shoe? He answered, clutching the tip of the shoelace, "So that when the bad things come in my dreams I can shoot them away."

". . . when the bad things come in my dreams."

Zen monks could contemplate their koans for years and not come close to the transformation I experienced when my child aimed his shoelace at me. Children are small and weak. The world is big and scary. Gabriel's need to feel safe so outweighed my own need to feel morally correct that the contest ended. From that night, we began building the armory until we achieved the overwhelming first-strike capability we have today.

I know what drives this war machine. It's a discovery of my own that I call the Q gene. The Q gene is that chromosomal imperative that compels little boys to pick up sticks and hair dryers; to chew their organically grown, wholegrain sandwiches into the shape of guns; to use whatever they can lay their murderous hands on, take aim and commence firing: "Kyew. Kyew. Kyew." The Q gene.

And here is my awful confession. I passed the Q gene on to my son. *10* As in male pattern baldness, I displayed none of the symptoms myself but carried it from both of my parents. My father an Air Force officer, my mother an Army nurse—I am the daughter of two warriors. I reflect on this heritage as my son stands beside a helicopter at nearby Camp Mabry. We have already examined the tanks and fighter jets parked on either side. Compared relative firepower. Discussed how each would fare in a battle with Tyrannosaurus rex. But my son pats the shark's grin painted on the helicopter and announces: "This is the one, Mom. This one is the best."

Watching him calls to mind a photograph of my father taken in the late fifties. He stands before a plane with a shark's smile painted on it, just beneath the inscription: 6091st Reconnaissance Squadron. My family lived in Japan then, conquerors grinning into the last minutes of a doomed colonialism. The crew with my father have their arms thrown around each other's shoulders, as heedless and glamorous as movie stars, frat boys, R.A.F. pilots, any gang of young men who know they will never grow old, never die.

Thirty years were to pass before I learned what it was my father did when he left us for weeks at a time. He and his smiling buddies would fly their "birds" over Russia and wait to be chased back into American airspace to test Soviet response time. That was when I understood why my mother, alone with six children, would burst into tears whenever an officer in uniform came to our front door.

I watch my son stroke the shark's grin and I want to whisper to him: "It is evil. All these machines are evil. You must never think about them again." But it can never be that simple.

I hear myself sometimes, times like this one right now. I see myself the way the mother shielding her children from the sight of my son opening up on the baby dolphins must have seen me, and I feel like a shill for the N.R.A. My position is indefensible, illogical, inconsistent. But love makes intellectual pretzels of us all. It's just that I know, long before I would like, there will come a moment when I can do nothing to chase away the bad things in my son's dreams. Until then, if I can give him a shoelace's worth of security I guess I will.

O.K., so I caved in on the white sugar, the TV, the war toys. There is, however, one moral issue that I have not wavered, have not wobbled, have not waffled on. I swore before my child was born that I would never buy a certain particularly insidious toy, and I am happy to report that I have held that line. There has never been, nor will ever be, a Barbie doll in my house.

15

Questions for Analysis

Logic
1. Bird claims in paragraph 6 that "I have lost an entire self-image and my deep Jeffersonian faith in the infinite perfectibility of man." Explain in your own words the rationale that Bird has lost. In particular what was the logic of her reasoning that man could be perfected with regard to the evils of violence?
2. Explain in your own words the logic of Bird's son with regard to his attitude toward means of violence.
3. Explain in your own words the rationale of Bird's claim in paragraph 5 that "we feast daily on banquets of our own words."

Character
1. Bird begins her essay with a mock confession and ends with a mock boast, both on the theme of "political correctness." What sense of her character does this aspect of her essay's organization tend to create? Explain the process that leads you to your conclusion.
2. In paragraph 2 we are told that "the frolicking Flippers ate hot lead." What point of view on the scene is implied by the *style* here? What quality of character is expressed in that point of view? Is it the same quality of character perceived by the mother who pulls her children away? Explain your answers.
3. Explain the sense of her character created by Bird's claim in paragraph 14 that "love makes intellectual pretzels of us all." Do you find her character in the essay as a whole to be that of an intellectual pretzel? Explain your answer.

Emotion

1. To what emotions in her reader does Bird appeal by her claim in paragraph 14 that "love makes intellectual pretzels of us all"? In what ways might this emotional appeal be expected to help her argument as a whole?
2. In paragraph 8 Bird claims to have experienced a transformation. Explain the emotional aspects of this transformation in your own words.
3. In paragraph 14 Bird says she sometimes sees herself as the woman in paragraph 2 must have seen her. To what emotions in her reader does this claim appeal? How might that appeal be expected to support her argument as a whole?

EXERCISES: TOYS FOR TOTS

Intertextual Questions

1. In paragraph 8 of her essay McDonough implies that children don't want their toys to be what they "really" are. According to her, what do they want their toys to be? Are her views shared by the other writers in the chapter? Support your answer with evidence.
2. In the last two essays each parent seems eager to understand his or her child. In what different ways is that sense of parental concern expressed in the writing? Find and analyze some examples.
3. The writer Cosimo Konstantine has said that "all literature is about love and death—of the innumerable subjects in reality only those stimulate the literary imagination." Are all *toys* about love and death, according to the authors in the chapter? Explain your answers with evidence.

Suggestions for Writing

1. Barbie is a figure that appears in easy essay. But is it the same Barbie? Write an essay in which you discuss the different senses of Barbie expressed by the writers in this chapter.
2. What were your own favorite toys as a child, and what were the bases of their appeal to you? Write an essay in which you argue for the value of your favorite toys.
3. If you were to become a parent what would your toy policy be? Write an essay in which you explain and defend your views.

13   *Euthanasia*

OFFERING EUTHANASIA CAN BE AN ACT OF LOVE

Derek Humphry

The American Medical Association's decision to recognize that artificial feeding is a life-support mechanism and can be disconnected from hopelessly comatose patients is a welcome, if tardy, acceptance of the inevitable.   1

Courts in California and New Jersey have already ruled this way, and although a Massachusetts court recently ruled in an opposite manner, this is being appealed to a higher court.

The AMA's pronouncement is all the more welcome because it comes at a time when the benefits of some of our modern medical technologies are in danger of being ignored because of the public's fear that to be on life-support machinery can create problems.

People dread having their loved ones put on such equipment if it means they are never likely to be removed if that proves later to be the more sensible course. As medical ethicist and lawyer George Annas has said, "People have rights, not technologies."

The argument by the pro-life lobby that food is a gift from God, no matter how it is introduced, and thus to deprive a comatose person of pipeline food is murder, is fallacious. A pipe is a manufactured item; the skill to introduce it into the body and maintain it there is a medical technology. Without the pipeline, the person would die. Food is common to all humans, but taking it through a pipeline is a technique carried out because the person has sustained an injury or suffers an illness which prevents normal feeding.   5

The pro-life lobby also harks back to Nazi excesses of the 1930s and 1940s as part of its argument for continued pipeline feeding. True, Nazi Germany murdered about one hundred thousand Aryan Germans who were mentally or physically defective because it considered them "useless eaters," detracting from the purity of the German race.

But neither the views of the victims nor their relatives were ever sought: they were murdered en masse in secret fashion and untruths concocted to cover the crimes.

No terminally ill or comatose person was ever helped to die by the Nazis. Moreover, their barbarous killing spree took in 6 million Jews and 10 million noncombatant Russians, Slavs, and gypsies. Life was cheapened by the Nazis to an appalling degree. What connection is there between the Nazis then and the carefully considered euthanasia today of a permanently comatose person who might, as Karen Quinlan did, lie curled up for ten years without any signs of what most of us consider life?

Helping another to die in carefully considered circumstances is part of good medicine and also demonstrates a caring society that offers euthanasia to hopelessly sick persons as an act of love.

Questions for Analysis

Logic
1. Where does Humphry suggest a definition of the "carefully considered circumstances" of his last paragraph?
2. Explain the logic of Humphrey's distinction between the Nazi murder of "useless eaters" and his own position on artificial feeding.
3. What in your view would be gained or lost for Humphry's argument if the essay were reorganized with the last paragraph made the second paragraph?

Character
1. What does the separation of the medical and legal issues in paragraphs 1 and 2 contribute to your sense of the author's character?
2. What attempts does Humphry make through his word choice to avoid a possible accusation of unfeeling brutality?
3. What sense of the author's character is created by the fact that almost all his sentences are declarative in their grammatical form?

Emotion
1. The phrase in paragraph 1, "acceptance of the inevitable," is one often used to describe dying. Do you think Humphry is making a joke here about the AMA? Explain your answer.
2. To what emotions does the author appeal in his characterization of his opponents as "the pro-life lobby" in paragraphs 5 and 6?
3. To what emotions does the author appeal by using the word *helping* in reference to euthanasia?

EUTHANASIA IS NOT THE ANSWER

Matthew E. Conolly

From the moment of our conception, each of us is engaged in a   *1*
personal battle that we must fight alone, a battle whose final outcome is
never in any doubt, for, naked, and all too often alone, sooner or later we
all must die.

We do not all make life's pilgrimage on equal terms. For some the
path is strewn with roses, and after a long and healthy life, death comes
swiftly and easily, for others it is not so. The bed of roses is supplanted by
a bed of nails, with poverty, rejection, deformity, and humiliation the
only lasting companions they ever know.

I know that many people here today carry this problem of pain in a
personal way, or else it has been the lot of someone close to you. Otherwise you would not be here. So let me say right at the outset, that those
of us who have not had to carry such a burden dare not criticize those
who have, if they should plead with us for an early end to their dismal
sojourn in this world.

HARD CASES MAKE BAD LAWS

Society in general, and the medical profession in particular, cannot
just turn away. We must do *something;* the question is—what?

The "what" we are being asked to consider today, of course, is   *5*
voluntary euthanasia. So that there be no confusion, let me make it quite
clear that to be opposed to the active taking of life, one does not have to
be determined to keep the heart beating at all costs.

I believe I speak for all responsible physicians when I say that there
clearly comes a time when death can no longer be held at bay, and when
we must sue for peace on the enemy's terms. At such a time, attending to
the patient's comfort in body, mind, and soul becomes paramount. There
is no obligation, indeed no justification, for pressing on at such a time
with so-called life-sustaining measures, be they respirators, intravenous
fluids, CPR, or whatever. I believe that there is no obligation to continue a treatment once it has been started, if it becomes apparent that it
is doing no good. Also, withholding useless treatment and letting nature
take its course is *not* equivalent to active euthanasia. Some people have
attempted to blur this distinction by creating the term "passive euthanasia." The least unkind thing that can be said about this term is that it is
very confusing.

Today's discussion really boils down to the question—do hard and
tragic cases warrant legalization of euthanasia? There can be no doubt

that hard and tragic cases do occur. However, the very natural tendency to want to alleviate human tragedy by legislative change is fraught with hazard, and I firmly believe that every would-be lawmaker should have tattooed on his or her face, where it can be seen in the mirror each morning, the adage that HARD CASES MAKE BAD LAWS.

If we take the superficially humane step of tailoring the law to the supposed wishes of an Elizabeth Bouvia (who, incidentally, later changed her mind), we will not only bring a hornet's nest of woes about our own ears, but, at a stroke, we will deny many relatives much good that we could have salvaged from a sad situation, while at the same time giving many *more* grief and guilt to contend with. Even worse, we will have denied our patients the best that could have been offered. Worst of all, that soaring of the human spirit to heights of inspiration and courage which only adversity makes possible will be denied, and we will all, from that, grow weaker, and less able to deal with the crisis of tomorrow.

UNLEASHING EUTHANASIA

Let's look at these problems one by one. The first problem is that once we unleash euthanasia, once we take to ourselves the right actively to terminate a human life, we will have no means of controlling it. Adolf Hitler showed with startling clarity that once the dam is breached, the principle somewhere compromised, death in the end comes to be administered equally to all—to the unwanted fetus, to the deformed, the mentally defective, the old and the unproductive, and thence to the politically inconvenient, and finally to the ethnically unacceptable. There is no logical place to stop.

The founders of Hemlock no doubt mean euthanasia only for those 10 who feel they can take no more, but if it is available for one it must be available for all. Then what about those precious people who even to the end put others before themselves? They will now have laid upon them the new and horrible thought that perhaps they ought to do away with themselves to spare their relatives more trouble or expense. What will they feel as they see their 210 days of Medicare hospice payments run out, and still they are alive. Not long ago, Governor Lamm of Colorado suggested that the old and incurable have a *duty* to get out of the way of the next generation. And can you not see where these pressures will be the greatest? It will be amongst the poor and dispossessed. Watts will have sunk in a sea of euthanasia long before the first ripple laps the shore of Brentwood. Is that what we mean to happen? Is that what we want? Is there nobility of purpose there?

It matters to me that my patients trust me. If they do so, it is because they believe that I will always act in their best interests. How could such trust survive if they could never be sure each time I approached the bed that I had not come to administer some coup de grace when they were not in a state to define their own wishes?

Those whose relatives have committed more conventional forms of suicide are often afterwards assailed by feelings of guilt and remorse. It would be unwise to think that euthanasia would bring any less in its wake.

A BETTER WAY

Speaking as a physician, I assert that unrelieved suffering need never occur, and I want to turn to this important area. Proponents of euthanasia make much of the pain and anguish so often linked in people's minds with cancer. I would not dare to pretend that the care we offer is not sometimes abysmal, whether because of the inappropriate use of aggressive technological medicine, the niggardly use of analgesics, some irrational fear of addiction in a dying patient, or a lack of compassion.

However, for many, the process of dying is more a case of gradually loosing life's moorings and slipping way. Oftentimes the anguish of dying is felt not by the patient but by the relatives: just as real, just as much in need of compassionate support, but hardly a reason for killing the patient!

But let us consider the patients who do have severe pain, turmoil, and distress, who find their helplessness or incontinence humiliating, for it is these who most engage our sympathies. It is wrong to assert that they must make a stark choice between suicide or suffering.

There is another way.

Experience with hospice care in England and the United States has shown repeatedly that in *every* case, pain and suffering can be overwhelmingly reduced. In many cases it can be abolished altogether. This care, which may (and for financial reasons perhaps must) include home care, is not easy. It demands infinite love and compassion. It must include the latest scientific knowledge of analgesic drugs, nerve blocks, antinausea medication, and so on. But it can be done, it can be done, it can be done!

LIFE IS SPECIAL

Time and again our patients have shown us that life, even a deformed, curtailed, and, to us, who are whole, an unimaginable life, can be made noble and worth living. Look at Joni Earickson—paraplegic from the age of seventeen—now a most positive, vibrant and inspirational person who has become world famous for her triumph over adversity. Time and time again, once symptoms are relieved, patients and relatives share quality time together, when forgiveness can be sought and given—for many a time of great healing.

Man, made in the image of his Creator, is *different* from all other animals. For this reason, his life is special and may not be taken at will.

We do not know why suffering is allowed, but Old and New   20
Testament alike are full of reassurances that we have not been, and will not ever be, abandoned by our God. "Yea, though I walk through the valley of the shadow of death, I will fear no evil *for thou art with me.*"

CALL TO CHANGE DIRECTION

Our modern tragedy is that man has turned his back on God, who alone can help, and has set himself up as the measure of all things. Gone then is the absolute importance of man, gone the sanctity of his life, and the meaning of it. Gone too the motivation for loving care which is our responsible duty to the sick and dying. Goodbye love. Hello indifference.

With our finite minds, we cannot know fully the meaning of life, but though at times the storms of doubt may rage, I stake my life on the belief that to God we are special, that with Him, murder is unacceptable, and suicide (whatever you call it) becomes unnecessary.

Abandon God, and yes, you can have euthanasia. But a *good* death it can never be, and no subterfuge of law like that before us today can ever make it so.

My plea to the Hemlock Society is: Give up your goal of self-destruction. Instead, lend your energy, your anger, your indignation, your influence and creativity to work with us in the building of such a system of hospice care that death, however it come, need no longer be feared. Is not this a nobler cause? Is not this a better way?

Questions for Analysis

Logic
1. How and where does Conolly separate the medical, legal, and religious implications of his argument? How and where are they combined?
2. What seems to be the reasoning behind Conolly's claim that with euthanasia "there is no logical place to stop"? [9]
3. Explain Conolly's reasoning at the end of his essay when he distinguishes between the idea of "good" and what he calls a "subterfuge of law."

Character
1. Conolly's argument is taken from a speech he delivered to the Hemlock Society—a group that favors euthanasia. What does this fact contribute to your sense of the author's character?

2. Conolly talks as a doctor, but what other personal attributes does he imply as defining characteristics of his identity?
3. Do you find the first sentence of paragraph 9—"Let's look at these problems one by one"—is representative of the author's style in general? Explain why or why not.

Emotion
1. What emotions does the author appeal to in the third paragraph?
2. What emotions are appealed to by the author's use of the term *unleash* in paragraph 9?
3. To what emotions in his audience does Conolly appeal by his discussion of his patients' trust in paragraph 11?

Conolly

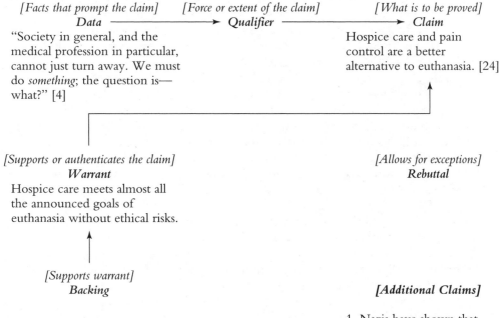

[Facts that prompt the claim]
Data ——————→

"Society in general, and the medical profession in particular, cannot just turn away. We must do *something*; the question is—what?" [4]

[Force or extent of the claim]
Qualifier ——————→

[What is to be proved]
Claim

Hospice care and pain control are a better alternative to euthanasia. [24]

[Supports or authenticates the claim]
Warrant

Hospice care meets almost all the announced goals of euthanasia without ethical risks.

[Allows for exceptions]
Rebuttal

[Supports warrant]
Backing

[Additional Claims]

1. Nazis have shown that there is no logical place to stop euthanasia. [9]

2. "Our modern tragedy is that man has turned his back on God, who alone can help, and has set himself up as the measure of all things." [21]

MUST THEY TINKER
WITH THE DYING?

Nancy M. Lederman

My grandmother, Freda Weinstein, was hospitalized for more than   *1*
four weeks after she was hit by a little girl riding a bicycle in a New York
playground. The unwary girl knocked her over, breaking her hip. It was
a bad fracture, the surgeon said. A week later, another surgeon said my
90-year-old grandmother had a perforated ulcer, and it was immediately
repaired. Then she had internal bleeding and a heart attack.

In hospital jargon, these are "events." The older the patient, the
more likely a hospital stay will trigger a succession of events leading to
one final event.

My grandmother's strength was impressive. She was tied to her bed
to keep her from pulling out the catheter and intravenous lines that supplied fluids, pain-killer and sedation. Despite the restraints, she pulled out
the ventilator tube that helped her breathe. Fighting the restraints, she
developed blisters on her forearms. She also had a gastro-nasal tube in
her nose.

The doctors wanted desperately to save her; that's what doctors are
programmed to do. To deal with the bleeding, they performed an endos-
copy, trailing another tube down her throat to her stomach. When that
didn't work, they wanted to do another. I said, enough. They wanted to
operate to stanch the bleeding, or do an angiogram, or both. Enough.
The prognosis kept changing. One doctor said, "I.C.U. psychosis." Another said, "How can you let her bleed to death?"

The odds were she would wind up where she most dreaded, in a   *5*
nursing home. At the least, she would need 24-hour care for a long time.
She would be "walker-dependent"—if she could walk at all. These things,
I knew, she emphatically did not want. I had her health care proxy. I had
drafted it. Although she had no living will, we discussed her wishes many
times. But we had not anticipated this.

She wasn't terminal. Once on the ventilator, she would stay there
as long as she needed it to breathe. Her body was fighting to live, as if
she was programmed to survive. Her mind was fighting, too. When I
squeezed her hand, she squeezed back. Hard.

If she could fully wake, what would she tell me? Would she say, Let
me die? In her pocketbook, I found speeches she had written, to be delivered to her senior center. I had a "eulogy" she had prepared months
before, to be read at her funeral. It was a letter to her family and friends
telling them not to grieve: she had lived a full life.

They say our ethics have yet to catch up to our technology. Medical advances are prolonging life for more and more people. Longer lives are not necessarily better ones.

They say you must have a living will or a health care proxy. Preferably both. Only then can you be assured that you or your chosen surrogate will be able to make critical health care decisions for you. They don't tell you what it's like to make those decisions for someone else—to play the odds with someone else's life.

My grandmother's "case" was used by the hospital ethicist on training rounds. Interns, nurses, and physicians' assistants discussed options. One resident said he couldn't understand why I refused the angiogram, why I had signed a "do not resuscitate" order if I was continuing to permit blood transfusions. *10*

As the doctors kept offering me interventions to save her, I began looking for a way out. I wanted her off that ventilator, sooner rather than later. Once she was off, I could refuse to let her back on.

How can you let her bleed to death? How could I not? I wasn't brave. But she was, and I had her proxy.

She died on Nov. 19. I wasn't there. I don't know what killed her. Respiratory failure, kidney failure, heart failure—it didn't matter. No experiments, she had said. None, I promised her. I kept my promise.

Questions for Analysis

Logic

1. Lederman's essay is organized partly by chronology. Do you see any other organizing principles at work? Explain your answer.
2. A large part of the author's appeal to reason takes place in the final paragraph. What elements in the reasoning there also appear elsewhere in the essay?
3. In what explicit and/or implicit ways does Lederman attempt to refute the arguments of her grandmother's doctors?

Character

1. Lederman is a lawyer by profession. In what ways do you think she does or does not attempt to express that aspect of her character in the essay?
2. In what ways does the author express the intensity of her concern for her grandmother? Point to specific uses of language that work to create this aspect of the author's character as expressed in the essay.
3. In what ways does the author create a sense of her grandmother's character? How does this sense of character support Lederman's argument?

Emotion

1. Explain the ways in which the word *tinker* in the essay's title appeals to the reader's emotions. Does the author appeal to the same emotions elsewhere in the essay? Explain.

2. How would you describe the emotions expressed by the general style of the essay and the tone of voice it creates? Point to some examples in explaining your answer.
3. What emotions does the author suggest were expressed by the doctors in charge of her grandmother? How does the author suggest them? Point to some particular moments and explain the operations of the specific language involved.

EXERCISES: EUTHANASIA

Intertextual Questions
1. Compare the uses that Humphry and Conolly make of the example of Nazi Germany in their arguments.
2. With what if anything would Humphry and Lederman take issue in Conolly's paragraph 6? Explain your answer.
3. Compare the roles that the writers see for love in what they consider to be the proper response to suffering.

Suggestions for Writing
1. Write an essay that compares the views of all the writers on the issue of personal versus medical responsibility in euthanasia.
2. Write a letter to the author with whom you most disagree and argue for your own views while answering his or hers.
3. Write an essay that analyzes the ways in which each writer attempts to bring an appropriate dignity of style to the great issues of life and death involved.

14   *What Books Should Students Read?*

PREFACE TO
THE GREAT CONVERSATION
Robert M. Hutchins

Until lately the West has regarded it as self-evident that the road to   *1*
education lay through great books. No man was educated unless he was
acquainted with the masterpieces of his tradition. There never was very
much doubt in anybody's mind about which the masterpieces were. They
were the books that had endured and that the common voice of mankind
called the finest creations, in writing, of the Western mind.

In the course of history, from epoch to epoch, new books have been
written that have won their place in the list. Books once thought entitled
to belong to it have been superseded; and this process of change will
continue as long as men can think and write. It is the task of every generation to reassess the tradition in which it lives, to discard what it cannot
use, and to bring into context with the distant and intermediate past the
most recent contributions to the Great Conversation. This set of books
is the result of an attempt to reappraise and re-embody the tradition of
the West for our generation.

The Editors do not believe that any of the social and political
changes that have taken place in the last fifty years, or any that now seem
imminent, have invalidated or can invalidate the tradition or make it irrelevant for modern men. On the contrary, they are convinced that the
West needs to recapture and re-emphasize and bring to bear upon its
present problems the wisdom that lies in the works of its greatest thinkers
and in the discussion that they have carried on.

This set of books is offered in no antiquarian spirit. We have not
seen our task as that of taking tourists on a visit to ancient ruins or to the
quaint productions of primitive peoples. We have not thought of providing our readers with hours of relaxation or with an escape from the
dreadful cares that are the lot of every man in the second half of the
twentieth century after Christ. We are as concerned as anybody else at
the headlong plunge into the abyss that Western civilization seems to be

taking. We believe that the voices that may recall the West to sanity are those which have taken part in the Great Conversation. We want them to be heard again—not because we want to go back to antiquity, or the Middle Ages, or the Renaissance, or the Eighteenth Century. We are quite aware that we do not live in any time but the present, and, distressing as the present is, we would not care to live in any other time if we could. We want the voices of the Great Conversation to be heard again because we think they may help us to learn to live better now.

We believe that in the passage of time the neglect of these books in the twentieth century will be regarded as an aberration, and not, as it is sometimes called today, a sign of progress. We think that progress, and progress in education in particular, depends on the incorporation of the ideas and images included in this set in the daily lives of all of us, from childhood through old age. In this view the disappearance of great books from education and from the reading of adults constitutes a calamity. In this view education in the West has been steadily deteriorating; the rising generation has been deprived of its birthright; the mess of pottage it has received in exchange has not been nutritious; adults have come to lead lives comparatively rich in material comforts and very poor in moral, intellectual, and spiritual tone.

We do not think that these books will solve all our problems. We do not think that they are the only books worth reading. We think that these books shed some light on all our basic problems, and that it is folly to do without any light we can get. We think that these books show the origins of many of our most serious difficulties. We think that the spirit they represent and the habit of mind they teach are more necessary today than ever before. We think that the reader who does his best to understand these books will find himself led to read and helped to understand other books. We think that reading and understanding great books will give him a standard by which to judge all other books.

We believe that the reduction of the citizen to an object of propaganda, private and public, is one of the greatest dangers to democracy. A prevalent notion is that the great mass of the people cannot understand and cannot form an independent judgment upon any matter; they cannot be educated, in the sense of developing their intellectual powers, but they can be bamboozled. The reiteration of slogans, the distortion of the news, the great storm of propaganda that beats upon the citizen twenty-four hours a day all his life long mean either that democracy must fall prey to the loudest and most persistent propagandists or that the people must save themselves by strengthening their minds so that they can appraise the issues for themselves.

Great books alone will not do the trick; for the people must have the information on which to base a judgment as well as the ability to make one. In order to understand inflation, for example, and to have an intelligent opinion as to what can be done about it, the economic facts in a given country at a given time have to be available. Great books cannot help us there. But they can help us to that grasp of history, politics, morals, and economics and to that habit of mind which are needed to form a valid judgment on the issue. Great books may even help us to know what information we should demand. If we knew what information to demand we might have a better chance of getting it.

Though we do not recommend great books as a panacea for our ills, we must admit that we have an exceedingly high opinion of them as an educational instrument. We think of them as the best educational instrument for young people and adults today. By this we do not mean that this particular set is the last word that can be said on the subject. We may have made errors of selection. We hope that this collection may some day be revised in the light of the criticism it will receive. But the idea that liberal education is the education that everybody ought to have, and that the best way to a liberal education in the West is through the greatest works the West has produced, is still, in our view, the best educational idea there is.

Questions for Analysis

Logic

1. Many of Hutchins's arguments have to do with refuting objections to the selections recommended by the series of books his essay introduces. Pick an example of this activity and explain the reasoning of his refutation.
2. Hutchins implies that his key term, *greatness,* is not defined as an eternal quality that is necessarily part of the nature of a book in itself. Explain the author's reasoning on the topics of "change" [2] and "progress" [5] in the selection of great books.
3. Explain the author's reasoning on the difference between a great book and one that embodies only "propaganda" [7].

Character

1. "Greatness" is a lofty subject. Exemplify and explain the ways in which you think the author's style does or does not suggest qualities of character that would make him a proper judge of greatness in writing. Do you think, for example, that he adopts a suitably lofty point of view?
2. In your view does the author seem to suggest a character that includes prejudice against other traditions than those of the West? Explain your answer with examples.
3. To what qualities of the imagined reader's character does the author appeal? Analyze an example of an appeal to the reader's character and explain its operation by referring to particular uses of language.

Emotion

1. What emotions in the reader are appealed to by the claim in the first paragraph, that until recently the main point the author argues has been "self-evident"?

2. Describe and explain the emotional appeal made by the author on the issue of "sanity" in paragraph 4.
3. The author does not hesitate to make judgments of value. To what emotions in his reader does this quality appeal? Explain your answer, using particular examples.

Hutchins

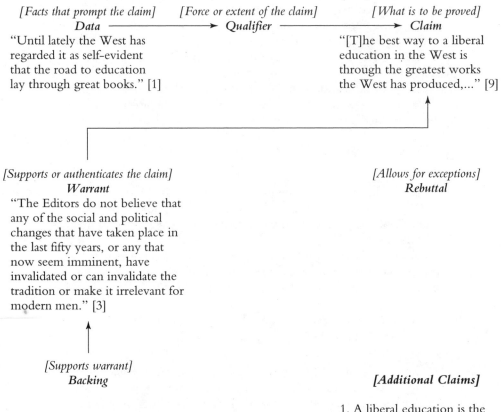

[Facts that prompt the claim]
Data ———→

"Until lately the West has regarded it as self-evident that the road to education lay through great books." [1]

[Force or extent of the claim]
Qualifier ———→

[What is to be proved]
Claim

"[T]he best way to a liberal education in the West is through the greatest works the West has produced,..." [9]

[Supports or authenticates the claim]
Warrant

"The Editors do not believe that any of the social and political changes that have taken place in the last fifty years, or any that now seem imminent, have invalidated or can invalidate the tradition or make it irrelevant for modern men." [3]

[Allows for exceptions]
Rebuttal

[Supports warrant]
Backing

[Additional Claims]

1. A liberal education is the best education. [9]

2. Great books will "recall the West to sanity." [4]

3. "Understanding great books" will lead to reading, understanding, and better judging other books. [6]

ON READING TRASH

Bob Swift

If you want kids to become omnivorous readers, let them read trash. *1*
That's my philosophy, and I speak from experience.

I don't disagree with The National Endowment for the Humanities,
which says every high school graduate should have read 30 great works
of literature, including the Bible, Plato, Shakespeare, Hawthorne, the
Declaration of Independence, "Catcher in the Rye," "Crime and Punishment" and "Moby Dick."

It's a fine list. Kids should read them all, and more. But they'll be
better readers if they start off on trash. Trash? What I mean is what some
might call "popular" fiction. My theory is, if you get kids interested in
reading books—no matter what sort—they will eventually go on to the
grander literature all by themselves.

In the third grade I read my first novel, a mystic adventure set in
India. I still recall the sheer excitement at discovering how much fun
reading could be.

When we moved within walking distance of the public library a *5*
whole new world opened. In the library I found that wonder of wonders,
the series. What a thrill, to find a favorite author had written a dozen or
more other titles.

I read a series about frontiersmen, learning about Indian tribes, beef
jerky and tepees. A Civil War series alternated young heroes from the
Blue and the Gray, and I learned about Grant and Lee and the Rock of
Chickamauga.

One summer, in Grandpa Barrow's attic, I discovered the Mother
Lode, scores of dusty books detailing the adventures of Tom Swift, The
Rover Boys, The Submarine Boys, The Motorcycle Boys and Bomba the
Jungle Boy. It didn't matter that some were written in 1919; any book
you haven't read is brand new.

Another summer I discovered Edgar Rice Burroughs. I swung
through jungles with Tarzan, fought green Martians with John Carter,
explored Pellucidar at the Earth's core, flew through the steamy air of
Venus with Carson Napier. Then I came across Sax Rohmer and, for
book after book, prowled opium dens with Nayland Smith, in pursuit of
the insidious Fu Manchu.

In the seventh grade, I ran across Booth Tarkington's hilarious Penrod books and read them over and over.

My cousin went off to war in 1942 and gave me his pulp magazines. *10*
I became hooked on Doc Savage, The Shadow, G8 and His Battle Aces,
The Spider, Amazing Stories. My folks wisely did not object to them as

trash. I began to look in second-hand book shops for past issues, and found a Blue Book Magazine, with an adventure story by Talbot Mundy. It led me back to the library, for more of Mundy's Far East thrillers. From Mundy, my path led to A. Conan Doyle's "The Lost World," Rudyard Kipling's "Kim," Jules Verne, H. G. Wells and Jack London.

Before long I was whaling with Herman Melville, affixing scarlet letters with Hawthorne and descending into the maelstrom with Poe. In due course came Hemingway, Dos Passos, "Hamlet," "The Odyssey," "The Iliad," "Crime and Punishment." I had discovered "real" literature by following the trail of popular fiction.

When our kids were small, we read aloud to them from Doctor Dolittle and Winnie the Pooh. Soon they learned to read, and favored the "Frog and Toad" and "Freddie the Pig" series.

When the old Doc Savage and Conan the Barbarian pulps were reissued as paperbacks, I brought them home. The kids devoured them, sometimes hiding them behind textbooks at school, just as I had. They read my old Tarzan and Penrod books along with Nancy Drew and The Black Stallion.

Now they're big kids. Each kid's room is lined with bookshelves, on which are stacked, in an eclectic mix, Doc Savage, Plato, Louis L'Amour westerns, Thomas Mann, Gothic romances, Agatha Christie, Sartre, Edgar Allen Poe, science-fiction, Saul Bellow, Shakespeare, Pogo, Greek tragedies, Hemingway, Kipling, Tarzan, Zen and the Art of Motorcycle Maintenance, F. Scott Fitzgerald, Bomba the Jungle Boy, Nietzsche, the Iliad, Dr. Dolittle, Joseph Conrad, Fu Manchu, Hawthorne, Penrod, Dostoevsky, Ray Bradbury, Herman Melville, Conan the Barbarian . . . more. Some great literature, some trash, but all good reading.

Questions for Analysis

Logic
1. In your view, is Swift's whole appeal to reason essentially contained in his first paragraph? If you think so, explain what the rest of the essay contributes to his appeal to reason within the categories of Toulmin's model of logic. For example, does the rest of the essay expand on the data? The claim? The warrant? The backing? If you don't think all the logical parts of the argument are essentially contained in the first paragraph, show where they are exemplified in the rest of the essay.
2. By what means does the author organize his essay? Explain how in your view the organization does or does not support the author's major point.
3. Explain some of the criteria by which the author creates throughout the essay a sense of the "eclectic mix" mentioned in his last paragraph.

Character

1. How would you characterize the general tone of voice Swift employs in the essay? Dignified? Chatty? Boasting? Describe what you hear in more than a word or two and explain the qualities of character that the author's tone seems designed to express.
2. What sense of character is created for you by the author's mentioning different family members throughout the essay?
3. What sense of character is created for you by the self-proclaimed eclecticism of the many lists of authors and books that the author gives throughout the essay?

Emotion

1. What emotions are evoked in general by the use of the term *trash* to describe many of the books the author mentions? Do you see any advantages for the author's use of that term rather than *popular fiction* [3]?
2. To what emotions in his audience does the author appeal when he says that "any book you haven't read is brand new" [7]?
3. To what emotions does the author appeal by his account of his children's reading habits? In what ways does the account advance his argument?

WHOSE CANON IS IT, ANYWAY?
IT'S NOT JUST ANGLO-SAXON

Henry Louis Gates, Jr.

I recently asked the dean of a prestigious liberal arts college if his   *1*
school would ever have, as Berkeley has, a 70 percent nonwhite enrollment. "Never," he replied. "That would completely alter our identity as a center of the liberal arts."

The assumption that there is a deep connection between the shape of a college's curriculum and the ethnic composition of its students reflects a disquieting trend in education. Political representation has been confused with the "representation" of various ethnic identities in the curriculum.

The cultural right wing, threatened by demographic changes and the ensuing demands for curricular change, has retreated to intellectual protectionism, arguing for a great and inviolable "Western tradition," which contains the seeds, fruit and flowers of the very best thought ever uttered in history. (Typically, Mortimer Adler has ventured that blacks "wrote no good books.") Meanwhile, the cultural left demands changes to accord with population shifts in gender and ethnicity. Both are wrongheaded.

I am just as concerned that so many of my colleagues feel that the rationale for a diverse curriculum depends on the latest Census Bureau report as I am that those opposed see pluralism as forestalling the possibilities of a communal "American" identity. To them, the study of our diverse cultures must lead to "tribalism" and "fragmentation."

The cultural diversity movement arose partly because of the frag- 5 mentation of society by ethnicity, class and gender. To make it the culprit for this fragmentation is to mistake effect for cause. A curriculum that reflects the achievement of the world's great cultures, not merely the West's, is not "politicized"; rather it situates the West as one of a community of civilizations. After all, culture is always a conversation among different voices.

To insist that we "master our own culture" before learning others— as Arthur Schlessinger Jr. has proposed—only defers the vexed question: What gets to count as "our" culture? What has passed as "common culture" has been an Anglo-American regional culture, masking itself as universal. Significantly different cultures sought refuge underground.

Writing in 1903, W. E. B. Du Bois expressed his dream of a high culture that would transcend the color line: "I sit with Shakespeare and he winces not." But the dream was not open to all. "Is this the life you grudge us," he concluded, "O knightly America?" For him, the humanities were a conduit into a republic of letters enabling escape from racism and ethnic chauvinism. Yet no one played a more crucial role than he in excavating the long buried heritage of Africans and African Americans.

The fact of one's ethnicity, for any American of color, is never neutral: One's public treatment, and public behavior, are shaped in large part by one's perceived ethnic identity just as by one's gender. To demand that Americans shuck their cultural heritages and homogenize themselves into a "universal" WASP culture is to dream of an America in cultural white face, and that just won't do.

So it's only when we're free to explore the complexities of our hyphenated culture that we can discover what a genuinely common American culture might actually look like.

Is multiculturalism un-American? Herman Melville didn't think so. 10 As he wrote: "We are not a narrow tribe, no . . . We are not a nation, so much as a world." We're all ethnics; the challenge of transcending ethnic chauvinism is one we all face.

We've entrusted our schools with the fashioning and refashioning of a democratic policy. That's why schooling has always been a matter of political judgment. But in a nation that has theorized itself as plural from its inception, schools have a very special task.

Our society won't survive without the values of tolerance, and cultural tolerance comes to nothing without cultural understanding. The challenge facing America will be the shaping of a truly common public culture, one responsive to the long-silenced cultures of color. If we relinquish the ideal of America as a plural nation, we've abandoned the very experiment America represents. And that is too great a price to pay.

Questions for Analysis

Logic

1. The word *canon* in the author's title refers to the books that a given culture considers its most valuable literary works. According to Gates, what is the reasoning of the "cultural right wing," and what arguments does he bring to refute that reasoning?
2. According to Gates, what is the reasoning of the cultural left wing, and what arguments does he bring to refute that reasoning?
3. Explain Gates's own reasoning on the meaning of the key term *tolerance*.

Character

1. What qualities of Gates's character are suggested by the anecdote with which he begins the essay?
2. What qualities of character in the author are suggested for you by the ways in which he responds to opposing viewpoints? Explain your answer using particular examples.
3. In what ways does the author seek to align his views with those of publicly acknowledged authorities? Explain your answer by using particular examples.

Emotion

1. The author refers to the "West," and to "Anglo-Saxon," and "Anglo-American" culture. What are the emotional appeals of each term? What is the emotional effect of using them interchangeably?
2. What is the emotional appeal created by the use of the term *white face* in paragraph 8?
3. To what emotions in his audience does the author appeal in paragraph 12 when he says that "society won't survive without the values of tolerance"?

EXERCISES: WHAT BOOKS SHOULD STUDENTS READ?

Intertextual Questions

1. Compare the ways in which each author takes into account the factor of historical change in his essay.
2. Both Hutchins and Gates use the metaphor of conversation to de-

scribe literary culture. Compare the ways in which each author understands and uses the implications of conversation in his argument.
3. Both Hutchins and Gates see the proper selection of books as a way
of solving problems. Compare the ways in which each author understands the criteria for choosing books as a matter of problems and
solutions.

Suggestions for Writing
1. Write an essay on the ways in which each author uses evidence as
a means of supporting his claims for the ideas about books that he
advances.
2. Literature is often said to combine delight and instruction. Write an
essay in which you analyze the ways in which each author addresses
the issues suggested by this dual definition.
3. Each writer imagines literature in some way as a "heritage." Write an
essay that analyzes the ways in which this metaphor is used implicitly
or explicitly to create appeals to emotion. Who or what, for example,
would *literally* be the one to give you an inheritance? What implications would there be for you in your receiving an inheritance? For
refusing to accept one? For not caring to know whether it exists or
not? Compare these implications to the simple act of refusing to read
or not caring to know about a book that someone else recommends.

15   *Modern Manners*

RUDENESS CAN BE LETHAL

Miss Manners

One of the leading causes of modern crime, Miss Manners gathers   1
from paying attention to the news reports, is senselessness.

"Another senseless shooting," they keep announcing.

"A senseless stabbing . . . a senseless murder . . . "

We used to have such sensible crime.

Miss Manners can't help wondering what went wrong.

Sensible crimes were ones committed for love or money. When   5
neither revenue nor revenge is involved, the modern crime seems to
strike people as unreasonable.

But Miss Manners has also been paying attention to what the criminals themselves give as their motives, and they make a certain deplorable
sense to her. People are now killing over—you're going to have a hard
time believing this one—etiquette.

One of our leading causes of murder is a perceived lack of respect.
Respect is a basic concept of manners, which features such principles as
dignity and compassion, rather than strict justice, which it leaves to the
law. Being treated respectfully is not one of our rights, nor is treating
others respectfully a legal obligation. Only manners require it.

Yet "dissin' "—showing real or apparent disrespect—is cited as the
motive in an amazing number of murders.

As a Washington, D.C., high-school football player said when dis-   10
cussing the shootings of members of his team—one dead, three wounded
last summer alone—"The biggest thing everybody is looking for is respect in the streets. It isn't money. They are just trying to make sure
you respect them. People are just pushing each other to the maximum to
get respect. And the maximum is death."

Remember what all those 18th-century Frenchmen in lace cuffs did
when they got fussed about people looking at them cross-eyed? The chief

difference now is that the duel has lost some of its frills, such as gloves, seconds and allowing both participants to shoot at the same time. In keeping with modern practicality, the idea caught on that it is more effective to shoot when your victim isn't looking.

Failure to provide road courtesies is given as the motivation for the new sport of car-to-car shootings. Law is supposed to regulate the highway, but traffic law does not cover such courtesies as letting others pass, not playing a car radio so loudly that it annoys people in other cars, and not going slowly in a fast lane. So highway murderers seem to think of themselves as encouraging drivers' etiquette.

Fairness is a concept that manners shares with law, but only etiquette requires it in such informal situations as waiting in line. Some months ago, there was a stabbing in a Bethesda, Maryland, grocery store over the fact that someone had broken into the checkout line out of turn.

Does all this sound as if Miss Manners is on the side of the criminals? She is, after all, devoted to stamping out rudeness, just as these people have claimed to be.

But she has her limits about how it can be done. And she makes   15
a strict division between the jurisdictions of the law and of manners. Crime is not merely lethal rudeness.

Without even squabbling, she and Miss Justice managed to divide the task of regulating social behavior so that the law, with its fierce sanctions, agreed to punish behavior that is seriously threatening to life, limb or property, while gentle Miss Manners tries to persuade people to avoid the kind of behavior that leads to such unpleasantness.

But when poor old etiquette fails, the law must take over. It was a humiliating defeat for manners when both smokers and nonsmokers refused to curb their rudeness toward one another, and the law had to take over what used to be in the jurisdiction of manners.

Miss Manners' point about the new etiquette-motivated crime is that when there is no recognition of the need to observe courtesies, everyone finds life unbearable. Asking the law to regulate petty conduct would trespass on our basic rights, but allowing individual impulses to go totally unrestrained leads to mayhem.

There is no use telling Miss Manners that no one cares about etiquette any more. Even outlaws are outraged when others do not follow its rules.

Questions for Analysis

Logic
1. Explain in your own words what Miss Manners takes to be the sense behind some "senseless" crimes.
2. Explain in your own words the rationale of "respect" explained in paragraphs 9 and 10.

3. Explain in your own words the distinction Miss Manners makes beginning in paragraph 15 between her own relationship to rudeness and that of criminals.

Character
1. What techniques of writing does Miss Manners employ to create a sense of her own character as a well-mannered one? Point to and analyze two examples.
2. What differences in character does Miss Manners attribute to duelists and drive-by shooters in paragraph 11? What uses of language work to create your sense of those differences?
3. What sense of character does Miss Manners create for Miss Justice in paragraph 16? What uses of language work toward creating this sense?

Emotion
1. Miss Manners speaks of herself always in the third person. What effect does this technique create with regard to the emotional range of feelings her essay expresses? Is the range a constrained one in your opinion? Explain your answer.
2. In the analysis of paragraph 10, the football player uses the word *just* twice. Read the sentences aloud with and without the word. What effect on the emotional content of his sentences does this word create?
3. To what emotions in her readers does Miss Manners appeal in her discussion of smoking regulations in paragraph 17? Explain the ways in which her uses of language create the appeal.

PUBLIC SERVANTS OFTEN BEHAVE LIKE MASTERS

Stephen Chapman

The other day, I arrived at the bus stop, where my bus was waiting, and walked up to the door behind two other commuters. They got on, but before I could board, a Chicago Transit Authority fare collector abruptly stepped in front of me, blocked the door, told the driver to close it and drive on, and then, when I asked for an explanation, strode away without a word, even though he apparently had nothing else to do.

The bus was half-empty during rush hour, there was no other bus in sight, and I was not holding things up. But for some strange reason, the guy in the CTA uniform decided he just had to prevent me from spending my money for the benefit of his employer.

When I called the agency's customer service line to report his badge number, the lady who took the information was perfectly polite, and she actually managed to sound surprised by my account. But if you have ever had the pleasure of dealing with urban transit workers, the idea of being abused for no conceivable purpose will strike you as perfectly normal.

The CTA, I am happy to report, has a lot of workers who do their jobs competently and helpfully. Probably a majority, I suspect. It also has many who think of mass transit patrons as an intolerable nuisance that keeps them from getting their paychecks with the least possible exertion.

It's a good day when a driver will advise you which stop you want   5
or a fare collector will tell you where a bus goes. A friend of mine, new to town, ventured into an L station and approached a CTA employee. "Excuse me," he said politely, "I'm trying to get to State and Randolph." Came the reply: "Buddy, who the hell's stopping you?"

The government takes all sorts of antitrust actions to prevent private companies from acquiring monopolies, but the only monopoly truly worth fearing is the one exercised by the government itself. In a democracy, public employees are supposed to be accountable to the people. In fact, their privileged status, safe from competing alternatives, often allows them to be indifferent to, and even contemptuous of, those they theoretically work for.

Our helpful fare collector is a good example. Can you imagine an employee at a movie theater, a hardware store or a fast-food restaurant physically preventing an unoffending customer from entering the establishment during normal business hours to make a purchase? Private companies offering goods and services for sale can't survive if they go out of their way to alienate consumers. Buyers can always go elsewhere.

In the public sector, workers are shielded from that horrid prospect. If you want to take a plane from O'Hare to New York or Dallas or Los Angeles, you have plenty of airlines to choose from. But if you want to take a bus across town, there's only one supplier. And if you don't like it, your local transit provider can get along just fine without you: It gets a subsidy extracted forcibly from the taxpayer at large.

A colleague of mine was recently reminded of the bleak realities of dealing with the public servants whose salaries she helps pay. Her 15-year-old son needed to take a written test for his learner's driving permit. But the licensing office is open only during the hours when she and her husband are unable to get there because of their jobs—with the sole exception of Saturday morning. So she and her son had to go on Saturday and wait two and a half hours for him to take a 20-minute test. The wait was necessitated solely by the refusal of public employees to make themselves available at times convenient to their patrons.

That's how most government offices function. You can get a pizza   10
delivered at 3 a.m., most commodities can be bought in well-appointed stores seven days a week, and computer help lines operate round the

clock. You can complete many transactions without ever leaving your home. But federal, state and municipal offices make few of the elementary concessions needed to accommodate ordinary people.

Of course, a lot of people who work in the private sector would also prefer to have their evenings and weekends free. But the nature of competition in the free market is that the consumer is sovereign—and the seller has to serve the consumer's needs or perish.

Government workers claim to serve the public, too, but in too many cases, their actions speak louder. Democracy, we are told, forces the government to respond to the bidding of the people. But it is not the nature of government, democratic or otherwise, to do that on a day-to-day basis. The imbalance of power is too large and too secure. Next time you're dealing with a sullen public employee, you should have no trouble figuring out who is the servant.

Questions for Analysis

Logic

1. According to Chapman, what reasons make it more pleasant to deal with workers in the private sector?
2. In paragraph 6 Chapman claims that "the only monopoly truly worth fearing is the one exercised by the government itself." Explain in your own words two ways in which he supports this claim logically.
3. Chapman does not argue explicitly for a solution to the problem of rudeness on the part of public employees. In your own words describe any implicit arguments he makes in this regard. Does he imply, for example, that we should change our form of government from democracy to something else to achieve better manners?

Character

1. Chapman argues that public employees are often ill mannered. What techniques of writing does he employ to create a sense of his own character as well mannered? Point to and analyze two examples.
2. In paragraph 4 Chapman allows that perhaps a majority of public employees act properly. What sense of Chapman's own character does this claim help to create?
3. In paragraph 9 Chapman speaks of working hours as the result of a "refusal"; in paragraph 11 he speaks of them in terms of preference. How does his choice of words help to create a sense of differing characters for workers in the public and private sectors?

Emotion

1. Point to three words in paragraph 1 that Chapman uses to create the sense of rudeness on the part of the fare conductor and explain their implications.

2. In paragraph 3 Chapman says that the customer service representative "actually managed to sound surprised." What does Chapman imply are her real emotions, and how does he use language to make this implication?

3. In paragraph 5 what emotions are expressed by the employee's remarks? Explain in particular how his use of the word *Buddy* helps to express them.

Chapman

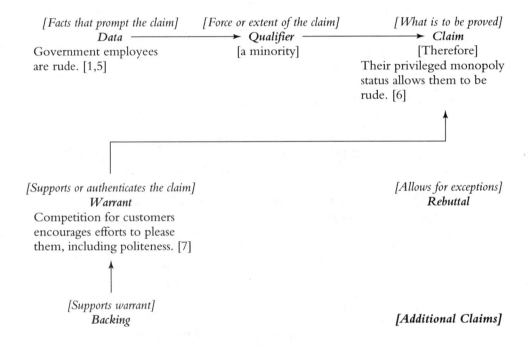

[Facts that prompt the claim] Data	[Force or extent of the claim] Qualifier	[What is to be proved] Claim
Government employees are rude. [1,5]	[a minority]	[Therefore] Their privileged monopoly status allows them to be rude. [6]

[Supports or authenticates the claim]
Warrant
Competition for customers encourages efforts to please them, including politeness. [7]

[Allows for exceptions]
Rebuttal

[Supports warrant]
Backing

[Additional Claims]

WHO'S HARASSING WHOM?

Marianne M. Jennings

Nearly 30 years in the workplace, and not once have I been sexually   *1*
harassed. I suppose I'm grateful, but given the action other working women seem to be getting, a part of me wonders: Exactly what's wrong with me? It's not as if I haven't been in high-risk environments. I began my legal career as an intern for the federal government. Yet I haven't had so much as a comment from a male coworker since the Reagan adminis-

tration. After the Anita Hill spectacle in 1991, I noticed men averting their eyes.

But what I resent more than the lack of attention is the assumption underlying the rules and court decisions governing sexual harassment: that I am incapable of handling unwanted sexual suggestion. My employer trusts me with budgeting, lobbying, fund-raising and shaping the minds of the next generation, but is forced by the Equal Employment Opportunity Commission and the courts to conclude that I can't handle the advances of knuckleheads.

I resent the women who bring sexual harassment suits and convince courts that we are as helpless and victimized as Melanie Wilkes in "Gone With the Wind." I come from a long line of unharassed women who taught me that the best defense against offensive male behavior is a good offense. The female arm has an appendage created for dealing with cads. Women in the 1940s used said appendage quite effectively to administer a slap in the face and thereby deter drunken sailors. And yet working women today can't handle a boor in wing tips and bifocals without the help of the Supreme Court?

The court's recent rulings on harassment make it easier to win damages against a company even if it is unaware that a supervisor is harassing an employee, and even if the plaintiff suffered no career damage. The likely result: Companies will redouble their already vigorous efforts aimed at preventing harassment.

But who's harassing whom when I'm forced to attend "sensitivity   5
training" seminars and reveal my personal feelings to coworkers with whom I don't even exchange recipes? At one Fortune 500 company, a sensitivity consultant instructed employees to conduct the following "group exercise": "I want all of the men to sit down on the floor in the center of the room. You are not allowed to speak while sitting down. The women are to stand around the men in a circle and begin to whistle and make sexist comments about the appearance and anatomy of the men." What if I don't *want* to talk about my colleagues' anatomy?

How innocent are the victims of harassment anyway? "Dateline NBC" recently ran a story on women who claimed they were harassed while working on the production lines at a Ford plant in Chicago. They tearfully told of sleeping with supervisors to keep their jobs and of being hospitalized for stress. These women defined their ethical dilemma as most people who make poor decisions do: Either I stay here and get harassed, or I leave and take another job for less pay but keep my sanity and virtue. To put it another way, the supervisors' brutish behavior was awful, but for $22 an hour the employees were willing to put up with it. Similarly, if you believe Anita Hill's story, she tolerated Clarence Thomas's misbehavior for years because riding to a career pinnacle on the tails of a shooting star was worth it.

Like tenants who claim "constructive eviction" due to horrible living conditions yet remain on the leased premises, the legal claim of women that their working environment is hostile doesn't jibe with their own decision to remain. Women define what's repulsive, stay in it and then file and win multimillion-dollar verdicts, which in many cases exceed the amounts awarded to children crippled in horrific accidents. The courtroom playing field reflects academic theories such as the following, touted in the Journal of Business Ethics: "Sexual harassment signifies to women that their presence is threatening to the dominant patriarchal order, that they are unwelcome, and works to maintain gender stratification." The guys at the Ford plant were interested in "gender stratification"? Sounds to me like they were just after a roll in the hay.

The most damaging result of sexual-harassment law is the chilling effect it has on men in the workplace. Mentoring, which I had from decent and honorable men and without which I would not have survived 30 years ago, is a lost art. Men who hold the keys and skills for advancement hestitate to involve themselves in one-on-one counseling of female employees. Men fear closing the office door during meetings with women. At the University of Nebraska, a graduate student was even ordered to remove a picture of his bikini-clad wife from his desk after two colleagues complained.

I see a fear in my male colleagues' eyes that they will unwittingly offend someone and will be the subject of a career-derailing investigation. The fear is justified. An accused rapist, after all, receives better treatment than an accused harasser. The rape defendant is entitled to due process, the presumption of innocence and his day in court. When a man is charged with sexual harassment, the employer's response will be swift, decisive and one-sided.

I resent that men in my office feel they must cast their eyes downward. It's not their sexual appetites they're holding back. It's candor. It's friendliness. It's lunch together. They're certainly not harassers, but they can no longer risk being my friends or mentors. Feminists claimed victory with these latest decisions because liability for sexual harassment now rests squarely with those responsible—employers. That's wrong. Employers don't cause sexual harassment. Women have defined it, capitalized on it and exacerbated it. We also possess the tools for handling it, without a federal judge or bureaucracy. Dear sisters, we have met the enemy and she is us.

10

Questions for Analysis

Logic

1. What assumption about ways to deal with sexual harassment in the reasoning of her opponents does Jennings most question? On what assumption does she rest her own argument?

2. Explain in your own words Jennings's objections to the logic of "innocent victims" beginning in paragraph 6.
3. Explain in your own words Jennings's reasoning on the subject of mentoring in the workplace.

Character
1. Jennings claims to be able to handle herself in the event of any harassment. Point to some uses of language that work to create a sense of self-reliance in her character.
2. What are Jennings's feelings about "personal feelings" in paragraph 5? What sense of her character is created by her objections here?
3. What qualities of character does Jennings attribute to the female auto workers? What to their supervisors? Explain your answers.

Emotion
1. Jennings claims several times to feel resentment. Besides the use of the word itself, what techniques of writing work to express this emotion? Point to and analyze two examples.
2. In paragraph 6 what are the emotions appealed to by the female workers? What emotions does Jennings herself invite us to feel about them? Analyze the techniques in each case.
3. In paragraph 7 what emotions are the readers invited to feel by the contrast between the dictional levels of "gender stratification" and "roll in the hay"? How might these two emotions be expected to gain support for Jennings's argument?

EXERCISES: MODERN MANNERS

Intertextual Questions
1. In paragraph 3 of his essay, Chapman invites his readers to agree that "being abused for no conceivable purpose" is "normal" for those dealing with public employees. He locates the problem in economics in the form of public monopolies. Discuss the ways in which the other two writers do or do not provide alternative ways of understanding the kind of rudeness that prompted Chapman's claim.
2. In paragraph 10 of her essay, Miss Manners reports an analysis of "dissin.'" Discuss the ways in which this analysis does or does not illuminate the difficulties of manners that are the subjects of the other two essays.
3. The political philosopher Hannah Arendt claims that one of the defining features of modern life has been "the conquest of society by the state." Discuss the ways in which the three authors in this chapter view the interaction between "society," where personal relations are controlled by convention, and "government," where personal relations are controlled by law.

Suggestions for Writing

1. The writer Roberta Conde has said: "Lord Acton didn't go far enough. While it is true that power corrupts and that absolute power corrupts absolutely, it is also true that petty power corrupts in petty ways." Write an essay in which you draw on your own experiences to attack, defend, or modify this claim as a way of understanding public and private rudeness.

2. Write an essay in the form of a letter addressed to someone who has been rude to you, in which you argue that the action was not only wrong in itself but also symptomatic of the larger social problem of modern manners.

3. Marianne Jennings rejects lawsuits and sensitivity training as proper responses to sexual harassment. Taking her position into account— whether to attack, modify, or defend it—write an essay in which you argue for the proper response to sexual harassment in school and the workplace.

16 *Should English Be the Official Language of the United States?*

IN SUPPORT OF OUR COMMON LANGUAGE . . .
U.S. English

ENGLISH, OUR COMMON BOND

Throughout its history, the United States has been enriched by the [1] cultural contributions of immigrants from many traditions, but blessed with one common language that has united a diverse nation and fostered harmony among its people.

As much by accident as by design, that language is English. Given our country's history of immigration and the geography of immigrant settlements, it might have been Dutch, or Spanish, or German; or it might have been two languages, as is the case in Canada, our neighbor to the north.

But English prevailed, and it has served us well. Its eloquence shines in our Declaration of Independence and in our Constitution. It is the living carrier of our democratic ideals.

English is a world language which we share with many other nations. It is the most popular medium of international communication.

THE SPREAD OF LANGUAGE SEGREGATION

The United States has been spared the bitter conflicts that plague so [5] many countries whose citizens do not share a common tongue. Historic forces made English the language of all Americans, though nothing in our laws designated it the official language of the nation.

But now English is under attack, and we must take affirmative steps to guarantee that it continues to be our common heritage. Failure to do so may well lead to institutionalized language segregation and a gradual loss of national unity.

The erosion of English and the rise of other languages in public life have several causes:

- Some spokesmen for ethnic groups reject the "melting pot" ideal; they label assimilation a betrayal of their native cultures and demand government funding to maintain separate ethnic institutions.
- Well-intentioned but unproven theories have led to extensive government-funded bilingual education programs, ranging from preschool through college.
- New civil-rights assertions have yielded bilingual and multi-lingual ballots, voting instructions, election site counselors, and government-funded voter registration campaigns aimed solely at speakers of foreign languages.
- Record immigration, concentrated in fewer language groups, is reinforcing language segregation and retarding language assimilation.
- The availability of foreign language electronic media, with a full range of news and entertainment, is a new disincentive to the learning of English.

U.S. ENGLISH: A TIMELY PUBLIC RESPONSE

In 1981, Senator S. I. Hayakawa, himself an immigrant and distinguished scholar of semantics, proposed a constitutional amendment designating English as the official language of the United States. Senator Hayakawa helped found U.S. ENGLISH in 1983 to organize and support a citizens' movement to maintain our common linguistic heritage.

U.S. ENGLISH is committed to promoting the use of English in the political, economic, and intellectual life of the nation. It operates squarely within the American political mainstream and rejects all manifestations of cultural or linguistic chauvinism.

OUR GUIDING PRINCIPLES

Our goal is to maintain the blessing of a common language—   10
English—for the people of the United States.

These principles guide us:

- In a pluralistic nation such as ours, government should foster the similarities that unite us rather than the differences that separate us.

- The nation's public schools have a special responsibility to help students who don't speak English to learn the language as quickly as possible.
- Quality teaching of English should be part of every student's curriculum, at every academic level.
- The study of foreign languages should be strongly encouraged, both as an academic discipline and for practical, economic, and foreign-policy considerations.
- *All* candidates for U.S. citizenship should be required to demonstrate the ability to understand, speak, read, and write simple English, and demonstrate basic understanding of our system of government.
- The rights of individuals and groups to use other languages and to establish *privately funded* institutions for the maintenance of diverse languages and cultures must be respected in a pluralistic society.

OUR ACTION PROGRAM

U.S. ENGLISH actively works to reverse the spread of foreign language usage in the nation's official life. Our program calls for:

- Adoption of a constitutional amendment to establish English as the official language of the United States.
- Repeal of laws mandating multilingual ballots and voting materials.
- Restriction of government funding for bilingual education to short-term transitional programs only.
- Universal enforcement of the English language and civics requirement for naturalization.
- Expansion of opportunities for learning English.

Toward these ends, U.S. ENGLISH serves as a national center for consultation and cooperation on ways to defend English as the sole official language of the United States. It directs its efforts to leading a public discussion on the best language policies for our multiethnic society; educating opinion leaders on the long-term implications of language segregation; encouraging research on improved methods of teaching English; and promoting effective programs of English language instruction.

WE NEED YOUR HELP

U.S. ENGLISH welcomes to membership all who are concerned about the prospect of entrenched language segregation and the possibility of losing our strongest national bond.

We hope that you will join us and defend our common language 15
against misguided policies that threaten our national unity.

———————

Questions for Analysis

Logic

1. Where in the essay do you find an attempt to meet the counter-arguments of opponents? Can you think of objections that have not been met?
2. Explain in your own words the logic of the claim in paragraph 6 that failure to defend English will lead to "language segregation."
3. In what ways does the document seek to avoid the objection that it is prejudiced? What reasons are mentioned that might seek to counter this charge?

Character

1. "In Support of Our Common Language . . ." was modified or approved by more than one author. Do you see any evidence of multiple authorship in any aspect of the document's style? Explain with examples.
2. What does the phrase "as much by accident as by design" in paragraph 2 contribute to the sense of character U.S. English projects? What motivations or rationales might be anticipated and rejected by the implications of the phrase?
3. What contribution does paragraph 4 make to the sense of character projected? What values and assumptions seem to underlie the statement? How does it expand the meaning of *our* in the section's title?

Emotion

1. What emotions are appealed to by the examples given in paragraph 3? Can you point to evidence for the same emotional appeal elsewhere in the document?
2. What emotional response seems invited by the example of Senator Hayakawa in paragraph 8?
3. The word *serve* appears in paragraphs 3 and 13. What are the emotional implications of the word, and what does it invite the audience to feel in each case? Does it act differently in each case? Explain your answer.

U.S. English

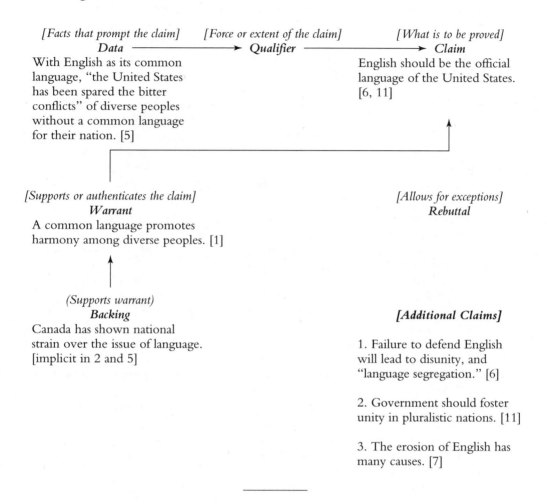

[Facts that prompt the claim]
Data ────────────▶ **Qualifier** ────────────▶ **Claim**
[Force or extent of the claim]   *[What is to be proved]*

Data
With English as its common
language, "the United States
has been spared the bitter
conflicts" of diverse peoples
without a common language
for their nation. [5]

Claim
English should be the official
language of the United States.
[6, 11]

[Supports or authenticates the claim]
Warrant
A common language promotes
harmony among diverse peoples. [1]

[Allows for exceptions]
Rebuttal

(Supports warrant)
Backing
Canada has shown national
strain over the issue of language.
[implicit in 2 and 5]

[Additional Claims]

1. Failure to defend English
will lead to disunity, and
"language segregation." [6]

2. Government should foster
unity in pluralistic nations. [11]

3. The erosion of English has
many causes. [7]

GAINS AND LOSSES

Richard Rodriguez

My *mother!* My *father!* After English became my primary language,   *1*
I no longer knew what words to use in addressing my parents. The old
Spanish words (those tender accents of sound) I had used earlier—*mamá*
and *papá*—I couldn't use anymore. They would have been too painful
reminders of how much had changed in my life. On the other hand, the

words I heard neighborhood kids call *their* parents seemed equally unsatisfactory. *Mother* and *Father; Ma, Papa, Pa, Dad, Pop* (how I hated the all-American sound of that last word especially)—all these terms I felt were unsuitable, not really terms of address for *my* parents. As a result, I never used them at home. Whenever I'd speak to my parents, I would try to get their attention with eye contact alone. In public conversations, I'd refer to 'my parents' or 'my mother and father.'

My mother and father, for their part, responded differently, as their children spoke to them less. She grew restless, seemed troubled and anxious at the scarcity of words exchanged in the house. It was she who would question me about my day when I came home from school. She smiled at small talk. She pried at the edges of my sentences to get me to say something more. (What?) She'd join conversations she overheard, but her intrusions often stopped her children's talking. By contrast, my father seemed reconciled to the new quiet. Though his English improved somewhat, he retired into silence. At dinner he spoke very little. One night his children and even his wife helplessly giggled at his garbled English pronunciation of the Catholic Grace before Meals. Thereafter he made his wife recite the prayer at the start of each meal, even on formal occasions, when there were guests in the house. Hers became the public voice of the family. On official business, it was she, not my father, one would usually hear on the phone or in stores, talking to strangers. His children grew so accustomed to his silence that, years later, they would speak routinely of his shyness. (My mother would often try to explain: Both his parents died when he was eight. He was raised by an uncle who treated him like little more than a menial servant. He was never encouraged to speak. He grew up alone. A man of few words.) But my father was not shy, I realized, when I'd watch him speaking Spanish with relatives. Using Spanish, he was quickly effusive. Especially when talking with other men, his voice would spark, flicker, flare alive with sounds. In Spanish, he expressed ideas and feelings he rarely revealed in English. With firm Spanish sounds, he conveyed confidence and authority English would never allow him.

The silence at home, however, was finally more than a literal silence. Fewer words passed between parent and child, but more profound was the silence that resulted from my inattention to sounds. At about the time I no longer bothered to listen with care to the sounds of English in public, I grew careless about listening to the sounds family members made when they spoke. Most of the time I heard someone speaking at home and didn't distinguish his sounds from the words people uttered in public. I didn't even pay much attention to my parents' accented and ungrammatical speech. At least not at home. Only when I was with them in public would I grow alert to their accents. Though, even then, their sounds caused me less and less concern. For I was increasingly confident of my own public identity.

I would have been happier about my public success had I not sometimes recalled what it had been like earlier, when my family had conveyed its intimacy through a set of conveniently private sounds. Sometimes in public, hearing a stranger, I'd hark back to my past. A Mexican farmworker approached me downtown to ask directions to somewhere. '¿Hijito . . . ?' he said. And his voice summoned deep longing. Another time, standing beside my mother in the visiting room of a Carmelite convent, before the dense screen which rendered the nuns shadowy figures, I heard several Spanish-speaking nuns—their busy, singsong overlapping voices—assure us that yes, yes, we were remembered, all our family was remembered in their prayers. (Their voices echoed faraway family sounds.) Another day, a dark-faced old woman—her hand light on my shoulder—steadied herself against me as she boarded a bus. She murmured something I couldn't quite comprehend. Her Spanish voice came near, like the face of a never-before-seen relative in the instant before I was kissed. Her voice, like so many of the Spanish voices I'd hear in public, recalled the golden age of my youth. Hearing Spanish then, I continued to be a careful, if sad, listener to sounds. Hearing a Spanish-speaking family walking behind me, I turned to look. I smiled for an instant, before my glance found the Hispanic-looking faces of strangers in the crowd going by.

Questions for Analysis

Logic
1. Make a list of the stated or implied reasons that English was a loss for Rodriguez in his private life.
2. Make a list of the stated or implied reasons that English was a gain for Rodriguez in his public life.
3. In your own words summarize the author's reasoning on the difference between literal and figurative silence.

Character
1. Does Rodriguez project a sense of character that seems fair-minded? Analyze some examples that support your answer.
2. Does Rodriguez project a sense of character that seems intelligent and reasonable? Analyze some examples.
3. Does the character suggested by the style of the essay seem to be founded on moral and ethical principles? Analyze the evidence that leads you to your response.

Emotion
1. In the narrative of the reactions of his family, compare the emotions Rodriguez suggests that he himself felt with those he seems to invite his audience to feel.
2. Of his mother Rodriguez says in paragraph 2 that "she pried at the

edges of my sentences." What emotions in his mother does the author's metaphor dramatize?

3. What differing emotions in his father does Rodriguez dramatize in paragraph 2 when he describes him speaking first in English and then in Spanish?

HOW NOT TO GET THE INFIDEL TO TALK THE KING'S TALK

Ishmael Reed

"How will we eradicate Black English?" Dick Cavett, public television's resident Anglo-lover, asked a group of linguists and John Simon. "You'd have to eradicate the black people," a linguist answered. Chilling thought, considering that there are historical precedents for people being exterminated because they didn't speak and write the way others thought they should.

When his arguments failed to convince the linguists of the existence of a "standard English," guest John Simon said that blacks should speak "'standard English' in order to get ahead," or as William Prashker wrote in the *New York Times* magazine section, "Black culture doesn't mean zip" when you're trying to impress "the man downtown." The Man downtown.

Of course, neither Prashker nor Simon and Cavett could explain the successes of Gerald Ford, or of New York City's Mayor Ed Koch, who confuses "each other" with "one another." Nor did they explain the triumphs of Dwight Eisenhower, who introduced the word "finalize" and whose press conference transcripts do not obey the rules of grammar.

Nelson Rockefeller, the late governor of New York, was a wealthy man, yet this man thought that the word "horrendous" was a word of praise. Really. The former President of the United States says "fahm" for what we call "farm." I was appalled to learn, in *The Brethren,* that Chief Justice Burger's decisions are so illiterate that the law clerk has to correct them so that they won't embarrass the Court.

If people who make these errors are "idiots," as Simon says, then many of our elected officials, industrialists, and writers are idiots: *As I Lay Dying* is filled with "errors" by Faulkner.

Did the powerful people who "rule" America—all white males according to the April 16, 1979, issue of *U.S. News and World Report*—"get ahead" by speaking like characters in a Henry James novel? Did oilmen? Did Teamster presidents? I doubt it.

You not gone make me give up Black English. When you ask me to give up my Black English you askin me to give up my soul. But for reasons of commerce, transportation-hassleless mobility in everyday life, I will talk to 411 in a language both the operator and I can understand. I will answer the highway patrolman who stops me, for having a broken rear light, in words he and I both know. The highway patrolman, who grew up on Elvis Presley, might speak Black English at home, because Black English has influenced not only blacks but whites too.

So when trying to get the infidel to talk so that the British Tea Company can keep an eye on the infidel, the missionaries should be aware that appeals to "getting ahead" will be seen through by the millions of Black English followers both overt and covert. The phantom legions.

Don't blame the mass defections from "standard English" on them; their rulers were the first to surrender.

The ironies don't end there. During an appearance before the   10
English-Speaking Union in San Francisco, John Simon spoke of reprimanding a young woman for saying "between Bill and I" instead of "Bill and me." He went on to say he didn't have the "foggiest notion who Bill or the woman speaking or the woman behind the counter *were*." As reporter Charles Haas pointed out in the December 17, 1979, issue of *New West* magazine, Simon should have said "was."

Questions for Analysis

Logic
1. What are the logical parallels of cause and effect that Reed implies between British rule of the American Colonies and standard English on the one hand and the Boston Tea Party and Black English on the other?
2. What are Reed's stated and implied reasons for wanting to keep Black English?
3. What are Reed's stated and implied reasons for wanting to keep a command of standard English?

Character
1. What does Reed's sentence structure, as exemplified in paragraph 3, contribute to our sense of his character? What does the relation between the sentences contribute to the structure of the paragraph and a further sense of Reed's character?
2. Reed could have pointed out the error mentioned in paragraph 10 himself or could have referred to a general grammar book. What does his having given credit to Charles Haas contribute to our sense of his character?
3. What does Reed's use of Black English in paragraph 7 contribute to our sense of his character? How is that style affected by the stylistic context of the rest of the essay?

Emotion
1. What emotions does Reed's use of Black English in paragraph 7 tend to evoke in his audience? If Reed were to imagine that audience as composed of speakers of both standard English and Black English, what emotions might be expected of each group?
2. What emotions does Reed invite by his emphasis on the word *eradicate* in paragraph 1? Are those emotions like the ones invited by his emphasis on *man/Man* in paragraph 2? Explain.
3. Do you understand the joke made by calling Dick Cavett an "Anglo-lover" in paragraph 1? If you do not, note carefully the differences it makes in your emotional relation to the paragraph when the joke is explained.

EXERCISES: SHOULD ENGLISH BE THE OFFICIAL LANGUAGE OF AMERICA?

Intertextual Questions
1. Do the three essays in this section all seem to operate on a common understanding of the definition of "standard English"? Explain your answer with examples.
2. The three essays may be seen as not directly opposing one another's positions. Pick examples of areas that overlap and explain some similarities in the positions taken.
3. What differences among the three essays are there in any area they all address? Explain your answer with examples.

Suggestions for Writing
1. Write a letter as though it were written by either Rodriguez or Reed to U.S. English, and explain the degree of support or opposition that you think the writer would express to the principles of the organization.
2. Write a letter from U.S. English to either Reed or Rodriguez that responds to the letter suggested in suggestion 1.
3. Write a short essay that argues for your own position on whether - "standard English" should be a national goal.

II Single Essays on Controversial Topics

Ellen Ullman, "Needed: Techies Who Know Shakespeare"
Craig R. Dean, "Legalize Gay Marriage"
Joanne Jacobs, "End the War on Drugs"
Nicholas Wade, "Method and Madness"
Cathy Young, "Women, Sex, and Rape"
Joseph Kuncewitch, "Only Hunting Trims Deer
    Reproduction"
Mona Charen, "Is Fertility Technology Good or Bad?"
Shira Feldman, "Corporations Are Looting Intellectual
    Property"
Dick Boland, "Serving Time the Old-Fashioned Way"
Walter E. Williams, "Government Is the Problem"

INTRODUCTION

All the earlier issues have been represented by multiple points of view and accompanied by extensive analytic apparatus. The idea of the following section is for you to practice the skills you have acquired by asking your own questions about the ways the authors argue through logic, character, and emotion and forming (if necessary) your own alternative opinions to those represented here. The range of topics includes many of those currently most controversial, and you will no doubt already have formed opinions on many of them. But whether you agree or disagree with the stance taken by these writers, you should be prepared both to analyze the ways in which their arguments operate and to respond to those arguments with supporting or opposing arguments of your own.

This section provides material for you to use in expanding and honing your analysis and argumentative writing skills without the help (or interference) of the editorial apparatus provided in the previous section. The selections have been made with the idea of giving one of the most controversial positions taken on controversial issues, so that you will have plenty of room to disagree with, modify, or support the author's point of view. Remember to pay attention to all sides of the rhetorical triangle whether analyzing the essays or responding to them with essays of your own.

NEEDED: TECHIES WHO KNOW SHAKESPEARE

Ellen Ullman

High-technology companies are so desperate for programmers, according to recent reports, that they are luring students out of the classroom with well-paying jobs. It's the schools' fault, say people in the industry and some computer-science professors. Students aren't being taught the skills they need and therefore don't see the point of getting a degree. [1]

But critics are forgetting that the very idea of the computer science degree is a relatively recent point on the short time line of the computer industry. Historically, most programmers had plenty of education, but little of it came from computer science departments. The problem is not the technical curriculum, but the undergraduate-computer science degree itself.

Computer programming has always been a self-taught, maverick occupation. Except for a brief moment in the late 1980s and early 1990s—what I think of as the Dilbert era—no one thought that programming was something you should learn in college.

Prospective programmers spent a great deal of time in school, but they typically studied something other than computers. Aside from a few famous dropouts—like Bill Gates, Steven Jobs and Stephen Wozniak—the profession has always attracted the very well-schooled.

Physicists and mathematicians created the industry just after World   5
War II and became the first programmers. As the need for such skills grew
in the 1970s, business and government had to look beyond people with
doctorates.

Fortunately, that demand coincided with the end of the 1960s,
when all sorts of overeducated people were on the loose, looking for a
way to earn a living.

That's where I came in: I'm a member of the generation that came
to computing as a second, third or fourth vocation. My first boss had two
master's degrees in social science and had spent years as a Sufi dancing
disciple. My next boss, a former bartender, had a master's degree in library science. The head of technical services at the same company had a
Ph.D. in anthropology, and she hired people who had completed all but
their dissertations in linguistics, archeology and classics. In this crowd, I
felt like the dunce with my undergraduate degree in English.

We had all taught ourselves computing. For us, it was just one more
difficult subject to learn. No one was intimidated by learning another
computer language—or anything else for that matter. What we knew
was how to learn, which is all that one can hang on to in a profession in
which change is relentless.

The generation of programmers who followed us were, well, disap-
pointing. They had engineering and computer science degrees, and none
of them seemed to have read anything but technical textbooks. They stood
mute among us when we said the occasional phrase in French. They
looked confused when we alluded to Shakespeare or Proust. If today's
would-be programmers are fleeing the sort of education that these people
received, well, that's wonderful.

A good friend of mine finished engineering school in the late   10
1980s. He managed to get his degree without having studied much of
what some still call Western civilization.

Poignantly, he knows he's missed something. He is now a principal
of a startup company developing E-mail services for the World Wide
Web. My friend is building connections around the planet, and he is
ashamed that he has never even studied a foreign language.

I don't mean for these stories to persuade aspiring programmers to
drop out of school. Quite the contrary, I hope it might make students
and professors realize that programming instruction can take place in a
few classes, and students can spend the rest of their time studying foreign
language, literature, linguistics, philosophy and history of science.

Schools might as well give up on teaching the latest skills, since
those skills will soon become obsolete anyway. Instead, they might stress
subjects that foster a flexible and open mind. Programmers seem to be
changing the world. It would be a relief, for them and for all of us, if they
knew something about it.

LEGALIZE GAY MARRIAGE

Craig R. Dean

In November 1990, my lover, Patrick Gill, and I were denied a   *1*
marriage license because we are gay. In a memorandum explaining the
District's decision, the clerk of the court wrote that "the sections of the
District of Columbia code governing marriage do not authorize marriage between persons of the same sex." By refusing to give us the same
legal recognition that is given to heterosexual couples, the District has
degraded our relationship as well as that of every other gay and lesbian
couple.

At one time, interracial couples were not allowed to marry. Gays
and lesbians are still denied this basic civil right in the U.S.—and around
the world. Can you imagine the outcry if any other minority group was
denied the right to legally marry today?

Marriage is more than a piece of paper. It gives societal recognition and legal protection to a relationship. It confers numerous benefits
to spouses; in the District alone, there are more than 100 automatic
marriage-based rights. In every state in the nation, married couples have
the right to be on each other's health, disability, life insurance and pension
plans. Married couples receive special tax exemptions, deductions and
refunds. Spouses may automatically inherit property and have rights of
survivorship that avoid inheritance tax. Though unmarried couples—
both gay and heterosexual—are entitled to some of these rights, they are
by no means guaranteed.

For married couples, the spouse is legally the next of kin in case
of death, medical emergency or mental incapacity. In stark contrast, the
family is generally the next of kin for same-sex couples. In the shadow of
AIDS, the denial of marriage rights can be even more ominous.

In November, Patrick and I filed suit against the District alleging   *5*
two-fold discrimination. First, the District violated its gender-neutral
marriage law: nowhere does its legal code state that a marriage must con-
sist of a man and a woman or that a married couple may not be of the
same sex.

Second, the District violated its own Human Rights Act, the strongest in the nation. According to the act, which was enacted in 1977, "every individual shall have an equal opportunity to participate in the economic, cultural and intellectual life of the District and to have an equal
opportunity to participate in all aspects of life."

The law is clearly on our side. In fact, cases interpreting the act have
held that the "eradication of sexual orientation discrimination is a com-

pelling governmental interest." Moreover, in 1987 the District Court of Appeals elevated anti-gay bias to the same level as racial and gender discrimination.

Some argue that gay marriage is too radical for society. We disagree. According to a 1989 study by the American Bar Association, eight to 10 million children are currently being reared in three million gay households. Therefore, approximately 6 percent of the U.S. population is made up of gay and lesbian families with children. Why should these families be denied the protection granted to other families?

Allowing gay marriage would strengthen society by increasing tolerance. It is paradoxical that mainstream America perceives gays and lesbians as unable to maintain long-term relationships while at the same time denying them the very institutions that stabilize such relationships.

Twenty-five years ago, one-third of the U.S. did not allow inter-   10
racial marriage. It took a 1967 Supreme Court decision, in *Loving* v. *Virginia,* a case similar to ours, to strike down these discriminatory prohibitions and redefine family and marriage. Then, as now, those who argued against granting civil rights spoke of morality, social tensions and protection of family values. But, now, as then, the real issue is justice vs. oppression.

END THE WAR ON DRUGS

Joanne Jacobs

President Clinton has inherited two costly, nasty and never-ending   *1*
wars from George Bush. I don't know what he should do about the war against Saddam Hussein, but I think he should end the war on drugs.

Bush drew a line in the snow, so to speak, and fought hard to make the hawkish supply-side strategies work. Drug war spending quadrupled, to nearly $13 billion a year for the federal effort alone, and Bush put 70 percent of the money into interdiction and enforcement.

The prison population doubled in the past 10 years, in large part due to more hawkish enforcement and long mandatory sentences for drug offenses.

"In California, the number of persons sent to prison for drug offenses tripled between 1980 and 1985, and tripled again in the following five years, rising from less than 1,000 to more than 10,000 over the decade," reports the Rand Research Review. No wonder the state is broke.

The result of this multibillion-dollar war: Less occasional drug use,   *5*
as much or more hard-core abuse. By one measure—emergency-room

admissions for cocaine and heroin overdoses—things are considerably worse.

Meanwhile, the murder rate has gone up in step with the drug-war budget. This is not a coincidence, observes Peter Reuter, a Rand drug-policy analyst. "Frequent harassment of street drug sellers increases the incentives to use violence to maintain market share."

Furthermore, our civil liberties have suffered collateral damage, as all Americans—but especially minorities—are subjected to drug tests, warrantless searches and long-distance snooping.

On the campaign trail, Clinton promised a "national crusade" that will spend more on treatment and prevention. He also pledged to provide federal funds for local police to suppress drugs.

A crusade is better than a war, but not much. Clinton's wording still implies a one-shot campaign leading to total victory, or perhaps total redemption.

The president has an opportunity for leadership toward some of that *10* change we've been hearing about: He can recast drug policy as a public-health issue.

After all, Clinton's half-brother is one of those drug criminals we've heard so much about. He served 15 months in federal prison for selling cocaine in 1984. Clinton participated in family therapy to aid his brother's treatment for addiction. He knows Roger Clinton Jr.'s criminal substance abuse is closely related to Roger Clinton Sr.'s legal substance abuse.

Perhaps Clinton guesses that if his brother had come from a poorer family—with no family friends to provide a job and no money to pay for therapy—his drug conviction would have ended his chances to find honest work or live a drug-free life.

The president of the Arkansas Senate was criticized this week for commuting two sentences while serving as acting governor: One was a murderer's life sentence; the other was a 50-year prison term for transporting cocaine. The drug carrier had served five years, and would not have been eligible for parole for another 18 years.

The foot-soldiers in the drug war are ready to change. Police chiefs and cops, probation officers, judges and prosecutors know that what they've been doing doesn't do any good. Most now advocate the pragmatic approach called "harm minimization." (Some favor decriminalization, but that much change isn't going to happen.)

What can Clinton do? *15*

Stop promising a "drug free" America, and drop the military rhetoric. Announce that drug abuse will be treated like alcohol abuse, a serious public-health problem causing harm to innocent victims as well as to abusers.

Cut the drug czar's bloated office—which in the past has been filled with political hacks—and transfer it to Health and Human Services.

Fund treatment programs with a record of success and rehabilitation programs for prisoners. Currently, there are enough federally funded treatment slots for fewer than one out of three serious drug abusers.

Don't put more money into prevention programs without evidence of effectiveness. Kids don't need more antidrug education. What they need is education to prepare for a future in which they'll have better choices than using or selling drugs.

(My sixth-grader just attended a school assembly featuring a guy   20
who demonstrated jumping rope and ventriloquism—including the singing of "Hava Nagila" for "our Jewish-American friends"—and led students in hope-not-dope and self-esteem chants. She threatened to start using drugs if forced to listen to one more antidrug spiel.)

Fund those cops on the beat to make neighborhoods safer for decent people. Sure, patrolling mean streets is not a federal responsibility, but as long as we're going to ignore that, make sure the money goes for community policing, not task forces and SWAT teams.

The money can come from eliminating the Drug Enforcement Administration. We've got the FBI; we don't need multiple agencies tripping over each other.

Take every dollar spent trying to interdict drug supplies and use it to pay for education, job training and drug treatment for inner-city kids.

Eliminate mandatory sentences that put first-time drug offenders behind bars for years longer than murderers and rapists, and fill jails with petty drug users. Some states are forced to release violent criminals early in order to make room for nonviolent drug offenders serving no-parole sentences.

Use the billions saved by reducing sentences to pay for locking up   25
violent criminals, for in-prison drug programs, for probation officers and for boarding schools (boot camps, if you prefer) for kids who get in trouble.

Finally, stop confiscating property unless there's proof it was bought with criminal proceeds. In some cases, cars, boats and homes have been seized without a criminal conviction, or with no evidence against the owner. This is the sort of arbitrary government power the Constitution is supposed to protect Americans against. The Supreme Court just agreed to hear a test case.

President Clinton is the first president to have smoked marijuana, even if he didn't inhale. I'd guess that almost all the Friends of Bill, and half his Cabinet, were drug criminals once.

U.S. drug policy casts millions of Americans as the enemy on whom war must be waged. It's time for a change.

METHOD AND MADNESS
Trials and Errors

Nicholas Wade

Science and the law are two systems of inquiry that diligently seek   1
truth. It's distressing enough when they arrive at discordant answers. But
in a number of recent cases, courts have endorsed legal theories of causation that merit credence only where the earth is flat.

The latest is that of silicone breast implants. Several manufacturers
have agreed in principle to pay $4.2 billion to women who believe they
have been harmed by the devices. You might suppose the courts had
found, by a preponderance of evidence, that breast implants are iniqui-
tously harmful.

But there was no such evidence. Epidemiological studies are only
now being completed. And the first three to be reported find no clear
sign of a link between silicone breast implants and disease. It's true such
studies should have been done years ago by the companies and plastic sur-
geons who profited from the devices; that lapse—not proof of harm—is
why in 1992 the Food and Drug Administration required cosmetic use
of the implants to cease. Nor does the present round of studies carry the
statistical weight to rule out the possibility that some rare disorders could
be made worse by leaking silicone.

But a $4 billion settlement in advance of any proof of harm makes
the courts look a little hasty, a trifle contemptuous of ascertainable scientific fact. And that's not free money the tort lawyers have extorted: the
insurance companies certainly plan to recover their share in stiffer pre-
miums, which in turn will mean higher prices or lost jobs.

So how did courts ever come to stray so far from the truth, at least   5
as it is understood by scientists? The fact is, science and law have such
entirely different touchstones for truth, it's surprising they're not at log-
gerheads more often.

Lawyers believe truth emerges from the contest between tenacious
advocates and their credibility to a jury, and that the best guarantee
against spurious scientific evidence is the cross-examination of witnesses
and careful instruction by the judge as to the burden of proof. But the
way scientists see it, some truths cannot be determined inside a courtroom. A single case is the equivalent of a mere anecdote, utterly useless
in deciding cause and effect. The truth does not lie in men's minds but
must be sought by cross-examining nature through rigorously objective trials.

Consider an egregious example of this cultural clash, in which a federal judge in Atlanta, sitting without a jury, ruled in 1986 that a contraceptive spermicide made by Ortho Pharmaceutical was the cause of a baby's birth defects. In awarding some $5 million in damages, the judge ignored the many clinical trials and the scientific community's clearly expressed consensus that spermicidal foams do not cause birth defects; what mattered to him was attitude. "The Court paid close attention to each expert's demeanor and tone," United States District Court Judge Marvin Shoob wrote in his decision. The companies' experts being deficient in the demeanor department, he found for the plaintiffs. Trial by ordeal worked sometimes, too.

For giving the government a hard time over Iraqgate, Judge Shoob has been likened by my colleague William Safire to a latter-day John Sirica, the Watergate judge. But on the humbler matter of spermicides Judge Shoob led the whole federal judiciary into a swamp of error; a Court of Appeals agreed that he had "found sufficient evidence of causation in a legal sense," and the Supreme Court refused to review the case.

The litigation over Agent Orange opened another eerie chasm between legal and scientific notions of causation. Vietnam veterans sued for damages, alleging ill health from dioxin, minuscule amounts of which contaminated the defoliant used during the war. Yet pilots who flew spraying missions and were drenched with Agent Orange every day have shown no pattern of unusual illness. Ground troops were exposed to far less.

Judge Jack B. Weinstein of the United States District Court in Brooklyn told the veterans' attorneys they had not proved causation, but that was just to get them to settle. Then he convinced the Agent Orange manufacturers that payment of a mere $180 million would let them walk away from an avalanche of litigation. Creative justice, maybe; so was Robin Hood's.

Bendectin, a drug to relieve morning sickness, provided another instance of the courts' failure to let truth suffice as a defense. Birth defects occur naturally in 2 to 3 percent of births, and inevitably the mothers of some of these children have taken Bendectin. Numerous scientific studies show Bendectin does not cause birth defects, but many women sued anyway. The manufacturer won most of the cases against it but quit making the drug: the costs of litigation were insupportable.

In each of these three cases—spermicides, Agent Orange and Bendectin—a scientific consensus built on many careful studies held that no harm had occurred, but courts punished the manufacturers almost as severely as if it had. What has gone wrong? Why don't the courts seem to respect the way scientists ascertain truth?

Part of the problem, of course, lies with scientists and doctors. There is no shortage of hired-gun experts who will depose as required.

The scientific community does not excommunicate these hacks, as they deserve, nor does it make its own consensus-forming processes very clear to outsiders.

Understandably enough, the courts have come to regard scientific and medical experts as mere advocates, whose defects and biases can be brought out by cross-examination. And courts have to make a decision: they can't enter the scientists' favorite verdict; more research is needed.

A year ago, in a Bendectin case known as *Daubert v. Merrell Dow*   *15* *Pharmaceuticals,* the United States Supreme Court decided that federal judges should act as gatekeepers of proffered scientific testimony and determine, through tests much the same as those used by scientists, whether the evidence's "underlying reasoning or methodology is scientifically valid."

Under the Daubert rule, judges have started to exclude evidence not generally accepted by the scientific community, like Bendectin birth defect claims, polygraphs and certain psychiatric testimony. That's a giant leap toward closing the gap between the two cultures in their mutual search for truth. Too bad the breast implant settlement seems to have escaped the new harrow of reason, but maybe it's the last weed in the field.

· ———————

WOMEN, SEX, AND RAPE
Have Some Feminists Exaggerated the Problem?

Cathy Young

The vast majority of Americans, women or men, undoubtedly   *1* take a positive view of changes the women's movement has brought about in attitudes toward rape. It is now widely accepted that a woman does not have to be a paragon of chastity to prove she has been raped; that her sexual history should not be put on trial; that even if she has been having drinks with a man or invited him in, he has no right to force sex on her. These advances, however, may be undermined by the efforts of some feminists to so enlarge the concept of rape as to demonize men, patronize women and offend the common sense of the majority of both sexes.

A recent example of this extremism was provided by the panel discussion on an ABC News special, "Men, Sex and Rape." Men and women in the audience as well as the panel were seated separately, implicitly reinforcing the message that *every man is a potential rapist.*

Five of the six women panelists, among them legal scholar Catherine MacKinnon and *Backlash* author Susan Faludi, backed the view that rape, far from being a pathology, reflects the norm in male-female relations in our society. As proof, MacKinnon asserted that 47 percent of all American women have been sexually assaulted and 25 percent raped. When a male panelist questioned these numbers, she retorted, "That means you don't believe women. It's not cooked, it's interviews with women by people who believed them when they said it."

But not all researchers on the topic do believe their female respondents. University of Arizona psychologist Mary Koss, whose studies in the field are among the most frequently cited, herself wrote in a 1988 article that of those women whom the researchers classified as victims of rape by nonromantic acquaintances, only 27 percent considered themselves rape victims. In situations involving dating partners, only 18 percent of the researcher-classified victims thought they had been raped. (In surveys that directly ask women about forced intercourse, fewer than 10 percent report such experiences.)

Do these feminists believe women, or do they believe that women   5
need expert guidance to know when they've been raped?

The reason for this startling "credibility gap" becomes clear when one looks at how the concept of rape has been broadened by the radical feminists. In their redefinition, physical force or threat of injury are no longer required.

In a recent volume of the *Journal of Social Issues,* for example, University of Kansas Professor Charlene Muehlenhard and three coauthors cite the finding that "the most common method men used to have sexual intercourse with unwilling women was ignoring their refusals *without using physical force* [emphasis mine]. . . . The prevalence of rape found in these studies would have been much lower if the definition had required physical force."

A couple is necking, and at some point she says, "Please don't," and perhaps pulls back a little; he keeps trying and she eventually goes along rather than push him away or repeat her refusal more forcefully. Is this rape? Yes, say the hardliners: She does not resist because of fear. Even if the man does not threaten her, his size and muscle implicitly do.

But many people, myself included, will find it hard to believe that most women are afraid their dates will beat them up if they resist. Indeed, many who are attacked by strangers and have far stronger reasons to fear injury still fight back or scream.

Women have sex after initial reluctance for a number of reasons,   10
and fear of being beaten up by their dates is rarely reported as one of them. Some may be ambivalent or confused; they may believe that they shouldn't want sex, and feel less guilty if they are "overpowered." Sometimes both the man and the woman are drunk, which adds to the confusion and miscommunication. Some women may change their mind, perhaps because they get sexually excited by the man's attentions. Others

may be genuinely unwilling but concerned about displeasing the man or hurting his feelings. As one student, prodded by a campus presentation on date rape to conclude that she was a victim, explained to a journalist, "I thought, 'Well, he's my friend . . . whatever happens, it's not going to be that bad' . . . no big deal."

Is it unfortunate that many women are brought up to be so anxious not to offend, to be liked? Yes. But the answer should be to encourage assertiveness, not make excuses for doormat behavior.

The redefinition of rape also includes "psychological coercion" such as "continual arguments." Muehlenhard and her coauthors suggest that if lack of resistance cannot be regarded as consent when a woman is threatened with being shot, it might be no different if she is threatened with being dumped. The old "If you loved me, you'd do it" line becomes a felony.

To the cutting-edge anti-date-rape activists, even a "no" is no longer necessary for a finding of coercion; the absence of an explicit "yes" will suffice. In the January/February issue of Ms., a scene of clearly consensual (but wordless) rough sex from "Basic Instinct" is described as one in which "a woman experiences date rape and then kisses the perp."

All these definitional shenanigans might be funny if they didn't have serious practical consequences. Young men on college campuses are now being told in rape prevention workshops (mandatory for male freshmen at some schools) that they may have raped some of their seemingly willing sexual partners; and young women are being encouraged to abdicate responsibility for their sexual behavior by labeling unsatisfactory experiences as coercive. Harvard's Date Rape Task Force recently issued a report recommending that university policy define rape as "any act of sexual intercourse that occurs without the expressed consent of the person," as well as sex with someone impaired by "intake of alcohol or drugs."

Of course, in the enterprise of redefining rape, there is no reason to stop at requiring verbal agreement. If a woman's failure to object to unwanted sex can be attributed to intimidation, so can explicit consent. Inevitably, on the outer limits, this patronizing line of thinking reaches the conclusion that in our oppressive society, *there can be no consensual sex.* Even if a woman thinks she wants it, that's only because her desire has been "constructed" by the patriarchy.

People have a right to the wackiest of ideas, but it is disturbing that some proponents of this theory are being treated as mainstream feminists. MacKinnon, who has emerged as a leading spokeswoman on sexual harassment and rape, has written such things as: "The similarity between the patterns, rhythms, roles and emotions, not to mention acts, which make up rape on one hand and intercourse on the other . . . makes

15

it difficult to sustain the customary distinctions between violence and sex. . . . The issue is less whether there was force and more whether consent is a meaningful concept." When she appears on television or is quoted in the press, this (one would think) very relevant aspect of her beliefs is tactfully omitted.

So anxious are they to extend the concept of rape, these crusaders become almost annoyed when discussions focus too much on violent attacks by strangers or near-strangers. They want to hammer in the point that the greatest danger to women comes from male friends, lovers, husbands. (University of Washington professor Marilyn Friedman has compared Rhett Butler sweeping up Scarlett O'Hara and carrying her upstairs to mass murderer Richard Speck.) They insist that rape at knifepoint in a parking lot is not different from an ambiguous encounter in which a woman is pushed further sexually than she wanted to go, and further, that women have no responsibility whatsoever to avert situations of the latter sort.

On the ABC panel, Naomi Wolf (author of *The Beauty Myth*) complained that "in this culture we tend to trivialize the harm that rape does to women." But if anything, much of the effort to broaden the definition of rape trivializes the horror of real sexual violence (by strangers or acquaintances).

The same program included footage of a treatment program for jailed sexual offenders, who were made to listen to a recording of a woman calling 911 just as a rapist breaks into her house. The terrified woman gasps, "He's here! He's here!" before her voice dissolves into screams and whimpers. One would have to be utterly removed from the real world to insist this is comparable to the experience of a woman who yields because she's tired of pushing away her date's roving hands.

A friend of mine, although acknowledging that some feminist rhetoric is excessive, believes that expanding the definition of rape to include noncoercive experiences is useful because it sensitizes the society to the pain that sexual pressure and manipulation often cause. But pressure and manipulation are not a one-way street; women can apply them too. Besides, the law is not there to ensure we have trauma-free relationships.

Trying to relabel insensitive behavior as illegal can only backfire: When a cad is accused of being a rapist, the unfairness of the charges may make him an object of sympathy, leading people to overlook his moral flaws.

While I, personally, do not think that "no-maybe-yes" games are the stuff of romance, or that the vanishing of feminine coyness would be a great loss, to replace those rituals with new ones based on suspiciousness, calculation and consent forms in triplicate would hardly be a gain.

ONLY HUNTING TRIMS DEER REPRODUCTION

Joseph Kuncewitch

Turns out things aren't going well for the wild deer penned up at *1* Cook College. It seems the experiments experts are conducting to find a one-shot contraceptive for New Jersey's burgeoning deer population have gone awry, and 19 of those once-wild, furry creatures dropped dead at the feet of their captors. The scientists say it was herpes. I say they died from broken hearts.

The scientists' forays into the woods of New Jersey might have been better spent if they simply handed out condoms to any unwitting deer they found. Perhaps this excursion could take place in, say, November, during which the male deer (you know, the one with the sharp sticks on his head) is most agreeable and accessible. By simply placing a few drops of doe estrus or buck urine abut the loins and buttocks of each researcher, he or she would have no problem locating these docile, nonterritorial creatures. Or a needle program in which the scientists pass out syringes to the deer and they can boot up their own contraceptives on their own time without infringing on the hooved ones' inalienable constitutional rights and all that.

I think the best one-shot contraceptive should not come from the hallowed halls of a higher learning institution, not from some high-minded laboratorians in their ivory towers concocting lotions, notions and potions. No. It must come from within. And also maybe from a PSE Thunderbolt bow with a 31-inch draw, 70 percent letoff and 65-pound peak weight hurling a three-bladed, 100 grain, well-sharpened broadhead projectile, in front of an Easton 2315 XX 75 Super Slam arrow. One shot of this and I would safely say that deer would never produce another offspring, with tremendous savings to the taxpayers, who probably are funding this and other state university programs.

IS FERTILITY TECHNOLOGY GOOD OR BAD?

Mona Charen

The first thing that must be said about the birth of the Mc- *1* Caughey septuplets is that it is a miracle. The human female is not de-signed to carry multiple fetuses, which is why any pregnancy involving more than one child is considered high risk. That Bobbie McCaughey was able to reach 31 weeks with seven is amazing. Any woman who has carried one baby to term must stand in awe of her physical fortitude.

The human uterus is about the size and shape of a small pear. Yet, during pregnancy, it stretches to the size of a beach ball. The expansion of the uterus is wondrous, but it is not unlimited, which is why multiple pregnancies almost always result in premature delivery—if not miscarriage. Twins are usually born four weeks premature. Triplets are usually seven weeks premature. A triplet is 12 times more likely to die within the first year of life than a singleton, and the risks increase with each added fetus. Among the common perils for very premature infants are blindness, cerebral hemorrhage, bowel infarctions, lung disease and cerebral palsy.

There are some Luddites (Jeremy Rifkin comes to mind) who see episodes like this, or the far more common instances of multiple pregnancies yielding severely impaired babies, and denounce the technology that made it possible.

There are also people in the prolife movement who decry the use of fertility treatments because so many clinics treat embryos as mere products.

Most Americans have only a fuzzy idea about how fertility treatments work and perhaps imagine that freakish pregnancies like McCaughey's are unavoidable when fertility drugs are used. That is not true.

Patients on Metrodin, the drug McCaughey took, are nearly always carefully monitored on a daily basis. Blood tests and ultrasound imaging give doctors a pretty good idea of how many follicles are forming on the surface of a woman's ovaries. Monitoring is both medically and ethically necessary. It is medically necessary because hyperstimulation of the ovaries can threaten a woman's life. It is ethically required precisely because of situations like the McCaugheys'.

If a woman's ovaries have produced so many eggs in one cycle as to risk a multiple-birth pregnancy above twins, the fertility doctors are under an obligation to advise the patient of this. At a well-equipped clinic, the cycle will not go to waste (the drugs alone cost thousands of dollars each month) because the eggs can be harvested, fertilized and frozen for implantation at a later date. But if the clinic is not equipped to perform in-vitro fertilization, the only prudent course when a woman has responded with too many eggs is to cancel the cycle and try again the following month with a reduced dosage.

Again, the McCaughey case is unique. In almost every other pregnancy featuring five or more fetuses, severe complications and death are almost certain.

The foregoing assumes that ethical people will not engage in the vile practice of "pregnancy reduction." Pregnancy reduction is the euphemism for selectively aborting some fetuses in a multiple pregnancy.

On Nov. 21, the *Wall Street Journal* ran a particularly graphic description of one such abortion. A woman carrying triplets lay watching the ultrasound screen as her doctor inserted a syringe filled with potassium chloride into the chest of one of her babies. The baby flailed its arms and legs and then lay motionless. The mother fled to the ladies' room and returned, much later, tearful and unable to speak.

In Britain, the law forbids putting more than three embryos into the womb at a time.   *10*

Fertility treatments have been a true godsend to millions of people. But the technology must be handled like the precious gift it is. Each new embryo, whether created the old-fashioned way or in a petri dish, is a new person and should be treated with the reverence and care a person deserves. Couples should be sure that however many embryos they create, they will implant. If that sometimes results in a larger family than they planned, that is the price for the joy of being able to have children at all. And once a pregnancy has begun, its result should be in the hands only of God.

CORPORATIONS ARE LOOTING INTELLECTUAL PROPERTY

Shira Feldman

Two pending bills concerning intellectual property may veer in   *1* opposite directions, but both move toward the same disturbing destination: the decline of American entrepreneurship. One bill would make patents less powerful, the other make copyrights stronger. Yet, paradoxically, both laws would achieve the same effect. By allowing corporations to commandeer individual energy and ingenuity, the laws would curb the profit that, according to distinguished American tradition, *should* arise from independent thinking.

S. 507, Senator Orrin Hatch's "Omnibus Patent" bill, proposes that all the details of every invention be made public 18 months after the invention is filed—even if a patent has not yet been issued. This bill, as Phyllis Schlafly has argued, would represent an outrageous violation of inventors' constitutional rights. The Constitution promises inventors "the exclusive right to their . . . discoveries," but a system undermining the secrecy of patent applications would render this injunction toothless. A product publicized before it's patented is a commodity begging to be stolen. S. 507, in fact, floodlights its corporate sponsors in all their voracious glory: once inventors' new ideas are abandoned, orphanlike, to the market, big industry will employ its bountiful resources to control all such innovations.

Another piece of legislation similarly violates the rightful intent behind intellectual property law. Picture this: a withered arm emerges from a lonely grave, stretches out far enough to collect piles and piles of money from the general public, and then, with a cold jangle of coins, rakes it all back underground. You have just envisioned H.R. 2589, a bill which attempts to strong-arm intellectual property—except that under this legislation, the proceeds would go to Disney, not the dead guy. Presently, copyrights last for the life of the author or artist plus an additional 50 years, and 75 years for a corporation. H.R. 2589 would extend them for 20 years beyond this already excessive term. Deceased authors, it seems clear enough, need royalties like the royalty needs frozen dinners. But powerful special interests, which want to collect on individuals' brainchildren, insist that authors' and artists' intellectual property remain *their* property. Such a policy would curb the natural dissemination of ideas, and lay a chokehold on public enjoyment of creative works. Moreover, it would illegitimately impress individual labor into the service of greedy corporations, transforming the authors name itself into an industry.

Like S. 507, which displaces intellectual property away from its originators and rechannels it into corporate pockets, H.R. 2589 undermines independent effort in favor of powerful interests. And independent initiative—the inspiration and perseverance of the little guy—is our country's glory, the star-spangled steam engine powering the national character. It is Congress's task to promote, not to discourage, personal brilliance.

Individual thinkers, who should be applauded by the American   5
public, are instead receiving an undeserved kick in the cerebrum. In the intersecting projectiles of these two antipodal initiatives lies an eloquent testament to corporate greed. Instead of serving individual effort up to entrenched interests, garnished with a cherry on top, Congress ought to leave intellectual property where it belongs—that is, in the author's intellect.

SERVING TIME THE OLD-FASHIONED WAY

Dick Boland

When it comes to correcting some of the ills that have plagued   1
our nation for years, we should once again look to California for guid-

ance. Gov. Pete Wilson is moving to eliminate many of the privileges inmates enjoy in California prisons.

He wants to remove weight-training equipment and enforce personal hygiene. These changes will not be popular with those who feel punishment should be confined to raising self-esteem. If you are laying out any of your hard-earned cash to go down to the health spa and lift weights, you will probably side with the governor.

He also wants to remove the law books from the prison library. Inmates use law books to challenge the courts that put them there. We have a system that is turning out musclebound paralegals. The prisoners complain that their rights are being violated. These are the people who killed and raped and committed all kinds of heinous crimes and now demand to be treated with dignity.

Prison officials are enforcing new grooming standards that require men's hair to be closely cropped. As a result, 100 inmates at Folsom Prison staged a hunger strike. This is good news for taxpayers, who have to feed these morons. Let's hope hunger strikes catch on. Prisoners will also be undergoing random drug tests and packages being sent directly to inmates will be examined. It appears that we are going to start treating inmates like they can't be trusted. Let's hope they can stand up under the pressure.

Of course, we have prisoners' rights advocates who claim these *5* measures are punitive. Imagine, punishing convicts. Everyone knows how well rehabilitation works. How do you rehabilitate a murderer? Would you care to have a rehabilitated murderer working for you or living next door? Only in the United States can a murderer be put to death on the one hand or spend his life lifting weights and watching TV on the other. I would say it is time for some prison reform.

Prison guards also object to any reduction in privileges in our overcrowded prisons, and you have to sympathize with them. The answer is to build more prisons or hire more guards. Surely if we can support thousands of prisoners for a good part of their lives, we can come up with the bucks to have an adequate guard force to do the job. Perhaps we should have a prisoner-exchange program with a country like Turkey, or even Mexico. Returning prisoners can explain how fortunate they are to have committed a crime in the United States.

The correctional system we have now does not hinder crime, nor will it ever until such time as being imprisoned becomes so unpleasant that one will think twice before taking a chance on going there. Prisoners should have minimal rights. Weight-lifting, television, telephone, free mail and law libraries should be removed from our penitentiaries.

If not, we should start calling prisons rest homes. How come I have to pay for all of the things the convict gets for nothing?

GOVERNMENT IS THE PROBLEM

Walter E. Williams

Which is more important, eyeglasses, books or schools? It's hard to tell. If you need eyeglasses, and don't have them, what good are books and schools? Eyeglasses and books are important for education, and we're doing well without much government control, doing so well that it never crossed your mind. Schools are completely controlled by government, and we have all sorts of customer dissatisfaction. Could there be a relationship between the level of government involvement and customer satisfaction?

Which is more important—marriage or work? Did you say marriage? If that's so, how come we have anti-discriminatory and equal-opportunity laws when it comes to work but not when it comes to marriage. Take me. Thirty-two years ago, when interviewing prospective spouses, I engaged in open discrimination. No interviews were offered to Oriental, Hispanic or white women, and men of any race. Moreover, there was no consideration of women given to intemperate drinking habits, foul language and criminal behavior. I'm sure my interview procedure violated all Equal Employment Opportunity Commission (EEOC) regulations for negotiating contracts, not to mention the Americans with Disabilities Act. Probably most men and women engage in similar grossly discriminatory behavior. But no sweat. Anybody who wants to be married tends to get married, even those that many consider undesirable. How is this happy outcome possible without government regulation?

How about language? Language is mankind's most important tool. Who discovered language? Who governs its use, deciding which words become part of the language and which get discarded from ordinary use? Nobody. Our language just evolved over time, adjusting itself to human uses, conditions and tastes; there were no government rules and dictates. Unlike the arrogant French, we anglicize anybody's word and make it a part of our vocabulary. That's one of the reasons why English is the world's most efficient language (efficiency measured as the number of bits of information conveyed per character).

All of these are examples of Williams' law: On balance, the less government is involved in something, the fewer the problems, the greater the level of satisfaction and the cheaper the cost.

Imagine that the decision of what kind of eyeglasses and books were to be produced, and delivered to whom at what time, was determined by Congress or state legislators. The resultant cruelty is unthinkable. Those who wanted paperback books would be in political conflict with those who wanted hardback. Similarly, those who wanted plastic lenses would be fighting those who wanted glass. It would resemble the fights between those who want prayers, the teaching of creationism and no sex education in school, and those who take the opposite view. Government allocation of resources always enhances the potential for human conflict.

Government control, such as the attempt to establish an official language, frequently leads to conflict, including wars and civil unrest, as we've seen in Quebec, Belgium, South Africa, Nigeria and other places. As our government creates bilingual legislation, we are seeing language become a focal point for conflict such as the ugly, racist-tainted "English Only" political campaigns in several states. The best state of affairs is to have no language laws at all.

Finally, there's the animal rights people. I'm wondering how they got the right to speak for animals and protect them from cruelty: Did the animals vote them in? Who's to say that animals don't like cruelty anyway? After all, cruelty seems to be a way of life among animals. When's the last time you saw cats and rats, lions and zebras, or birds and worms respect each other's rights? Only humans don't treat animals like animals.

III   *Moving to Longer Arguments*

Jonathan Swift, "A Modest Proposal"
M. F. K. Fisher, "The Indigestible"
Martin Luther King, Jr., "Letter from Birmingham Jail"

INTRODUCTION

Because many introductory writing courses and almost all students eventually move on to the consideration of longer arguments, this section provides material for that transition. It includes three classic essays by Jonathan Swift, M. F. K. Fisher, and Martin Luther King, Jr., for your enjoyment and analysis. You should be prepared by now to analyze these longer works, because all big arguments are made up of smaller ones. Don't forget to consider all sides of the rhetorical triangle—that is, to take into account not only the reasoning involved, but also the appeals to character and emotion.

A MODEST PROPOSAL

Jonathan Swift

It is a melancholy object to those who walk through this great   1
town or travel in the country, when they see the streets, the roads, and

cabin doors, crowded with beggars of the female sex, followed by three, four, or six children, all in rags and importuning every passenger for an alms. These mothers, instead of being able to work for their honest livelihood, are forced to employ all their time in strolling to beg sustenance for their helpless infants, who, as they grow up, either turn thieves for want of work, or leave their dear native country to fight for the Pretender in Spain, or sell themselves to the Barbados.

I think it is agreed by all parties that this prodigious number of children in the arms, or on the backs, or at the heels of their mothers, and frequently of their fathers, is in the present deplorable state of the kingdom a very great additional grievance; and therefore whoever could find out a fair, cheap, and easy method of making these children sound, useful members of the commonwealth would deserve so well of the public as to have his statue set up for a preserver of the nation.

But my intention is very far from being confined to provide only for the children of professed beggars; it is of a much greater extent, and shall take in the whole number of infants at a certain age who are born of parents in effect as little able to support them as those who demand our charity in the streets.

As to my own part, having turned my thoughts for many years upon this important subject, and maturely weighed the several schemes of other projectors, I have always found them grossly mistaken in their computation. It is true, a child just dropped from its dam may be supported by her milk for a solar year, with little other nourishment; at most not above the value of two shillings, which the mother may certainly get, or the value in scraps, by her lawful occupation of begging; and it is exactly at one year old that I propose to provide for them in such a manner as instead of being a charge upon their parents or the parish, or wanting food and raiment for the rest of their lives, they shall on the contrary contribute to the feeding, and partly to the clothing, of many thousands.

There is likewise another great advantage in my scheme, that it will prevent those voluntary abortions, and that horrid practice of women murdering their bastard children, alas, too frequent among us, sacrificing the poor innocent babes, I doubt, more to avoid the expense than the shame, which would move tears and pity in the most savage and inhuman breast.

The number of souls in this kingdom being usually reckoned one million and a half, of these I calculate there may be about two hundred thousand couples whose wives are breeders; from which number I subtract thirty thousand couples who are able to maintain their own children, although I apprehend there cannot be so many under the present distress of the kingdom; but this being granted, there will remain an hundred and seventy thousand breeders. I again subtract fifty thousand for those women who miscarry, or whose children die by accident or disease within the year. There only remain an hundred and twenty thousand children of poor parents annually born. The question therefore is, how this number shall be reared and provided for, which, as I have already said, under the present situation of affairs, is utterly impossible by all the methods hitherto proposed. For we can neither employ them in handicraft nor agriculture; we neither build houses (I mean in the country) nor cultivate land. They can very seldom pick up a livelihood by stealing till they arrive at six years old, except where they are of towardly parts; although I confess they learn the rudiments much earlier, during which time they can however be looked upon only as probationers, as I have been informed by a principal gentleman in the county of Cavan, who protested to me that he never knew above one or two instances under the age of six, even in a part of the kingdom so renowned for the quickest proficiency in that art.

I am assured by our merchants that a boy or a girl before twelve years old is no salable commodity; and even when they come to this age, they will not yield above three pounds, or three pounds and half a crown at most on the Exchange; which cannot turn to account either to the parents or the kingdom, the charge of nutriment and rags having been at least four times that value.

I shall now therefore humbly propose my own thoughts, which I hope will not be liable to the least objection.

I have been assured by a very knowing American of my acquaintance in London, that a young healthy child well nursed is at a year old a most delicious, nourishing, and wholesome food, whether stewed, roasted, baked, or boiled; and I make no doubt that it will equally serve in a fricassee or a ragout.

I do therefore humbly offer it to public consideration that of the *10*
hundred and twenty thousand children, already computed, twenty thousand may be reserved for breed, whereof only one fourth part to be males, which is more than we allow to sheep, black cattle, or swine; and my reason is that these children are seldom the fruits of marriage, a circumstance not much regarded by our savages, therefore one male will be sufficient to serve four females. That the remaining hundred thousand may at a year old be offered in sale to the persons of quality and fortune through the kingdom, always advising the mother to let them suck plentifully in the last month, so as to render them plump and fat for a good table. A child will make two dishes at an entertainment for friends; and when the family dines alone, the fore or hind quarter will make a reasonable dish, and seasoned with a little pepper or salt will be very good boiled on the fourth day, especially in winter.

I have reckoned upon a medium that a child just born will weigh twelve pounds, and in a solar year if tolerably nursed increaseth to twenty-eight pounds.

I grant this food will be somewhat dear, and therefore very proper for landlords, who, as they have already devoured most of the parents, seem to have the best title to the children.

Infant's flesh will be in season throughout the year, but more plentiful in March, and a little before and after. For we are told by a grave author, an eminent French physician, that fish being a prolific diet, there are more children born in Roman Catholic countries about nine months after Lent, than at any other season; therefore, reckoning a year after Lent, the markets will be more glutted than usual, because the number of popish infants is at least three to one in this kingdom; and therefore it will have one other collateral advantage, by lessening the number of Papists among us.

I have already computed the charge of nursing a beggar's child (in which list I reckon all cottagers, laborers, and four fifths of the farmers) to be about two shillings per annum, rags included; and I believe no gentleman would repine to give ten shillings for the carcass of a good fat child, which, as I have said, will make four dishes of excellent nutritive meat, when he hath only some particular friend or his own family to dine with him. Thus the squire will learn to be a good landlord, and grow popular among the tenants; the mother will have eight shillings net profit, and be fit for work till she produces another child.

Those who are more thrifty (as I must confess the times require) may flay the carcass; the skin of which artificially dressed will make admirable gloves for ladies, and summer boots for fine gentlemen.   *15*

As to our city of Dublin, shambles may be appointed for this purpose in the most convenient parts of it, and butchers we may be assured will not be wanting; although I rather recommend buying the children alive, and dressing them hot from the knife as we do roasting pigs.

A very worthy person, a true lover of his country, and whose virtues I highly esteem, was lately pleased in discoursing on this matter to offer a refinement upon my scheme. He said that many gentlemen of his kingdom, having of late destroyed their deer, he conceived that the want of venison might be well supplied by the bodies of young lads and maidens, not exceeding fourteen years of age nor under twelve, so great a number of both sexes in every country being now ready to starve for want of work and service; and these to be disposed of by their parents, if alive, or otherwise by their nearest relations. But with due deference to so excellent a friend and so deserving a patriot, I cannot be altogether in his sentiments; for as to the males, my American acquaintance assured me from frequent experience that their flesh was generally tough and lean, like that of our schoolboys, by continual exercise, and their taste disagreeable; and to fatten them would not answer the charge. Then as to the females, it would, I think with humble submission, be a loss to the public, because they soon would become breeders themselves; and besides, it is not improbable that some scrupulous people might be apt to censure such a practice (although indeed very unjustly) as a little bordering upon cruelty; which, I confess, hath always been with me the strongest objection against any project, how well soever intended.

But in order to justify my friend, he confessed that this expedient was put into his head by the famous Psalmanazar, a native of the island Formosa, who came from thence to London above twenty years ago, and in conversation told my friend that in his country when any young person happened to be put to death, the executioner sold the carcass to the persons of quality as a prime dainty; and that in his time the body of a plump girl of fifteen, who was crucified for an attempt to poison the emperor, was sold to his Imperial Majesty's prime minister of state, and other great mandarins of the court, in joints from the gibbet, at four hundred crowns. Neither indeed can I deny that if the same use were made of several plump young girls in this town, who without one single groat to their fortunes cannot stir abroad without a chair, and appear at the playhouse and assemblies in foreign fineries which they never will play for, the kingdom would not be the worse.

Some persons of a desponding spirit are in great concern about that vast number of poor people who are aged, diseased, or maimed, and I have been desired to employ my thoughts what course may be taken to ease the nation of so grievous an encumbrance. But I am not in the least pain upon that matter, because it is very well known that they are every day dying and rotting by cold and famine, and filth and vermin, as fast as can be reasonably expected. And as to the younger laborers, they are now in almost as hopeful a condition. They cannot get work, and consequently pine away for want of nourishment to a degree that if any time they are accidentally hired to common labor, they have not strength to perform it; and thus the country and themselves are happily delivered from the evils to come.

I have too long digressed, and therefore shall return to my subject. *20* I think the advantages by the proposal which I have made are obvious and many, as well as of the highest importance.

For first, as I have already observed, it would greatly lessen the number of Papists, with whom we are yearly overrun, being the principal breeders of the nation as well as our most dangerous enemies; and who stay at home on purpose to deliver the kingdom to the Pretender, hoping to take their advantage by the absence of so many good Protestants, who have chosen rather to leave their country than to stay at home and pay tithes against their conscience to an Episcopal curate.

Secondly, the poorer tenants will have something valuable of their own, which by law may be made liable to distress, and help to pay their landlord's rent, their corn and cattle being already seized and money a thing unknown.

Thirdly, whereas the maintenance of an hundred thousand children, from two years old and upwards, cannot be computed at less than ten shillings a piece per annum, the nation's stock will be thereby increased fifty thousand pounds per annum, besides the profit of a new dish introduced to the tables of all gentlemen of fortune in the kingdom who have any refinement in taste. And the money will circulate among ourselves, the goods being entirely of our own growth and manufacture.

Fourthly, the constant breeders, besides the gain of eight shillings sterling per annum by the sale of their children, will be rid of the charge for maintaining them after the first year.

Fifthly, this food would likewise bring great custom to taverns, where the vintners will certainly be so prudent as to procure the best receipts for dressing it to perfection, and consequently have their houses frequented by all the fine gentlemen, who justly value themselves upon their knowledge in good eating; and a skillful cook, who understands how to oblige his guests, will contrive to make it as expensive as they please.

Sixthly, this would be a great inducement to marriage, which all wise nations have either encouraged by rewards or enforced by laws and penalties. It would increase the care and tenderness of mothers toward their children, when they were sure of a settlement for life to the poor babes, provided in some sort by the public, to their annual profit instead of expense. We should see an honest emulation among the married women, which of them could bring the fattest child to the market. Men would become as fond of their wives during the time of their pregnancy as they are now of their mares in foal, their cows in calf, or sows when they are ready to farrow; nor offer to beat or kick them (as is too frequent a practice) for fear of a miscarriage.

Many other advantages might be enumerated. For instance, the addition of some thousand carcasses in our exportation of barreled beef, the propagation of swine's flesh, and improvements in the art of making good bacon, so much wanted among us by the great destruction of pigs, too frequent at our tables, which are no way comparable in taste or magnificence to a well-grown, fat, yearling child, which roasted whole will make a considerable figure at a lord mayor's feast or any other public entertainment. But this and many others I omit, being studious of brevity.

Supposing that one thousand families in this city would be constant customers for infants' flesh, besides others who might have it at merry meetings, particularly weddings and christenings, I compute that Dublin would take off annually about twenty thousand carcasses, and the rest of the kingdom (where probably they will be sold somewhat cheaper) the remaining eighty thousand.

I can think of no one objection that will possibly be raised against this proposal, unless it should be urged that the number of people will be thereby much lessened in the kingdom. This I freely own, and it was

25

indeed one principal design in offering it to the world. I desire the reader will observe, that I calculate my remedy for this one individual kingdom of Ireland and for no other that ever was, is, or I think ever can be upon earth. Therefore, let no man talk to me of other expedients: of taxing our absentees at five shillings a pound: of using neither clothes nor household furniture except what is of our own growth and manufacture: of utterly rejecting the materials and instruments that promote foreign luxury: of curing the expensiveness of pride, vanity, idleness, and gaming in our women: of introducing a vein of parsimony, prudence, and temperance: of learning to love our country, in the want of which we differ even from Laplanders and the inhabitants of Topinamboo: of quitting our animosities and factions, nor acting any longer like the Jews, who were murdering one another at the very moment their city was taken: of being a little cautious not to sell our country and conscience for nothing: of teaching landlords to have at least one degree of mercy toward their tenants: lastly, of putting a spirit of honesty, industry, and skill into our shopkeepers; who, if a resolution could now be taken to buy only our native goods, would immediately unite to cheat and exact upon us in the price, the measure, and the goodness, nor could ever yet be brought to make one fair proposal of just dealing, though often and earnestly invited to it.

Therefore, I repeat, let no man talk to me of these and the like   *30* expedients, till he hath at least some glimpse of hope that there will ever be some hearty and sincere attempt to put them in practice.

But as to myself, having been wearied out for many years with offering vain, idle, visionary thoughts, and at length utterly despairing of success, I fortunately fell upon this proposal, which, as it is wholly new, so it hath something solid and real, of no expense and little trouble, full in our own power, and whereby we can incur no danger in disobliging England. For this kind of commodity will not bear exportation, the flesh being of too tender a consistence to admit a long continuance in salt, although perhaps I could name a country which would be glad to eat up our whole nation without it.

After all, I am no so violently bent upon my own opinion as to reject any offer proposed by wise men, which shall be found equally innocent, cheap, easy, and effectual. But before something of that kind shall be advanced in contradiction to my scheme, and offering a better, I desire the author or authors will be pleased maturely to consider two points. First, as things now stand, how they will be able to find food and raiment for an hundred thousand useless mouths and backs. And secondly, there being a round million of creatures in human figure throughout this kingdom, whose sole subsistence put into a common stock would leave them in debt two millions of pounds sterling, adding those who are beggars by profession to the bulk of farmers, cottagers, and laborers, with their wives and children who are beggars in effect; I desire those politicians who dislike my overture, and may perhaps be so bold to attempt an answer, that they will first ask the parents of these mortals whether they would not at this day think it a great happiness to have been sold for food at a year old in this manner I prescribe, and thereby have avoided such a perpetual scene of misfortunes as they have since gone through by the oppression of landlords, the impossibility of paying rent without money or trade, the want of common sustenance, with neither house nor clothes to cover them from the inclemencies of the weather, and the most inevitable prospect of entailing the like or greater miseries upon their breed forever.

I profess, in the sincerity of my heart, that I have not the least personal interest in endeavoring to promote this necessary work, having no other motive than the public good of my country, by advancing our trade, providing for infants, relieving the poor, and giving some pleasure to the rich. I have no children by which I can propose to get a single penny; the youngest being nine years old, and my wife past childbearing.

THE INDIGESTIBLE
The Language of Food

M. F. K. Fisher

Hunger is, to describe it most simply, an urgent need for food. It *1* is a craving, a desire. It is, I would guess, much older than man as we now think of him, and probably synonymous with the beginning of sex. It is strange that we feel that anything as intrinsic as this must continually be wooed and excited, as if it were an unwilling and capricious part of us. If someone is not hungry, it indicates that his body does not, for a time and a reason, want to be fed. The logical thing, then, is to let him rest. He will either die, which he may have been meant to do, or he will once more feel the craving, the desire, the urgency to *eat*. He will have to do that before he can satisfy most of his other needs. Then he will revive again, which apparently he was meant to do.

It is hard to understand why this instinct to eat must be importuned, since it is so strong in all relatively healthy bodies. But in our present Western world, we face a literal bombardment of cajolery from all the media to eat this or that. It is as if we had been born without appetite, and must be led gently into an introduction to oral satisfaction and its increasingly dubious results, the way nubile maidens in past centuries were prepared for marriage proposals and then their legitimate defloration.

The language that is developing, in this game of making us *want* to eat, is far from subtle. To begin with, we must be made to feel that we really find the whole atavistic process difficult, or embarrassing or boring. We must be coaxed and cajoled to crave one advertised product rather than another, one taste, on presentation of something that we might have chosen anyway if let alone.

The truth is that we are born hungry and in our own ways will die so. But modern food advertising assumes that we are by nature bewildered and listless. As a matter of fact, we come into the world howling for Mother's Milk. We leave it, given a reasonable length of time, satisfied with much the same bland if lusty precursor of "pap and pabulum," tempered perhaps with a brush of wine on our lips to ease the parting of body and spirit. And in between, today, now, we are assaulted with the most insulting distortion of our sensory linguistics that I can imagine. We are treated like innocents and idiots by the advertisers, here in America and in Western Europe. (These are the only two regions I know, even slightly, but I feel sure that this same attack on our innate common sense is going on in the Orient, in India, in Brazil. . . .)

We are told, on radio and television and in widely distributed publications, not only how but what to eat, and when, and where. The pictures are colorful. The prose, often written by famous people, is deliberately persuasive, if often supercilious in a way that makes us out as clumsy louts, gastronomical oafs badly in need of guidance toward the satisfaction of appetites we are unaware of. And by now, with this constant attack on innate desires, an attack that can be either overt or subliminal, we apparently feel fogged-out, bombed, bewildered about whether we really crave some peanut butter on crackers as a post-amour snack, or want to sleep forever. And first, before varied forms of physical dalliance, should we share with our partner a French aperitif that keeps telling us to, or should we lead up to our accomplishments by sipping a tiny glass of Sicilian love potion?

The language for this liquid aphro-cut is familiar to most of us, thanks to lush ads in all the media. It becomes even stronger as we go into solid foods. Sexually the ads are aimed at two main groups—the Doers and the Dones. Either the reader/viewer/listener is out to woo a lover, or has married and acquired at least two children and needs help to keep the machismo-level high. Either way, one person is supposed to feed another so as to get the partner into bed and then, if possible, to pay domestic maintenance—that is, foot the bills.

One full-page color ad, for instance, shows six shots of repellently mingled vegetables, and claims boldly that these combinations "will do almost anything to get a husband's attentions." They will "catch his passing fancy . . . on the first vegetables he might even notice." In short, the ad goes on with skilled persuasion, "they're vegetables your husband can't ignore." This almost promises that he may not ignore the cook either, a heartening if vaguely lewd thought if the pictures in the ad are any intimation of his tastes.

It is plain that if a man must be kept satisfied at table, so must his progeny, and advertisers know how to woo mothers as well as plain sexual companions. Most of their nutritional bids imply somewhat unruly family life, that only food can ease: "No more fights over who gets what," one ad proposes, as it suggests buying not one but three different types of frozen but "crisp hot fried chicken at a price that take-out can't beat": thighs and drumsticks, breast portions and wings, all coated with the same oven-crunchy-golden skin, and fresh from freezer to stove in minutes. In the last quarter of this family ad there is a garishly bright new proposal, the "no-fire, sure-fire, barbecue-sauced" chicken. Personal experience frowns on this daring departure from the national "finger-lickin'" syndrome: with children who fight over who gets what, it would be very messy.

It is easy to continue such ever-loving family-style meals, as suggested by current advertising, all in deceptively alluring color in almost any home-oriented magazine one finds. How about enjoying a "good family western," whatever that may be, by serving a mixture of "redy-rice" and leftover chicken topped with a blenderized sauce of ripe avocado? This is called "love food from California," and it will make us "taste how the West was won." The avocado, the ad goes on, will "open new frontiers of wholesome family enjoyment." And of course the pre-spiced-already-seasoned "instant" rice, combined with cooked chicken, will look yummy packed into the hollowed fruit shells and covered with nutlike green stuff. All this will help greatly to keep the kids from hitting each other about who gets what.

The way to a man's heart is through his stomach, we have been assured for a couple of centuries, and for much longer than that good wives as well as noted courtesans have given their time and thought to keeping the male belly full (and the male liver equally if innocently enlarged). By now this precarious mixture of sex and gastronomy has come out of the pantry, so to speak, and ordinary cookbook shelves show *Cuisine d'amour* and *Venus in the Kitchen* alongside Mrs. Rombauer and Julia Child. *10*

In order to become a classic, which I consider the last two to be, any creation, from a potato soufflé to a marble bust or a skyscraper, must be honest, and that is why most cooks, as well as their methods, are never known. It is also why dishonesty in the kitchen is driving us so fast and successfully to the world of convenience foods and franchised eateries.

If we look at a few of the so-called cookbooks now providing a kind of armchair gastronomy (to read while we wait for the wife and kids to get ready to pile in the car for supper at the nearest drive-in), we understand without either amazement or active nausea some such "homemade" treat as I was brought lately by a generous neighbor. The recipe she proudly passed along to me, as if it were her great-grandmother's secret way to many a heart, was from a best-selling new cookbook, and it included a large package of sweet chocolate bits, a box of "Butter Fudge" chocolate cake mix, a package of instant vanilla pudding, and a cup of imitation mayonnaise. It was to be served with synthetic whipped cream sprayed from an aerosol can. It was called *Old-Fashion Fudge Torte.*

This distortion of values, this insidious numbing of what we once knew without question as either True or False, can be blamed, in part anyway, on the language we hear and read every day and night about the satisfying of such a basic need as hunger. Advertising, especially in magazines and books devoted to such animal satisfaction, twists us deftly into acceptance of the new lingo of gastronomical seduction.

A good example: an impossibly juicy-looking pork chop lies like a Matisse odalisque in an open microwave oven, cooked until "fall-from-the-bone-tender." This is a new word. It still says that the meat is so overcooked that it will fall off its bone (a dubious virtue!), but it is supposed to beguile the reader into thinking that he or she (1) speaks a special streamlined language, and (2) deserves to buy an oven to match, and (3) appreciates all such finer things in life. It takes *know-how,* the ad assures us subliminally, to understand all that "fall-from-the-bone-tender" really means!

This strange need to turn plain descriptive English into hyphen- 15 ated hyperbole can be found even in the best gastronomical reviews and articles as well as magazine copy. How about "fresh-from-the-oven apple cobbler," as described by one of the more reputable food writers of today? What would be wrong, especially for someone who actually knows syntax and grammar, in saying "apple cobbler, fresh from the oven"? A contemporary answer is that the multiple adjective is more . . . uh . . . contemporary. This implies that it should reach the conditioned brain cells of today's reader in a more understandable, coherent way—or does it?

The vocabulary of our kitchen comes from every part of the planet, sooner or later, because as we live, so we speak. After the Norman Conquest in 1066, England learned countless French nouns and verbs that are now part of both British and American cooking language: *appetite, dinner, salmon, sausage, lemon, fig, almond,* and so on. We all say *roast, fry, boil,* and we make *sauces* and put them in *bowls* or on *plates.* And the German kitchen, the Aztecan: they too gave us words like *cookie* and *chocolate.* We say *borscht* easily (Russian before it was Yiddish). From slave-time Africa there is the word *gumbo,* for okra, and in *benne* biscuits there is the black man's sesame. Some people say that *alcohol* came from the nonalcoholic Arabs.

But what about the new culinary language of the media, the kind we now hear and view and read? What can "freezer-fresh" mean? *Fresh* used to imply new, pure, lively. Now it means, at best, that when a food was packaged, it would qualify as ready to be eaten: "oven-fresh" cookies a year on the shelf, "farm-fresh" eggs laid last spring, "corn-on-the-cob fresh" dehydrated vegetable soup-mix. . . .

Personal feelings and opinions and prejudices (sometimes called skunners) have a lot to do with our reactions to gastronomical words, and other kinds. I know a man who finally divorced his wife because, even by indirection, he could not cure her of "calling up." She called up people, and to her it meant that she used the telephone—that is, she was not calling across a garden or over a fence, but was calling up when she could not *see* her friends. Calling and calling up are entirely different, she and a lot of interested amateur semanticists told her husband. He refused to admit this. "Why not simply *telephone* them? To telephone you don't say telephone *up*," he would say. Her phrase continued to set his inner teeth, the ones rooted directly in his spiritual law, on such an edge that he finally fled. She called up to tell me.

This domestic calamity made me aware, over many years but never with such anguish, how *up* can dangle in our language. And experience has shown me that if a word starts dangling, it is an easy mark for the careless users and the overt rapists of syntax and meaning who write copy for mass-media outlets connected, for instance, with hunger, and its current quasi-satisfactions. Sometimes the grammatical approach is fairly conventional and old-fashioned, and the *up* is tacked onto a verb in a fairly comprehensible way. "Perk up your dinner," one magazine head-line begs us, with vaguely disgusting suggestions about how to do it. "Brighten up a burger," a full-page lesson in salad-making with an instant powder tells us. (This ad sneaks in another call on home unity with its "unusually delicious . . . bright . . . tasty" offering: "Sit back and listen to the cheers," it says. "Your family will give them to this tasty-zesty easy-to-make salad!")

Of course *up* gets into the adjectives as well as the verbs: *souped up chicken* and *souped up dip* are modish in advertising for canned pudding-like concoctions that fall in their original shapes from tin to saucepan or mixing bowl, to be blended with liquids to make fairly edible "soups," or to serve in prefab sauces as handy vehicles for clams or peanuts or whatever is added to the can-shaped glob to tantalize drinkers to want one more Bloody Mary. They dip up the mixture on specially stiffened packaged "chips" made of imitation tortillas or even imitation recondi-tioned potatoes, guaranteed not to crumble, shatter, or otherwise mess up the landscape. . . .

Verbs are more fun than adjectives, in this game of upmanship. And one of the best/worst of them is creeping into our vocabularies in a thoroughly unsubtle way. It is *to gourmet up*. By now the word *gourmet* has been so distorted, and so overloaded, that to people who know its real meaning it is meaningless. They have never misused it and they refuse to now. To them a gourmet is a person, and perforce the word is a noun. Probably it turned irrevocably into an adjective with descriptive terms like *gourmet-style* and *gourmet-type*. I am not sure. But it has come to mean fancy rather than fastidious. It means expensive, or exotic, or pseudoelegant and classy and pricey. It rarely describes enjoyment. It describes a style, at best, and at worst a cheap imitation of once-stylish and always costly affectation.

There is gourmet food. There are gourmet restaurants, or gourmet-style eating places. There are packaged frozen cubes of comestibles called gourmet that cost three times as much as plain fast foods because, the cunningly succulent mouth-watering ads propose, their sauces are made by world-famous chefs, whose magical blends of spices and herbs have been touched off by a personalized fillip of rare old Madeira. In other words, at triple the price, they are worth it because they have been gourmeted up. Not long ago I heard a young woman in a supermarket say to a friend who looked almost as gaunt and harried as she, "Oh god . . . why am I here? You ask! Harry calls to say his sales manager is coming to dinner, and I've got to gourmet up the pot roast!"

I slow my trundle down the pushcart aisle.

"I could slice some olives into it, maybe? Pitted. Or maybe dump in a can of mushrooms. Sliced. It's got to be more expensive."

The friend says, "A cup of wine? Red. Or sour cream . . . a kind of Stroganoff . . . ?"

I worm my way past them, feeling vaguely worried. I long to tell them something—perhaps not to worry.

There are, of course, even more personal language shocks than the one that drove a man to leave his dear girl because she had to call people up. Each of us has his own, actively or dimly connected with hunger (which only an adamant Freudian could call his!). It becomes a real embarrassment, for example, when a friend or a responsible critic of cookbooks or restaurants uses words like *yummy*, or *scrumptious*. There is no dignity in such infantile evasions of plain words like *good*—or even *delicious* or *excellent*.

My own word aversion is longstanding, and several decades from the first time I heard it I still pull back, like the flanges of a freshly opened oyster. It is the verb *to drool*, when applied to written prose, and especially to anything I myself have written. Very nice people have told me, for a long time now, that some things they have read of mine, in books or magazines, have made them drool. I know they mean to compliment me. They are saying that my use of words makes them oversalivate, like hap-

25

less dogs waiting for a bell to say "Meat!" to them. It has made them more alive than they were, more active. They are grateful to me, perhaps, for being reminded that they are still functioning, still aware of some of their hungers.

I too should be grateful, and even humble, that I have reminded people of what fun it is, vicariously or not, to eat/live. Instead I am revolted. I see a slavering slobbering maw. It dribbles helplessly, in a Pavlovian response. It *drools*. And drooling, not over a meaty bone or a warm bowl of slops, is what some people have done over my printed words. This has long worried me. I feel grateful but repelled. They are nice people, and I like them and I like dogs, but dogs *must* drool when they are excited by the prospect of the satisfaction of alerted tastebuds, and two-legged people do not need to, and in general I know that my reaction to the fact that some people slobber like conditioned animals is a personal skunner, and that I should accept it as such instead of meeting it like a stiff-upper-lipped Anglo-Saxon (and conditioned!) nanny.

I continue, however, to be regretfully disgusted by the word *drool*   30 in connection with all writing about food, including my own. And a few fans loyal enough to resist being hurt by this statement may possibly call me up.

It is too easy to be malicious, but certainly the self-styled food experts of our current media sometimes seem overtly silly enough to be fair game. For anyone with half an ear for the English-American language we write and speak, it is almost impossible not to chuckle over the unending flow of insults to our syntax and grammar, not to mention our several levels of intelligence.

How are we supposed to react to descriptive phrases like "crisply crunchy, to snap in your mouth"? We know this was written, and for pay, by one or another of the country's best gastronomical hacks. We should not titter. He is a good fellow. Why then does he permit himself to say that some corn on the cob is so tender that "it dribbles milk down your chin"? He seems, whether or not he means well, to lose a little of the innate dignity that we want from our gourmet-judges. He is like a comedian who with one extra grimace becomes coarse instead of funny, or like an otherwise sensitive reader who says that certain writing makes him drool.

Not all our food critics, of course, are as aware of language as the well-known culinary experts who sign magazine articles and syndicated columns. And for one of them, there are a hundred struggling copywriters who care less about mouth-watering prose than about filling ad space with folksy propaganda for "kwik" puddings and suchlike. They say shamelessly, to keep their jobs, that Mom has just told them how to make instant homemade gravy taste "like I could never make before!" "*Believe* me," they beg, "those other gravies just aren't the same! This has a real homemade flavor and a rich brown color. Just add it to your pot drippings." And so on.

Often these unsung kitchen psalmists turn, with probable desperation, to puns and other word games. They write, for instance, that frozen batter-fried fish are so delicious that "one crunch and you're hooked!" Oh, hohoho ha ha. And these same miserable slaves produce millions of words, if they are fortunate enough to find and keep their jobs, about things like synthetic dough that is "pre-formed" into "old-fashioned shapes that taste cooky-fresh and crunchy" in just fifteen minutes from freezer to oven to the kiddies' eager paws and maws.

When the hacks have proved that they can sling such culinary lingo, *35* they are promoted to a special division that deals even more directly with oral satisfaction. They write full-page ads in juicy color, about cocktail nibbles with "a fried-chicken taste that's lip-lickin' good." This, not too indirectly, is aimed to appeal to hungry readers familiar with a franchised fried chicken that is of course known worldwide as finger-lickin' good, and even packaged Kitty Krums that are whisker-lickin good. (It is interesting and reassuring, although we must drop a few *g*'s to understand it, that modern gastronomy still encourages us to indulge in public tongueplay.)

Prose by the copywriters usually stays coy, but is somewhat more serious about pet foods than humanoid provender. Perhaps it is assumed that most people who buy kibbles do not bother to read the printed information on all four sides of their sacks, but simply pour the formula into bowls on the floor and hope for the best. Or perhaps animal-food companies recognize that some of their slaves are incurably dedicated to correct word usage. Often the script on a bag of dry pet food is better written than most paperback novels. Possibly some renegade English instructor has been allowed to explain "Why Your Cat Will Enjoy This." He is permitted tiny professorial jokes, now and then: "As Nutritious As It Is Delicious," one caption says, and another section is called "Some Reading on Feeding," and then the prose goes all out, almost euphorically, with "Some Raving on Saving." The lost academician does have to toss in a few words like *munchy* to keep his job, but in general there is an enjoyably relaxed air about the unread prose on pet-food packages, as opposed to the stressful cuteness of most fashionable critics of our dining habits.

Of course the important thing is to stay abreast of the lingo, it seems. Stylist restaurants go through their phases, with beef Wellington and chocolate mousse high in favor one year and strictly for Oskahoola, Tennessee, the next. We need private dining-out guides as well as smart monthly magazines to tell us what we are eating tonight, as well as what we are paying for it.

A lot of our most modish edibles are dictated by their scarcity, as always in the long history of gastronomy. In 1978, for instance, it became *de rigueur* in California to serve caviar in some guise, usually with baked or boiled potatoes, because shipments from Iran grew almost as limited as they had long been from Russia. (Chilled caviar, regal fare, was paired with the quaintly plebeian potato many years ago, in Switzerland I think, but by 1978 its extravagant whimsy had reached Hollywood and the upper West Coast by way of New York, so that desperate hostesses were buying and even trying to "homemake" caviar from the Sacramento River sturgeons. Results: usually lamentable, but well meant.)

All this shifting of gustatory snobbism should probably have more influence on our language than it does. Writers for both elegant magazines and "in" guides use much the same word-appeal as do the copywriters for popular brands of convenience foods. They may not say "lip-smackin" or "de-lish," but they manage to imply what their words will make readers do. They use their own posh patter, which like the humbler variety seldom bears any kind of scrutiny, whether for original meaning or plain syntax.

How about "unbelievably succulent luscious scallops which boast   40
a nectar-of-the-sea freshness"? Or "a *beurre blanc,* that ethereally light, grandmotherly sauce"? Or "an onion soup, baked *naturellement,* melting its knee-deep crust of cheese and croutons"? Dressings are "teasingly-tart," not teasing or tart or even teasingly tart. They have "breathtakingly visual appeal," instead of looking yummy, and some of them, perhaps fortunately, are "almost too beautiful to describe," "framed in a picture-perfect garnish of utter perfection and exquisiteness," "a pinnacle of gastronomical delight." (Any of these experiences can be found, credit card on the ready, in the bistros-of-the-moment.)

It is somewhat hard to keep one's balance, caught between the three stools of folksy lure, stylist gushing, and a dictionary of word usage. How does one *parse,* as my grandfather would say, a complete sentence like "The very pinkness it was, of mini-slices"? Or "A richly eggy and spiritous Zabaglione, edged in its serving dish with tiny dots of grenadine"? These are not sentences, at least to my grandfather and to me, and I think *spirituous* is a better word in this setting, and I wonder whether the dots of grenadine were wee drops of the sweet syrup made from pomegranates or the glowing seeds of the fruit itself, and how and why anyone would preserve them for a chic restaurant. And were those pink mini-slices from a lamb, a calf? Then there are always verbs to ponder on, in such seductive reports on what and where to dine. One soup "packs chunks" of something or other, to prove its masculine heartiness in a stylish lunchtime brasserie. "Don't forget to special-order!" Is this a verb, a split infinitive, an attempt of the reporter to sound down-to-earth?

Plainly it is as easy to carp, criticize, even dismiss such unworthy

verbiage as it is to quibble and shudder about what the other media dictate, that we may subsist. And we continue to carp, criticize, dismiss—
and to *eat,* not always as we are told to, and not always well, either! But
we were born *hungry.*

LETTER FROM BIRMINGHAM JAIL

Martin Luther King, Jr.

April 16, 1963

My Dear Fellow Clergymen:
    While confined here in the Birmingham city jail, I came across
your recent statement calling my present activities "unwise and untimely." Seldom do I pause to answer criticism of my work and ideas. If
I sought to answer all the criticisms that cross my desk, my secretaries
would have little time for anything other than such correspondence in
the course of the day, and I would have no time for constructive work.
But since I feel that you are men of genuine good will and that your
criticisms are sincerely set forth, I want to try to answer your statement
in what I hope will be patient and reasonable terms.
    I think I should indicate why I am here in Birmingham, since you
have been influenced by the view which argues against "outsiders coming in." I have the honor of serving as president of the Southern Christian Leadership Conference, an organization operating in every southern
state, with headquarters in Atlanta, Georgia. We have some eighty-five
affiliated organizations across the South, and one of them is the Alabama
Christian Movement for Human Rights. Frequently we share staff, educational and financial resources with our affiliates. Several months ago the
affiliate here in Birmingham asked us to be on call to engage in a nonviolent direct-action program if such were deemed necessary. We readily
consented, and when the hour came we lived up to our promise. So I,
along with several members of my staff, am here because I was invited
here. I am here because I have organizational ties here.
    But more basically, I am in Birmingham because injustice is here.
Just as the prophets of the eighth century B.C. left their villages and
carried their "thus saith the Lord" far beyond the boundaries of their
home towns, and just as the Apostle Paul left his village of Tarsus and
carried the gospel of Jesus Christ to the far corners of the Greco-Roman
world, so am I compelled to carry the gospel of freedom beyond my own
home town. Like Paul, I must constantly respond to the Macedonian call
for aid.
    Moreover, I am cognizant of the interrelatedness of all communities

and states. I cannot sit idly by in Atlanta and not be concerned about what happens in Birmingham. Injustice anywhere is a threat to justice everywhere. We are caught in an inescapable network of mutuality, tied in a single garment of destiny. Whatever affects one directly, affects all indirectly. Never again can we afford to live with the narrow, provincial "outside agitator" idea. Anyone who lives inside the United States can never be considered an outsider anywhere within its bounds.

You deplore the demonstrations taking place in Birmingham. But your statement, I am sorry to say, fails to express a similar concern for the conditions that brought about the demonstrations. I am sure that none of you would want to rest content with the superficial kind of social analysis that deals merely with effects and does not grapple with underlying causes. It is unfortunate that demonstrations are taking place in Birmingham, but it is even more unfortunate that the city's white power structure left the Negro community with no alternative.

In any nonviolent campaign there are four basic steps: collection of the facts to determine whether injustices exist; negotiation; self-purification; and direct action. We have gone through all these steps in Birmingham. There can be no gainsaying the fact that racial injustice engulfs this community. Birmingham is probably the most thoroughly segregated city in the United States. Its ugly record of brutality is widely known. Negroes have experienced grossly unjust treatment in the courts. There have been more unsolved bombings of Negro homes and churches in Birmingham than in any other city in the nation. These are the hard, brutal facts of the case. On the basis of these conditions, Negro leaders sought to negotiate with the city fathers. But the latter consistently refused to engage in good-faith negotiation.

Then, last September, came the opportunity to talk with leaders of Birmingham's economic community. In the course of the negotiations, certain promises were made by the merchants—for example, to remove the stores' humiliating racial signs. On the basis of these promises, the Reverend Fred Shuttlesworth and the leaders of the Alabama Christian Movement for Human Rights agreed to a moratorium on all demonstrations. As the weeks and months went by, we realized that we were the victims of a broken promise. A few signs, briefly removed, returned; the others remained.

As in so many past experiences, our hopes had been blasted, and the shadow of deep disappointment settled upon us. We had no alternative except to prepare for direct action, whereby we would present our very bodies as a means of laying our case before the conscience of the local and the national community. Mindful of the difficulties involved, we decided to undertake a process of self-purification. We began a series of workshops on nonviolence, and we repeatedly asked ourselves: "Are you able to accept blows without retaliating?" "Are you able to endure the ordeal of jail?" We decided to schedule our direct-action program for the Easter season, realizing that except for Christmas, this is the main shopping period of the year. Knowing that a strong economic-withdrawal program would be the by-product of direct action, we felt that this would be the best time to bring pressure to bear on the merchants for the needed change.

Then it occurred to us that Birmingham's mayoralty election was coming up in March, and we speedily decided to postpone action until after election day. When we discovered that the Commissioner of Public Safety, Eugene "Bull" Connor, had piled up enough votes to be in the run-off, we decided again to postpone action until the day after the run-off so that the demonstrations could not be used to cloud the issues. Like many others, we waited to see Mr. Connor defeated, and to this end we endured postponement after postponement. Having aided in this community need, we felt that our direct-action program could be delayed no longer.

You may well ask: "Why direct action? Why sit-ins, marches and   10
so forth? Isn't negotiation a better path?" You are quite right in calling for negotiation. Indeed, this is the very purpose of direct action. Nonviolent direct action seeks to create such a crisis and foster such a tension that a community which has constantly refused to negotiate is forced to confront the issue. It seeks so to dramatize the issue that it can no longer be ignored. My citing the creation of tension as part of the work of the nonviolent resister may sound rather shocking. But I must confess that I am not afraid of the word "tension." I have earnestly opposed violent tension, but there is a type of constructive, nonviolent tension which is necessary for growth. Just as Socrates felt that it was necessary to create a tension in the mind so that individuals could rise from the bondage of myths and half-truths to the unfettered realm of creative analysis and objective appraisal, so must we see the need for nonviolent gadflies to create the kind of tension in society that will help men rise from the dark depths of prejudice and racism to the majestic heights of understanding and brotherhood.

The purpose of our direct-action program is to create a situation so crisis-packed that it will inevitably open the door to negotiation. I therefore concur with you in your call for negotiation. Too long has our beloved Southland been bogged down in a tragic effort to live in monologue rather than dialogue.

One of the basic points in your statement is that the action that I and my associates have taken in Birmingham is untimely. Some have asked: "Why didn't you give the new city administration time to act?" The only answer that I can give to this query is that the new Birmingham administration must be prodded about as much as the outgoing one, before it will act. We are sadly mistaken if we feel that the election of Albert

Boutwell as mayor will bring the millennium to Birmingham. While Mr. Boutwell is a much more gentle person than Mr. Connor, they are both segregationists, dedicated to maintenance of the status quo. I have hope that Mr. Boutwell will be reasonable enough to see the futility of massive resistance to desegregation. But he will not see this without pressure from devotees of civil rights. My friends, I must say to you that we have not made a single gain in civil rights without determined legal and nonviolent pressure. Lamentably, it is an historical fact that privileged groups seldom give up their privileges voluntarily. Individuals may see the moral light and voluntarily give up their unjust posture; but, as Reinhold Niebuhr has reminded us, groups tend to be more immoral than individuals.

We know through painful experience that freedom is never voluntarily given by the oppressor; it must be demanded by the oppressed. Frankly, I have yet to engage in a direct-action campaign that was "well timed" in the view of those who have not suffered unduly from the disease of segregation. For years now I have heard the word "Wait!" It rings in the ear of every Negro with piercing familiarity. This "Wait" has almost always meant "Never." We must come to see, with one of our distinguished jurists, that "justice too long delayed is justice denied."

We have waited for more than 340 years for our constitutional and God-given rights. The nations of Asia and Africa are moving with jetlike speed toward gaining political independence, but we still creep at horse-and-buggy pace toward gaining a cup of coffee at a lunch counter. Perhaps it is easy for those who have never felt the stinging darts of segregation to say, "Wait." But when you have seen vicious mobs lynch your mothers and fathers at will and drown your sisters and brothers at whim; when you have seen hate-filled policemen curse, kick and even kill your black brothers and sisters; when you see the vast majority of your twenty million Negro brothers smothering in an airtight cage of poverty in the midst of an affluent society; when you suddenly find your tongue twisted and your speech stammering as you seek to explain to your six-year-old daughter why she can't go to the public amusement park that has just been advertised on television, and see tears welling up in her eyes when she is told that Funtown is closed to colored children, and see ominous clouds of inferiority beginning to form in her little mental sky, and see her beginning to distort her personality by developing an unconscious bitterness toward white people; when you have to concoct an answer for a five-year-old son who is asking: "Daddy, why do white people treat colored people so mean?"; when you take a cross-country drive and find it necessary to sleep night after night in the uncomfortable corners of your automobile because no motel will accept you; when you are humiliated day in and day out by nagging signs reading "white" and "colored"; when your first name becomes "nigger," your middle name becomes "boy" (however old you are) and your last name becomes "John," and your wife and mother are never given the respected title "Mrs."; when you are harried by day and haunted by night by the fact that you are a Negro, living constantly at tiptoe stance, never quite knowing what to expect next, and are plagued with inner fears and outer resentments; when you are forever fighting a degenerating sense of "nobodiness"— then you will understand why we find it difficult to wait. There comes a time when the cup of endurance runs over, and men are no longer willing to be plunged into the abyss of despair. I hope, sirs, you can understand our legitimate and unavoidable impatience.

You express a great deal of anxiety over our willingness to break 15 laws. This is certainly a legitimate concern. Since we so diligently urge people to obey the Supreme Court's decision of 1954 outlawing segregation in the public schools, at first glance it may seem rather paradoxical for us consciously to break laws. One may well ask: "How can you advocate breaking some laws and obeying others?" The answer lies in the fact that there are two types of laws: just and unjust. I would be the first to advocate obeying just laws. One has not only a legal but a moral responsibility to obey just laws. Conversely, one has a moral responsibility to disobey unjust laws. I would agree with St. Augustine that "an unjust law is no law at all."

Now, what is the difference between the two? How does one determine whether a law is just or unjust? A just law is a man-made code that squares with the moral law or the law of God. An unjust law is a code that is out of harmony with the moral law. To put it in the terms of St. Thomas Aquinas: An unjust law is a human law that is not rooted in eternal law and natural law. Any law that uplifts human personality is just. Any law that degrades human personality is unjust. All segregation statutes are unjust because segregation distorts the soul and damages the personality. It gives the segregator a false sense of superiority and the segregated a false sense of inferiority. Segregation, to use the terminology of the Jewish philosopher Martin Buber, substitutes an "I-it" relationship for an "I-thou" relationship and ends up relegating persons to the status of things. Hence segregation is not only politically, economically and sociologically unsound, it is morally wrong and sinful. Paul Tillich has said that sin is separation. Is not segregation an existential expression of man's tragic separation, his awful estrangement, his terrible sinfulness? Thus it is that I can urge men to obey the 1954 decision of the Supreme Court, for it is morally right; and I can urge them to disobey segregation ordinances, for they are morally wrong.

Let us consider a more concrete example of just and unjust laws. An unjust law is a code that a numerical or power majority group compels a minority group to obey but does not make binding on itself. This is *difference* made legal. By the same token, a just law is a code that a majority compels a minority to follow and that it is willing to follow itself. This is *sameness* made legal.

Let me give another explanation. A law is unjust if it is inflicted on a minority that, as a result of being denied the right to vote, had no part in enacting or devising the law. Who can say that the legislature of Alabama which set up that state's segregation laws was democratically elected? Throughout Alabama all sorts of devious methods are used to prevent Negroes from becoming registered voters, and there are some counties in which, even though Negroes constitute a majority of the population, not a single Negro is registered. Can any law enacted under such circumstances be considered democratically structured?

Sometimes a law is just on its face and unjust in its application. For instance, I have been arrested on a charge of parading without a permit. Now, there is nothing wrong in having an ordinance which requires a permit for a parade. But such an ordinance becomes unjust when it is used to maintain segregation and to deny citizens the First-Amendment privilege of peaceful assembly and protest.

I hope you are able to see the distinction I am trying to point out.   20
In no sense do I advocate evading or defying the law, as would the rabid segregationist. That would lead to anarchy. One who breaks an unjust law must do so openly, lovingly, and with a willingness to accept the penalty. I submit that an individual who breaks a law that conscience tells him is unjust, and who willingly accepts the penalty of imprisonment in order to arouse the conscience of the community over its injustice, is in reality expressing the highest respect for law.

Of course, there is nothing new about this kind of civil disobedience. It was evidenced sublimely in the refusal of Shadrach, Meshach and Abednego to obey the laws of Nebuchadnezzar, on the ground that a higher moral law was at stake. It was practiced superbly by the early Christians, who were willing to face hungry lions and the excruciating pain of chopping blocks rather than submit to certain unjust laws of the Roman Empire. To a degree, academic freedom is a reality today because Socrates practiced civil disobedience. In our own nation, the Boston Tea Party represented a massive act of civil disobedience.

We should never forget that everything Adolf Hitler did in Germany was "legal" and everything the Hungarian freedom fighters did in Hungary was "illegal." It was "illegal" to aid and comfort a Jew in Hitler's Germany. Even so, I am sure that, had I lived in Germany at the time, I would have aided and comforted my Jewish brothers. If today I lived in a Communist country where certain principles dear to the Christian faith are suppressed, I would openly advocate disobeying that country's anti-religious laws.

I must make two honest confessions to you, my Christian and Jewish brothers. First, I must confess that over the past few years I have been gravely disappointed with the white moderate. I have almost reached the regrettable conclusion that the Negro's great stumbling block in his stride toward freedom is not the White Citizen's Counciler or the Ku Klux Klanner, but the white moderate, who is more devoted to "order" than to justice; who prefers a negative peace which is the absence of tension to a positive peace which is the presence of justice; who constantly says: "I agree with you in the goal you seek, but I cannot agree with your methods of direct action"; who paternalistically believes he can set the timetable for another man's freedom; who lives by a mythical concept of time and who constantly advises the Negro to wait for a "more convenient season." Shallow understanding from people of good will is more frustrating than absolute misunderstanding from people of ill will. Lukewarm acceptance is much more bewildering than outright rejection.

I had hoped that the white moderate would understand that law and order exist for the purpose of establishing justice and that when they fail in this purpose they become the dangerously structured dams that block the flow of social progress. I had hoped that the white moderate would understand that the present tension in the South is a necessary phase of the transition from an obnoxious negative peace, in which the Negro passively accepted his unjust plight, to a substantive and positive peace, in which all men will respect the dignity and worth of human personality. Actually, we who engage in nonviolent direct action are not the creators of tension. We merely bring to the surface the hidden tension that is already alive. We bring it out in the open, where it can be seen and dealt with. Like a boil that can never be cured so long as it is covered up but must be opened with all its ugliness to the natural medicines of air and light, injustice must be exposed, with all the tension its exposure creates, to the light of human conscience and the air of national opinion before it can be cured.

In your statement you assert that our actions, even though peaceful, must be condemned because they precipitate violence. But is this a logical assertion? Isn't this like condemning a robbed man because his possession of money precipitated the evil act of robbery? Isn't this like condemning Socrates because his unswerving commitment to truth and his philosophical inquiries precipitated the act by the misguided populace in which they made him drink hemlock? Isn't this like condemning Jesus because his unique God-consciousness and never-ceasing devotion to God's will precipitated the evil act of crucifixion? We must come to see that, as the federal courts have consistently affirmed, it is wrong to urge an individual to cease his efforts to gain his basic constitutional rights because the quest may precipitate violence. Society must protect the robbed and punish the robber.

I had also hoped that the white moderate would reject the myth concerning time in relation to the struggle for freedom. I have just re-

25

ceived a letter from a white brother in Texas. He writes: "All Christians know that the colored people will receive equal rights eventually, but it is possible that you are in too great a religious hurry. It has taken Christianity almost two thousand years to accomplish what it has. The teachings of Christ take time to come to earth." Such an attitude stems from a tragic misconception of time, from the strangely irrational notion that there is something in the very flow of time that will inevitably cure all ills. Actually, time itself is neutral; it can be used either destructively or constructively. More and more I feel that the people of ill will have used time much more effectively than have the people of good will. We will have to repent in this generation not merely for the hateful words and actions of the bad people but for the appalling silence of the good people. Human progress never rolls in on wheels of inevitability; it comes through the tireless efforts of men willing to be coworkers with God, and without this hard work, time itself becomes an ally of the forces of social stagnation. We must use time creatively, in the knowledge that the time is always ripe to do right. Now is the time to make real the promise of democracy and transform our pending national elegy into a creative psalm of brotherhood. Now is the time to lift our national policy from the quicksand of racial injustice to the solid rock of human dignity.

You speak of our activity in Birmingham as extreme. At first I was rather disappointed that fellow clergymen would see my nonviolent efforts as those of an extremist. I began thinking about the fact that I stand in the middle of two opposing forces in the Negro community. One is a force of complacency, made up in part of Negroes who, as a result of long years of oppression, are so drained of self-respect and a sense of "somebodiness" that they have adjusted to segregation; and in part of a few middle-class Negroes who, because of a degree of academic and economic security and because in some ways they profit by segregation, have become insensitive to the problems of masses. The other force is one of bitterness and hatred, and it comes perilously close to advocating violence. It is expressed in the various black nationalist groups that are springing up across the nation, the largest and best-known being Elijah Muhammad's Muslim movement. Nourished by the Negro's frustration over the continued existence of racial discrimination, this movement is made up of people who have lost faith in America, who have absolutely repudiated Christianity, and who have concluded that the white man is an incorrigible "devil."

I have tried to stand between these two forces, saying that we need emulate neither the "do-nothingism" of the complacent nor the hatred and despair of the black nationalist. For there is the more excellent way of love and nonviolent protest. I am grateful to God that, through the influence of the Negro church, the way of nonviolence became an integral part of our struggle.

If this philosophy had not emerged, by now many streets of the South would, I am convinced, be flowing with blood. And I am further convinced that if our white brothers dismiss as "rabble-rousers" and "outside agitators" those of us who employ nonviolent direct action, and if they refuse to support our nonviolent efforts, millions of Negroes will, out of frustration and despair, seek solace and security in black-nationalist ideologies—a development that would inevitably lead to a frightening racial nightmare.

Oppressed people cannot remain oppressed forever. The yearning   *30* for freedom eventually manifests itself, and that is what has happened to the American Negro. Something within has reminded him of his birthright of freedom, and something without has reminded him that it can be gained. Consciously or unconsciously, he has been caught up by the *Zeitgeist,* and with his black brothers of Africa and his brown and yellow brothers of Asia, South America and the Caribbean, the United States Negro is moving with a sense of great urgency toward the promised land of racial justice. If one recognizes this vital urge that has engulfed the Negro community, one should readily understand why public demonstrations are taking place. The Negro has many pent-up resentments and latent frustrations, and he must release them. So let him march; let him make prayer pilgrimages to the city hall; let him go on freedom rides— and try to understand why he must do so. If his repressed emotions are not released in nonviolent ways, they will seek expression through violence; this is not a threat but a fact of history. So I have not said to my people: "Get rid of your discontent." Rather, I have tried to say that this normal and healthy discontent can be channeled into the creative outlet of nonviolent direct action. And now this approach is being termed extremist.

But though I was initially disappointed at being categorized as an extremist, as I continued to think about the matter I gradually gained a measure of satisfaction from the label. Was not Jesus an extremist for love: "Love your enemies, bless them that curse you, do good to them that hate you, and pray for them which despitefully use you, and persecute you." Was not Amos an extremist for justice: "Let justice roll down like waters and righteousness like an ever-flowing stream." Was not Paul an extremist for the Christian gospel: "I bear in my body the marks of the Lord Jesus." Was not Martin Luther an extremist: "Here I stand; I cannot do otherwise, so help me God." And John Bunyan: "I will stay in jail to the end of my days before I make a butchery of my conscience." And Abraham Lincoln: "This nation cannot survive half slave and half free." And Thomas Jefferson: "We hold these truths to be self-evident, that all men are created equal . . ." So the question is not whether we will be extremists, but what kind of extremists we will be. Will we be extremists for hate or for love? Will we be extremists for the preservation of injustice or for the extension of justice? In that dramatic scene on Calvary's hill three men were crucified. We must never forget that all three were crucified for the same crime—the crime of extremism. Two were extremists for immorality, and thus fell below their environment. The other, Jesus Christ, was an extremist for love, truth and goodness, and thereby rose above his environment. Perhaps the South, the nation and the world are in dire need of creative extremists.

I had hoped that the white moderate would see this need. Perhaps I was too optimistic; perhaps I expected too much. I suppose I should have realized that few members of the oppressor race can understand the deep groans and passionate yearnings of the oppressed race, and still fewer have the vision to see that injustice must be rooted out by strong, persistent and determined action. I am thankful, however, that some of our white brothers in the South have grasped the meaning of this social revolution and committed themselves to it. They are still all too few in quantity, but they are big in quality. Some—such as Ralph McGill, Lillian Smith, Harry Golden, James McBride Dabbs, Ann Braden and Sarah Patton Boyle—have written about our struggle in eloquent and prophetic terms. Others have marched with us down nameless streets of the South. They have languished in filthy, roach-infested jails, suffering the abuse and brutality of policemen who view them as "dirty nigger-lovers." Unlike so many of their moderate brothers and sisters, they have recognized the urgency of the moment and sensed the need for powerful "action" antidotes to combat the disease of segregation.

Let me take note of my other major disappointment. I have been so greatly disappointed with the white church and its leadership. Of course, there are some notable exceptions. I am not unmindful of the fact that each of you has taken some significant stands on this issue. I commend you, Reverend Stallings, for your Christian stand on this past Sunday, in welcoming Negroes to your worship service on a nonsegregated basis. I commend the Catholic leaders of this state for integrating Spring Hill College several years ago.

But despite these notable exceptions, I must honestly reiterate that I have been disappointed with the Church. I do not say this as one of those negative critics who can always find something wrong with the church. I say this as a minister of the gospel, who loves the church; who was nurtured in its bosom; who has been sustained by its spiritual blessings and who will remain true to it as long as the cord of life shall lengthen.

When I was suddenly catapulted into the leadership of the bus *35* protest in Montgomery, Alabama, a few years ago, I felt we would be supported by the white church. I felt that the white ministers, priests and rabbis of the South would be among our strongest allies. Instead, some have been outright opponents, refusing to understand the freedom movement and misrepresenting its leaders; all too many others have been more cautious than courageous and have remained silent behind the anesthetizing security of stained-glass windows.

In spite of my shattered dreams, I came to Birmingham with the hope that the white religious leadership of this community would see the justice of our cause and, with deep moral concern, would serve as the channel through which our just grievances could reach the power structure. I had hoped that each of you would understand. But again I have been disappointed.

I have heard numerous southern religious leaders admonish their worshipers to comply with a desegregation decision because it is the law, but I have longed to hear white ministers declare: "Follow this decree because integration is morally right and because the Negro is your brother." In the midst of blatant injustices inflicted upon the Negro, I have watched white churchmen stand on the sideline and mouth pious irrelevancies and sanctimonious trivialities. In the midst of a mighty struggle to rid our nation of racial and economic injustice, I have heard many ministers say: "Those are social issues, with which the gospel has no real concern." And I have watched many churches commit themselves to a completely other-worldly religion which makes a strange, un-Biblical distinction between body and soul, between the sacred and the secular.

I have traveled the length and breadth of Alabama, Mississippi and all the other southern states. On sweltering summer days and crisp autumn mornings I have looked at the South's beautiful churches with their lofty spires pointing heavenward. I have beheld the impressive outlines of her massive religious-education buildings. Over and over I have found myself saying: "What kind of people worship here? Who is their God? Where were their voices when the lips of Governor Barnett dripped with words of interposition and nullification? Where were they when Governor Wallace gave a clarion call for defiance and hatred? Where were their voices of support when bruised and weary Negro men and women decided to rise from the dark dungeons of complacency to the bright hills of creative protest?"

Yes, these questions are still in my mind. In deep disappointment I have wept over the laxity of the church. But be assured that my tears have been tears of love. There can be no deep disappointment where there is not deep love. Yes, I love the church. How could I do otherwise? I am in the rather unique position of being the son, the grandson and the great-grandson of preachers. Yes, I see the church as the body of Christ. But, oh! How we have blemished and scarred that body through social neglect and through fear of being nonconformists.

There was a time when the church was very powerful—in the time *40* when the early Christians rejoiced at being deemed worthy to suffer for

what they believed. In those days the church was not merely a ther-
mometer that recorded the ideas and principles of popular opinion; it was
a thermostat that transformed the mores of society. Whenever the early
Christians entered a town, the people in power became disturbed and
immediately sought to convict the Christians for being "disturbers of the
peace" and "outside agitators." But the Christians pressed on, in the conviction that they were "a colony of heaven," called to obey God rather
than man. Small in number, they were big in commitment. They were
too God-intoxicated to be "astronomically intimidated." By their effort
and example they brought an end to such ancient evils as infanticide and
gladiatorial contests.

Things are different now. So often the contemporary church is a
weak, ineffectual voice with an uncertain sound. So often it is an arch-
defender of the status quo. Far from being disturbed by the presence of
the church, the power structure of the average community is consoled by
the church's silent—and often even vocal—sanction of things as they are.

But the judgment of God is upon the church as never before. If
today's church does not recapture the sacrificial spirit of the early church,
it will lose its authenticity, forfeit the loyalty of millions, and be dismissed
as an irrelevant social club with no meaning for the twentieth century.
Every day I meet young people whose disappointment with the church
has turned into outright disgust.

Perhaps I have once again been too optimistic. Is organized religion
too inextricably bound to the status quo to save our nation and the
world? Perhaps I must turn my faith to the inner spiritual church, the
church within the church, as the true *ekklesia* and the hope of the world.
But again I am thankful to God that some noble souls from the ranks of
organized religion have broken loose from the paralyzing chains of con-
formity and joined us as active partners in the struggle for freedom. They
have left their secure congregations and walked the streets of Albany,
Georgia, with us. They have gone down the highways of the South on
tortuous rides for freedom. Yes, they have gone to jail with us. Some have
been dismissed from their churches, have lost the support of their bishops
and fellow ministers. But they have acted in the faith that right defeated
is stronger than evil triumphant. Their witness has been the spiritual salt
that has preserved the true meaning of the gospel in these troubled times.
They have carved a tunnel of hope through the dark mountain of disappointment.

I hope the church as a whole will meet the challenge of this decisive
hour. But even if the church does not come to the aid of justice, I have
no despair about the future. I have no fear about the outcome of our
struggle in Birmingham, even if our motives are at present misunderstood. We will reach the goal of freedom in Birmingham and all over
the nation, because the goal of America is freedom. Abused and scorned

though we may be, our destiny is tied up with America's destiny. Before the pilgrims landed at Plymouth, we were here. Before the pen of Jefferson etched the majestic words of the Declaration of Independence across the pages of history, we were here. For more than two centuries our forebears labored in this country without wages; they made cotton king; they built the homes of their masters while suffering gross injustice and shameful humiliation—and yet out of a bottomless vitality they continued to thrive and develop. If the inexpressible cruelties of slavery could not stop us, the opposition we now face will surely fail. We will win our freedom because the sacred heritage of our nation and the eternal will of God are embodied in our echoing demands.

Before closing I feel impelled to mention one other point in your 45 statement that has troubled me profoundly. You warmly commended the Birmingham police force for keeping "order" and "preventing violence." I doubt that you would have so warmly commended the police force if you had seen its dogs sinking their teeth into unarmed, nonviolent Negroes. I doubt that you would so quickly commend the policemen if you were to observe their ugly and inhumane treatment of Negroes here in the city jail; if you were to watch them push and curse old Negro women and young Negro girls; if you were to see them slap and kick old Negro men and young boys; if you were to observe them, as they did on two occasions, refuse to give us food because we wanted to sing our grace together. I cannot join you in your praise of the Birmingham police department.

It is true that the police have exercised a degree of discipline in handling the demonstrators. In this sense they have conducted themselves rather "nonviolently" in public. But for what purpose? To preserve the evil system of segregation. Over the past few years I have consistently preached that nonviolence demands that the means we use must be as pure as the ends we seek. I have tried to make clear that it is wrong to use immoral means to attain moral ends. But now I must affirm that it is just as wrong, or perhaps even more so, to use moral means to preserve immoral ends. Perhaps Mr. Connor and his policemen have been rather nonviolent in public, as was Chief Pritchett in Albany, Georgia, but they have used the moral means of nonviolence to maintain the immoral end of racial injustice. As T. S. Eliot has said: "The last temptation is the greatest treason: To do the right deed for the wrong reason."

I wish you had commended the Negro sit-inners and demonstrators of Birmingham for their sublime courage, their willingness to suffer and their amazing discipline in the midst of great provocation. One day the South will recognize its real heroes. They will be the James Merediths, with the noble sense of purpose that enables them to face jeering and hostile mobs, and with the agonizing loneliness that characterizes the life of the pioneer. They will be old, oppressed, battered Negro women, symbolized in a seventy-two-year-old woman in Montgomery, Alabama, who rose up with a sense of dignity and with her people decided not to ride segregated buses, and who responded with ungrammatical profundity to one who inquired about her weariness: "My feets is tired, but my soul is at rest." They will be the young high school and college students, the young ministers of the gospel and a host of their elders, courageously and nonviolently sitting in at lunch counters and willingly going to jail for conscience' sake. One day the South will know that when these disinherited children of God sat down at lunch counters, they were in reality standing up for what is best in the American dream and for the most sacred values in our Judaeo-Christian heritage, thereby bringing our nation back to those great wells of democracy which were dug deep by the founding fathers in their formulation of the Constitution and the Declaration of Independence.

Never before have I written so long a letter. I'm afraid it is much too long to take your precious time. I can assure you that it would have been much shorter if I had been writing from a comfortable desk, but what else can one do when he is alone in a narrow jail cell, other than write long letters, think long thoughts and pray long prayers?

If I have said anything in this letter that overstates the truth and indicates an unreasonable impatience, I beg you to forgive me. If I have said anything that understates the truth and indicates my having a patience that allows me to settle for anything less than brotherhood, I beg God to forgive me.

I hope this letter finds you strong in the faith. I also hope that circumstances will soon make it possible for me to meet each of you, not as an integrationist or a civil-rights leader but as a fellow clergyman and a Christian brother. Let us all hope that the dark clouds of racial prejudice will soon pass away and the deep fog of misunderstanding will be lifted from our fear-drenched communities, and in some not too distant tomorrow the radiant stars of love and brotherhood will shine over our great nation with all their scintillating beauty.

Yours for the cause of Peace and Brotherhood,
Martin Luther King, Jr.

50

IV A Minicasebook on Censoring Rock and Rap

INTRODUCTION

This section is designed to provide you with material on which
to base a longer argument in greater depth. The topic is one of today's
most controversial and important issues, and the material varies widely in
length, level, type of publication, and point of view. The selections range
from op-ed pieces to senatorial speeches and academic articles; they

include a satirical cartoon and a debate in a national magazine. The two professional academic articles are given complete with footnotes in professional form.

You can use the information here either alone or in conjunction with further research of the sort described in the "Guide to Finding and Using Information" at the end of the book. Good luck with your project!

A SELECTED CHRONOLOGY OF MUSICAL CONTROVERSY

Fred Bronson

FEBRUARY 1954

Rep. Ruth Thompson (R.-Mich.) introduces a bill in the House that would ban mailing any phonograph record or "other article capable of producing sound" that was "obscene, lewd, lascivious, or filthy." Punishment would include fines up to $5,000 and five years imprisonment.

OCTOBER 1954

WDIA in Memphis bans "Work With Me, Annie" and "Annie Had a Baby" by the Midnighters as well as "Honey Love" by the Drifters because of "offensive lyrics."

JANUARY 1957

Elvis Presley makes his third and final appearance on "The Ed Sullivan Show," but the camera operators are directed not to pan below the waist.

MARCH 1957

Cardinal Stritch, head of the Catholic archdiocese in Chicago, bans rock 'n' roll from schools because of its "tribal rhythms" and "encouragement to behave in a hedonistic manner."

JANUARY 1959

Link Wray's instrumental "Rumble" is dropped by many radio stations because the title refers to teenage gang violence. On "American

Bandstand," Dick Clark introduces Wray but does not mention the title of the song.

JANUARY 1962

In Buffalo, N.Y., Bishop Burke forbids students from dancing, singing about or listening to "The Twist" in any school or parish or at any youth event.

FEBRUARY 1962

The Radio Trade Practices Committee recommends that lyrics of all pop songs be screened by the NAB Code Committee "due to the proliferation of songs dealing with raw sex and violence beamed directly and singularly at children and teenagers."

FEBRUARY 1963

CBS tells Bob Dylan he cannot sing "Talking John Birch Society Blues," his take on the right-wing organization, on "The Ed Sullivan Show." Dylan refuses to appear.

FEBRUARY 1964

Gov. Matthew Welsh of Indiana deems "Louie Louie" by the Kingsmen to be pornographic and asks the state broadcasters association to ban the song.

FEBRUARY 1965

After splitting his pants during a London concert, P. J. Proby is *10* banned from appearing on ABC-TV's "Shindig."

JUNE 1965

Many American radio stations refuse to play the Rolling Stones' "(I Can't Get No) Satisfaction" because of "suggestive lyrics."

MARCH 1966

In an interview with London's *The Evening Standard,* John Lennon talks about Christianity and says of the Beatles, "We're more popular than Jesus Christ right now." As a result, burnings of Beatles records take place around the world.

JUNE 1966

The Beatles' "Yesterday And Today" album is released with "the butcher cover," featuring the Fab Four sitting with pieces of meat and decapitated baby dolls. The cover is withdrawn from stores and replaced by an innocuous photo of the Beatles.

JANUARY 1967

The Rolling Stones perform "Let's Spend The Night Together" on "The Ed Sullivan Show" after Jagger agrees to substitute the lyrics with "Let's spend some time together." Later, he claims to have sung the original words, but says he slurred them.

SEPTEMBER 1967

The Doors appear on "The Ed Sullivan Show." Jim Morrison is asked to delete the lyric, "Girl we couldn't get much higher" from "Light My Fire," but doesn't. *15*

SEPTEMBER 1968

One month after the Democratic convention, radio stations in Chicago ban the Rolling Stones' single "Street Fighting Man," fearful it might incite people to riot.

JANUARY 1969

Some 30,000 copies of John Lennon and Yoko Ono's "Two Virgins" album, featuring the couple nude on the cover, are seized by police at Newark airport in New Jersey. In Chicago, a record store displaying the cover is closed down by the vice squad.

FEBRUARY 1969

Protests greet the original Blind Faith LP cover of a nude 11-year-old girl holding a phallic-looking model airplane. Atco releases the album with two different covers so retailers can choose which they prefer to stock.

APRIL 1969

Detroit rockers MC5 agree to delete an expletive from the title song of their album "Kick Out The Jams." But Elektra drops the quintet after the members write another expletive on company letterhead and personally deliver the stationery to stores that refused to stock their album.

JULY 1969

Almost half of the Top 40 stations in the U.S. refuse to play the [20] Beatles' new single, "The Ballad Of John And Yoko," because of the lyric, "Christ, you know it ain't easy. . . ."

SEPTEMBER 1969

A two-page ad in the *Seattle Post-Intelligence* calls for criminal prosecution against "rock festivals and their drug-sex-rock-squalor culture." The spread, paid for by the city's Roman Catholic archdiocese, includes photos from local festivals with nudity and drug use blacked out.

OCTOBER 1970

President Richard Nixon tells radio broadcasters that rock lyrics should be screened and any songs suggesting drug use should be banned.

MARCH 1971

WNBC radio in New York bans "One Toke Over The Line" by Brewer & Shipley because of alleged drug references. Songwriter Tom Shipley compares pulling a record from the airwaves in the '70s to book-burning in the '30s.

APRIL 1971

The Illinois Crime Commission publishes a list of "drug-oriented rock records," including "Puff The Magic Dragon," "Yellow Submarine," "A Whiter Shade Of Pale" and "Hi-De-Ho (That Old Sweet Roll)."

APRIL 1973

On the syndicated "Soul Train," Curtis Mayfield is censored when [25] references to drugs are deleted from his song "Pusherman."

NOVEMBER 1975

In Tallahassee, Rev. Charles Boykin of the Lakeswood Baptist Church burns rock 'n' roll records, calling them the "devil's music."

DECEMBER 1976

In an interview on British television, the Sex Pistols land in hot water when bassist Glen Matlock utters an expletive. As a result, their U.K. tour collapses as most venues refuse to book the group. A month later, EMI drops the group from its roster. A&M signs the group and ends the deal nine days later without releasing any product.

MAY 1977

Virgin Records signs the Sex Pistols. The song "God Save The Queen" is banned from British radio because of "treasonous sentiments," but hits No. 2 on the chart anyway.

MAY 1985

The Parents' Music Resource Center (PMRC) is established by a group of mainly wives of Washington politicians, including co-chairs Susan Baker and Tipper Gore. Identifying five basic negative themes in rock music—free love/sex, sadomasochism, rebellion, the occult and drugs—the group fights for a rating system in order to alert parents to explicit lyrics.

FEBRUARY 1989

The City Council of New Iberia, La., passses an emergency or- 30
dinance requiring that materials that might fall under the state's definitions of obscenity be placed out of view of unmarried people under the
age of 17. Violation carries a penalty of 60 days in jail and a $500 fine.

After Yusef Islam, once known as Cat Stevens, endorses the Ayatol-
lah Khomeni's call for the execution of "Satanic Verses" author Salman
Rushdie, radio stations around the U.S. drop Stevens from their playlists.
KFI talk show host Tom Leykis holds a Cat Stevens record burning.

JANUARY 1990

A bill introduced in the Missouri legislature prohibits the sale of records that contain lyrics that are violent, sexually explicit, or perverse, unless they have an affixed parental advisory warning label and the lyrics printed on the album cover. Similar proposals follow in Maryland, Dela-ware, Florida and Kansas.

Police in Dade County, Fla., investigate incidents in which three re-tailers were caught in a sting set up by attorney Jack Thompson. Thomp-son says that the three stores sold unedited versions of 2 Live Crew's album to a 16-year-old. As a result, the 52-store Spec's Music chain institutes an 18-to-purchase policy on stickered product.

RAISED ON ROCK-AND-ROLL

Anna Quindlen

Mister Ed is back on television, indicating that, as most middle-of-the-road antique shops suggests, Americans cannot discriminate between things worth saving and things that simply exist. *The Donna Reed Show* is on, too, and *My Three Sons,* and those dopey folks from *Gilligan's Island.* There's *Leave It to Beaver* and *The Beverly Hillbillies* and even *Lassie,* whose plaintive theme song leaves my husband all mushy around the edges.

Social historians say these images, and those of Howdy Doody and Pinky Lee and Lamb Chop and Annette have forever shaped my consciousness. But I have memories far stronger than that. I remember sitting cross-legged in front of the tube, one of the console sets with the ersatz lamé netting over the speakers, but I was not watching puppets or pratfalls. I was born in Philadelphia, a city where if you can't dance you might as well stay home, and I was raised on rock-and-roll. My earliest television memory is of *American Bandstand,* and the central question of my childhood was: Can you dance to it?

When I was fifteen and a wild devotee of Mitch Ryder and the Detroit Wheels, it sometimes crossed my mind that when I was thirty-four years old, decrepit, wrinkled as a prune and near death, I would have moved on to some nameless kind of dreadful show music, something akin to Muzak. I did not think about the fact that my parents were still listening to the music that had been popular when they were kids; I only thought that they played "Pennsylvania 6-5000" to torment me and keep my friends away from the house.

But I know now that I'm never going to stop loving rock-and-roll, all kinds of rock-and-roll: the Beatles, the Rolling Stones, Hall and Oates, Talking Heads, the Doors, the Supremes, Tina Turner, Elvis Costello, Elvis Presley. I even like really bad rock-and-roll, although I guess that's where my age shows; I don't have the tolerance for Bon Jovi that I once had for the Raspberries.

We have friends who, when their son was a baby, used to put a record on and say, "Drop your butt, Phillip." And Phillip did. That's what I love: drop-your-butt music. It's one of the few things left in my life that makes me feel good without even thinking about it. I can walk into any bookstore and find dozens of books about motherhood and love and human relations and so many other things that we once did through

1

5

a combination of intuition and emotion. I even heard recently that some school is giving a course on kissing, which makes me wonder if I'm missing something. But rock-and-roll flows through my veins, not my brain. There's nothing else that feels the same to me as, say, the faint sound of the opening dum-doo-doo-doo-doo-doo of "My Girl" coming from a radio on a summer day. I feel the way I felt when I first heard it. I feel good, as James Brown says.

There are lots of people who don't feel this way about rock-and-roll. Some of them don't understand it, like the Senate wives who said that records should have rating stickers on them so that you would know whether the lyrics were dirty. The kids who hang out at Mr. Big's sub shop in my neighborhood thought this would make record shopping a lot easier, because you could choose albums by how bad the rating was. Most of the people who love rock-and-roll just thought the labeling idea was dumb. Lyrics, after all, are not the point of rock-and-roll, despite how beautifully people like Bruce Springsteen and Joni Mitchell write. Lyrics are the point only in the case of "Louie, Louie"; the words have never been deciphered, but it is widely understood that they are about sex. That's understandable, because rock-and-roll is a lot like sex: If you talk seriously about it, it takes a lot of the feeling away—and feeling is the point.

Some people over-analyze rock-and-roll, just as they over-analyze everything else. They say things like "Bruce Springsteen is the poet laureate of the American dream gone sour," when all I need to know about Bruce Springsteen is that the saxophone bridge on "Jungleland" makes the back of my neck feel exactly the same way I felt the first time a boy kissed me, only over and over and over again. People write about Prince's "psychedelic masturbatory fantasies," but when I think about Prince, I don't really think, I just feel—feel the moment when, driving to the beach, I first heard "Kiss" on the radio and started bopping up and down in my seat like a seventeen-year-old on a day trip.

I've got precious few things in my life anymore that just make me feel, that make me jump up and dance, that make me forget the schedule and the job and the mortgage payments and just let me thrash around inside my skin. I've got precious few things I haven't studied and considered and reconsidered and studied some more. I don't know a chord change from a snare drum, but I know what I like, and I like feeling this way sometimes. I love rock-and-roll because in a time of talk, talk, talk, it's about action.

Here's a test: Get hold of a two-year-old, a person who has never read a single word about how heavy-metal musicians should be put in jail or about Tina Turner's "throaty alto range." Put "I Heard It Through the Grapevine" on the stereo. Stand the two-year-old in front of the stereo. The two-year-old will begin to dance. The two-year-old will drop his butt. Enough said.

ON "JUNK FOOD FOR THE SOUL"
In Defense of Rock and Roll

Frank Zappa

THE NATURE OF MUSIC

> Music is the soul's primitive and primary speech . . . without
> articulate speech or reason. It is not only not reasonable, it is
> hostile to reason. . . . Civilization . . . is the taming or domesti-
> cation of the soul's raw passions. . . . Rock music has one appeal
> only, a barbaric appeal, to sexual desire—not love, not eros, but
> sexual desire undeveloped and untutored . . .
>
> —*A. Bloom*

This is a puff pastry version of the belief that music is the work 1
of the Devil: that the nasty ol' Devil plays his fiddle and people dance
around and we don't want to see them twitching like that. In fact, if one
wants to be a real artist in the United States today and comment on our
culture, one would be very far off the track if one did something delicate
or sublime. This is not a noble, delicate, sublime country. This is a mess
run by criminals. Performers who are doing the crude, vulgar, repulsive
things Bloom doesn't enjoy are only commenting on that fact.

In general, antirock propositions began when rock 'n' roll began,
and most of these were racially motivated. In the fifties, petitions were
circulated which said, "Don't allow your children to buy Negro records."
The petitions referred to the "raw unbridled passion" of screaming people
with dark skin who are going to drive our children wild. Some things
never go out of fashion in certain ideological camps. They are like tenets
of the faith.

Music's real effect on people is a new field of science called psycho-
acoustics—the way an organism deals with wiggling air molecules. Our
ears decode the wiggling air molecules, and that gives us the information
of a particular musical sound. Our brain says, "This is music, this is a
structure," and we deal with it based on certain tools we have acquired.

I personally make music because I want to ask a question, and I
want to get an answer. If that question and answer amuse me, then statistically, there are a certain number of other people out there who have
the same amusement factor. If I present my work to them, they will be
amused by it, and we will all have a good time.

I need to be amused because I get bored easily and being amused 5
entertains me. If I could be easily amused, like many people who like
beer and football, I would never do anything because everything that

would be beautiful for my life would already be provided by American television.

But beer and television bore me, so what am I going to do? I am going to be alive for X number of years. I have to do something with my time besides sleep and eat. So, I devise little things to amuse myself. If I can amuse somebody else, great. And if I can amuse somebody else and earn a living while doing it, that is a true miracle in the twentieth century!

MUSIC AND THE DARK FORCES OF THE SOUL

> To Plato and Nietzsche, the history of music is a series of attempts to give form and beauty to the dark, chaotic, premonitory forces in the soul—to make them serve a higher purpose, an ideal, to given man's duties a fullness.
>
> —*A. Bloom*

This is a man who has fallen for rock's fabricated image of itself. This is the worst kind of ivory tower intellectualism. Anybody who talks about dark forces is right on the fringe of mumbo jumbo. Dark forces? What is this, another product from Lucasfilm? The passions! When was the last time you saw an American exhibit any form of passion other than the desire to shoot a guy on the freeway? Those are the forces of evil as far as I am concerned.

If there are dark forces hovering in the vicinity of the music business, they are mercantile forces. We meet the darkness when we meet the orchestra committees, when we get in touch with funding organizations, when we deal with people who give grants and when we get into the world of commerce that greets us when we arrive with our piece of art. Whether it's a rock 'n' roll record or a symphony, it's the same machinery lurking out there.

The reason a person writes a piece of music has got nothing to do with dark forces. I certainly don't have dark forces lurking around me when I'm writing. If someone is going to write a piece of music, in fact they are preoccupied with the boring labor and very hard work involved. That's what's really going on.

WHAT MAKES MUSIC CLASSICAL

> Rock music . . . has risen to its current heights in the education of the young on the ashes of classical music, and in an atmosphere in which there is no intellectual resistance to attempts to tap the rawest passions. . . . Cultivation of the soul uses the pas-

sions and satisfies them sublimating them and giving them an artistic unity. . . . Bach's religious intentions and Beethoven's revolutionary and humane ones are clear enough examples.

—*A. Bloom*

This is such nonsense. All the people recognized as great classical composers are recognized at this point for two reasons:

One, during the time these composers were alive and writing they had patrons who liked what they did and who therefore paid them money or gave them a place to live so that the composers would stay alive by writing dots on pieces of paper. If any of the compositions these men wrote had not been pleasing to a church, a duke, or a king, they would have been out of work and their music would not have survived.

There is a book called *Grove's Dictionary of Music and Musicians,* with thousands of names in it. You have never heard of most of the people in that book, nor have you heard their music. That doesn't mean they wrote awful music, it means they didn't have hits.

So basically, the people who are recognized as the genuises of classical music had hits. And the person who determined whether or not it was a hit was a king, a duke, or the church or whoever paid the bill. The desire to get a sandwich or something to drink had a lot to do with it. And the content of what they wrote was to a degree determined by the musical predilections of the guy who was paying the bill.

Today, we have a similar situation in rock 'n' roll. We have kings, dukes, and popes: the A&R guy who spots a group or screens the tape when it comes in; the business affairs guy who writes the contract; the radio station programmers who choose what records get air play.

The other reason the classical greats survived is their works are played over and over again by orchestras. The reasons they are played over and over again are: (1) all the musicians in the orchestra know how to play them because they learned them in the conservatory; (2) the orchestra management programs these pieces because the musicians already know them and therefore it costs less to rehearse them; (3) the composers are dead so the orchestras pay no royalties for the use of the music.

Today, survivability is based on the number of specimens in the market place—the sheer numbers of plastic objects. Many other compositions from this era will vanish, but Michael Jackson's *Thriller* album will survive because there are 30 million odd pieces of plastic out there. No matter what we may think of the content, a future generation may pick up that piece of plastic and say, "Oh, they were like this."

I suppose somewhere in future there will be other men like Bloom certifying that the very narrow spectrum of rock 'n' roll which survives composes the great works of the later half of the twentieth century.

THE DIFFERENCE BETWEEN CLASSICAL MUSIC AND ROCK 'N' ROLL

> Rock music provides premature ecstasy and, in this respect, is like the drugs with which it is allied. . . . These are the three great lyrical themes: sex, hate and a smarmy, hypocritical version of brotherly love. . . . Nothing noble, sublime, profound, delicate, tasteful or even decent can find a place in such tableaux.
>
> —*A. Bloom*

Again, Bloom is not looking at what is really going on here. The ugliness in this society is not a product of unrefined art, but of unrefined commerce, wild superstition, and religious fanaticism.

The real difference between the classics and rock 'n' roll is mostly a matter of form. In order to say we have written a symphony, the design we put on a piece of paper has to conform to certain specifications. We have an exposition that last a certain amount of time, then modulation, development, and recapitulation. It's like a box, like an egg carton. We must fill all the little spaces in the egg carton with the right forms. If we do, we can call it a symphony because it conforms to the spaces in that box.

Compare that creative process to rock 'n' roll. If we want to have an AM hit record, we have another egg carton to fill. We have an intro, a couple of verses, a bridge, another verse, and then a fade out. All of which requires a "hook." That's a very rigid form. If we wander away from that form, our song's not going to go on the radio because it doesn't sound like it fits into their format.

Now, whether the person writing the song graduated from a conservatory or whether they came out of a garage, they know that in order to finish a piece they have to do certain things to make it fit into a certain form. In the classical period the sonata or a concerto or symphony had to be that certain size and shape or else the king was not going to like it. One could die. These were literally matters of life and death, but not in the way Bloom defines them.

THE ROCK BUSINESS

> The family spiritual void has left the field open to rock music. . . . The result is nothing less than parents' loss of control over their children's moral education at a time when no one else is seriously concerned with it. This has been achieved by an alliance between the strange young males who have the gift of divining the mob's emergent wishes—our versions of Thrasymachus, Socrates' rhetorical adversary—and the record-holding executives, the new robber barons, who mine gold out of rock.
>
> —*A. Bloom*

There is some truth to that, but how did we get to this point and what do we do about it?

We got here because teenagers are the most sought-after consumers. The whole idea of merchandising the prepubescent masturbational fantasy is not necessarily the work of the songwriter or the singer, but the work of the merchandiser who has elevated rock 'n' roll to the commercial enterprise it is.

In the beginning, rock 'n' roll was young kids singing to other kids about their girlfriends. That's all there was. The guys who make these records came from Manual Arts High School. They went into a recording studio, were given some wine, $25, and a bunch of records when their song came out as a single—which made them heroes at school. That was their career, not, "Well, we're not going to sing until we get a $125 thousand advance."

Today, rock 'n' roll is about getting a contract with a major company, and pretty much doing what the company tells you to do. The company promotes the image of rock 'n' roll as being wild and fun when in fact it's just a dismal business. 25

Record companies have people who claim to be experts on what the public really wants to hear. And they inflict their taste on the people who actually make the music. To be a big success, you need a really big company behind you because really big companies can make really big distribution deals.

Even people who are waiting to get into the business know it's a business. They spend a great deal of time planning what they will look like and getting a good publicity photo before they walk in the door with their tape. And the record companies tend to take the attitude that it doesn't make too much difference what the tape sounds like as long as the artists look right, because they can always hire a producer who will fix up the sound and make it the way they want it—so long as the people wear the right clothes and have the right hair.

RETAINING CLASSICAL MUSIC

> Classical music is dead among the young. . . . Rock music is as unquestioned and unproblematic as the air the students breathe, and very few have any acquaintance at all with classical music. . . . Classical music is now a special taste, like Greek language or pre-Columbian archeology, not a common culture of reciprocal communication and psychological shorthand.
>
> —*A. Bloom*

On this point, Bloom and I can agree, but how can a child be blamed for consuming only that which is presented to him? Most kids have never been in contact with anything other than this highly merchanised stuff.

When I testified in front of the Senate, I pointed out that if they don't like the idea of young people buying certain kinds of music, why don't they stick a few dollars back into the school system to have music appreciation? There are kids today who have never heard a string quartet; they have never heard a symphony orchestra. I argued that the money for music appreication courses, in terms of social good and other benefits such as improved behavior or uplifting the spirit, is far less than the cost of another set of uniforms for the football team. But I frankly don't see people waving banners in the street saying more music appreciation in schools.

When I was in school, we could go into a room and they had 30 records there. I could hear anything I wanted by going in there and putting on a record. I won't say I enjoyed everything that was played for me, but I was curious, and if I had never heard any of that music I wouldn't know about it.

Once we're out of school, the time we can spend doing that type of research is limited because most of us are out looking for a job flipping hamburgers in the great tradition of the Reagan economic miracle. When all is said and done, that's the real source of America's barren and arid lives.

CURBING THE SEXPLOITATION INDUSTRY

Tipper Gore

I can't even count the times in the last three years, since I began to 1 express my concern about violence and sexuality in rock music, that I have been called a prude, a censor, a music hater, even a book burner. So let me be perfectly clear: I detest censorship. I'm not advocating censorship but rather a candid and vigorous debate about the dangers posed for our children by what I call the "exploitation industry."

We don't need to put a childproof cap on the world, but we do need to remind the nation that children live in it, too, and deserve respect and sensitive treatment.

When I launched this campaign in 1985 (long before my husband dreamed of running for president), I went to the source of the problem, sharing my concerns and proposals with the entertainment industry. Many producers were sympathetic. Some cooperated with my efforts.

But others have been overtly hostile, accusing me of censorship and suggesting, unfairly, that my motives are political.

This resistance and hostility has convinced me of the need for a two-pronged campaign, with equal effort from the entertainment industry and concerned parents. Entertainment producers must take the first step, by labeling sexually explicit material.

But the industry cannot be expected to solve the problem on its own. Parents should encourage producers to cooperate and praise them when they do. Producers need to know that parents are aware of the issue and are reading their advisory labels. Above all, they need to know that somebody out there cares, that the community at large is not apathetic about the deep and lasting damage being done to our children.

What's at issue is not the occasional sexy rock lyric. What troubles—indeed, outrages—me is far more vicious: a celebration of the most gruesome violence, coupled with the explicit message that sadomasochism is the essence of sex.

We're surrounded by examples—in rock lyrics, on television, at the movies and in rental videos. One major TV network recently aired a preview of a soap opera rape scene during a morning game show.

The newest craze in horror movies is something called the "teen slasher" film, and it typically depicts the killing, torture and sexual mutilation of women in sickening detail. Several rock groups now simulate sexual torture and murder during live performances. Others titillate youthful audiences with strippers confined in cages on stage and with half-naked dancers, who often act out sex with band members. Sexual brutality has become the common currency of America's youth culture and with it the pervasive degradation of women.

Why is this graphic violence dangerous? It's especially damaging for young children because they lack the moral judgment of adults. Many children are only dimly aware of the consequences of their actions, and, as parents know, they are excellent mimics. They often imitate violence they see on TV, without necessarily understanding what they are doing or what the consequences might be.

One 5-year-old boy from Boston recently got up from watching a teen slasher film and stabbed a 2-year-old girl with a butcher knife. He didn't mean to kill her (and luckily he did not). He was just imitating the man in the video.

Nor does the danger end as children grow older. National health officials tell us that children younger than teen-agers are apt to react to excessive violence with suicide, satanism, drug and alcohol abuse. Even grown-ups are not immune. One series of studies by researchers at the University of Wisconsin found that men exposed to films in which women are beaten, butchered, maimed and raped were significantly desensitized to the violence. Not only did they express less sympathy for the victims, they even approved of lesser penalties in hypothetical rape trials.

Sadomasochistic pornography is a kind of poison. Like most poisons, it probably cannot be totally eliminated, but it certainly could be labeled for what it is and be kept away from those who are most vulnerable.

The largest record companies have agreed to this—in principle at least. In November 1985, the Recording Industry Association of America adopted my proposal to alert parents by having producers either put warning labels on records with explicitly sexual lyrics or display the lyrics on the outside of the record jackets. Since then, some companies have complied in good faith, although others have not complied at all.

This is where we parents must step in. We must let the industry know we're angry. We must press for uniform voluntary compliance with labeling guidelines. And we must take an active interest at home in what our children are watching and listening to. After all, we can hardly expect that the labels or printed lyrics alone will discourage young consumers.

Some parents may want to write to the record companies. Others can give their support to groups like the Parent Teacher Association, which have endorsed the labeling idea. All of us can use our purchasing power. We have more power than we think, and we must use it. For the sake of our children, we simply can't afford to slip back into apathy.

My concern for the health and welfare of children has nothing to do with politics: It is addressed to conservatives and liberals alike. Some civil libertarians believe it is wrong even to raise these questions—just as some conservatives believe that the government should police popular American culture. I reject both these views. I have no desire to restrain artists or cast a "chill" over popular culture. But I believe parents have First Amendment rights, too.

The fate of the family, the dignity of women, the mental health of children—these concerns belong to everyone. We must protect our children with choice, not censorship. Let's start working in our communities to forge a moral consensus for the 1990s. Children need our help, and we must summon the courage to examine the culture that shapes their lives.

THE EFFECT OF CENSORSHIP ON ATTITUDES TOWARD POPULAR MUSIC

Brian K. Simmons

Recent years have seen a resurgence of interest in the content of popular music. Efforts by powerful activist groups such as the Parents' Music Resource Center, Congressional testimony by popular music artists and *2 Live Crew's* obscenity trial have refocused national attention on the timeless problem of defining the limits of acceptable expression. With increased frequency, censorship of lyrics is being advocated as a solution.

There are many who feel that rather than curbing instances of undesirable content, censorship officials instead fuel the desire for controversial material. Anecdotal evidence seems to support such a contention. For example, when the Sex Pistol's "God Save the Queen" came under fire from the BBC, airplay on commercial radio stations and retail sales of the record increased dramatically (Frith). Furthermore, recording artist Frank Zappa warns that censoring objectionable popular music will only make the targeted audience want that music more. Zappa's intriguing notion provides the focus of this study.

There has been no basic empirical investigation of the relationship between the censorship of popular music and its perceived desirability. In this study, whether participants' knowledge of a popular album's censorship affected their desire to hear the material was evaluated experimentally in a field setting.

REVIEW OF LITERATURE

Controlling exposure to popular music through censorship is not a new idea. In surveying the history of the censorship of rock lyrics, McDonald notes that "an examination of the history of rock and roll reveals that the concerns of the Parent's Music Resource Center are certainly not new or original, since both individuals and organizations have long complained of the negative influence of rock and roll songs" (294). He further notes that numerous artists and songs have been the censorship targets of various entities. There has been no investigation of the effects of such actions.

The theoretical basis for examining the impacts of censorship can   5
be found in the literature of psychological reactance theory. Reactance theory holds that whenever a person's free choice is threatened the result is for him or her to want those choices even more (Brehm, *Theory of Psychological Reactance*). Thus, when freedom is lost (as when censoring an album prevents its purchase), the expected result would be reactance against the proscribing agent (the censor) and a measurable increase in the desire to possess the prohibited object (the censored album).

Reactance has been demonstrated in several social settings and over a wide span of ages (Brehm, *Psychological Reactance;* Brehm and Weintraub). The obstinate behavior of two-year-old children during this period is explained by their developing awareness of individual choice in the face of parental imposed limits on their behavior. Researchers also found evidence of reactance in adult consumer choices. Mazis and Mazis, Settle and Leslie examined the effects of a law which banned phosphates in all laundry detergents sold in two South Florida counties. The researchers discovered that consumers became more favorably disposed toward the detergents with phosphates only after the law was enacted. Similarly, a study by Broeder revealed that juries react favorably to information judges deemed inadmissible by valuing it more.

Adolescents (who comprise the largest audience for popular music) are especially vulnerable to psychological reactance. For example, when Driscoll, Davis and Lipetz studied adolescent romantic relationships they found that a teen's desire and love for a member of the opposite sex was positively related to the extent the relationship was marked by parental interference.

Investigation into the effects of censorship on opinion change, however, has been negligible. As Cialdini notes, "although much data exist concerning our reactions to observing various kinds of potentially censorable material—media violences, pornography, radical political rhetoric—there is surprisingly little evidence on our reaction to the censoring of material" (239). The first empirical studies in this area were conducted by Ashmore, Ramchandra and Jones. In this experiment, college students were told that a controversial speech they were scheduled to hear had been censored by administrators at the college. Compared to control groups, participants' opinion about the position advocated in the scheduled speech became more favorable, while their estimation of the college administration became less favorable. These findings were interpreted in terms of psychological reactance.

Worchel and Arnold confirmed these findings in a slightly modified version of Ashmore et al.'s experiment. Worchel and Arnold note that "censorship whether by a positive, negative, or neutral source, enhances the desires of the potential audience to hear the communication and causes them to change their opinion in the direction of the censored communication. . . . The experiment yielded results suggesting that, in some cases, the audience may lower its opinion of a group if it takes on the role of censor" (374). Later, Worchel, Arnold and Baker found that when students learned about the banning of a speech favoring coed dorms, they were more in favor of the idea of coed dorms. Finally, Zellinger, Fromkin, Speller and Kohn (1974) demonstrated similar results using acts of censorship such as age restrictions. In their study, college students were shown advertisements for a novel which included a warning that the book was restricted to those 21 years of age and older. When the students were later asked to state their feelings toward the restricted book, they not only wanted to read it more than those in the control group, their estimated enjoyment of the book also rose.

METHODOLOGY

The extant research regarding the results of censoring information is minimal. And, no known research has been conducted in the area   10 of popular music censorship. However, recent developments seem to call for inquiry in this area. The present study sought to investigate the following null hypothesis: There is no statistically significant difference between a potential music listeners' opinion toward an album when they know it is censored and when they do not.

A pretest-posttest with control group experiment was conducted involving 65 college students at a small Midwestern university. The pretest phase of the experiment began when two groups of randomly selected participants were given a slip of paper with the titles of nine rock albums arranged alphabetically by artist. Eight of the albums and artists were "legitimate," while one was fictitious. The subjects were then asked to rank order each of the albums according to which they would most like to hear. The statistical mean of each album was then calculated.

One week later, one-half the same subjects were told that in the previous session many students apparently were not familiar with each of the albums, and that they would be given some new information and asked to rank order the same ones again. This time, next to each album title and artist was a one-sentence description of the album's contents, e.g. "'Combat Rock' The Clash (This is the album containing 'Rock the Casbah' etc.)." The lone fictitious entry (the treatment) was "'By the Sword' by A.R.I. (This is the only album to have been declared legally obscene in Great Britain)." These descriptions were intended to serve as a point of reference for the subjects and to disguise the treatment. The other half of the pretest group was simply told the first set of rankings was lost and was asked to repeat their original rankings using the same information, the statistical mean of each album was calculated.

Afterwards, a paired *t*-Test was used to analyze the statistical significance of the differences between the pretest and posttest means of the fictitious album. The assumption was that the new information about the fictitious album being declared legally obscene in Great Britain would cause the subjects to desire to hear the album more than before they knew of the censorship. Thus, the hypothesized relationship between a potential listener's opinion toward an album they know is censored and one that is not could be empirically tested.

RESULTS AND DISCUSSION

The experiment found that there was a statistical difference in the pretest and posttest means of the fictitious album as ranked by the group receiving the treatment. The album's pretest mean was 6.30303, while its posttest mean was was 4.166667 ($t=4.94$, $p>.05$). The difference in the album's mean as ranked by the control group was not statistically significant (4.261539 vs 4.907692, $t=1.57$, $p>.05$). Hence the above stated null hypothesis was rejected.

The present study would seem to lend credence to the notion   *15*
that the censoring of rock music can lead to an increased desire on the
part of the listeners to hear the censored material. As noted above, one
explanation for this is psychological reactance theory, which holds that
people seek to re-establish freedoms forcibly taken from them.

The findings of this experiment contain several implications. First,
the study indicates that those seeking to control people's access to rock
music lyrics are actually making the problem worse by fostering a desire
to hear the banned communication. This is especially true when the present study's findings are linked with previous research which found adolescents to be particularly susceptible to psychological reactance (Driscoll,
Davis and Lipetz; Worchel and Arnold).

Second, the study lends some support to psychological reactance as
an explanation for the phenomenon, rather than balance theory. Other
researchers have suggested that if there is a "boomerang effect" when
censoring materials it is the result of subjects seeking to reconcile their
orientations toward the artist, the music, and the censor, as balance theory
would hold. However, Worchel and Arnold reported that their experiment indicated that such was not the case, and that reactance theory was
a better supported explanation for their discovery of a "boomerang effect." Similarly, the present study's findings can best be seen in light of
reactance theory.

Third, the study would seem to indicate that the lyrical content of
an album is possibly a factor in the subject's desire to hear a communication. Since the only knowledge subjects had of the fictitious album was
that it had been declared legally obscene in Great Britain, it stands to reason
that they were aware of the objectionable lyrical content, and that this was
the driving reason behind their desire to hear the communication. However, this conclusion is tenuous at best as previous research suggests that
listeners may not be attentive to lyrical content in any substantive way
(Prinsky and Rosenbaum). Interestingly, if this is so then the entire premise on which banning objectionable lyrics stands is dubious.

The present study also has some limitations which must be noted.
First, the method of revealing the subjects' desire to hear the communication is somewhat artificial. Asking the subjects to rank order an inclu-
sive list of albums according to their desire to hear them is different than
determining if they would actually purchase the album. Also, forcing
the subjects to rank order the albums does not necessarily mean that the
subject actually wants to hear a particular album. Third, there are other
things which might also determine the subject's desire to hear the communication. Perhaps the fictitious album did not fall into the subjects'
range of musical taste, Perhaps they had never heard of some of the albums even after additional information was given to them.

Future research is needed in this area. The present study, being   *20* one of the first in the area, is exploratory in nature. The conclusions reached here are tentative. Minimally, further research with a greater degree of generalizability is called for. In addition, the notion that censoring rock lyrics causes listeners to have lower esteem for the censor needs to be empirically tested. Experiments need to be designed which will control the other factors which might influence a person's desire to hear a popular music selection (other than knowledge that it was censored). Finally, the entire line of inquiry needs to be evaluated in light of research suggesting that listeners do not attend to rock lyrics.

In conclusion, the present study sought to test the relationship between a potential music listener's knowledge of a censored song and his/her desire to hear that communication. It was found that there is a statistically significant relationship between the two. In other words, there does seem to be a "boomerang effect" associated with censoring popular music albums. Potential listeners do have an increased desire to hear the censored material after they know it has been censored. While this is not good news for those seeking to widen the scope of censored materials, it does provide some preliminary scientifically-grounded answers to an area previously dominated by mere conjecture.

WORKS CITED

Ashmore, R.D., V. Ramchandra, and R.A. Jones. "Censorship as an Attitude Change Induction." Presented at Eastern Psychological Association Convention, 1971.

Brehm, J.W. *A Theory of Psychological Reactance.* New York: Academic P, 1966.

Brehm, S.S. "Psychological Reactance and the Attractiveness of Unattainable Objects: Sex Differences in Children's Responses to an Elimination of Freedom." *Sex Roles* 7 (1981): 937–49.

Brehm, S.S., and M. Weintraub. "Physical Barriers and Psychological Reactance: Two-year-olds' Responses to Threats to Freedom." *Journal of Personality and Social Psychology* 35 (1977): 830–36.

Broder, D. "The University of Chicago Jury Project." *Nebraska Law Review* 38 (1959): 744–60.

Cialdini, R.B. *Influence: Science and Practice,* 2nd. ed. Glenview, IL: Scott Foresman, 1989.

Driscoll, R., K.E. Davis, and M.E. Lipetz, "Parental Influence and Romantic Love: The Romeo and Juliet Effect." *Journal of Personality and Social Psychology* 24 (1972): 1–10.

Frith, S. *Sound Effects: Youth, Leisure, and the Politics of Rock 'n' Roll.* New York: Pantheon, 1981.

Mazis, M.B. "Antipollution Measures and Psychological Reactance Theory: A Field Study." *Journal of Personality and Social Psychology* 31 (1975): 954–66.

Mazis, M.B., R.B. Settle, and D.C. Leslie. "Elimination of Phosphate Detergents and Psychological Reactance." *Journal of Marketing Research* 10 (1973): 390–95.

McDonald, J. "Censoring Rock Lyrics: A Historical Analysis of the Debate." *Youth & Society* 19 (1988): 294–313.

Prinsky, L.E., and J.L. Rosenbaum. "Leer-ics or Lyrics: Teenage Impressions of Rock 'n' roll." *Youth and Society* 18 (1987): 384–97.

Worchel, S., and S. Arnold. "The Effects of Censorship and Attractiveness of the Censor on Attitude Change." *Journal of Experimental Social Psychology* 9 (1973): 365–77.

Worchel, S., S. Arnold, and M. Baker. "The Effect of Censorship on Attitude Change: The Influence of Censor and Communicator Characteristics." *Journal of Applied Social Psychology* 5 (1975): 222–39.

Zappa, F. Statement to congress, U.S. Senate, 99th Congress, 1st Session, Committee on Commerce, Science and Transportation. *Record labeling.* Hearing, Sept. 19, 1985 (S. Hrg. 99/529). Washington D.C.: Government Printing Office, 1985.

Zellinger, D.A., H.L. Fromkin, D.E. Speller, and C.A. Kohn. *A Commodity Theory Analysis of the Effects of Age Restrictions on Pornographic Materials.* Paper No. 440, Lafayette, IN: Purdue U, Institute for Research in the Behavioral, Economic and Management Sciences, 1974.

ICE-T: THE ISSUE IS SOCIAL RESPONSIBILITY

MICHAEL KINSLEY

How did the company that publishes this magazine come to produce a record glorifying the murder of police?   *1*

> I got my 12-gauge sawed off
> I got my headlights turned off
> I'm 'bout to bust some shots off
> I'm 'bout to dust some cops off . . .
> Die, Die, Die Pig, Die!

So go the lyrics to *Cop Killer* by the rapper Ice-T on the album *Body Count.* The album is released by Warner Bros. Records, part of the Time Warner media and entertainment conglomerate.

In a *Wall Street Journal* op-ed piece laying out the company's position, Time Warner Co-CEO Gerald Levin makes two defenses. First, Ice-T's *Cop Killer* is misunderstood. "It doesn't incite or glorify violence . . . It's his fictionalized attempt to get inside a character's head . . . *Cop Killer* is no more a call for gunning down the police than *Frankie and Johnny* is a summons for jilted lovers to shoot one another." Instead of "finding ways to silence the messenger," we should be "heeding the anguished cry contained in his message."

This defense is self-contradictory. *Frankie and Johnny* does not pretend to have a political "message" that must be "heeded." If *Cop Killer* has a message, it is that the murder of policemen is a justified response to police brutality. And not in self-defense, but in premeditated acts of revenge against random cops. ("I know your family's grievin'—f___ 'em.")

Killing policemen is a good thing—that is the plain meaning of   *5* the words, and no "larger understanding" of black culture, the rage of the streets or anything else can explain it away. This is not Ella Fitzgerald telling a story in a song. As in much of today's popular music, the line between performer and performance is purposely blurred. These are political sermonettes clearly intended to endorse the sentiments being expressed. Tracy Morrow (Ice-T) himself has said, "I scared the police, and they need to be scared." That seems clear.

The company's second defense of *Cop Killer* is the classic one of free expression: "We stand for creative freedom. We believe that the worth of what an artist or journalist has to say does not depend on preapproval from a government official or a corporate censor."

Of course Ice-T has the right to say whatever he wants. But that doesn't require any company to provide him an outlet. And it doesn't relieve a company of responsibility for the messages it chooses to promote. Judgment is not "censorship." Many an "anguished cry" goes unrecorded. This one was recorded, and promoted, because a successful artist under contract wanted to record it. Nothing wrong with making money, but a company cannot take the money and run from the responsibility.

The founder of *Time,* Henry Luce, would snort at the notion that his company should provide a value-free forum for the exchange of ideas. In Luce's system, editors were supposed to make value judgments and promote the truth as they saw it. *Time* has moved far from its old Lucean rigidity—far enough to allow for dissenting essays like this one. That evolution is a good thing, as long as it's not a handy excuse for abandoning all standards.

No commercial enterprise need agree with every word that appears under its corporate imprimatur. If Time Warner now intends to be "a global force for encouraging the confrontation of ideas," that's swell. But a policy of allowing diverse viewpoints is not a moral free pass. Pro and con on national health care is one thing; pro and con on killing policemen is another.

A bit of sympathy is in order for Time Warner. It is indeed a   *10*
"global force" with media tentacles around the world. If it imposes rigorous standards and values from the top, it gets accused of corporate censorship. If it doesn't, it gets accused of moral irresponsibility. A dilemma.
But someone should have thought of that before deciding to become a
global force.

And another genuine dilemma. Whatever the actual merits of *Cop
Killer,* if Time Warner withdraws the album now the company will be
perceived as giving in to outside pressure. That is a disastrous precedent
for a global conglomerate.

The Time-Warner merger of 1989 was supposed to produce corporate "synergy": the whole was supposed to be more than the sum of
the parts. The *Cop Killer* controversy is an example of negative synergy.
People get mad at *Cop Killer* and start boycotting the movie *Batman
Returns.* A reviewer praises *Cop Killer* ("Tracy Morrow's poetry takes a
switchblade and deftly slices life's jugular," etc.), and *Time* is accused of
corruption instead of mere foolishness. Senior Time Warner executives
find themselves under attack for—and defending—products of their
company they neither honestly care for nor really understand, and doubt-
less weren't even aware of before controversy hit.

Anyway, it's absurd to discuss *Cop Killer* as part of the "confrontation of ideas"—or even as an authentic anguished cry of rage from the
ghetto. *Cop Killer* is a cynical commercial concoction, designed to titillate
its audience with imagery of violence. It merely exploits the authentic
anguish of the inner city for further titilation. Tracy Morrow is in business for a buck, just like Time Warner. *Cop Killer* is an excellent joke
on the white establishment, of which the company's anguished apologia
("Why can't we hear what rap is trying to tell us?") is the punch line.

ICE-T: THE ISSUE IS FREE SPEECH

BARBARA EHRENREICH

Ice-T's song *Cop Killer* is as bad as they come. This is black an-   *1*
ger—raw, rude and cruel—and one reason the song's so shocking is that
in postliberal America, black anger is virtually taboo. You won't find it
on TV, not on the *McLaughlin Group* or *Crossfire,* and certainly not in the
placid features of Arsenio Hall or Bernard Shaw. It's been beaten back
into the outlaw subcultures of rap and rock, where, precisely because it
is taboo, it sells. And the nastier it is, the faster it moves off the shelves.
As Ice-T asks in another song on the same album, "Goddamn what a
brotha gotta do/ To get a message through/ To the red, white and blue?"

But there's a gross overreaction going on, building to a veritable paroxysm of white denial. A national boycott has been called, not just of the song or Ice-T, but of all Time Warner products. The President himself has denounced Time Warner as "wrong" and Ice-T as "sick." Ollie North's Freedom Alliance has started a petition drive aimed at bringing Time-Warner executives to trial for "sedition and anarchy."

Much of this is posturing and requires no more courage than it takes to stand up in a VFW hall and condemn communism or crack. Yes, *Cop Killer* is irresponsible and vile. But Ice-T is as right about some things as he is righteous about the rest. And ultimately, he's not even dangerous— least of all to the white power structure his songs condemn.

The "danger" implicit in all the uproar is of empty-headed, suggestible black kids, crouching by their boom boxes, waiting for the word. But what Ice-T's fans know and his detractors obviously don't is that *Cop Killer* is just one more entry in pop music's long history of macho hyperbole and violent boast. Flip to the classic-rock station, and you might catch the Rolling Stones announcing "the time is right of violent revoloo-shun!" from their 1968 hit *Street Fighting Man*. And where were the defenders of our law-enforcement officers when a white British group, the Clash, taunted its fans with lyrics: "When they kick open your front door/How you gonna come/With your hands on your head/Or on the trigger of your gun?"

"Die, Die, Die Pig" is strong speech, but the Constitution protects *5* strong speech, and it's doing so this year more aggressively than ever. The Supreme Court has just downgraded cross burnings to the level of bonfires and ruled that it's no crime to throw around verbal grenades like "nigger" and "kike." Where are the defenders of decorum and social stability when prime-time demagogues like Howard Stern deride African Americans as "spear chuckers?"

More to the point, young African Americans are not so naive and suggestible that they have to depend on a compact disc for their sociology lessons. To paraphrase another song from another era, you don't need a rap song to tell which way the wind is blowing. Black youths know that the police are likely to see them through a filter of stereotypes as miscreants and potential "cop killers." They are aware that a black youth is seven times as likely to be charged with a felony as a white youth who has committed the same offense, and is much more likely to be imprisoned.

They know, too, that in a shameful number of cases, it is the police themselves who indulge in "anarchy" and violence. The U.S. Justice Department has received 47,000 complaints of police brutality in the past six years, and Amnesty International has just issued a report on police brutality in Los Angeles, documenting 40 cases of "torture or cruel, inhuman or degrading treatment."

Menacing as it sounds, the fantasy in *Cop Killer* is the fantasy of the powerless and beaten down—the black man who's been hassled once too often ("A pig stopping me for nothin'!"), spread-eagled against a police car, pushed around. It's not a "responsible" fantasy (fantasies seldom are). It's not even a very creative one. In fact, the sad thing about *Cop Killer* is that it falls for the cheapest, more conventional image of rebellion that our culture offers: the lone gunman spraying fire from his AK-47. This is not "sedition"; it's the familiar, all-American, Hollywood-style pornography of violence.

Which is why Ice-T is right to say he's no more dangerous than George Bush's pal Arnold Schwarzenegger, who wasted an army of cops in *Terminator 2.* Images of extraordinary cruelty and violence are marketed every day, many of far less artistic merit than *Cop Killer.* This is our free market of ideas and images, and it shouldn't be any less free for a black man than for other purveyors of "irresponsible" sentiments, from David Duke to Andrew Dice Clay.

Just, please, don't dignify Ice-T's contribution with the word sedition. The past masters of sedition—men like George Washington, Toussaint-Louverture, Fidel Castro or Mao Zedong, all of whom led and won armed insurrections—would be unimpressed by *Cop Killer* and probably saddened. They would shake their heads and mutter words like "infantile" and "adventurism." They might point out that the cops are hardly a noble target, being, for the most part, honest working stiffs who've got stuck with the job of patrolling ghettos ravaged by economic decline and official neglect.   *10*

There is a difference, the true seditionist would argue, between a revolution and a gesture of macho defiance. Gestures are cheap. They feel good, they blow off some rage. But revolutions, violent or otherwise, are made by people who have learned how to count very slowly to ten.

———

FREE SPEECH: LYRICS, LIBERTY, AND LICENSE

Sam Brownback

Good afternoon. I want to thank the City Club of Cleveland for its hospitality, and the students who run the Youth Forum for the invitation, their top-notch administrative skills, and the opportunity to speak to you today.   *1*

I want to talk with you today about music and freedom about lyrics, liberty and license. This is an issue that is important to me—as it is, I suspect, important to you. I can't think of a more fitting place for this discussion here, at a forum dedicated to upholding the principle of free speech, in Cleveland, the home of the Rock and Roll Hall of Fame.

As many of you know, I recently held a Senate hearing on the impact of violent music lyrics on young people. During this hearing, we heard a variety of witnesses testify on the effects of music lyrics that glorified rape, sexual torture, violence and murder. Some of these lyrics are almost unbelievably awful but they are backed by huge, powerful, prestigious corporations. I have grown more and more concerned about the content and the impact of these lyrics. And I have publicly criticized the entertainment executives who produce, promote, and profit from such music.

I am also the only Senator on the Commerce Committee to vote against a very popular bill that would coerce TV stations into labeling their programs.

I publicly opposed V-chip legislation. I have consistently voted   5
against any sort of government involvement in regulating or rating music or television.

Some people don't think the two go together. They think that if you talk about some music lyrics being degrading and violent, then you must be in favor of censorship. Others think that if you vote against various government restrictions on television programs, or music content, you must approve of those programs and songs. Both views are mistaken.

And today, I'd like to talk about legislating in a way to maximize freedom, and agitating for civility and decency, and why the two not only can go together, but should—and indeed, if we are to preserve freedom, they must.

Most of you here have strong ideas about music. As indeed, you should. Music is powerful. It changes our mood, shapes our experience, affects our thoughts, alters our pulse, touches our lives. The rhythm, the beat, and the lyrics all impress us with their message. Thousands of years ago, the great philosopher Plato stated, "Musical training is a more potent instrument than any other, because rhythm and harmony find their way into the inward places of the soul, on which they mightily fasten."

As such, music lyrics have profound public consequences. In many ways, the music industry is more influential than anything that happens in Washington. After all, most people spend a lot more time listening to music than watching C-Span or reading the newspaper. They're more likely to recognize musicians than Supreme Court Justices. Most of us spend more time thinking about music than laws, bills, and policies. And that's probably a good thing.

And as many of you know, no one spends more time listening to   10
music than young people. In fact, one recent study conducted by the Carnegie Foundation concluded that the average teenager listens to music around four hours a day. In contrast, less than an hour is spent on

homework or reading, less than 20 minutes a day is spent talking to Mom, and less than five minutes is spent talking with Dad. If this is true, there are a lot of people who spend more time listening to shock-rock artist Marilyn Manson or Snoop Doggy Dogg than Mom or Dad. In fact, Marilyn Manson himself said: "Music is such a powerful medium now. The kids don't even know who the President is, but they know what's on MTV. I think if anyone like Hitler or Mussolini were alive now, they would have to be rock stars."

In short, because of the power of music, the time we spend listening to it, and the potency of its messages, music has a powerful public impact. It affects us, not only privately, but publicly. It helps shape our attitudes and assumptions, and thus, our decisions and behavior—all of which has a public dimension, and merits public debate.

Frankly, I believe there needs to be more public discourse over music. It is too important to ignore. Its influence reaches around the world. American rock and rap are popular exports. They are listened to by billions, in virtually every nation on earth. And for good or bad, our music shapes the way in which many people around the world view the U.S.—American music is the most pervasive (and loudest) ambassador we have. Unfortunately, its message is too often a destructive one.

Over the past few years, I have grown concerned about the popularity of some lyrics—lyrics which glorify violence and debase women. Some recent best-selling albums have included graphic descriptions of murder, torture, and rape. Women are objectified, often in the most obscene and degrading ways. Songs such as Prodigy's single "Smack My Bitch Up" or "Don't Trust a Bitch" by the group, 'Mo Thugs, encourage animosity and even violence toward women. The alternative group Nine Inch Nails enjoyed both critical and commercial success with their song "Big Man with a Gun" which describes forcing a woman into oral sex and shooting her in the head at pointblank range.

Shock-rock bands such as Marilyn Manson or Cannibal Corpse go even further, with lyrics describing violence, rape, and torture. Consider just a few song titles by the group Cannibal Corpse; "Orgasm by Torture," or "Stripped, Raped and Strangled." As their titles indicate, the lyrics to these songs celebrate hideous crimes against women.

Many of you may already know the kind of lyrics I am talking *15* about. If not, it is useful to read some of them—they won't be hard to find; they are quite popular. Then ask youself: what are the real-world affects of these lyrics? What do these lyrics celebrate, and what do they ridicule or denounce? What are the consequences of glorifying violence and glamorizing rape? Have record companies behaved responsibly when they produce music that debases women? You and your friends may come up with different answers. But they are good questions to think about. And I hope recording industry executives think about them as well.

It is a simple fact of human nature that what we hear and see, what we experience, affects our thoughts, our emotions, and our behavior. If it did not, commercials wouldn't exist, and anyone who ever spent a dollar on advertising would be a complete fool. But advertising is a multibillion dollar business because it works. It creates an appetite for things we don't need, it motivates us to buy things we may not have otherwise. What we see and hear changes how we act.

Now think back to the music we have been talking about. How do these lyrics affect their fans? Different people will be affected in different ways. Some teens are more vulnerable than others. Young people who grow up in strong families, going to good schools, with adults who are committed to them, are probably going to be just fine. But let's consider what happens in some of America's inner cities, where many young men grow up without fathers, without good schools, surrounded by violence—how does this affect the way they think about, and treat women? Moreover, there have already been several studies done that have pointed to a loss of self-esteem among girls and young women. How does the fact that some of the best-selling albums feature songs that refer to them exclusively as "those, bitches and sluts" affect them?

There are no easy answers to these questions. It is impossible to quantify the ways in which such lyrics affect us. But it is equally impossible to believe they have no effect at all.

Of course, most rock and rap do not have hyperviolent or perverse lyrics. In the grand scale of things, it is a small number of songs from an even smaller number of bands that produce these sort of lyrics. They are the exception, not the rule.

It is also true that people will disagree over which music is offensive. Some people thought the Beach Boys were a problem, and some think the Spice Girls are. I do not happen to be one of them. There will always be songs about which reasonable people with good judgment will disagree. *20*

But there should also be some things that we can all agree upon. And one of those things is that music which glorifies rape, violence and bigotry is wrong. It may be constitutionally protected. The huge entertainment corporations that produce, promote and profit from this sort of record may have a right to do so. But it is not the right thing to do.

So this past November, I held a hearing on the impact of music lyrics which glorified violence and debased women. We heard from a variety of witnesses—a parent, a representative from the American Academy of Pediatrics, a Stanford Professor, the head of the Recording Industry Association, and the head of the National Political Congress of Black Women, who has campaigned against gangsta rap. Should any of you want to see the record of the hearing, you may do so by logging on to my senate web site.

I held this hearing for two reasons: 1) to raise public awareness of some of these lyrics, so that potential consumers can make more informed judgments before they buy the music, 2) to examine, through hearing from witnesses from the medical and academic communities, the impact of such lyrics on youth attitudes and well-being.

It is a particularly important time to do so. Actual and virtual violence have dramatically increased over the last few decades. Over the last thirty years, violent juvenile crime has jumped over 500%. Teen suicide has tripled.

Crimes against women have increased. Casual teen drug use has   *25* jumped by almost 50 percent in the last four years alone.

There is also a sense that we have lost ground in ways that defy easy measurement. There is a feeling that we as a society have grown coarser, meaner, more alienated. Violence seems not only more widespread but less shocking. We have become more accustomed, and more tolerant, of tragedy, violence, and hate.

At the same time, there has been a marked increase in violence and misogyny in popular music. Now, this is not to say that music violence was the cause of real-life violence. Music is only one slice of the entertainment world, a small part of the popular culture. Whatever impact music has on our attitudes and behavior is bound to be complex and variant. But the best way, I believe—then and now—to determine what that impact is, what influence violent lyrics exert, is to encourage research, debate and discussion.

During the hearing, we did not call for censorship. We did not propose, consider, or tolerate any restriction of free speech. We did not ask for legislation, regulation, litigation, or any other machination of government that would prohibit even the most racist, violent antiwoman lyrics. When it comes to First Amendment issues, I vote as a libertarian. I have voted against labels, against restrictions, against government meddling. But it is not enough to merely legislate in a mannner to protect freedom. It is also necessary to agitate for the cultural conditions that safeguard freedom. Let me explain what I mean.

For free societies to endure, there must be a distinction between what is allowed and what is honored. I believe that the First Amendment assures the widest possible latitude in allowing various forms of speech— including offensive, obnoxious speech. But the fact that certain forms of speech should be allowed does not mean that they should be honored, or given respectability. There are many forms of speech that should be thoroughly critized, even as they are protected. Freedom of expression is not immunity from criticism.

The proper response to offensive speech is criticism—not cen-   *30* sorship, and not apathy. Vigorous criticism of the perverse, hateful, and violent refects a willingness on the part of citizens to take ideas seriously, evaluate them accordingly, and engage them directly. A cultural predisposition to care about ideas and to judge between them, while protecting the liberty of others, is the best bulwark of a free society. A citizenry that evaluates ideas, that discerns the true from the false, that values reason over reaction, that affirms that which is edifying, and that refutes that which is wrong is exactly the society most likely to value, to have, and to keep free speech.

What we honor says as much about out national character as what we allow. There is an old saying "Tell me what you love, and I'll tell you who you are." The same can be said of societies, as well as individuals. What we honor and esteem as a people reflects and affects our culture. We grow to resemble what we honor, we become less like what we disparage. What we choose to honor, then, forecasts our cultural condition.

That is important, because there are cultural conditions which make democracy possible, markets open, and societies free. Democracy cannot endure in a society that has lost respect for the law or an interest in self-government. Societies become less free when they become more violent. The more culturally chaotic we become, the more restrictions, laws and regulations are imposed to maintain order.

Glorifying violence in popular music is dangerous, because a society that glorifies violence will grow more violent. Similarly, when we refuse to criticize music that debases women, we sent the message that treating women as chattel is not something to be upset about. Record companies that promote violent music implicitly push the idea that more people should listen to, purchase, and enjoy the sounds of slaughter. When MTV named Marilyn Manson the "best new artist of the year" last year, they held Manson up as an example to be aspired and emulated. Promoting violence as entertainment corrodes our nation from within.

This is not a new idea. Virtually all of the founding Fathers agreed—even assumed—that nations rise and fall based on what they honor and what they discourage. Samuel Adams, an outspoken free speech advocate, said the following: "A General dissolution of principles and manners will more surely overthrow the liberties of America than the whole force of the common enemy."

Unfortunately, in many circles, liberty is being redefined as "license"—the idea that anything goes, that all speech is morally equivalent. According to this view, we cannot judge or criticize speech no matter how offensive we may find it. After all, what is offensive to one person, the reasoning goes, may be acceptable, even enjoyable to someone else. Thus, the idea of honoring certain forms of speech and stigmatizing others become seen as infringements on liberty. This assumes that to have freedom of speech, you can't give a rip over what is said—and that tolerance is achieved by apathy. Their motto can be summed up in one word: "whatever."

This is dead wrong. A philosophy of "whatever" is poison to the body politic. Civility, decency, courtesy, compassion, and respect should

35

not be matters of indifference to us. We should care about these things—care about them deeply. We should allow both honorable and offensive forms of speech. But just as certainly, we should honor that which is honorable, and criticise that which is not. If we, as a society, come to the place where we think anything goes, the first thing to go will be freedom.

The great southern author Walker Percy once stated that his greatest fear for our future was that of "seeing America, with all its great strength and beauty and freedom . . . gradually subside into decay through default and be defeated . . . from within by weariness, boredom, cynicism, greed and in the end, helplessness before its great problems."

I am optimistic about our future, but his point is an important one. America is at a place in history where our great enemies have been defeated.

Communism, with all of its shackles on the human spirit, has fallen. The Cold War is over. Our economy is strong, our incomes up, our expectations high. We are, in a sense, the only remaining world superpower.

Certainly, the future looks bright. But our continued success is not   40
a historical certainty. It will be determined by the character of our nation—by the condition of our culture as much as our economy, or our policies. What we value, and what we disparage, are good predictors to what we soon shall be.

This is why I have both legislated in a libertarian manner, and agitated against hateful, racist, violent music lyrics. For those of us who are concerned about the loss of civility in society, and the glorification of hate, violence, and misogyny in popular music, our goal must be not to coerce, but to persuade. We should aim to change hearts and minds, rather than laws. Analyzing, evaluating, and sometimes criticizing lyrics is not only compatible with, but essential to, liberty.

May rock roll on, and freedom ring.

————

SUPPORT FOR CENSORSHIP OF VIOLENT AND MISOGYNIC RAP LYRICS
An Analysis of the Third-Person Effect

Douglas M. McLeod, William P. Eveland, Jr., Amy I. Nathanson

Recent calls for censorship or rap music have demonstrated the need to rest the perceptual and especially the behavioral components of Davison's third-person effect hypothesis. The hypothesis states that people perceive media content to have a greater impact on others than on themselves (perceptual component), and that these perceptions lead people to take actions, such as censorship, to prevent the impact (behavioral component). Results of a survey of college students ($N = 202$) using rap lyrics as the context revealed strong support for both components of the hypothesis. Limited support was found for the social distance corollary of the perceptual component, while the knowledge corollary of the perceptual component was not supported. A new target corollary to the perceptual component was proposed; it predicts that those groups seen as likely targets of a communication will produce larger third-person perceptions than will generalized others.

[Censors] are never worried about their own ability to differentiate between fantasy and reality, to resist being seized by uncontrollable urges to commit violent or immoral acts, or to remain decent, law-abiding human beings who do not wish to hurt or degrade others. But they are *very* worried about *your* ability to do so.

—*(Dority, 1991, p. 44)*

During the last decade or so in the United States, may people have   1 expressed concern that rap music—especially rap with violent or misogynic lyrics—is harmful to not only the youth of society but also to society itself (Leo, 1993). Prominent politicians, including presidential candidates in the 1996 primary campaign, have called for record companies to engage in self-censorship to protect people from the negative effects of antisocial lyrics ("Time Warner," 1995). In response to such demands, some record company executives have cloaked themself in the First Amendment (Bowman, 1992) and some have made concessions such as labeling or self-censorship (Dority, 1991; "Time Warner," 1995). The discourse surrounding this controversy is rarely based on research about the negative impact of rap music. Instead, it is founded primarily on perceptions of rap's powerful harmful effects on others. Research on the third-person effect suggests that individuals who advocate censorship believe in powerful effects on others but, ironically, not necessarily on themselves. In short, many people believe that they are able to resist negative media effects but that others are less capable (or willing) to do so and must be protected by censorship.

Formalized over a decade ago by public opinion researcher W. Phillips Davison, the third-person effect hypothesis states:

People will tend to overestimate the influence that mass communications have on the attitudes and behavior of others. More specifically, individuals who are members of an audience that is exposed to a persuasive communication . . . will expect the communication to have a greater effect on others than themselves. And whether or not these individuals are among the *ostensible* audience for the message, the impact that they expect this communication to have on others may lead them to take some action. (Davison, 1983, p. 3)

The third-person effect hypothesis has two components: perceptual and behavioral. The perceptual component (or third-person *perceptions*), which has received frequent research attention and considerable empirical support, states that people will estimate the effects of media messages on themselves to be less than the effects on others. This first component of the third-person effect, however, is at most an interesting perceptual phenomenon. The perceptual tendency predicted by the third-person effect becomes more meaningful if it is linked with real-world consequences as hypothesized by Davison.

The behavioral component, which has typically been ignored by theorists and rarely tested by researchers (Mutz, 1994), proposes that these perceptions of media impact will lead to behavior intended to protect the public from perceived negative effects. Other students have suggested that third-person perceptions held by public officials can lead them to take policy actions to quell public outcries (Cook et al., 1983). Although third-person perceptions may have many implications for public policy, the present study examines one behavioral component—expressed support for censorship of allegedly harmful media content.

The purpose of this analysis, which is part of a larger study of third-person effect, is to replicate findings on third-person perceptions and to add to the small but growing pool of evidence on the behavioral component. This study examines the relationship between third-person perceptions in the context of violent and misogynic rap lyrics and support for censorship of this content.

LITERATURE REVIEW AND HYPOTHESES

Evidence of Third-Person Effects:
The Perceptual Component

The past decade has brought about numerous tests of the perceptual component of the third-person effect hypothesis using several different methodologies, including sample surveys and experiments. Researchers have examined third-person perceptions from media content such as libelous newspaper articles, pornography, the television movie *Amerika,* product advertisements, public service announcements, and various forms of political communication.

According to Perloff (1993), 13 of the 14 studies on the third-person effect at that time found support for the perceptual component of the hypothesis. Recent research has continued to demonstrate support (e.g., Gunther & Hua, 1966; Lee & Yang, 1996; Price, Tewksbury, & Huang, 1996). In the initial formulation, Davison (1983) suggested that third-person perceptions were caused by the overestimation of effects on others but relatively accurate estimates of effects on self. For the most part, the literature indicates that people do in fact overestimate the effects of media content on others (Cohen et al., 1988; Gunther, 1991; Gunther & Thorson, 1992; Perloff et al., 1992; Price et al., 1996). This is consistent with the literature on pluralistic ignorance showing that people are typically inaccurate in their perceptions of the climate of opinion (e.g., Miller & Prentice, 1994; O'Gorman, 1986; Toch & Klofas, 1984). However, the evidence on whether people can accurately assess media effects on themselves is mixed, with some studies finding underestimates of effects on self (Cohen et al., 1988), some finding relatively accurate estimates (Gunther, 1991; Perloff et al., 1992), and some finding overestimates (Gunther & Thorson, 1992).

One condition for the perceptual effect is that the media impact must be perceived to be negative by respondents (Gunther & Mundy, 1993). This condition is especially important because it supports assertions (e.g., Gunther & Mundy, 1993; Gunther & Thorson, 1992) that third-person perceptions are a special case of the "it can't happen to me" syndrome, identified in social psychology under terms such as "unrealistic optimism" (Weinstein, 1980). In fact, messages believed to produce positive effects may cause a "reverse third-person effect" (Gunther & Thorson, 1992). Both third-person perceptions and reverse third-person perceptions can be explained by a general tendency for people to fall prey to some form of self-serving bias (e.g., Brown, 1986; Zuckerman, 1979), which leads people to compare themselves favorably to others for ego enhancement reasons.[1]

We expected to replicate previous findings of the perceptual component of the third-person effect. Using antisocial messages in the form of either violent or misogynic rap lyrics, in which we presume respondents to perceive negative effects, we predicted the following:

H1: Perceived effects of antisocial rap lyrics on others will be greater than perceived effects on self.

Davison (1983) noted, "In the view of those trying to evaluate the effects of a communication, its greatest impact will not be on 'me' or 'you,' but on 'them'—the third persons" (p. 3). Consistent with Davison's intuition, Cohen et al. (1988) found that the size of the third-person perception differential increased as the social distance between self and other increased. That is, respondents assessed increasingly larger media impact as the "other" was changed from "other Stanford students" to "other Californians" to "public opinion at large."

Since this initial research, several studies have addressed the social   *10*
distance corollary of the third-person perception. Gunther (1991) found
that University of Minnesota students perceived greater effects on "other
Minnesota residents" than on "other University of Minnesota students,"
which is consistent with the social distance corollary. However, Cohen
and Davis (1991), using "people from your home state," "people from
your region of the country," and "people in the U.S. in general" as the
comparison groups in their study, found no support for increased third-
person perceptions for more socially distant groups.

Despite Cohen and Davis's (1991) null findings, we expected to find
an effect of social distance on the strength of third-person perceptions.
Because individuals are likely to believe they are more similar to members
of their own social group than to members of other social groups (Brewer
& Kramer, 1985), it is possible that the size of the third-person effect
will increase as the social distance between self and other increases. We
expected that respondents would perceive the social distance between
themselves and other groups to increase as they moved from students at
their own university (due to similarities in age, geography, and academic
interests) to youths from New York and Los Angeles (due to age similarities) to the "average person," an analog to Cohen et al.'s (1988) "public
opinion at large" or Cohen and Davis's (1991) "people in the U.S. in
general." Therefore, our predictions are informed by the social distance
corollary as follows:

H2: The size of the third-person perception will increase as the social distance of the comparison group increases.

Finally, research hints that third-person perceptions are linked to
perceived knowledge about the content area (Lasorsa, 1989). However,
measures of actual knowledge have been found to be unrelated to third-
person perceptions (Lasorsa, 1989; Price & Tewksbury, 1994). The logic
behind this knowledge corollary is that perceptions of oneself as more
knowledgeable about a topic should lead to perceptions that one is better
able to defend against negative media effects and thus is less easily influenced than novices. Therefore, we predicted that students who perceived
themselves to be more knowledgeable about rap music would be particularly susceptible to third-person perceptions.

H3: Perceived knowledge of rap music will be positively associated
with third-person perceptions.

Evidence of Third-Person Effects:
The Behavioral Component

The behavioral component states that third-person perceptions will
lead to actions to redress negative media effects, such as censorship (or

support for censorship) or public policy change (Davison, 1983). Despite the fact that most studies have tested this hypothesis as third-person perceptions (not simply perceived effects on self or others), few have explained why this is the appropriate test. We assert that the reason one would expect the third-person effect differential to be a stronger predictor of censorship attitudes than either of the perceived effects on self or perceived effects on other components is based on the nature of people who support or engage in censorship.

Salmon (1989, p. 38) has noted that social interventions that "do not consider the persons's capacity to make an informed decision "are instances of "strong paternalism." In our view, censorship of media content is the epitome of strong paternalism in social intervention because it inherently assumes that people are not capable of screening content for themselves and, if they are exposed, they (or society) will be harmed in some way. We believe that censorship is based on this paternalistic foundation.

It has been argued that censorship is supported by people in order   *15*
to protect relatively "helpless" others (e.g., Dority, 1991; Frohnmayer, 1994). Censorship advocates do not see a need for censorship for themselves because they either are smart enough to resist negative effects or can simply avoid harmful media content when necessary. In the view of a censor, it is those who are not "smart enough" or "wholesome" enough to do the right thing who need the protection that censorship provides. This seems to set up a necessary comparison of self and other. Indeed, Frohnmayer (1994, p. 47) discusses censorship as being closely linked to "the urge to be ethically pure, morally superior," especially in times of social stress. Similarly, Dority (1991) states, "The censor's most visible and striking characteristic is a flagrantly displayed belief in his or her own moral and spiritual superiority" (p. 44). Davison (1983) himself notes, "Insofar as faith and morals are concerned, at least, it is difficult to find a censor who will admit to having been adversely affected by the information whose dissemination is to be prohibited. . . . It is the general public that must be protected" (p. 14). In all of these comments about the characteristics of censors it is clear that there is a comparison with others, since superiority is an inherently relative concept. Thus it should not be simple perceived effects of media content on others but the perceived effects of media on others relative to oneself that spurs people to support censorship.

The paternalistic perception of superiority may be another manifestation of the illusion of control (Langer, 1975) or general self-serving bias (Brown, 1986), of which, as we noted above, the third-person effect may be a special case. That is, censors believe that the content is not dangerous to themselves personally (because they are immune to influence) but that others lack the self-control, knowledge, intelligence, goodness, and so on to protect themselves from harmful media content. Just as third-person perceptions may be founded on a need to maintain an illusion of control or superiority over others, Frohnmayer (1994) notes that censorship is also "an issue of control, of power over what others will or will not have the opportunity to experience" (p. 47). It may be, then, that this illusion of control that generates third-person perceptions could also lead people to want to take control over others, meaning that the link between third-person perceptions and behaviors is spurious. Unfortunately, we will not be able to test the possibility of spuriousness in the present study.

Gunther (1995) argues that people consider the level of media impact on themselves—whatever the level that happens to be—to be acceptable. Their judgment of an unacceptable level of influence is made by comparison to the acceptable (presumably inconsequential) impact on themselves. The more unacceptable the impact on others—that is, the greater relative to themselves—the more likely they are to support censorship to protect others. This interpretation is consistent with our paternalism argument. Essentially, people feel that the level of effect media have upon themselves is acceptable, but any deviation from this level toward greater effects is harmful. The greater the deviation from effects on themselves, the greater the need for censorship.

In summary, it is not simply the perceived impact of media content on oneself or on others that should lead to support for censorship. Instead, support for censorship should be most prevalent among those who hold the paternalistic or morally superior perception that they are relatively immune to the negative effects of media content compared to the masses (the third-person perception).[2]

Only a few studies have directly tested the behavioral component of the third-person effect hypothesis (Mutz, 1994), and only very recently have researchers tested the relationship between third-person perceptions and the desire for censorship. Thompson, Chaffee, and Oshagan (1990) found that perceptions of the negative effects of pornography on others were *negatively* associated with desire for censorship, but they did not fully interpret what they admitted was an unexpected finding. Although this finding would seem contrary to the third-person effect hypothesis, their research did not actually test the relationship between third-person perceptions and desire for censorship. As we have noted, the desire for censorship should be related to the *difference* between perceived effects on self and perceived effects on others (i.e., third-person perceptions), so Thompson et al.'s finding should not be interpreted as evidence against the behavioral component of the third-person effect hypothesis.

Rucinski and Salmon (1990), however, did test the behavioral component of the third-person effect by examining the relationship between third-person perceptions and support for independent monitoring

20

of political media content. Although their dependent variable is not truly censorship of the offensive media content, the finding is applicable. They found that neither perceived effects on self nor third-person perceptions had an impact on support for monitoring. Perceived effects on others did have a small positive effect. This finding is inconsistent with the behavioral component of the third-person effect hypothesis.

Two published studies provide evidence supporting the relationship between third-person perceptions and desire for censorship. Gunther's (1995) national study of pornography indicated that the size of third-person perceptions was positively related to favoring restrictions on pornographic material, although perceived effects on self also made a strong contribution. The relationship between third-person perceptions and regulation of pornography was even stronger when Gunther excluded participants who did not demonstrate the third-person perception for pornographic content.

Similarly, Rojas, Shah, and Faber (1996) demonstrated that third-person perceptions were positively associated with the desire to censor violence on television, and pornography, and support for censorship in general. In addition, they found that a measure of hypothetical censorship behaviors was also strongly predicted by third-person perceptions.[3]

The present research was designed to provide an additional test of the relationship between the perceptual and behavioral components of the third-person effect hypothesis and to clarify whether it is perceived effects on self, perceived effects on others, or the third-person perception that is most strongly related to censorship attitudes. Following Davison (1983), Gunther (1995), and Rojas et al. (1996), we predicted:

> H4: Third-person perceptions about the effects or rap will be positively associated with support for censorship of rap.

METHOD

Questionnaires were administered to 202 students in two introductory mass communication courses at the University of Delaware.[4] These courses draw students from a wide variety of academic majors (62% of the respondents were from majors other than communication); however, the sample was disproportionately female (70%). The mean age of respondents in this sample was just over 20 years old.

Respondents were randomly given one of two versions of a nine-page questionnaire, which were identical except for the third page.[5] This page presented the stimulus material—rap lyrics adapted from actual songs. One set of lyrics constituted the violent rap stimulus; the other constituted the misogynic rap stimulus. The different stimuli were used to provide more than one context for third-person effects. The violent stimulus portrays the life of a "gangsta" who is not afraid to use a gun to settle his problems. In the misogynic stimulus, a man uses a woman for sex but is embarrassed to be seen with her in public; he clearly treats her as little more than temporary sexual gratification.

Lyrics were chosen that celebrated values considered by the authors to be antisocial. In order to test whether our respondents also considered the lyrics antisocial (thus enabling a third-person perception), respondents were asked to rate their perceptions of the lyrics on an 11-point scale ranging from 0 (*very antisocial*) to 10 (*very prosocial*). Both sets of lyrics were considered antisocial by respondents ($M = 1.98$ and $M = 2.4$ for violent and misogynic lyrics, respectively).

Respondents were instructed to read the lyrics carefully and encouraged to refer back to them as they filled out the remainder of the questionnaire. Following the lyrics and the social desirability question where the items used to create four scales for the third-person perceptions measures. Respondents were asked to estimate the effects of "listening to songs with these types of lyrics" on the knowledge, attitudes, and behaviors of each of the following referent groups: "you," "other University of Delaware students," "people your age in cities like New York and Los Angeles," and "the average person." [6]

The instrument used to measure third-person perceptions was an 11-point scale ranging from 0 (*no effect*) to 10 (*a great deal of effects*). Perceived effects on knowledge, attitudes, and behaviors were summed to create the scales for each referent group (effects on self Cronbach's $\alpha = .79$, effects on the Delaware students $\alpha = .82$, effects on New York/Los Angeles youth $\alpha = .85$, effects on the average person $\alpha = .85$). These four scales are used in the analyses displayed in Table 1. Difference scores between self and each of the three comparison groups were also computed to represent third-person perceptions. The reliabilities for the self versus Delaware students, self versus average person, and self versus New York/Los Angeles youth were .61, .60, and .74, respectively. [7]

The next set of measures was seven items used to create the support for censorship scale ($\alpha = .87$). Subjects were asked to think again about the song lyrics as they responded to the seven (5-point) Likert-type items. The seven statements dealt with support for industry self-censorship, banning airplay during hours when children might be listening, support for federal or local laws, and banning sale of the content.

A single item was used to measure perceived knowledge or rap music. Subjects were asked how knowledgeable they were about each of several types of music using an 11-point scale ranging from 0 (*not at all*) to 10 (*a great deal*).

Due to their expected relationship to censorship attitudes and third-person perceptions, three additional variables (gender, conservatism, and liking of rap) were measured and used as controls in the regression anal-

30

Table 1

*t Tests of Differences Between Perceived Effects on Self and Delaware Students,
New York/Los Angeles Youth, and the Average Person*

| | | Comparison Group | | |
	Self versus	Delaware Students	New York/ Los Angeles Youth	Average Person
Violent rap ($df = 98-100$)	5.56	8.96	15.14	8.74
Misogynic rap ($df = 98$)	3.26	8.17	12.75	7.46
Total ($df = 197-199$)	4.43	8.58	13.95	8.10

Note: Mean figures for the self reported here are based on the comparison with the largest number of cases possible. Significance tests are based on the actual number of cases in the analysis. All differences between self and the three comparison groups (for the total sample as well as for the violent rap and misogynic rap subsamples) are significant at the $p \leq .01$ level.

ysis. Conservatism was created by summing responses to two items asking about respondent's political orientations on social and economic issues ($r = .53$). For both items, 7-point scales ranging from *very liberal* to *very conservative* were used to measure responses. Two items also were used to measure liking of rap. The first indicator in the scale was part of a set of items that asked respondents to rank order by preference nine different music types, one of which was rap. Rankings for this item were reversed so that higher values represented greater preference for rap compared to other musical genres. The second indicator was part of a group of items that asked respondents how much they liked each of the nine music types using an 11-point scale ranging from 0 (*not at all*) to 10 (*a great deal*). These two items ($r = .79$) were standardized and then summed to create the liking of rap variable.

To test Hypotheses 1 and 2, t tests of the size of the difference between perceived effects on self and perceived effects on others were conducted. Hypothesis 3 was tested using bivariate correlation analysis. Hypothesis 4 was tested using a regression technique called the "diamond model" as advocated by Whitt (1983) for dealing with hypotheses that predict an effect for a difference score variable (third-person perceptions in this case) above and beyond the effects of its components (perceived effects on self and perceived effects on others). For the regression analyses in Table 2, the final block of variables entered into the equation contain the self plus other variable and the third-person perception variable for each of the three comparison groups. According to Whitt (1983), when these two variables are entered simultaneously into a regression equation,

Table 2

Hierarchical Multiple Regression Model Predicting
Attitudes Toward Censorship of Rap Lyrics

	Comparison Group		
Independent Variable	Delaware Students	New York/ Los Angeles Youth	Average Person
Block 1			
Gender (female)			
$\beta 1$	.11	.11	.11
$\beta 2$	.11	.12	.10
Conservatism			
$\beta 1$	.27**	.27**	.27**
$\beta 2$	.24**	.23**	.24**
R^2 (%)	7.5**	7.5**	7.5**
Block 2			
Social desirability			
$\beta 1$	$-.10$	$-.10$	$-.10$
$\beta 2$	$-.03$	.00	$-.05$
Incremental R^2 (%)	0.9	0.9	0.9
Block 3			
Liking of rap			
$\beta 1$	$-.13$	$-.13$	$-.13$
$\beta 2$	$-.11$	$-.11$	$-.10$
Knowledge of rap			
$\beta 1$	$-.02$	$-.02$	$-.02$
$\beta 2$	$-.05$	$-.06$	$-.03$
Incremental R^2 (%)	1.8	1.8	1.8
Block 4			
Self + other perceptions			
$\beta 2$	.04	.07	.05
Third-person perceptions			
$\beta 2$	.17*	.22**	.15*
Incremental R^2 (%)	2.8*	5.6**	2.3
Final R^2 (%)	13.0*	15.8**	12.5

Note: $N = 189$. $\beta 1 =$ standardized beta upon entry of block into equation (thus controlling for previous and current blocks); $\beta 2 =$ standardized beta from full model (final beta
controlling for all variables in the model).
*$p < .05$; **$p < .01$.

a significant effect for the difference score variable should be interpreted as support for the hypothesis.

RESULTS

Hypotheses 1–3: The Perceptual Component

Hypothesis 1 predicted that the perceived effects of the rap lyrics on others would be greater than perceived effects on self. Table 1 presents the results of *t* tests that demonstrate strong support for this hypothesis. Overall, the third-person perception differentials were significant for comparisons of self to other Delaware students, self to youth from New York and Los Angeles, and self to the average person. In addition, separating out the perceptual difference by condition (violent vs. misogynic rap) revealed that both conditions induced a perceptual third-person effect (Table 1).

Hypothesis 2 stated that the size of third-person perceptions should increase as comparisons were made with referent groups more socially distant from the perceiver. There was only limited support for this hypothesis (Table 1). The group was expected to be most socially distant, the average person, did not produce the greatest third-person perception. Instead, youth from New York and Los Angeles demonstrated the largest perceptual difference from self, significantly greater than the difference between self and other Delaware students was not significantly less than the difference between self and the average person.

Hypothesis 3 predicted a positive association between perceived knowledge of rap and third-person perceptions. Our results failed to support this hypothesis; in none of the three tests (Delaware students, New York/Los Angeles youth, or average person) was there a significant relationship between third-person perceptions and perceived knowledge of rap. The nonsignificant correlations ranged from −.03 (average person) to +.09 (Delaware students). Although inconsistent with our hypothesis, these findings are consistent with studies that have tested the relationship between *actual* knowledge and third-person perceptions.

Hypothesis 4: The Behavioral Component

Hypothesis 4 linked third-person perceptions with support for censorship of the presumably harmful content of rap music. To test this hypothesis, we used the diamond model in a multiple regression analysis (Whitt, 1983). The first block of the regression equation entered gender and conservatism as predictor variables, revealing that conservatives were more likely to support censorship of antisocial rap lyrics, but revealing no significant effect for gender.[8] Second, because previous research had indicated that "perceived harm" is an important predictor of willingness to support government regulations of media content (Rucinski & Salmon,

1990), our measure of perceived social desirability of the "message" in the rap lyrics was entered into the regression equation next. The effect of social desirability on support for censorship was not significant. Our third control block included perceived knowledge of rap as well as our index of liking of rap. Both of these variables were significantly related to opposition to censorship at the zero-order level; however, both were reduced to nonsignificance after controls for the first two regression blocks.

The final block of the regression equation in Table 2 provided the test for Hypothesis 4. Here, both perceived effects on self and perceived effects on others (combined into two-item indices) and third-person perceptions (two-item difference scores) were entered into the equation simultaneously. The evidence indicates that for each of the three comparison groups, third-person perceptions were significantly related to censorship attitudes, while self and other perceptions were in no case significantly related to support for censorship. The strongest relationship between third-person perceptions and support for censorship comes from the New York/Los Angeles comparison group, although all three comparison groups produced similar regression coefficients. Thus our data indicated strong support for Hypothesis 4 in each of three separate tests.[9]

DISCUSSION

The results of this study provide solid support for both the perceptual and behavioral components of the third-person effect hypothesis. Consistent with past research, our respondents perceived others to be more influenced by negative media messages than themselves. In addition, this perception was strongly related to support for censorship, even after controlling for other important variables. The study provided less support for the knowledge and social distance corollaries of the perceptual component of the third-person effect hypothesis. However, our findings may shed some light on these areas of third-person effect research and lead to more fruitful research in the future.

The present study makes several contributions to the literature on third-person effects. Using a unique material (rap music), it replicated findings on the third-person perception. The supposed impact of antisocial rap lyrics is currently a hotly debated topic in news media, political discussions, and on the presidential campaign trail. Antisocial rap provides, then, a socially relevant context in which to study third-person effects.

The current political climate makes tests of the link between the *40* perceptual and behavioral components of the hypothesis important. Politicians from both the Left and the Right have recently called for (at least) industry self-censorship or rap music in order to protect the masses. The present study adds to the small body of literature (required to add relevance to third-person perceptions) by assessing the relationship between these perceptions and support for censorship. In so doing, it investigates one plausible cause for the desire to censor media content. If it is the case (as research seems to indicate) that third-person perceptions are based on an overestimation of effects on others, the desire for censorship caused by third-person perceptions is built on a flawed foundation. Any censorship that results from misperceptions may in fact be unnecessary censorship.

The present study, like any single research effort, has its limitations. For instance, our test of the behavioral component actually used an attitudinal measure as the dependent variable. That is, we were unable to measure censorship behaviors directly, and therefore we were forced to rely on self-report measures of support for censorship. This may not be a severe limitation, however, since public policy, such as restrictions on objectionable media content, is often based on public opinion.

Another limitation of this study is our inability to make strong causal inferences. Our cross-sectional data and limited number of controls restrict a conclusion of association between third-person perceptions and support for censorship. Future research might attempt to experimentally manipulate third-person perceptions in much the way the climate of opinion has been manipulated in studies of impersonal influence (Mutz, 1992). This would strengthen inferences about the direction of causality.

Finally, our homogeneous and gender-biased student sample may have provided greater third-person perceptions than those of the population. Davison (1983) suggests that third-person perceptions are greater among those who believe they are "experts" in a particular domain, and enrollment in a course in mass communication may have led our respondents to consider themselves experts in the domain of media effects. This sample issue is one common to many third-person effect studies (e.g., Cohen et al., 1988; Gunther, 1991; Mutz, 1989; Perloff, 1989).

These limitations, however, do not cast serious doubt on the major findings of the study, which help to move third-person effect research forward. Regarding our first hypothesis, our results indicated a consistent pattern of perceiving three groups of others (other Delaware students, New York and Los Angeles youth, and the average person) to be more influenced by both violent and antisocial rap lyrics than oneself. This finding adds to the substantial research demonstrating a perceptual third-person effect for negative media messages.

The social distance corollary (H2) predicted that the size of the perceptual bias will increase as the referent group becomes more socially distant from the perceiver. We operationalized social distance by assuming a priori that respondents would believe that other students at their university would be the most similar, people in their age group in New

45

York and Los Angeles would be a little less similar, and people in the average person group would be the least similar. The social distance corollary held with the exception of the average person comparison group, which was perceived as similar to the other Delaware students group.

The most likely explanation of this finding is that the respondents considered the average person to be older than themselves, generally outside the target audience of rap music and hence less likely to be influenced. By contrast, the youth of large urban cities may be considered a prime target for rap, and therefore more likely to be influenced by it. We suggest that future research take into account "target groups" in studies of the third-person effect.

The results of this study reveal that there may be two separate perceptual evaluations that regulate the size of the third-person perception—perceived social distance and perceived likelihood of exposure to the content (the target corollary). In this study, the effect of the target corollary seemed to be more powerful than the impact of social distance. However, it may also be that perceived social distance was not specified correctly in our a priori assumptions. This indicates the need for future research to directly measure perceived social distance to test these assumptions.

The results of this test of the social distance corollary point to the importance of considering the relationship of the third-person comparison group to the target market of the media content. Although the target market corollary seemed to outweigh the social distance corollary in our test, there are some questions about how important the target market consideration is with regard to judgments about effects on self. Perceived effects on self (more or less part of the target audience in this study) were seen as being less than the impact on the average person (somewhat outside the target audience). This may reflect the fact that the social distance corollary was not completely overrun by the target market corollary. It may also be that respondents do not consider target markets when they make judgments about themselves—instead, they see themselves as unlikely to be influenced by media content despite their membership in its target market. This explanation has some support in our data; while we do not have direct measures of exposure, the zero-order correlations between perceived effects on self and knowledge of rap ($r = .03$) and liking of rap ($r = .13$) are nonsignificant. Research examining the link between exposure and perceived effects on self, however, has generally found significant results (Rucinski & Salmon, 1990).

Clearly, the social distance corollary and the target corollary merit further research. Such research should also investigate an alternative interpretation of the target corollary. Conceivably, respondents could be passing judgment on the typical education level of members of the third-person comparison groups and making the assumption that less educated people are more susceptible to negative media influence (a possibility that is consistent with paternalistic notions that may account for linkages between third-person perceptions and the desire for censorship). Future research could measure perceived educational levels, perceived social distance (i.e., dissimilarity), and the perceived likelihood of exposure to the stimulus genre (e.g., rap music) of each of the comparison groups in order to investigate the various explanations for these results.

Our results did not support the knowledge corollary predicted by the third hypothesis. Although some research has indicated that perceived knowledge of a content domain leads to greater third-person perceptions (Lasorsa, 1989), our results indicated no significant effect. This finding is similar to those of Lasorsa (1989) and Price and Tewksbury (1994), who found that actual knowledge was not related to third-person effects. It is possible that respondents in our study had no incentive to exaggerate their knowledge of rap music (as is likely for Lasorsa's measure of perceived political knowledge), and therefore their perceptions in fact were an accurate representation of their actual knowledge. It is possible that the knowledge corollary may only hold in situations where perceived knowledge is an overestimate of actual knowledge.

Finally, our data provide strong support for the behavioral component of the third-person effect (H4), which states that perceiving others as more influenced by media content than oneself is related to support for taking actions to protect others. In several tests comparing the impact of the third-person perception with additive indices of perceived effects on self and perceived effects on others, the third-person perception was consistently a significant predictor while the additive index was in no case significant. The impact of third-person perceptions on support for censorship was strong despite controls for several correlates of censorship (gender, conservatism, social desirability of the content, and knowledge of and liking of the content, in question).

Findings of a strong relationship between third-person perceptions and support for censorship provide insight into the real-world impact of third-person perceptions. Whereas some might question the importance of a perceptual error, regardless of its consistency, few media researchers would dispute the importance of a perceptual bias that leads to support for censorship. By providing correlational evidence for the behavioral component of the third-person effect hypothesis, we have bared the "teeth" of the third-person effect.

It is possible that the effects of third-person perceptions go beyond support for censorship. Future third-person research should attempt to link third-person perceptions to more broad public opinion processes. For instance, are those who exhibit third-person perceptions more likely to participate in the public opinion formation and change processes (regarding censorship or otherwise) as radio talk show callers or protestors? Are those who hold third-person perceptions consistently more likely to hold strong attitudes on public issues, whatever the valence? Future third-person effect research may benefit most from links to more broad public opinion research and to psychological research on the concept of pluralistic ignorance.

Researchers from both social science and legal perspectives should further explore the impact of third-person perceptions on attitudes toward media censorship. In a time when the political climate is replete with calls for censorship of not only rap lyrics but also other forms of media content, this research is all the more important.

APPENDIX

Social Desirability

On a scale from 0 to 10, circle the number that indicates how you rate the message in the lyrics in terms of its antisocial/prosocial content.

Liking of Rap

Please rank the following types of music in order of your preference: country (e.g., Garth Brooks, Clint Brooks, Mary Chapin Carpenter, etc.), classic rock (e.g., Led Zeppelin, Rolling Stones, Aerosmith, etc.), heavy metal (e.g., Metallica, AC/DC, Megadeath, etc.), rap/hip-hop (e.g., Public Enemy, Salt 'N' Peppa, Snoop Doggy Dog, etc.), alternative (e.g., Pearl Jam, Nine-Inch Nails, Nirvana, etc.), classical (e.g., Bach, Beethoven, Mozart, etc.), jazz (e.g., Miles Davis, Wynton Marsalis, Pat Metheny, etc.), reggae (e.g., Bob Marley, Peter Tosh, UB40, etc.), pop (e.g., Whitney Houston, Madonna, Phil Collins, etc.).

On a scale from 0 to 10, 0 being *not at all* and 10 being *a great deal,* circle the number that indicates how much you *like* each of the following types of music. . . .

Knowledge of Rap

On a scale from 0 to 10, 0 being *not at all* and 10 being *a great deal,* circle the number that indicates how *knowledgeable* you are about the artists and lyrics of each of the following types of music. . . .

Perceived Effects of Rap

(a) Overall, how much do you think *you* would learn from listening to songs with these types of lyrics? (b) Overall, how much would you say *your* attitudes would be influenced by listening to songs with these types of lyrics? (c) Overall, how much would you say that *your* behavior would be affected by listening to songs with these types of lyrics? (These same three questions were asked with other University of Delaware students, people your age in New York and Los Angeles, and the average person as the referent groups).

Support for Censorship

(a) Songs with these types of lyrics should be banned from radio play during hours when children might be listening. (b) Songs with these types of lyrics should be banned from radio play during any time of the day. (c) Songs with these types of lyrics should be required to carry a parental advisory label to warn consumers about the possible negative effects of their content. (d) Songs with these types of lyrics should be banned from MTV and other music video programs. (e) Songs with these types of lyrics should be self-censored by record companies. (f) Songs with these types of lyrics should be removed from music store shelves by local ordinance. (g) Sale of albums with songs containing these types of lyrics should be banned by federal law.

Conservatism

The terms "liberal" and "conservative" may mean different things to people depending on the kind of issue one is considering. (a) In terms of economic issues, would you say you are very liberal, liberal, somewhat liberal, neutral, somewhat conservative, conservative, very conservative. (b) Now, thinking in terms of social issues, would you say you are very liberal, liberal, somewhat liberal, neutral, somewhat conservative, conservative, very conservative.

NOTES

1. The motivational interpretation for the third-person effect has not gone unchallenged, however (see Perloff, 1993). The same can be said for attribution biases (e.g., Perloff & Fetzer, 1986) and pluralistic ignorance (e.g., Mullen, 1983) research paradigms in psychology, on which the third-person effect motivational explanation is based. We agree with Tetlock and Levi (1982), however, that the debate over motivational versus cognitive explanations is not fruitful until the theories have been developed enough to provide a critical test. It is most likely, we think (see also Perloff, 1993), that both motivational and cognitive biases occur simultaneously, as demonstrated by Sherman, Presson, and Chassin (1984) in a study of the causes of pluralistic ignorance. However, the motivational bias is stressed here because the bulk of evidence and theory in the third-person effect literature supports a motivational interpretation.

2. Although it may seem counterintuitive to predict that the causal force in the third-person effect is not absolute perceived effects on self or perceived effects on others but instead the difference between them, the third-person effect is not the only hypothesis that proposes that perceived differences between self and others may be the basis for holding political opinions or taking political actions. Relative deprivation theory has been applied to political science in order to explain why some people engage in protest activities (e.g., Barnes, Farah, & Heunks, 1979; Barnes & Kaase, 1979). This theory predicts that it is not absolute deprivation (in terms of one's

life as a whole or standard of living) but the perceived deprivation by comparison to expectations or comparable reference groups that leads people to engage in political protest.

3. Three recent conference papers present somewhat contradictory evidence on this point, however. Lee and Yang (1996) found a significant relationship between third-person perceptions and support for censorship of sexually explicit television content in Korea, and Gunther and Hua (1996) found similar support for censorship among those evidencing greater third-person perception across a range of television content types in Singapore. However, Price et al. (1996) reported no significant relationship between third-person perceptions and support for censorship of a potentially offensive advertisement beyond the zero-order level. However, the relationship was at least in the predicted direction in this study.

4. A question at the end of the questionnaire asked respondents if they had ever heard of the third-person effect. Of the few who reported knowing about the third-person effect, none was able to correctly answer an open-ended follow-up question about the nature of the hypothesis. For that reason, all subjects were retained for the analysis.

5. Question wordings are included in the appendix.

6. Several studies (Gunther, 1991, 1995; Price & Tewksbury, 1994; Tiedge, Silverblatt, Havice, & Rosenfeld, 1991) have found that there are no effects for the ordering of the self versus other questions. Price and Tewksbury (1994) also demonstrated that the observed third-person perceptual bias was not due to a contrast effect (i.e., making comparisons regardless of the order). Therefore, we made no attempt to randomize the order of the comparison groups.

7. Although the reliability of a difference score cannot be tested directly via Cronbach's alpha, Cohen and Cohen (1983) provide a formula to calculate it. The reliability of a difference score is calculated by subtracting the correlation between the two components of the difference score from the average of their reliabilities, then dividing by one minus the correlation between the component scores.

8. One of the anonymous reviewers of this manuscript suggested that the relationship between political ideology and censorship might be nonlinear, such that not only strong conservatives but also strong liberals (e.g., feminists) might support censorship. However, analyses using power polynomials (see Cohen & Cohen, 1983) to test for a quadratic (inverted U) effect of conservatism on censorship attitudes revealed no significant deviation from linearity of this form in our data. Despite this, it should be noted that support for censorship is not necessarily limited to the conservative end of the ideological continuum and may be based instead on the group whose speech is going to be censored (see Sullivan, Pierson, & Marcus, 1983).

9. One of the anonymous reviewers of this manuscript suggested that another analytical strategy, the Taylor model, would be a more stringent test of our hypothesis. Taylor (1973) argues that in order to test a hypothesis of effects of a difference score above and beyond its components' combined effects while avoiding linear dependence, the two components should be entered individually into the regression equation (unlike the diamond model,

which combines them into an index). Then, instead of using the difference score as a predictor, the absolute size of the difference score and a
pair of dummy variables (representing the possible directions of the difference score: positive, negative, and no difference) should be entered into
the equation as an indirect representation of the difference score. The results of this analytical technique for the present data produced null findings
for H4. In none of the three regressions did either the size of the difference
between self and other or the direction of the difference between self and
other significantly predict support for censorship. Examination of the final
beta coefficients for self and other (separately) also showed null findings in
two of the three tests. Only for the Delaware students comparison group
did perceived impact on self (negatively) and others (positively) significantly predict support for censorship. We do not believe, however, that
the results of this analytical strategy are meaningful. Although the Taylor
model does avoid the linear dependence problem that prevents the test of
the difference score and its two components in the same regression equation (because they are correlated at 1.0), even Taylor himself notes that
severe multicollinearity remains a problem in this model (Taylor, 1973).
Our data reveal evidence to support this assertion. In addition to indirect
indications of multicollinearity, such as regression coefficients that are reversed in sign for their zero-order counterparts and large beta weights that
do no attain statistical significance (e.g., $\beta = .20$), more direct tests, such
as the multiple correlation between predictor variables (as large as .95 in
the New York/ Los Angeles regression model) and the variance inflation
factor (see Neter, Kutner, Nachtsheim, & Wasserman, 1996) all indicated
high levels of multicollinearity in our regression equations. It is for this
reason that we have chosen to interpret the results of the diamond model
only—we believe that the low levels of multicollinearity in this model
reveal the true relationships betwen the independent and dependent variables. However, we leave it to the reader to decide which strategy seems
more appropriate.

REFERENCES

Barnes, S. H., Farah, B. G., & Heunks, F. (1979). Personal dissatisfaction. In
S. Barnes & M. Kaase (Eds.), *Political action* (pp. 381–407). Beverly Hills,
CA: Sage.

Barnes, S. H., & Kaase, M. (1979). Introduction. In S. Barnes & M. Kaase (Eds.),
Political action (pp. 13–26). Beverly Hills, CA: Sage.

Bowman, J. (1992, July). Plain brown rappers. *National Review,* pp. 36–38, 53.

Brewer, M. B., & Kramer, R. M. (1985). The psychology of intergroup attitudes
and behavior. *Annual Review of Psychology, 36,* 219–243.

Brown, J. D. (1986). Evaluations of self and others: Self-enhancement biases in
social judgments. *Social Cognition, 4,* 353–376.

Cohen, J., & Cohen, P. (1983). *Applied multiple regression/correlation analysis for the
behavioral sciences* (2nd ed.). Hillsdale, NJ: Lawrence Erlbaum.

Cohen, J., & Davis, R. G. (1991). Third-person effects and the differential impact in negative political advertising. *Journalism Quarterly, 68,* 680–688.

Cohen, J., Mutz, D., Price, V., & Gunther, A. (1988). Perceived impact of defamation: An experiment on third-person effects. *Public Opinion Quarterly, 52,* 161–173.

Cook, F. L., Tyler, T., Goetz, E. G., Gordon, M. T., Protess, D., Leff, D. R., & Molotch, H. L. (1983). Media and agenda setting: Effects on the public, interest group leaders, policy makers, and policy. *Public Opinion Quarterly, 47,* 16–35.

Davison, W. P. (1983). The third-person effect in communication. *Public Opinion Quarterly, 47,* 1–15.

Dority, B. (1991, January/February). Profile of a censor. *The Humanist,* pp. 43–44.

Frohnmayer, J. (1994). *Out of tune: Listening to the First Amendment.* The Freedom Forum First Amendment Center, Vanderbilt University.

Gunther, A. (1991). What we think others think: Cause and consequence in the third-person effect. *Communication Research, 18,* 355–372.

Gunther, A. (1995). Overrating the X-rating: The third-person perception and support for censorship of pornography. *Journal of Communication, 45*(1), 27–38.

Gunther, A. C., & Hua, A. P. (1996, May). *Public perceptions of television influence and opinions about censorship in Singapore.* Paper presented at the annual meeting of the International Communication Association, Chicago.

Gunther, A. C., & Mundy, P. (1993). Biased optimism and the third-person effect. *Journalism Quarterly, 70,* 58–67.

Gunther, A. C., & Thorson, E. (1992). Perceived persuasive effects of product commercials and public service announcements: Third-person effects in new domains. *Communication Research, 19,* 574–596.

Langer, E. J. (1975). The illusion of control. *Journal of Personality and Social Psychology, 32,* 311–328.

Lasorsa, D. L. (1989). Real and perceived effects of "Amerika." *Journalism Quarterly, 66,* 373–378, 529.

Lee, C., & Yang, S. (1996, August). *Third-person perceptions and support for censorship of sexually explicit visual content: A Korean case.* Paper presented at the annual meeting of the Association for Education in Journalism and Mass Communication, Anaheim, CA.

Leo, J. (1993, December 20). At a cultural crossroads. *U.S. News & World Report,* p. 14.

Miller, D. T., & Prentice, D. A. (1994). Collective errors and errors about the collective. *Personality and Social Psychology Bulletin, 20,* 541–550.

Mullen, B. (1983). Egocentric biases in estimates of consensus. *Journal of Social Psychology, 121,* 31–38.

Mutz, D. C. (1989). The influence of perceptions of media influence: Third person effects and the public expression of opinions. *International Journal of Public Opinion Research, 1,* 3–23.

Mutz, D. C. (1992). Impersonal influence: Effects of representations of public opinion on political attitudes. *Political Behavior, 14,* 89–122.

Mutz, D. C. (1994). The political effects of perceptions of mass opinion. *Research in Micropolitics, 4,* 143–167.

Neter, J., Kutner, M. H., Nachtsheim, C. J., & Wasserman, W. (1996). *Applied linear regression models* (3rd ed.). Chicago: Irwin.

O'Gorman, H. J. (1986). The discovery of pluralistic ignorance: An ironic lesson. *Journal of the History of the Behavioral Sciences, 22,* 333–347.

Perloff, L. S., & Fetzer, B. K. (1986). Self-other judgments and perceived vulnerability to victimization. *Journal of Personality and Social Psychology, 50,* 502–510.

Perloff, R. M. (1989). Ego-involvement and the third person effect of televised news coverage. *Communication Research, 16,* 236–262.

Perloff, R. M. (1993). Third-person effect research 1983–1992: A review and synthesis. *International Journal of Public Opinion Research, 5,* 167–184.

Perloff, R. M., Neuendorf, K., Giles, D., Change, T. K., & Jeffres, L. W. (1992). Perceptions of "Amerika." *Mass Communication Review, 19*(3), 42–48.

Price, V., & Tewksbury, D. (1994, November). *The roles of question order, contrast, and knowledge in the third-person effect.* Paper presented at the annual conference of the Midwest Association for Public Opinion Research, Chicago.

Price, V., Tewksbury, D., & Huang, L. N. (1996, May). *Denying the Holocaust: Third-person effects and decisions to publish a controversial advertisement.* Paper presented at the annual meeting of the American Association for Public Opinion Research, Salt Lake City, UT.

Rojas, H., Shah, D. V., & Faber, R. J. (1996). For the good of others: Censorship and the third-person effect. *International Journal of Public Opinion Research, 8,* 163–186.

Rucinski, D., & Salmon, C. T. (1990). The "other" as the vulnerable voter: A study of the third-person effect in the 1988 U.S. presidential campaign. *International Journal of Public Opinion Research, 2,* 345–368.

Salmon, C. T. (1989). Campaigns for social "improvement": An overview of values, rationales, and impacts. In C. T. Salmon (Ed.), *Information campaigns: Balancing social values and social change* (pp. 19–53). Newbury Park, CA: Sage.

Sherman, S. J., Presson, C. C., & Chassin, L. (1984). Mechanisms underlying the false consensus effect: The special role of threats to the self. *Personality and Social Psychology Bulletin, 10,* 127–138.

Sullivan, J. L., Pierson, J., & Marcus, G. E. (1983). *Political tolerance and American democracy.* Chicago: University of Chicago Press.

Taylor, H. F. (1973). Linear models of consistency: Some extensions of Blalock's strategy. *American Journal of Sociology, 78,* 1192–1215.

Tetlock, P. E., & Levi, A. (1982). Attribution bias: On the inconclusiveness of the cognition-motivation debate. *Journal of Experimental Social Psychology, 18,* 68–88.

Thompson, M. E., Chaffee, S. H., & Oshagan, H. H. (1990). Regulating pornography: A public dilemma. *Journal of Communication, 40*(3), 73–83.

Tiedge, J. T., Silverblatt, A., Havice, M. J., & Rosenfeld, R. (1991). Discrepancy between perceived first-person and perceived third-person mass media effects. *Journalism Quarterly, 68,* 141–154.

Time Warner abandons raps—and a bit more. (1995, October 9). *U.S. News & World Report,* p. 18.

Toch, H., & Klofas, J. (1984). Pluralistic ignorance, revisited. In G. M. Stephenson & J. H. Davis (Eds.), *Progress in applied social psychology* (Vol. 2, pp. 129–159). New York: John Wiley & Sons.

Weinstein, N. D. (1980). Unrealistic optimism about future life events. *Journal of Personality and Social Psychology, 39,* 806–820.

Whitt, H. P. (1983). Status inconsistency: A body of negative evidence or a statistical artifact? *Social Forces, 62,* 201–233.

Zuckerman, M. (1979). Attribution of success and failure revisited: The motivational bias is alive and well in attribution theory. *Journal of Personality, 47,* 245–287.

CARTOON: CENSORSHIP BEGINS AT HOME

DAN MORAN

V A Guide to Finding and Using Information

Conducting research in a college or university library or on the Internet may at first seem like a daunting task: The sheer number of sources available to you can appear overwhelming. However, taking the time to learn what kinds of research materials your library and the Internet provide and how to use them will ultimately lend depth as well as validity to your essays.

When they hear the word *library,* most people naturally think first of books. But a library contains numerous other sources, such as academic and scientific journals, magazines, newspapers, government publications, dissertation abstracts, and **bibliographies.** Any of these sources may prove invaluable to your research. Books can provide a thorough treatment of some particular issue, and articles in journals and newspapers can provide up-to-the-minute information on the same subject. This current information is especially important in disciplines where new experiments and research are almost constantly altering past findings and conclusions.

Nothing will be more helpful to your discovery of the library's resources than the assistance of trained research librarians. These members of the library's staff are usually located at the reference desk. Before you begin searching for sources for a particular paper, consult a research librarian to help you identify the sources that are best suited for the level of research necessary for the paper. Never be embarrassed to ask the reference librarians anything about the library or its workings: Their job is to assist you, and their expertise is wasted unless it is used.

As you uncover the wealth of resources available in the library and on the Internet, keep in mind that the purpose of research is to expand your argument, not to replace it with a series of statistics or quotations.

Some material in this chapter is adapted from Ebest, et al., *Writing from A to Z* (Mayfield: 2000).

The sample paper at the end of this chapter illustrates the appropriate use of the material you find in your research.

LOCATING INFORMATION IN THE LIBRARY AND ON THE INTERNET

One of the first steps in writing an essay or a research paper is to find an appropriate topic, one that is neither too broad nor too narrow. If you have only a general subject in mind but not a specific topic, looking in the library catalog and in the books in the relevant shelves of the stacks can help.

For a general overview of a broad topic, articles in encyclopedias can also be helpful, and they often end with a list of recommended books. However, because the information in encyclopedias is often general and always dated, you should use it only to help you find appropriate sources for your paper, not as a source itself.

The Library and the Internet

The library and the Internet each have strengths and limitations. In the library, the staff can help you find what you need quickly and efficiently. On the Internet, you are on your own, and it is easy to get caught in the Web.

RELIABILITY The books and periodicals in the library have gone through a screening process for accuracy and reliability. The publishers decided that the works were worth publishing, and the library decided that they were worth buying. On the Internet, anyone can publish anything. No one monitors the content for credibility or accuracy. You may find interesting nuggets on the Internet, but you are the one who has to decide whether a Web site is credible. Begin your basic research in the library; use the Internet to add details.

COMPREHENSIVENESS VERSUS CONVENIENCE Relatively few books are available on the Internet; the full texts of most periodical articles are available on-line only for a fee or through a database such as Lexis/Nexis. However, the library may not own the particular book or periodical you need (although interlibarary loans can increase what is available), or someone may have checked it out. On the Internet, the information is always there. Moreover, you can access information from all around the world (for example, newspapers from every continent at ⟨http://www.mediainfo.com/emedia⟩), and on-line reference documents may be updated more frequently than the ones on the library shelves. Use the library for basic information and the Internet for up-to-the-minute news or data.

THE MEDIUM The printed page is static; hypertext Web documents are interactive and searchable. Sometimes a book fits your needs, and sometimes the Internet is the answer. For example, searching for a particular word or phrase in an Internet document (say, in one of Shakespeare's plays at ⟨http://www.psrg.cs.usyd.edu.au/~matty/Shakespeare⟩) is much faster and more efficient than searching through a book line by line. On the other hand, reading an entire book or play on screen is difficult, and you cannot underline or write in the margins. Use the Internet to locate a particular piece of information in a large document; use a book when you need to study an entire work.

In short, the Internet offers convenience, currency, and interactivity; the library offers reliable and comprehensive sources. Use the Internet for the extras it can offer; don't let it replace the library for your research.

LOCATING BOOKS

The Library Catalog

The library catalog is a record of all the library's books, classified alphabetically by their authors, titles, and subjects. It may be in the form of computer terminals or a card catalog. If you know the title or author of a specific book you want, simply look for it in the author or title listings in the computer or in the author or title section of the card catalog. For example, if you wanted to find a copy of *Walden* by Henry David Thoreau, you would type in the book title or the author's last name to reach a computer screen resembling this one:

Call No:	P3541 Thor
Author:	Thoreau, Henry David, 1817–1862.
Main Title:	Walden : or Life in the woods / by Henry David Thoreau; with an introduction by Harold Smith.
Publisher:	New York : Random House, 1983.

Or you would look for the title in the W section of the card catalog or for the author in the T section to locate a card resembling this one:

```
P3541      Thoreau, Henry David

Thor              Walden.   With an introduction

           by Harold Smith.   New York:

           Random House, 1983.
```

The call number on the first line of the computer screen and in the upper left corner of the card is the book's "address" within the library. If you go to the shelf that houses books with this call number, you will be able to locate your book unless it has been checked out. Computerized catalogs often provide information about the loan status of a book.

When you go through the library catalog, always have a piece of paper handy on which to record call numbers, and be sure to copy them completely and accurately. You may waste time looking for PZ4014 because you forgot that the proper number of your book is really PZ4014(t). The extra seconds you spend writing down call numbers could save you minutes when searching the shelves (commonly called "stacks").

The subject catalog is slightly different from the author and title catalogs. It allows you to look up a particular subject (which can be a person, event, or issue) and find a list of books in the library that address the topic. For example, if you were researching animal rights, you would look under "animal rights" to find a number of computer entries or cards identifying books on the topic.

If the library catalog provides no works dealing with your specific topic, try looking under related topics before stopping your search. If, for example, you were researching a paper on some aspect of artificial intelligence, you might find under the main heading, "Artificial Intelligence," a cross-reference entry for "Artificial Intelligence—Computers" or a card that reads "See Also: Computers." In addition to using these cross-references, try to think of other headings, such as "Robotics," to be sure you do not overlook what might be an important source. You might find it helpful to consult the *Library of Congress Subject Headings* (LCSH), usually located near the catalog. This reference book shows the particular wording that most libraries use to name subjects; for example, "Flying Saucers," not "UFOs," is the subject heading for information about unidentified flying objects. For each subject heading, LCSH also lists subtopics and related subjects.

Online Catalogs and Databases

Some libraries subscribe to large databases that are used across the United States and Canada. The chief virtue of a database is that it usually provides up-to-date listings for specific articles and books concerning topics in different fields and disciplines. If you would like to search a database, your library may allow you to do so yourself, or a reference librarian may do it for you. Since online computer time can be expensive, your library may charge a fee for this service. Some of the more popular online databases are

> Bibliographical Retrieval Services (BRS)
> Dialog (a compendium of databases)
> Educational Resources Information Center (ERIC)
> Research Libraries Information Network (RLIN)
> Online Computer Library Center (OCLC)

Remember that if you are given a book title from a database, you will then have to look it up in the library catalog to find out whether your library owns the book and where it is shelved.

Search Engines

The overwhelming amount of information available electronically may be most efficiently explored by the sorting and retrieval power of search engines. Although they differ slightly, each works when prompted by the key words you enter to produce a list of links that may be appropriate. Some of the most popular search engines are

Alta Vista	http://www.altavista.digital.com
InfoSeek	http://www.guide.infoseek.com
Lycos	http://www.lycos.com
Excite	http://www.excite.com
WebCrawler	http://webcrawler.com
Yahoo	http://www.yahoo.com

Call Numbers and the Stacks

Libraries use one of two systems to assign call numbers to books. The first is the older Dewey Decimal System, which uses numbers to classify books according to their categories:

000–099 General Works
100–199 Philosophy
200–299 Religion
300–399 Social Sciences
400–499 Language
500–599 Natural Science
600–699 Technology
700–799 Fine Arts
800–899 Literature
900–999 History and Geography

These divisions are further subdivided by groups of ten to classify works more narrowly within their broader fields. For example, 800–899 indicates literature in general, and the numbers 810–819 indicate American literature. Many public libraries still use this system to classify their books.

The Library of Congress system begins with letters to classify books within 21 general categories:

A   General Works
B   Philosophy, Psychology, and Religion
C   Auxiliary Sciences of History
D   History (General)
E,F   American History (North and South)
G   Geography, Anthropology, and Recreation
H   Social Sciences
J   Political Science and Official Documents
K   Law
L   Education
M   Music
N   Visual Arts
P   Language and Literature
Q   Science
R   Medicine
S   Agriculture
T   Technology
U   Military Science
V   Naval Science
W   Bibliography and Library Science

Like the Dewey Decimal System, these categories are further subdivided according to more specific topics. Most university libraries now classify their books according to the Library of Congress system; however, some of those libraries still classify their older holdings by the Dewey Decimal System.

Once you have compiled your list of call numbers, you are ready to search your library's stacks. Simply go to the shelf that houses works on the subject depicted by your book's call number. For example, if your call number was PN1899.W5, you might find it on a shelf marked PN1860–2000. Larger, multifloor libraries often feature maps near elevators or staircases. Consult these to save time.

After you find your book, it is a good idea to scan its "home shelf" for other books on the same topic. Since the library uses a classification system based on subjects, books concerning the same subject will be housed together. This check will show you the range of titles the library offers on your topic. It will also provide a rough idea of the extent to which people have written about your topic; for example, the number of books on the death penalty will be considerably larger than the number of books on the death of Socrates. You also may find some titles you overlooked when searching the library catalog. Finally, if the book you seek has been slightly misplaced, you may find it near its proper position.

Recalls and Interlibrary Loans

If the book you want has been lent to another patron, many libraries allow you to recall the book and then borrow it for a designated length of time. If you want a book not owned by your library, you may acquire the book by requesting an interlibrary loan in which your library will try to borrow the book from another library and then lend it to you. Both recalls and interlibrary loans are performed by the library's staff; consult the circulation librarian for specific details.

LOCATING ARTICLES IN PERIODICALS

A periodical is any newspaper, magazine, or academic journal published on a regular basis. Most libraries subscribe to a number of periodicals, which they keep on their periodical shelves for a predetermined length of time. After this time is up, the periodicals are bound in covers (usually marked according to volume number) and housed in a different part of the library. Almost any research project must feature periodicals, because they are the primary sources for current information and opinions.

When searching for periodicals, proceed in the same manner as you would when searching for books: Keep a list handy to which you add complete citations as you research your topic, and, after compiling your initial list, search the library's periodical stacks for the articles. After finding roughly ten citations, search for the articles. Keep in mind, however, that your library may not subscribe to all the periodicals you need; if this happens, you may want to talk to your circulation librarian about an interlibrary loan.

Indexes

Because the library catalog lists only books, you will need to consult periodical indexes, which are usually located in the periodical section of the library, to find articles about your topic. These indexes may be published as printed volumes, on CD-ROMs, or on-line (on-line indexes can usually be accessed from either a modem or a terminal in the library). In general, one volume of a printed index covers only one year of articles, but on-line and CD-ROM indexes usually contain bibliographic listings for several years and may include abstracts of articles as well. Your research librarian can help you locate specific indexes or collections of periodicals.

THE *READERS' GUIDE TO PERIODICAL LITERATURE* Available in print, on CD-ROM, and on-line, the *Readers' Guide to Periodical Literature* is the most widely consulted periodical index. It lists all the articles in more than 230 general-interest magazines and the *New York Times*.

To use the *Readers' Guide,* simply look up your subject, which will be listed alphabetically. For example, if you were researching the ethics of genetic engineering, you might find the following entry:

Engineering, Genetic
Change for the Better? [scientists debate
virtues of gen. eng.] W. Waltz. il *Scientific
Quarterly* 11:17–22 Nov 7 '92

This entry tells you that the article "Change for the Better?" was written by W. Waltz, is illustrated (il), and appears on pages 17 through 22 of *Scientific Quarterly,* volume 11, which is dated November 7, 1992. The bracketed passage is a summary of the article. The *Readers' Guide* features such summaries only when the title of the article does not connote in some way the subject of the article.

Your library may have other periodical indexes in addition to *Readers' Guide*. The InfoTrac series of indexes, available on-line and on CD-ROM, covers general-interest magazines and scholarly journals, a number of major newspapers, and U.S. legislative documents. University Microfilms (UMI) also publishes electronic indexes, including the ProQuest series, for general-interest magazines and newspapers. These indexes use a format similar to the one employed by the *Readers' Guide;* if you have difficulty understanding the codes, instructions on how to read them appear in the index's preface.

NEWSPAPER INDEXES For background information and overviews, magazine articles are usually better sources than newspaper articles. But for a detailed chronicle of events as they develop, newspaper articles are better. Some widely circulating newspapers, such as the *New York Times* and *Wall Street Journal,* provide their own indexes, arranged by subject. NewsBank is a monthly index to newspapers from over 500 cities in the United States. Texts of the indexed articles are available on microfiche.

INDEXES TO SCHOLARLY JOURNALS Articles in the journals of various academic disciplines are listed in specialized indexes, which may be available on CD-ROM and on-line as well as in print. Some of the most common indexes are

> *Social Sciences Index* for fields such as anthropology, psychology, sociology, economics, and political science
> *Education Index* for all areas of educational theory and child development
> *Humanities Index* for an interdisciplinary variety of topics, including history, classics, folklore, religion, philosophy, and the arts
> *Index Medicus* (print) and *Medline* (electronic) for biomedical literature, nursing, and dentistry
> *MLA International Bibliography* for books and articles on literature, modern languages, linguistics, and folklore
> *PAIS [Public Affairs Information Service] International in Print* for social and economic issues and international relations

Abstracts

An abstract is a short summary of the main points of a book or article. Collections of abstracts allow you to "skim" a number of articles in one sitting without having to look for the articles themselves. Although you will eventually have to read a number of articles carefully, reading abstracts can save you time by helping you narrow your search to articles that pertain directly to your topic. Abstracts are especially helpful to those researching a scientific issue, for they frequently summarize the findings of experiments and research. Some of the most popular collections are

> *Biological Abstracts*
> *Book Review Digest*
> *Chemical Abstracts*
> *Historical Abstracts*
> *Physics Abstracts*
> *Women's Studies Abstracts*

Government Documents

Many university libraries are listed as United States Government Depositories. Every time any branch of the government releases a publi-

cation (such as the results of a study, the findings of a congressional committee, or an analysis of information from the last census), a copy of that
publication is sent to each of these libraries. Even if your library is not a
government depository, it should still own the current indexes to these
publications, and should be able to acquire the ones you need through
interlibrary loan. You can access many government publications on-line
through FedWorld at ⟨www.fedworld.gov/⟩.

Finding Your Periodicals

Once you have compiled your list of citations, find out whether
your library subscribes to the periodicals you need by consulting the library's Union List of Serials, an alphabetical listing of all your library's
periodical holdings. Next look on the periodical shelves to see how long
your library keeps its periodicals before binding them. If the articles you
need are already bound, find out where your library keeps its bound periodicals, and locate your article there. Some periodicals may be kept on
microfiche; ask your research librarian for details.

TAKING NOTES

Some sources are so useful that you'll want to take many notes;
others may be worth only a sentence or two of general summary; still
others may turn out not to be useful at all. Before you start taking notes,
skim the table of contents or the subheads. This quick look may tell you
that the source isn't one you can use. If, however, it does seem to contain
relevant information, read through it. Then take notes, which can be
your responses to the source as well as a report of what the source says.
Just be sure to indicate somehow which notes are your own evaluations.
You can write your notes on index cards; you can type your notes—or
keep just the bibliographical information—on a computer; or you can
annotate photocopies and highlight key passages. Or you can use some
combination of techniques. Many writers like to photocopy articles so
that they can refer to them throughout the drafting process, as they
sharpen the focus of the paper and build their argument. Although every
writer has a different system for taking research notes, there are two basic
guidelines to follow as you develop a system for yourself:

- Be organized.
- Summarize and paraphrase instead of copying long quotations.

Be Organized

Use a new page or a new index card for each new note or piece of
information so that you can easily rearrange your notes as you draft your
paper. (Make sure you identify the source on each note.) Arranging the

information in different ways can give you a feel for the different ways your paper could be organized. For example, what you may at first regard as a piece of evidence for your "backing," you may later decide to treat as a separate "claim."

Keep all your notes together. As you conduct your research, you may find an argument that sounds similar or flatly contradictory to one you previously encountered. Having all your notes in one place will make it easy to cross-reference arguments and facts.

Record the complete bibliographical information for each source you consult. It is much easier to delete information about sources you don't end up using than to try to retrace your steps and find missing information about sources you do use. Some writers keep bibliographical notes on 3×5 cards and content notes on 4×6 cards so that the two kinds can be easily differentiated. Those who keep their notes on computer make a separate file for their source notes, which they can alphabetize with a simple command (if the entries begin with the author's last name). If you choose to keep the source information on note cards (one source per card) or to photocopy it directly from the sources, you can arrange the cards or photocopies in alphabetical order when it's time to type the "Works Cited" page of references or works cited for your paper.

Summarize, Paraphrase, and Quote

Before you begin making notes about a source, read through it. Then make a note that summarizes the article or chapter. Next, consider whether there are any particularly important or useful ideas expressed in the work; if so, paraphrase them. Writing a **paraphrase** requires using your own words to express an idea in a source. Make a note of a quotation only if the idea needs to be expressed in the exact words of the source. Figures 1, 2, and 3 are examples of a summary note, a paraphrase note, and a quotation note based on the following paragraphs. (Notice that the source, including the page number, is indicated at the top of each note.)

> Human actions bring about scarcities of renewable resources in three principal ways. First, people can reduce the quantity or degrade the quality of these resources faster than they are renewed. This phenomenon is often referred to as the consumption of the resource's "capital": the capital generates "income" that can be tapped for human consumption. A sustainable economy can therefore be defined as one that leaves the capital intact and undamaged so that future generations can enjoy undiminished income. Thus, if topsoil creation in a region of farmland is 0.25 millimeter per year, then average soil loss should not exceed that amount.

"Environmental Change," Homer-Dixon,
Boutwell, and Rathjens, p. 40

The major human causes of shortages of renewable
resources are (1) overconsumption, (2) overpopulation,
and (3) unequal distribution.

Figure 1. Summary Note Card.

"Environmental Change," Homer-Dixon,
Boutwell, and Rathjens, p. 40

There are three major causes of shortages of
human resources. (1)People consume the resources or
dilute their quality faster than the resources can
regenerate. (In this regard, a sustainable economy is one
that uses resources only as fast as they can be renewed.)
(2) Population increases put excessive demand on
the supply of resources. (3) A few people take control
of the resources and restrict distribution of them.

Figure 2. Paraphrase Note Card.

"Environmental Change," Homer-Dixon,
Boutwell, and Rathjens, p. 40

Homer-Dixon, Boutwell, and Rathjens use financial terms
to describe resource consumption. Depleting resources
faster than they can be renewed is "the consumption
of the resource's 'capital.'" Accordingly, a sustainable
economy is one that "leaves the capital intact and
undamaged so that future generations can enjoy
undiminished income."

Figure 3. Quotation Note Card.

The second source of scarcity is population growth. Over time, for instance, a given flow of water might have to be divided among a greater number of people. The final cause is change in the distribution of a resource within a society. Such a shift can concentrate supply in the hands of a few, subjecting the rest to extreme scarcity.

—Thomas Homer-Dixon, Jeffrey Boutwell, and George Rathjens, "Environmental Change and Violent Conflict," *Scientific American* Feb. 1993: 38–45.

USING YOUR NOTES

Your paper should not be a "quotation dump" in which you string together a large number of quotations without any interpretation or remarks. Instead it should express your own ideas and opinions, which you have developed and refined in the course of your research. The appropriate use of quotations is as *evidence that supports the claim or warrant at hand.* If you are relying on a warrant with the backing of expert testimony or statistics, quoting that material will strengthen your argument's ethos by showing your reader that your opinion is an informed one.

Always integrate quotations gracefully into your text; don't just drop them in. Quoted material should flow into your prose. Compare these two treatments of a quotation:

Incorrect: Samuel Johnson also praised London. "When a man is tired of London, he is tired of life."

| Correct: | As Samuel Johnson once remarked, "When a man is tired of London, he is tired of life" (Boswell 231). |

Notice how the quotation in the second example is part of the sentence. A common way to incorporate quotations is to use phrases such as "once remarked," "as one expert has said," "as one critic has observed," and "as one study has found."

Notice also that the second example leaves no doubt about who said the quoted words and indicates where they can be found. The parenthetical reference between the end quotation marks and the period identifies the author and the page number of the work where the quotation can be found. The full bibliographical information for the source is at the end of the paper under the author's name in the list of works cited.

Plagiarism

Plagiarism means taking someone else's words or ideas and passing them off as your own. However minor or innocent such an act might seem to you, any attempt to deceive one's audience violates the spirit of the objective pursuit of truth. Institutions of higher learning always expect you to act as part of this great tradition, and the penalties for plagiarism are stiff, ranging from an F to expulsion.

. The most obvious kind of plagiarism is to use someone's exact words as if they were your own—for example, to repeat Samuel Johnson's aphorism, "When a man is tired of London, he is tired of life," without acknowledging that the words are Johnson's. But there are other forms of plagiarism, such as writing, "When a man is tired of Manhattan, he is tired of life." To avoid plagiarism, you would need to add a phrase like "to paraphrase Samuel Johnson."

Another kind of plagiarism occurs when a paraphrase does not acknowledge the source. Here is an example:

| Original Passage: | "Anyone who knows the frantic temper of the present schools will understand the transvaluation of values that would be effected by [the abolition of grades]. For most of the students, the competitive grade has become the essence. The naive teacher points to the beauty and the ingenuity of the research; the shrewd student asks if he is responsible for that on the final exam."—Paul Goodman, p. 34 |
| Example of Plagiarism: | If grades were abolished, our entire set of educational values would be upset. Many students see their grades as the essence of academic success; while their teachers may concern themselves only with their subject matter, the students want to know what they will need to know to pass an exam. |

Although only a few exact words from the original appear in the example (*values, essence*) the exact idea is repeated without any credit to Paul Goodman. An example of quoting without plagiarizing would be:

> Correctly   Paul Goodman has argued that abolishing grades
> Quoted: would result in a "transvaluation of values" concern-
>   ing education as a whole. Many students view their
>   grades as the "essence" of education and are more
>   concerned with what they need to know for exams
>   than with the "beauty and ingenuity" of their subject
>   matters (Goodman 34).

When in doubt, provide a citation. This will save you the embarrassment of being accused of academic dishonesty.

DOCUMENTING SOURCES

The most obvious purpose of parenthetical references is to tell your readers the source of information or a quotation. The parenthetical references are keyed to a list at the end of the paper. There are several systems for citing references. This text explains the MLA (Modern Language Association) and APA (American Psychological Association) systems.

The MLA System

The Modern Language Association (MLA) format for identifying sources is used primarily by scholars in English, foreign languages, and other humanities disciplines. The parenthetical references in the text, which identify the author and usually the pages, refer to a list of works cited, which are arranged alphabetically by author.

PARENTHETICAL REFERENCES Parenthetical references include the author's last name and the page number of the source; for example,

    (Goodman 34),

as shown on page 311 at the end of the correctly quoted version of the passage by Paul Goodman.

If the author's name is mentioned in the sentence, only the page number is needed in the parenthetical reference immediately after the author's name.

If you are discussing an entire work, you do not need to include page numbers in the parenthetical reference.

If you consulted more than one work by the same author, include a shortened version of the title in your citation (underline titles of books; enclose titles of essays and articles in quotation marks):

(Goodman, <u>Growing Up</u> 34).

If the work has two or three authors, use all their names:

(Goodman and Strong 143-44).

If the work has more than three authors, use the first name and *et al.*:

(Goodman et al. 134).

If the work, such as a brief newspaper article, is not signed, identify it with a short version of the title:

("Education" 44).

If a statement has two or more sources, separate them with a semicolon:

(Goodman 34; Strong 98-99).

If you consulted sources by authors with the same last name, differentiate them by including their first initials or first names in the parenthetical references:

(Paul Goodman 34; Percival Goodman 178-79).

LIST OF WORKS CITED The complete information about the works identified in the parenthetical references comes on a separate page, titled "Works Cited," at the end of the paper. The entries are double-spaced, and the second and subsequent lines of each entry are indented half an inch (five spaces if you are using a typewriter).

The formats for common and not-so-common sources can be found in the fourth edition of the *MLA Handbook for Writers of Research Papers* (New York: Modern Language Association of America, 1995). Every writer of research papers should consult that handbook when preparing his or her final draft. However, here are examples of formats for most of the kinds of sources you are likely to use.

Books

Book by a Single Author

Willeford, Charles. <u>New Hope for the Dead</u>. New York: Ballantine, 1985.

Book by Two or Three Authors

Killiam, James, and Robert Cole. <u>Medical Ethics in America</u>. Boston: Globe, 1991.

Olds, Sally B., Marcia L. London, and Patricia E.
Ladewig. <u>Maternal Newborn Nursing</u>. 3rd ed.
Menlo Park: Addison-Wesley, 1988.

Book by More Than Three Authors

Barker, Francis, et al. <u>1642: Literature and Power
in the Seventeenth Century</u>. Essex: U of Essex,
1981.

Two or More Books by the Same Author

Sullivan, Michael. <u>The Arts of China</u>. Berkeley:
U of California P, 1967.
- - -. <u>The Birth of Landscape Painting in China</u>.
Berkeley: U of California P, 1961.
- - -. <u>The Meeting of Eastern and Western Art</u>.
Berkeley: U of California P, 1989.

Book by a Corporate Author

Editors, Inc. <u>How to Write Effective Prose</u>. New
York: Editors, 1990.

Edited Book

Peil, Manfred, ed. <u>Modern Views on Classic Films</u>.
Los Angeles: Smithdon, 1992.

Book with an Author and an Editor

Donne, John. <u>Poetical Works</u>. Ed. H. J. C. Grierson.
2 vols. Oxford: Oxford UP, 1912.

Book without an Author or an Editor

<u>Merriam-Webster Dictionary of English Usage</u>.
Springfield: Merriam-Webster, 1989.

Translated Book

>Trebelli, Salvatore. <u>My Life on Stage</u>. Trans. Erin
>   Cairns. New York: Musicland, 1972.

Book Edition Other Than the First

>de Man, Paul. <u>Blindness and Insight: Essays in the
>   Rhetoric of Contemporary Criticism</u>. 2nd ed.
>   Minneapolis: U of Minnesota P, 1983.

Republished Book

>Mitchell, Juliet. <u>Woman's Estate</u>. 1971. New York:
>   Vintage, 1973.

Multivolume Series

>Chambers, E. K. <u>The Elizabethan Stage</u>. 5 vols.
>   Oxford: Clarendon, 1923.

Volume in a Multivolume Series

>Twichett, Denis, and Michael Lowe, eds. <u>The Ch'in
>   and Han Empires, 221 B.C.-A.D. 220</u>. New York:
>   Cambridge UP, 1986. Vol. 1 of <u>The Cambridge
>   History of China</u>. 15 vols. to date. 1978-.

Book in a Series

>Bruner, Charlotte H., ed. <u>The Heinemann Book of
>   African Women's Writing</u>. Heinemann African
>   Writers Series. London: Heinemann, 1993.

Parts of Books

Selection in an Anthology or Compilation

>Neary, Adam. "The Impossibility of Utopia." <u>Essays
>   in Modern Political Theory</u>. Ed. Lenore
>   Kingsmore. New York: Political, 1982. 176-92.

Signed Article in an Encyclopedia

> Ruoff, A. Lavonne Brown. "Native American Prose and
> Poetry." Benét Reader Encyclopedia of American
> Literature. Ed. George Perkins, Barbara
> Perkins, and Phillip Leininger. New York:
> Harper, 1991.

Unsigned Article in an Encyclopedia

> "Coffee." Encyclopaedia Britannica. 1992 ed.

Introduction, Preface, Foreword, or Afterword

> Sirr, Lauren. Preface. School Certification and Its
> Critics. Chicago: Copper, 1982. v-xii.

Periodicals

Newspaper Article

> Donner, Matthew. "The Plight of the Intern." New
> York Times 1 Apr. 1990, sec. 2: 1+.

Article in a Monthly Magazine

> Pinho, Genero. "Revitalizing Traditional Opera."
> Opera Monthly Feb. 1991: 77-89.

Article in a Journal Paginated by Year or Volume

> Gale, Richard P. "The Environmental Movement and the
> Left: Antagonists or Allies?" Sociological
> Inquiry 53 (1983): 179-99.

Article in a Journal Paginated by Issue

> Stevenson, Warren. "'The Tyger' as Artefact." Blake
> Studies 2.1 (1969-70): 9.

Unsigned Article or Editorial

> "Finally a Solution." Editorial. Nation 16 Dec.
> 1988: 12.

Review

> Cather, Willa. Rev. of The Awakening, by Kate
> Chopin. Pittsburgh Leader, 8 July 1899: 6.

Other Sources

Unpublished Dissertation

> Yount, Neala Schleuning. "'America: Song We Sang
> Without Knowing'--Meridel Le Sueur's America."
> Diss. U of Minnesota, 1978.

Government Document

> United States. General Accounting Office. Siting of
> Hazardous Waste Landfills and Their Correlation
> with Racial and Economic Status of Surrounding
> Communities. Washington: GPO, 1983.

Lecture, Speech, or Address

> Freudenberg, Nicholas. "The Grass Roots Environmen-
> tal Movement: Not in Our Backyards." Annual
> meeting of American Assoc. for the Advancement
> of Science. New Orleans. 15 Feb. 1990.

Film

> 12 Monkeys. Dir. Terry Gilliam. Perf. Bruce Willis,
> Brad Pitt, and Madeline Stowe. Universal, 1995.

Television or Radio Program

> "Satanic Cults and Children." Geraldo. CBS. WCBS,
> New York. 19 Nov. 1987.

Recording

> Barber, Samuel. "Adagio for Strings," op. 11. Perf.
> Smithsonian Chamber Players. Cond. Kenneth
> Slowik. <u>Metamorphosis</u>. BMG, 1995.

Live Performance

> <u>The Tempest</u>. By William Shakespeare. Dir. Carey
> Perloff. Perf. David Strathairn, Graham Beckel,
> David Patrick Kelly, and Vera Farmiga. Geary
> Theater, San Francisco. 30 Jan. 1996.

Work of Art

> Vermeer, Jan. <u>Young Woman with a Water Jug</u>.
> Metropolitan Museum of Art, New York.

Court Decision

> Brown v. Board of Ed. 347 US 483. 1954.

Interview, Unpublished Letter, E-mail, or Other Personal Communication

> Moreno, Gloria. Personal interview. 29 Mar. 1999.
> Meredith, Lloyd. E-mail to the author. 14 Jan. 1999.

Current MLA Guidelines for Documenting Electronic Sources

If you do a lot of research with electronic sources, you may find it useful to consult *The Columbia Guide to Online Style,* by Janice Walker and Todd Taylor, which can be accessed at 〈http://www.cas.usf.edu/english/walker/janice.html〉, or *Electronic Style: A Guide to Citing Electronic Information,* by Xia Li and Nancy Crane (Westport, CT: Mecklermedia, 1996), which may be available in your library. This book covers a wide variety of electronic sources.

The fifth edition of the *MLA Handbook for Writers of Research Papers,* published in 1999, contains extensive guidelines for documenting electronic sources. These have been revised to reflect recent advances in computer technology and the growth of the Internet. For specific information concerning MLA format, and for recent updates, visit the MLA web site at: ⟨http://www.mla.org⟩.

The following is a list of the basic requirements for citing an Internet or electronic source according to MLA style.

1. Author or editor name, followed by a period.
2. The title of the article or short work (such as a short story or poem) enclosed by quotation marks.
3. The name of the book, journal, or other longer work in italics.
4. Publication information, followed by a period:
   City, publisher, and date for books
   Volume and year for journals
   Date of a magazine
   Date and description of government documents.
5. The date on which you accessed the information (no period).
6. The URL, placed within angle brackets, followed by a period.

Selected models follow.

Online reference database or scholarly project

> Victorian Women Writers Project. Ed. Perry Willett.
>
>   22 Feb. 1999. Indiana U. 26 Feb. 1999
>
>   ⟨http://www.indiana.edu/~letrs/vwwp⟩.

Book

> James, Henry. Daisy Miller. New York: Harper, 1892.
>
>   10 Mar. 1999 ⟨http://eldred.ne.mediaone.net/
>
>   hjj/dm/daisy0.html⟩.

Article in a scholarly journal

> Haviland, Beverly. "The Return of the Alien: Henry
>
>   James in New York, 1904." The Henry James
>
>   Review 16.3 (1993). 26 Feb. 1999 ⟨http://
>
>   musc.jbu.edu/journals/henry_james_review/⟩.

Article in a magazine

> Peyser, Marc. "Home of the Gray." Newsweek 1 Mar.
>
>   1999. 25 Feb. 1999 ⟨http://newsweek.com/nw-srv/
>
>   printed/us/front.htm⟩.

Article from an online encyclopedia

> "Toni Morrison." Encyclopaedia Britannica
>
>> Online. 1994-1999. Encyclopaedia Britannica,
>>
>> 4 Mar. 1999 〈http://members.cb.com/bol/
>>
>> topic?eu=55183&setn=#s_top〉.

CD-ROM

> The Civil War: A Newspaper Perspective. Nashville;
>
>> Folio, 1990. CD-ROM. Accessible Archives, 1994.

The APA System

The chief alternative to the MLA system for documenting sources is the system used by the American Psychological Association (APA), described in the *Publication Manual of the American Psychological Association,* 4th edition (Washington, DC: APA, 1994). This system is primarily used in psychology, sociology, and other social science disciplines. The main differences from MLA style are that the parenthetical references show the date of publication and that the list of works cited is called "References" and has the date as the second element of the entries.

PARENTHETICAL REFERENCES As with the MLA style, the APA style requires short parenthetical references within the text. Unlike the MLA style, these references include the date of publication, but page numbers are included only for direct quotations. Here is an example of a parenthetical reference in APA style (note that the author's name does not appear in the parentheses here, because the name appears in the text):

> Paul Goodman (1962, p. 34) argued that abolishing
>
>> grades would have revolutionary consequences,
>>
>> because "the competitive grade has become the
>>
>> essence" for most students.

If you do not mention the author's name in the text, include it in the parenthetical reference:

> (Goodman, 1962, p. 34).

If your sources include two works by an author in the same year, differentiate them by putting a letter after the date, both in the parenthetical reference and in the reference list:

> (Goodman, 1962a).

If your sources include two authors with the same last name, use their initials in the parenthetical citations:

(P. S. Goodman, 1962).

If a work has two authors, use an ampersand between their names in the parenthetical reference:

(Goodman & Strong, 1962).

If the work, such as a brief newspaper article, is not signed, refer to it by the first few words of the title, starting with the first important word (underline book titles; enclose article and essay titles in quotation marks):

("Education," 1962, p. 34).

If you cite two or more works by the same author in one parenthetical reference, follow the author's name with the years in chronological order, separated by commas:

(Goodman, 1962, 1972).

If you cite two or more sources in one parenthetical reference, give them in alphabetical order and separate them with semicolons:

(Goodman, 1962; Strong, 1958).

Personal communications, such as letters, e-mail messages, and telephone conversations, do not need to be included in the list of references. They can simply be identified in the parenthetical reference in the text:

(Goodman, personal communication, January 8, 1970).

LIST OF REFERENCES The MLA and APA requirements for the list of works cited are different on several counts. The first is that APA titles this page "References" rather than "Works Cited."

Notice also that MLA gives authors' first names, whereas APA shows only initials. APA style reverses last name and initials on all authors of a multiauthor work, not just the first author, as MLA does. Additionally, in APA style, only the first word of titles and subtitles of books and magazine articles is capitalized. However, APA style for the title of periodicals is like MLA style; namely, all important words are capitalized. Unlike the MLA, the APA includes the state abbreviation for cities of publication that are "not well known."

Finally, in APA style, the first line of each entry is indented five to seven spaces, and the subsequent lines begin at the left margin. Some instructors, however, may prefer a hanging indentation (that is, the first line is flush with the left margin and subsequent lines are indented), which is the style used in the MLA system and in printed APA publications as well.

Books

Book by a Single Author

>Anderson, B. (1992). <u>Modern sport psychology</u>. New York: Jacobson Press.

Book by Two or More Authors

>Bennet, M., & Juran, S. (1989). <u>Inventing culture</u>. Boston: Globe.

Book by a Corporate Author

>National Association of Anglers. (1990). <u>The ten best bass rivers in America: A guide</u>. Seattle: Nature Press.

Edited Book

>Kagan, J., & Coles, R. (Eds.). (1972). <u>Twelve to sixteen: Early adolescence</u>. New York: Norton.

Book without an Author or an Editor

><u>Merriam-Webster dictionary of English usage</u>. (1989). Springfield, MA: Merriam-Webster.

Translated Book

>Segouin, J. (1976). <u>Selling the sunset</u> (S. Moccio, Trans.). New York: Brookson.

Book Edition Other Than the First

>Bennett, W. L. (1988). <u>News: The politics of illusion</u> (2nd ed.). New York: Longman.

Separately Titled Volume in a Multivolume Work

>Schultz, J. (Ed.). (1982). <u>The history of thought: Vol. 11. The Elizabethan world</u>. New York: Edgeboro.

Parts of Books

Selection in an Anthology or Compilation

> Tobias, A. L. (1988). Bulimia: An overview. In K. Clark, R. Parr, & W. Castelli (Eds.), Evaluation and management of eating disorders. Champaign, IL: Life Enhancement Publications.

Article in an Encyclopedia

> Haseltine, W. A. (1992). AIDS. In Encyclopedia Americana (Vol. 1, pp. 334-336). Danbury, CT: Grolier.

Periodicals

Article in a Daily Newspaper

> Keane, V. (1990, July 21). More trouble for the troublemakers. New York Newsday, p. A21.

Article in a Magazine

> Dahlin, R. (1996, April 1). Laughing halfway to the bank. Publishers Weekly, 42-46.

Article in Journal Paginated by Volume or Year

> Crisp, A. H., Palmer, R. L., & Kalucy, R. S. (1976). How common is anorexia nervosa? A prevalence study. British Journal of Psychiatry, 128, 549-554.

Article in Journal Paginated by Issue

> Hansen, G. B. (1988). Layoffs, plant closings, and worker displacement in America: Serious problems that need a national solution. Journal of Social Issues, 44(4), 153-171.

Two or More Articles by Same Author in Same Year

> Steinberg, L. (1987a). The impact of puberty on family relations: Effects of pubertal status and pubertal timing. Developmental Psychology, 23, 451-460.

> Steinberg, L. (1987b). Recent research on the family at adolescence: The extent and nature of sex differences. Journal of Youth and Adolescence, 16, 191-197.

Unsigned Article or Editorial

> Fortune Global Service 500: The 50 largest retail companies. (1991, August 26). Fortune, 37, 179.

Review

> Giles, J. (1996, January 22). A cold, bleak Caribbean [Review of the book The autobiography of my mother]. Newsweek, 62.

Other Sources

Unpublished Dissertation

> Hall, C. (1993). Social networks and availability factors: Mobilizing adherents for social movement participation. Unpublished doctoral dissertation, Purdue University, Lafayette, IN.

Government Document

> U.S. Department of Justice. (1991). Criminal victimization, 1990 (Special Report No. NCJ-122743). Washington, DC: Bureau of Justice Statistics.

Research Report or Monograph

>   Robertson, M. J., Ropers, R., & Boyer, R.
>   (1985). <u>The homeless of Los Angeles County: An</u>
>   <u>empirical evaluation</u> (Document No. 4). Los Angeles:
>   University of California, Los Angeles, Basic Shelter
>   Research Project, School of Public Health.

Unpublished Paper Presented at a Meeting

>   Allgeier, E. (1986, August). <u>Coercive versus</u>
>   <u>consensual sexual interactions</u>. Paper presented at
>   the annual meeting of the American Psychological
>   Association, Washington, DC.

Film or Videotape

>   Stein, P. L. (Producer), & Levy, P. R.
>   (Director). (1994). <u>Neighborhoods: The hidden cities</u>
>   <u>of San Francisco</u> [Videotape]. San Francisco: KQED.

Court Decision

>   Brown v. Board of Educ., 347 U.S. 483 (1954).

Current APA Guidelines for Documenting Electronic Sources

ELECTRONIC SOURCES If material is available in both print and electronic forms, the APA prefers references to the print form. For documents available only in electronic form, provide enough information so that the version of the source you used can be retrieved.

ONLINE SOURCES Since the fourth edition of APA's *Publication Manual*, citation styles for online sources have been becoming more uniform, and the APA has updated its guidelines with an online document ⟨http://www.apa.org/journals/webref.html⟩; that style is reflected in the examples here.

In general, provide the author, date, and title information as you would for a print source. After the title, add a brief description of the type of online document (enclosed in square brackets). At the end of the citation, provide the date the information was retrieved and the URL.

Web Site

James, L. (1998, October 9). Highlights of the results. <u>DrDriving Road Rage Survey</u> [Web page]. Retrieved December 10, 1998, from the World Wide Web; http://www.aloha.net/~dyc/surveys/highlights.html

Article from Online Journal

Kraut, R., Lundmark, V., Patterson, M., Kiesler, S., Mukopadhyay, T., & Scherlis, W. (1998, September). Internet paradox: A social technology that reduces social involvement and psychological well-being? <u>American Psychologist, 53</u>, 1017-1031. Retrieved October 31, 1998 from the World Wide Web: http://www.apa.org/journals/amp/amp5391017.html

Newspaper Article Online

Young, J. R. (1998, November). Gender and electoral politics: Scholar's book rides the historical coattails of family values. <u>The Chronicle of Higher Education</u>, p. A14 [Newspaper article online]. Retrieved Nobember 14, 1998 from the World Wide Web: http://chronicle.com/weekly/v45/ill/11a01401.htm

Online Posting (Listserv/Mailing List or Usenet/Discussion List)

Kenyon, E. (1998, July 22). Safety and the lone researcher 2#. <u>Biog-Methods Archives</u> [Online discussion list archive]. Retrieved November 2, 1998 from the World Wide Web: http://www.mailbase.ac.uk/lists/biog-methods/1998-07/0002.html

CD-ROMs and Portable Databases

Steinhausen, H. C., & Vollrath, M. (1993). The self-image of adolescent patients with eating disorders. [CD-ROM]. International Journal of Eating Disorders, 13(2), 221-227. Abstract from: SilverPlatter File: PsycLIT Item: 80-33985

SAMPLE RESEARCH PAPER: MLA AND APA FORMATS

The sample research paper on pages 321–341 illustrates MLA style and makes a cogent argument for transracial adoption. Page 342 is a cutaway that shows the same paper set in APA style.

Kimberley Waibel

Professor Moekle

Writing 39C

Date

In the Best Interest of the Child?

Transracial adoption has historically followed a pattern
much like that of a roller coaster; one year it is favored, the
next year it is opposed. While the roller coaster has taken many
twists and turns, the motor propelling it has never changed.
Like many things, transracial adoption's past has been the
result of the racial views and prejudices of the judicial
system, the adoption agencies, and special interest groups.
This is evident when one looks closely at the court rulings and
social service practices that have been the driving force in
transracial adoption practices. Also obvious are discrepancies
in agency procedures and legal decisions. Consequently, minority
children available for adoption have suffered at the hands of
those who are charged with protecting them. The present system
has failed our children and we must do something to change it.
In order to bring transracial adoption's roller coaster ride to
an end, we must understand its past and the dynamics surrounding
it. We begin in one of the most racially volatile eras in U.S.
history--the 1940s.

The end of World War II came at a time when prevailing
social attitudes were steeped in racism. Many Blacks worked as
domestic help in the homes of wealthy and middle-class White
families. Bathrooms and drinking fountains were separated Black

Waibel 2

from White, and communities were far from culturally mixed. Minorities in general were having a difficult time being accepted as equals in the eyes of the White society. This is the climate in which transracial adoption surfaced in this country. It began with the end of the War, which left many children all over the world without parents and without homes (Simon and Alstein, Adoption, Race, and Identity 1-2). In addition, many of the American troops created illegitimate children in the countries to which they had been deployed (Bagley 135). As a result, many American families began to adopt children from foreign countries. Known as intercountry adoption, this practice was, and still is, very controversial. Yet it was through the efforts of the practitioners of intercountry adoption that transracial adoption, within our own country, came to be recognized as a feasible solution to the predicament adoption agencies faced concerning minority children. In 1948, in Minneapolis, Minnesota, a Black social worker named Laura Gaskin, placed a Black child with a White adoptive family (Hermann 150). Thus, transracial adoption was born.

The atmosphere of the forties and fifties no doubt gave rise to fierce opposition regarding interracial adoption. The families who ventured into the unknown realm of transracial adoption were likely condemned by their families, friends, and communities. These families were torn apart by the legal system as well. In 1955, a case known as In re Adoption of a Minor was decided in the District of Columbia. The case involved an illegitimate child born to a White couple, the birth mother and her new husband, a Black man. With the mother's permission, the Black man filed a petition to adopt the child. The court refused, citing that the child would lose the social status of a White man by virtue of the fact that his father of record would be Black (Simon and Alstein, A.R.I. 40). While the court of appeals reversed the district court's ruling, the district court's ruling represents the deeply rooted prejudices of this time period.

In 1958, the Child Welfare League of America published its Standards for Adoption Service (SAS). In it were guidelines upon which, had it been published only three years earlier, the D.C. district court could have based its decision. The SAS explicitly promoted inracial (same-race) adoption as the only acceptable form of adoption. Under the subtitle "Matching," the CWLA held that, "Physical resemblances should not be a determining factor in the selection of a home, with the possible exception of such racial characteristics as color" (Simon and Alstein, A.R.I. 4). Concurrently, the rate of transracial adoption diminished, and while specific statistics are unavailable, it is safe to assume that the position stated by the CWLA influenced many adoption agencies against practicing transracial adoption. Fortunately, the sexual revolution and the Civil Rights Movement were soon to follow, forcing the CWLA to reevaluate its position.

The sexual revolution brought about many changes in society, not the least of which was the increased availability of contraception and abortion. However, such services were primarily available to middle- and upper-class White people,

5

Waibel 4

due to the cost of things like birth control pills and doctors'
visits. What resulted was not a total reduction in the number of
children available for adoption, but a reduction in the number
of White children available for adoption (Simon and Alstein,
A.R.I. 2). Furthermore, the historical treatment of minorities
by adoption agencies was one that seemed to either exclude or
discourage participation. Statistics show that many more White
families were accepted as adoptive parents than minority families (Simon and Alstein, Transracial Adoptees and Their Families
9). These factors left adoption agencies facing an interesting
predicament. Should they continue to promote inracial adoption,
thereby leaving hundreds of children without homes? Or should
they place minority children with White families that could give
them stability and happiness? The sexual revolution left these
questions to be answered by the agencies.

At the same time, Martin Luther King, Jr., was leading the
nation's Civil Rights Movement, which promoted racial harmony
and the full integration of Black people into society. This allowed the adoption agencies to feel that transracial adoption
could be acceptable and would further the cause of racial integration. Consequently, in the late 1960s, the CWLA reversed its
earlier position, now stating that "...families who have the capacity to adopt a child whose racial background is different
from their own...should be encouraged to consider such a child"
(McRoy 149). Also interesting is that the National Association
for the Advancement of Colored People (NAACP) and the National
Urban League both made statements endorsing transracial adoption

as a reasonable alternative to traditional adoption (McRoy 149).
As a result, the frequency of transracial adoptions increased
nationwide, and between 1967 and 1972, while different sources
cite very different statistics, approximately 5,000 to 10,000
transracial adoptions occurred across the country.

In 1972, a new influence made its voice heard. In a national conference, the National Association of Black Social
Workers (NABSW) presented a viewpoint ardently opposed to transracial adoption. The 5,000 member association passed a resolution against transracial adoption, stating that "Black children
in white homes are cut off from the healthy development of themselves as Black people" (McRoy 150). Furthermore the NABSW went
so far as to call transracial adoption a form of genocide (Simon
and Alstein, A.R.I. 15). Support for the NABSW came from
African-American separatists who surfaced in response to the
Civil Rights Movement. These separatists reinforced the NABSW's
position by stating that the adoption of Black children by White
families would be detrimental to the African American community
as a whole (Hayes 305). As a result, the CWLA again reversed its
position, restating the importance of inracial placements in order to facilitate a child's integration into its adoptive family
(McRoy 150). Following the announcements made by the NABSW and
the CWLA, the rate of transracial adoptions decreased dramatically. In 1975, the last year the federal government collected
information on adoption statistics, the number of transracial
adoptions was 831, as reported by the Department of Health, Education and Welfare. This is much lower than the record high in

Waibel 6

1971, when 2,574 transracial adoptions were recorded (Simon and Alstein, Transracial Adoptees and Their Families 5). It is important to remember that minorities still constituted the bulk of the adoptable population. We can conclude that, while 831 children were adopted, many more were left without families.

Until this point in transracial adoption's history, the U.S. Supreme Court had refused to get involved, on the basis that such cases were domestic issues (Simon and Alstein, A.R.I. 48). In 1977, Drummond vs. Fulton County came before the Supreme Court. A White couple from Georgia had been the foster parents of a three-year-old boy since he was one month old. The agency denied the petition to adopt the child when he was one year old, and the Fifth Circuit Court of Appeals upheld the agency's decision on the grounds that there were racial differences between the parents and the child (Simon and Alstein, A.R.I. 42). The U.S. Supreme Court, staying true to its history of rejecting domestic cases, refused to hear the case stating, "It is obvious that race did enter into the decision of the Department" (Simon and Alstein, A.R.I. 42). However, the Court declared its confidence that race was not the only factor in the Department's decision. While this assertion may have been true, the Court unknowingly established a precedent that allowed race to be a factor, although not the only one, in cases concerning adoption. This started the resurgence of opposition to transracial adoption. More fuel was added to the opposition's fire in 1978, when the Indian Child Welfare Act was passed. The Act was passed to ensure that Indian children removed from their biological parents would be placed with families that were representative of the American Indian's culture and heritage (McRoy 150). By providing that a minority group deserved special consideration during adoption proceedings with regard to their culture, the federal government advanced the anti-transracial adoption movement. However, the opposition's influence on adoption law and standards did not last long. This was due to the changing racial attitudes in society approaching the eighties. While far from totally equal, Black people were, at this point, seen as social equals and had been integrated into society for some time. Therefore, the NABSW had a much harder time promoting their views to a society that, as a whole, no longer believed in separation of the races.

In 1984, a landmark case was decided. Surprisingly, the Supreme Court overlooked tradition and got involved in the case known as Palmore vs. Sidoti. A married White couple got divorced and the mother was awarded custody of their three-year-old daughter. When the mother became involved with a Black man, the father sought custody of his daughter. When the mother and her boyfriend married, the state court revoked the mother's custody and awarded custody to the father. The court stated that "a racially mixed household would have a detrimental effect on the child if she remained there" (Hermann 154). The U.S. Supreme Court, in a unanimous decision, reversed the lower court's decision based on the Fourteenth Amendment's Equal Protection Clause, which states that, "No state shall...deny to any person within its jurisdiction the equal protection of the laws" (Gro-

Waibel 8

lier's). Four years later, in 1988, the CWLA's <u>Standards for Adoption Services</u> presented a much diluted position concerning transracial adoption. While still maintaining inracial adoption to be the best alternative, the 1988 <u>SAS</u> states, "If aggressive, ongoing recruitment efforts are unsuccessful in finding families of the same ethnicity or culture, other families should be considered" (Simon and Alstein, <u>A.R.I.</u> 32). As of the most recent research, the CWLA's position has not changed, despite the fact that the NABSW renews its vehement position against transracial adoption yearly.

Despite the recent legal efforts to abolish race as a determinant in adoption, transracial adoption is still not a completely accepted practice. Other factors still influence whether or not minority children are adopted by White families. First of all, there is a prevailing attitude that transracial adoption is not an ideal, nor is it an equal alternative to inracial adoption. When children are placed transracially, it is seen as a subordinate decision; "second best" (Simon and Alstein, <u>A.R.I.</u> 32). Such an attitude creates a situation in which adoption agencies go to extreme measures to find same-race homes for a child, allowing the child to spend additional time in foster or institutional care. The older the child gets, the more developed his identity is, the more difficult it is for him to integrate into an adoptive family. However, one of the biggest influences on the state of transracial adoption today lies in the ambiguity of the views of not only the adoption agencies, but the federal government as well. State by state,

10

the guidelines regarding transracial adoption have differed greatly throughout its history. This is evident when one looks at the individual states' statistics. From 28 agencies in California, 62 children were placed transracially in 1974, as compared to the 37 children placed transracially from 27 agencies in Michigan (Simon and Alstein, Transracial Adoption 32). Even in the present day, courts in individual states decide transracial adoption cases differently. Michigan, Maryland, and Pennsylvania have all been involved in cases where children were removed from custody based solely on their race, Matter of "Male" Chiang, Queen vs. Queen, and McLaughlin vs. Pernsley, respectively (Simon and Alstein, A.R.I. 49-50). Oftentimes a lower court will rule in favor of the adoption agency removing a child placed transracially, and a higher court will reverse the ruling. This inconsistency in decision making is detrimental to the children, as they will often be shuffled from one place to the other, back and forth from adoptive parents to foster care, and back again.

This discrepancy doesn't exist solely at the state level. In 1972, the same year the NABSW came out against transracial adoptions, the U.S. Supreme Court declared all antimiscegenation (interracial marriage) laws unconstitutional. The Court, essentially, has upheld that race is not a determinant for who can and cannot be a family. Yet, the Court has failed to extend this judgment to rulings against transracial adoption. The adoption agencies, however, are the most ambiguous with regard to transracial adoption. Agencies will place Black children in White

Waibel 10

foster homes, often for years at a time, but not allow those
same families to adopt their foster children. In 1989, in Napa
Valley, California, several White families were recruited to
provide temporary (45 days) foster care for Black infants born
addicted to drugs. Several years later, when the families tried
to adopt their foster children, the department of social services began removing the children and placing them with Black
foster parents (Simon and Alstein, <u>A.R.I.</u> 54). Not only are
such actions detrimental to the foster child, but they create
emotional strains for the foster family as well. People fall
in love with the children they care for, and when one is taken
away, whether by accident or purposefully, it is devastating to
all parties involved.

Social service organizations, funded by the government and
our tax dollars, have been denying adoptable children homes in
this manner since the 1940s without the public's knowledge. Essentially, transracial adoption has been an issue ignored by
much of the popular media, preventing the general public from
forming any kind of opinion on the subject. Unfortunately, this
leaves this issue to be decided by special interest groups like
the NABSW who use their influence to frame adoption standards
through the CWLA. The views of such groups have proven to be
physically and emotionally harmful to the children whom they are
trying to protect. While adoption agencies try to search for a
racial match for a child, that child spends unnecessary time in
foster or institutional care. In addition, adoption agencies
have actually lowered their applicant requirements in order to

Waibel 11

make an inracial placement. A young Black boy in Ohio was killed
by his adoptive Black parents after social workers failed to acknowledge potential warning signs about the couple's qualifica-
tions (Hermann 155). The present structure has failed our children and will continue to do so if it is left alone. What is
needed is a major restructuring of the adoption system as we
know it. Within a new system, all kinds of changes can be made
in order to find the most loving and suitable home for orphaned
children. However, it is impossible for each individual state to
come up with its own system without there being discrepancies
across state lines. A federal agency needs to be formed in order
to regulate, investigate, and assist the adoption agencies in
this country. Such an agency would serve as an umbrella organization to which all adoption agencies, public or private, would
answer. Hopefully, this restructuring would also include the
passage of a law banning any restrictions based on the race of
the child or the adoptive parent. In the words of the NABSW,
"Human beings are products of their environment and develop
their sense of values, attitudes, and self-concept within their
family structure" (McRoy 150). Restructuring the adoption system
will give minority children a better chance of finding what the
NABSW says they need most, a family.

    As has been shown, the adoption services available in this
country are sorely inadequate. Rectifying this situation will
not only take a lot of manpower, but it will require that federal funds be allocated in order to meet the demands of creating
and operating a new system. In addition, this proposal is, in

Waibel 12

fact, a long-term solution and we will obviously need to implement short-term solutions as well. While the government is busy
trying to change the adoption situation, children are still going to require adoption and foster services, and some short-term
objectives will create an atmosphere in which adoption and foster care can still flourish.

The first step in this long-term plan is the passage
of a law banning race as a determinant in the selection of prospective adoptive parents. This can be achieved in one of three
ways. Proponents of transracial adoption can write to their con-
gressmen and ask them to draft a bill to be introduced on the
House floor. The bill is then revised as needed and, if passed,
sent to the Senate and, ultimately, the President's office. Unfortunately, this process takes an inordinate amount of time.
Taking this route only agitates the problem because of the
amount of time it takes, leaving adoptable children and adoptive
parents in the same boat as they are in now, while politicians
fight over every word in the proposed bill.

Another possibility is to get a law passed by an   15
Executive Order. This is when the bill bypasses the House of
Representatives and the Senate, and the President signs the bill
without their approval. After the President signs the bill, it
automatically becomes law. Unfortunately, this takes quite a lot
of time as well, due to the amount of time it would take to
alert the President to the urgency of the situation. The number
of people one has to go through in order to get to the President
is absolutely incredible, and, like previously mentioned, the

children and the parents trying to adopt them pay the price by not being allowed to legally call themselves a family.

The only other possibility would be to find a couple willing to fight their case all the way to the U.S. Supreme Court using the 1972 ruling against antimiscegenation (interracial marriage) laws as a precedent, in addition to the Fourteenth Amendment. Agreeably, this would also take some time, however, there are many foster parents out there fighting to become legal parents of their foster children, and undoubtedly a family willing to do this can be found. Ultimately, the decision is in the hands of the Supreme Court, but with the 1972 ruling as a basis, a competent lawyer should be able to convince 9 people that race is not a valid requirement when it comes to adoption, or anything else, for that matter. While this would not actually create a law, it would establish a strong precedent that lower courts in this country would base their rulings on, and make adoption agencies think twice about denying someone parentage based on skin color.

While a law against using race as a determinant is ideal, it is not completely necessary in order to put the rest of the plan into action. The next step would be for the Department of Health and Human Services to add a fifth division to its Department, the Office of Adoption and Foster Care. In the beginning, this organization would be charged with the reformation of the adoption system, and would later oversee and govern the new system. In order for this office to regulate adoption fairly, it is important that all adoption agencies be required by law to fol-

Waibel 14

low the policies established by the office. To ensure the public
that their local agencies are legal, the office needs to establish a membership of agencies which can promote themselves as
such. Nonmembership agencies would be subject to investigation
from the office and would eventually die out due to lack of
funding, as all public funds would be directed through the office to its membership.

Adoption agencies are not the only players in the adoption
game, however, and other useful organizations need to be targeted for membership as well. Interim-care facilities, such as
group homes like Orangewood Children's Home in Orange, California, provide children with a positive environment in which to
grow while they are separated from their natural parents, or
while they are waiting for a foster or adoptive family. Such organizations are integral to the adoption process and would benefit from the government membership system. Such a system of membership not only allows for fair regulation, but reassures those
who seek out such services that the agency they have chosen will
follow certain procedures in order to ensure a quick and successful adoption.

Secondly, the new office must sit down to establish a set
of rules and procedures that agencies must follow. Covered in
this set of rules would be things such as placing a ceiling over
adoption fees, limiting the amount of time a child spends in
foster or group care, and speeding up the paperwork process involved in adoption. These three subjects are universal concerns
with regard to adoption, transracial or not. Transracial adop-

Waibel 15

tion, however, needs to be an issue of utmost concern to this office, and at the top of this list would be a rule stating that race cannot be an impediment to the adoption process, nor will race be a factor when determining the appropriateness of a family for a particular child. The important thing here is that race not be used as an excuse for why a child is without a family.

Social workers need to stop looking at transracial   20
adoption as a second-rate alternative and start treating it as an equally valuable alternative to inracial adoption. In a study done by William Feigelman and Arnold R. Silverman of Nassau Community College, they found that "[transracially adopted] children's adjustments were generally similar to those of White in-racially adopted children" (600). In fact, little proof has been given to support the opposition's claims that transracially adopted children are maladjusted and have identity problems. We can conclude, then, that transracial adoption can and should be practiced with no more possible risk than any other type of adoption. From this point on, the Office of Adoption and Foster Care would be charged with overseeing and investigating the actions of adoption agencies. It would create a system of regulation that safeguards the children and the parents, rather than special interest groups and politicians.

While maintaining the adoption system, the office would also offer a wide variety of support and educational services for adopted and foster children and their families. Such services would include: regular group meetings for adopted

Waibel 16

children, regular meetings for adoptive parents, workshops on
special-needs adoption, including transracial adoption and adoption of children with disabilities, and a widespread media campaign to promote the uniqueness of families formed through
adoption as well as to recruit prospective families. In addition, the office needs to actively recruit minorities as prospective adoptive parents, not to promote inracial adoption, but
to create as diverse a database of prospective parents as possible. This is achieved by setting up agencies in primarily minority areas staffed by a multi-ethnic group of people as has
been previously recommended (McRoy 156-157). Not only does this
create a more heterogeneous group from which to choose, but it
also allays the fears of anti-transracial adoption groups that
minorities will continue to be excluded from the adoption
process.

The benefits of this restructuring will certainly outweigh
its costs. The government already pays for a vast majority of
the country's social workers, thus the main budgetary increase
would come from staffing the new Office. Since the Office would
be a part of the already-established Department of Health and
Human Services, it is possible that some staff members from
other areas could be utilized here as well. Adoption has always
been a state's issue, thus each individual state has a budget
set aside for adoption services. Since the federal government
would be relieving the states of many of their responsibilities
regarding adoption, it would be fair for the states to be required to hand the money they set aside for adoption services

over to the government. Not only does this relieve some of the
federal government's budgetary tensions, but it allows for a
smaller increase in taxes on the public, due to the fact that
they are already paying for these services. The only difference
is that the money goes to the federal government instead of the
state government. However, there will have to be either an increase in taxes or a decrease in spending to help pay for
this restructuring. The increase in taxes could be achieved by
increasing property taxes on property worth over $500,000. Other
revenue could be acquired by increasing interest rates on luxury
loans over $500,000. Spending can be cut in every department
with regard to the perks that agency officials receive.
While the amount that this would generate is unknown, it is conceivable that this office could be maintained with minimal tax
increases and spending decreases. However it is done, we have,
in the end, ensured a future for abandoned children, something
that has no price tag.

Unfortunately, this is a long-term process, and there
are a few things we can do in the meantime in order to keep
transracial adoption alive. First, all of the small organizations that have been formed over the years that promote transracial adoption, such as Parents to Adopt Minority Youngsters
(PAMY), Families for Interracial Adoption, and Opportunity, need
to come together to form a single advocacy group. This group
should then create a database of transracial adoptees and their
families and invite them to become part of the organization.
Then they need to hire a professional lobbyist to give them a

Waibel 18

voice in Washington D.C. By combining these groups of people,
this alliance would prove to be fruitful in expediting the implementation of the preceding proposal.

The second thing that is essential in promoting transracial
adoption is the widespread involvement of the media. The media
is so important to the cause of transracial adoption, and it has
already proven to be a very powerful force. On September 9,
1992, the state of Texas removed a Black boy from his White foster parents, Lana and Phillip Jenkins. In October of that same
year, the Jenkins appeared on The Phil Donahue Show. The show
aired a tape of the Jenkins' son, Christopher, being taken away
from his parents kicking and screaming. As a result, the Jenkin-
ses received calls and letters in support of their cause, and
the national attention was beneficial because, on January 15,
1993, the Jenkins got Christopher back. Through the media, the
state of Texas was forced to change its laws to allow transracial adoption. James Myart, the attorney for the Jenkins, told
Phil Donahue that "It was the national attention brought by you
[Donahue], quite frankly, that got the people in the state of
Texas, and throughout this country, to rally in support of this
White family and this Black child" (Donahue 15 March 1994). More
media attention like this is needed to get the general public
involved in this issue so they can pressure their representatives in Washington to do something about it.

While the most ideal of all situations is for all children
to be born into a family that could provide them with the love
and support they need to grow into a productive adult, this is

25

not likely to ever be the case. Thus we must provide those children who don't have the benefits of a loving family with the resources to find one. The adoption system we presently use is inefficient and inconsistent. The very children it strives to
protect are the ones who suffer the most. Minority children have
suffered the most because of the controversies and conflicting
viewpoints regarding transracial adoption. The very title
"transracial adoption" places a stigma upon the practice, making
it sound like placing a minority child in a White family is the
process of stepping over a specific line, of crossing a set
boundary. This is not the case. Transracial adoption is not
about color or political agendas; it is about love. With the
help of the media, the public and the federal government, it is
possible to put the love back into the adoption process for all
of the adoptable children.

Waibel 20

Works Cited

Austin, Judy, ed. <u>Adoption: The Inside Story</u>. New York: Barn Owl
    Books, 1985.

Bagley, Christopher, Loretta Young, and Anne Scully.
    <u>International and Transracial Adoptions</u>. Brookfield,
    Vermont: Ashgate Publishing Company, 1993.

Brophy, Beth. "The Unhappy Politics of Interracial Adoption."
    <u>U.S. News and World Report</u> 13 Nov. 1989: 72-74.

Day, Dawn. <u>The Adoption of Black Children</u>. London: Souvenir
    Press Ltd., 1984.

Feigelman, William, and Arnold R. Silverman. "The Long-Term
    Effects of Transracial Adoption." <u>Social Service Review</u> 58
    (1984): 588-602.

Hayes, Peter. "Transracial Adoption: Politics and Ideology."
    <u>Child Welfare</u> 72 (1993): 301-310.

Hermann, Valerie Phillips. "Transracial Adoption: 'Child-Saving'
    or 'Child-Snatching'?" <u>National Black Law Journal</u> 13 (1993):
    147-164.

Kallgren, Carl A., and Pamela J. Caudill. "Current Transracial
    Adoption Practices: Racial Dissonance or Racial Awareness?"
    <u>Psychological Reports</u> 72 (1993): 551-558.

McRoy, Ruth G. "An Organizational Dilemma: The Case of
    Transracial Adoptions." <u>The Journal of Applied Behavioral
    Science</u> 25.2 (1989): 145-160.

<u>The Phil Donahue Show</u>. NBC. KNBC, Los Angeles, 15 Mar. 1994.

Rosenthal, Donna. "Did Cultures Clash Over 'Schindler's'?" <u>Los
    Angeles Times</u> 22 January 1994: F1, F9.

Waibel 21

Simon, Rita James, and Howard Alstein. Transracial Adoption. New
    York: John Wiley and Sons, Inc., 1977.

---. Transracial Adoptees and Their Families. New York: Praeger
    Publishers, 1987.

---. Adoption, Race, and Identity. New York: Praeger Publishers,
    1992.

Wheeler, David L. "Black Children, White Parents." The Chronicle
    of Higher Education 15 Sept. 1993: A9, A16.

Zastrow, Charles H. Outcome of Black Children-White Parents
    Transracial Adoptions. San Francisco: R&E Research
    Associates, Inc., 1977.

Sample Paper Format: APA Style

In the Best Interest of the Child?   4

References

Bagley, J. (Ed.). (1985). Adoption: The inside story.
New York: Barn Owl Books.

Bagley, C., Young, L., & Scully, A. (1993).
International and transracial adoptions. Vermont: Ashgate.

Brophy, B. (1989, November 13). The unhappy politics
of interracial adoption. U.S. News & World Report, 45,
72-74.

In the Best Interest of the Child?   3

a feasible solution to the predicament adoption agencies
faced concerning minority children. In 1948, in
Minneapolis, Minnesota, a Black social worker named Laura
Gaskin placed a Black child with a white adoptive family

at least 1" ↕

at least 1" ↔

In the Best Interest of the Child?   2

center title

5 spaces

In the Best Interest of the Child?

Transracial adoption has historically followed a
pattern much like that of a roller coaster: one year it is
favored, the next year it is opposed. Athough the roller
coaster has taken many twist and turns, the motor
propelling it has never changed. Like many things,

5 spaces

In the Best Interest of the Child?   1

at least 1" ↔

Running head: IN THE BEST INTEREST OF THE CHILD?

In the Best Interest of the Child?
Kimberly Waibel
Rutgers University

center title, name, school

GLOSSARY

ad hominem Latin for "to the man"; personal attack on an opponent instead of on the opponent's arguments

ad populum Latin for "to the people"; an argument that appeals to general sentiments or prejudices

allusion A reference to a person or fact (for example, the American Revolution) that the audience is expected to know without explanation

analogy A comparison for purposes of explanation, usually between something concrete and something abstract

analysis The breaking down of complete matters into simpler ones

appeal A traditional name for the method by which the arguer hopes to convince the reader; for example, the appeal to reason

argument Language organized and used to convince others

assertion A declaration of belief

assumption Ideas or values that the writer takes as givens

audience The imagined readers of your argument

authority A reliable, expert source of support

backing The authority or evidence on which a warrant is based

begging the question An attempt to assume in advance what needs to be proved

bibliography A list of works on a subject

claim The conclusion your argument is attempting to prove

cliché An expression so worn out as to convey little meaning

connotation The associations inspired by a word; its flavor or spirit, as opposed to the strict meaning, its denotation

data Facts that prompt you to make your argument

deductive reasoning Reasoning from general principles to particular conclusions

demonstration The provision of reasons and evidence to support assertions

denotation The literal, dictionary definition of a word

diction Word choice: "high" diction is formal, "low" diction informal

enthymeme A syllogism whose parts are not all clearly stated

ethos The qualities of character, intelligence, and morality that an arguer conveys through the manner of argument

equivocate To deliberately use ambiguous words to confuse the issue

grounds A term in Toulmin's system that is equivalent to "data"

hyperbole A statement exaggerated for effect

hypothesis A conditionally held theory to aid in exploring the meaning of what you seek to explain

inference The intuitive act of recognizing an implication

inductive reasoning The type of reasoning that proceeds from particular facts to general explanations

irony Intentionally saying one thing to convey another

logos The traditional name for the appeal to reason or logic

metaphor A comparison that illustrates meaning through figurative language, for example, "Babe Ruth was the Sultan of Swat."

non sequitur A statement that does not follow from a previous statement

paradox An apparent contradiction that contains a deeper meaning, for example, "nothing is so invisible as the obvious"

paraphrase Restating a point in your own words

pathos The traditional name for the appeal to emotion or feeling

persona The implied character created by the writer to speak for him or her; for example, at a given time a writer's persona may seem to be a joker, but the writer is a *person* whose complex identity may not be reduced to a role played at a particular time

persuasion The act of seeking to convince others

plagiarism Using someone else's words or ideas without giving proper credit

point of view The attitude with which a writer approaches the subject

post hoc, ergo propter hoc Latin for "after this, therefore because of this"; the false assumption that, because one event happened after another, the first somehow caused the second

premise The underlying assumption from which one begins to make a point

qualifier A restriction or modification in the extent of an argued claim

rebuttal The part of an argument that allows for exceptions without having to give up the claim as generally true

refutation The process of meeting and overcoming the arguments of your opponent

rhetoric Traditionally, the art and study of persuasion; now loosely used to suggest an emphasis on manner at the expense of matter

rhetorical question A question asked figuratively, for effect, rather than literally, for information

simile Using "like" or "as" in acknowledgment that one is using figurative language: "In the world of baseball, Babe Ruth was like a giant."

syllogism A classical method of deductive reasoning in which two premises considered together lead with certainty to a conclusion

syntax Word order

thesis The central idea of an argument or essay

tone The way a writer "sounds"; the writer's attitude

Toulmin system The method of reasoned argument invented by Stephen Toulmin and emphasized in the appeals to reason analyzed in this book

transition A link between points or sections in writing

trope A name for "figure of speech"

warrant The underlying generalization (explicit or implicit) that the writer expects the reader to share and that connects the data with the claim

writing process A general term for the stages involved from prewriting through the production of a final draft

ACKNOWLEDGMENTS

PETER ALSON, "Raking It In," September 10, 1995. Copyright © 1995 by The New York Times. Reprinted by permission.

CLEVELAND AMORY, "Needless Cruelty to Animals," September 17, 1989. Copyright © 1989 by The New York Times. Reprinted by permission.

ROBERT ATWAN, "A Meditation on Barbie Dolls." Used with permission of the author.

DOUG BANDOW, "Eliminate the Minimum Drinking Age," June 6, 1998. Reprinted by permission of Copley News Service.

RICK BERMAN, "Should We Adopt a Lower National Blood Alcohol Threshold for Drunk Driving? No!," April 5, 1998. Reprinted with permission of Knight-Ridder/Tribune Information Services.

PAPIA BHATTACHARYYA, "Bad Associations." Reprinted by permission of the author.

SARA BIRD, "The Q Gene," May 1, 1994. Copyright © 1994 by The New York Times. Reprinted by permission.

DICK BOLAND, "Serving Time the Old-Fashioned Way," March 4, 1998. By permission of the author and the Creators Syndicate.

LINDA BOWLES, "Big Brother's Two Minute Hate" from "Tobacco Scam Is Format for Tyranny," May 13, 1998. By permission of the author and the Creators Syndicate.

FRED BRONSON, "A Selected Chronology of Musical Controversy," Billboard, March 26, 1994. Copyright © BPI Communications, Inc. Used with permission.

SAM BROWNBACK, "Free Speech: Lyrics, Liberty, and License," May 15, 1998, Vital Speeches, City News Publishing Co. Reprinted by permission.

RHONDA BURNS, "Downsizing the Middle Class." Used with permission of the author.

STEPHEN CHAPMAN, "Public Servants Often Behave Like Masters," March 11, 1998. By permission of the author and the Creators Syndicate.

MONA CHAREN, "Is Fertility Technology Good or Bad?," December 12, 1998. By permission of the author and the Creators Syndicate.

SALLY CHEN, "Smoking Is Bad for Everyone So It Should Be Illegal." Used with permission of the author.

MATTHEW E. CONOLLY, "Euthanasia Is Not the Answer." Used with permission of the author.

CRAIG R. DEAN, "Legalize Gay Marriage," September 28, 1991. Copyright © 1991 by The New York Times. Reprinted by permission.

HELEN DODGE, "Special Crimes Need Special Laws." Used with permission of the author.

BARBARA EHRENREICH, "Ice-T: Is the Issue Social Responsibility or Free Speech?" Time, July 20, 1992, p. 88. Copyright © 1992 Time Inc. Reprinted by permission.

DON FEDER, "An Amendment Is Not the Way to Honor the Flag." By permission of the author and the Creators Syndicate.

SHIRA FELDMAN, "Corporations Are Looting Intellectual Property." Used with permission of the author.

M. F. K. FISHER, "The Indigestible: The Language of Food." Copyright © 1979 by M. F. K. Fisher. Originally appeared in The New York Review of Books. This usage granted by permission.

SAMUEL FRANCIS, "Hate Crimes Change the Law" from "Liberal British Magazine Scorns 'Hate Crime' Laws," June 27, 1998. Copyright © 1998 Tribune Media Services, Inc. All Rights Reserved. Reprinted with permission.

HENRY LOUIS GATES, JR., "Whose Culture Is It Anyway? It's Not Just Anglo-Saxon." Copyright © 1991 by Henry Louis Gates, Jr. Originally published in *The New York Times*. Reprinted by permission of the author.

TIPPER GORE, "Curbing the Sexploitation Industry," March 14, 1988. Copyright © 1988 by The New York Times. Reprinted by permission.

MEG GREENFIELD, "In Defense of the Animals," Newsweek, April 17, 1989. Reprinted by permission of the author.

JEFFREY HART, "Ethnic Studies Are a Delusion." Reprinted with permission from King Features Syndicate.

MARIA HERNANDEZ, "My Flag—Burn It and Burn." Used with permission of the author.

DEREK HUMPHRY, from *Dying With Dignity*. Copyright © 1992 by Derek Humphry. Published by arrangement with Carol Publishing Group. A Birch Lane Press Book.

ROBERT M. HUTCHINS, "Preface to *The Great Conversation*." Reprinted from *Great Books of the Western World*. Copyright © 1952, 1990 Encyclopaedia Britannica, Inc.

ICE-T, lyrics from "Cop Killer." Words and Music by Ernest Cunnigan and Tracy Marrow. Copyright © 1992 PolyGram International Publishing, Inc., Ernkneesea Music and Rhyme Syndicate Music. International Copyright © Secured. All Rights Reserved.

JOANNE JACOBS, "End the War on Drugs." Reprinted by permission of Tribune Media Services.

MARIANNE M. JENNINGS, "Who's Harrassing Whom?" *The Wall Street Journal*, July 6, 1998. Reprinted with permission of *The Wall Street Journal*. Copyright © 1998 Dow Jones & Company, Inc. and Marianne Jennings. All rights reserved.

MICHAEL KINSLEY, "Ice-T: Is the Issue Social Responsibility or Free Speech?" *Time*, July 20, 1992, p. 88. Copyright © 1992 Time Inc. Reprinted by permission.

NANCY LEDERMAN, "Must They Tinker with the Dying?" January 16, 1993. Copyright © 1993 by The New York Times. Reprinted by permission.

MARTIN LUTHER KING, JR., "Letter from Birmingham Jail." Copyright © 1963 by Martin Luther King, Jr., copyright renewed 1991 by The Estate of Martin Luther King.

RON KLINE, "A Scientist: 'I Am the Enemy.'" Used with permission of the author.

JOSEPH KUNCEWITCH, "Only Hunting Trims Deer Reproduction." Reprinted with permission from the author.

MICHAEL LEWIS, "Rainbow, Inc.," December 8, 1996. Copyright © 1996 by The New York Times. Reprinted by permission.

MISS MANNERS (JUDITH MARTIN), "Rudeness Can Be Lethal." From "Rudeness Turns Outs to Be Lethal When Respect Is Life or Death Issue," February 21, 1994. Copyright © 1998 by Judith Martin. Distributed by United Feature Syndicate, Inc.

YONA ZELDIS MCDONOUGH, "What Barbie Really Taught Me," from *The Barbie Chronicles: A Real Doll Turns 40* by Yona Zeldis McDonough. Copyright © 1999 by Yona Zeldis McDonough. Reprinted with permission of the author and the publisher, Fireside, a registered trademark of Simon & Schuster, Inc.

DOUGLAS M. MCLEOD, WILLIAM P. EVELAND, JR., AMY I. NATHANSON, "Support for Censorship of Violent and Misogynic Rap Lyrics, An Analysis of the Third-Person Effect," Communication Research, Vol. 24, No. 2, April 1997, 153–174. Copyright © 1997 Sage Publications, Inc. Reprinted by permission of the publisher.

MARNIE MONIERE, "How to Win Every Time." Used with permission from the author.

DAVID PELLICANE, "Alone with My E-Mail," Simpleton.com. November 18, 1997. With permission from the author.

DAN MORAN, "King's Ransom" and "Censorship Begins at Home." Used with permission of the author.

ANNA QUINDLEN, "Raised on Rock and Roll," February 25, 1987. Copyright © 1987 by The New York Times. Reprinted by permission.

ISHMAEL REED, "How Not to Get the Infidel to Talk the King's Talk." Copyright © 1982 Ishmael Reed. Reprinted by permission of the author.

CHARLEY REESE, "Hate Crimes Laws Are a Bad Idea," November 4, 1997. Reprinted with permission from King Features Syndicate.

PAUL CRAIG ROBERTS, "The Poor Have Enslaved the Rich," November 19, 1997. By permission of the author and the Creators Syndicate.

RICHARD RODRIGUEZ, "Gains and Losses" from *The Hunger of Memory* by Richard Rodriguez. Copyright © 1982 by Richard Rodriguez. Reprinted by permission of David R. Godine, Publisher, Inc.

PAULA ROTHENBERG, "Critics of Attempts to Democratize the Curriculum Are Waging a Campaign to Misrepresent the Work of Responsible Professors." Used with permission from the author.

PHYLLIS SCHLAFLY, "Clinton May Get Toasted By 'Global Warming,'" November 26, 1997. Reprinted by permission of Copley News Service.

BRIAN K. SIMMONS, "The Effect of Censorship on Attitudes toward Popular Music," *Popular Music and Society,* Vol. 16, Issue 4, pp. 61–67. Reprinted with permission from the publisher.

THOMAS SOWELL, "A World of Virtual Reality" and "Global Warming Is a Grab for Power," December 24, 1997. By permission of the author and the Creators Syndicate.

BRENT STAPLES, "The Quota Bashers Come In from the Cold," April 12, 1998. Copyright © 1998 by The New York Times. Reprinted by permission.

JUDITH LEE STONE, "Should We Adopt a Lower National Blood Alcohol Threshold for Drunk Driving, Yes!," April 5, 1998. Reprinted with permission of Knight-Ridder / Tribune Information Services.

BOB SWIFT, "On Reading Trash," *The Miami Herald,* April 28, 1988. Reprinted with permission of *The Miami Herald.*

CAL THOMAS, "Burned Up over Flag Burning." Copyright © 1995 Los Angeles Times Syndicate. Reprinted with permission.

GREG TUCULESCU, "If You Wish to Speak With a Computer, Please Choose from the Following Levels of Frustration." Used with permission from the author.

U. S. ENGLISH FOUNDATION, "In Support of Our Common Language." Reprinted with permission.

ELLEN ULLMAN, "Needed: Techies Who Know Shakespeare," July 8, 1998. Copyright © 1998 by The New York Times. Reprinted by permission.

NICHOLAS WADE, "Method and Madness," July 24, 1994. Copyright © 1994 by The New York Times. Reprinted by permission.

GEORGE F. WILL, "Gambling with Our National Character." Copyright © 1993 Washington Post Writers Group. "Radical English." Copyright © 1991 Washington Post Writers Group. Reprinted with permission.

WALTER E. WILLIAMS, "Government Is the Problem" and "The Tyranny of the Majority," June 17, 1998. By permission of the author and the Creators Syndicate.

CATHY YOUNG, "Women, Sex, and Rape." Used with permission from the author.

FRANK ZAPPA, "On Junk Food for the Soul: In Defense of Rock & Roll," *New Perspectives Quarterly,* Winter 1988, pp. 27–29. Reprinted with permission from Blackwell Publishers.

INDEX OF AUTHORS AND TITLES